SCHIZOID PHENOMENA
OBJECT-RELATIONS
AND THE SELF

By the same author

*

PSYCHOLOGY FOR MINISTERS AND SOCIAL WORKERS

YOU AND YOUR NERVES

MENTAL PAIN AND THE CURE OF SOULS

MIDDLE AGE

(*With L. J. Tizard*)

PERSONALITY STRUCTURE AND HUMAN INTERACTION

SCHIZOID PHENOMENA OBJECT-RELATIONS AND THE SELF

HARRY GUNTRIP

Fellow of the British Psychological Society
Psychotherapist and Lecturer, Leeds University
Department of Psychiatry

INTERNATIONAL UNIVERSITIES PRESS, INC.
NEW YORK
1969

SECOND PRINTING 1970
Library of Congress Catalog Card Number: 68–56426

CONTENTS

PART 4
SOME IMPLICATIONS FOR PSYCHOTHERAPY

PART 5
OBJECT-RELATIONS THEORY AND EGO-THEORY

'There is a great deal of unmapped country within us which would have to be taken into account in an explanation of our gusts and storms.'

(George Eliot, *Daniel Deronda*, p. 206.)

'It may be reserved for psycho-analysis to lead psychiatry out of the impasse of therapeutic nihilism.'

(Karl Abraham, *Selected Papers on Psycho-Analysis*, p. 156.)

ACKNOWLEDGMENTS

I HAVE acknowledged my indebtedness to Fairbairn and Winnicott, and also to Dicks (first Nuffield Professor of Psychiatry at Leeds) in my Introduction. It is a pleasure also to acknowledge my debt to Dicks' successors as Head of the Leeds University Department of Psychiatry. Professors MacCalman, Hargreaves and Hamilton have each in turn confirmed the appointment Dicks made, leaving me free to carry on long-term research in psychoanalytically orientated psychotherapy in my own way. Much of the material used in this book has been gathered in clinical work done in the Department. I would like at this stage to thank Dr J. D. Sutherland and Mr Masud R. Khan, who at various stages have read and commented on the chapters previously published in the Journals, and the MSS. of the new chapters, and have given generous encouragement.

I owe a particular debt to Miss A. Hutchinson, Secretary to the Editor of The International Psycho-Analytical Library, for going over the entire MS. in great detail and putting it in order for presentation to the Publishers. Lastly, I take this opportunity of thanking my wife for help in proof-reading.

INTRODUCTION

This book is a sequel to and a development from my earlier historical study of trends in psychoanalytic theory, *Personality Structure and Human Interaction* (Hogarth Press, 1961). That book gave the theoretical background of a research on schizoid conditions. This book was originally planned as a clinical clarification of the implications for psychotherapeutic treatment of the shift of emphasis from depressive to schizoid problems: but it has grown into a more complete development of the basic theory. In it I have sought to rethink as a coherent whole the developing material of papers written since 1960, together with fresh clinical data. The total study, theoretical and clinical, has convinced me that, given time, psychoanalysis is destined to bring about a far-reaching change of viewpoint from which all human problems must be studied. Hitherto, *the moral standpoint* has dominated thinking; the need for the control of anti-social impulses and for the production of properly socialized characters by training and discipline, education and religion, authoritative guidance and direction by 'reason' and the value of the spiritual life. *This moral standpoint is relevant where a well-developed and integrated 'self' exists, where basic ego-strength renders the 'person' capable of accepting moral responsibility, and social education.*

When Freud, in the 1880's, began to investigate psychoneurosis in an ever more psychological way, and gradually created psychoanalysis, he found himself dealing with problems which involved at one and the same time both moral issues and illness. Ever since, there has been vague confusion as to where and how to draw the dividing line. The issue has often been put bluntly if crudely in the question 'Are neurotics really ill or only selfish?' After starting with the study of hysteria, psychoanalysis in its first great creative period analysed thoroughly the moral and pseudo-moral (or pathologically moral) level of human experience, the area of the control of impulses of sex and aggression working antisocially, generating guilt, and leading to obsessional neurosis and depression.

But Freud's very success in this task opened the way to a deeper and more primitive level of our psychic life, denoted by the term 'the schizoid problem'. This is as yet very far from having been exhaustively studied, but it is clear that it involves a fundamentally different point of view from that of the moral approach. Instead of assuming an individual strong enough to be able to respond to the appeal of moral values and capable of accepting training and education of character, the difficulties of schizoid individuals present us with a quite different situation. Here, the great problem is that the foundations of an adequate 'self' were prevented from growing in infancy. We are dealing with individuals who, however much they may have been trained to adult social and moral obligations and values at the ordinary conscious level of their personality of everyday living, are unable to maintain themselves on that level because the underlying, unconscious strata of their personalities are on the pre-moral level of infantile fear, ego-weakness, and flight from life.

I was fortunate in my undergraduate days to make my first acquaintance with psychoanalysis in the classroom of Professor Flugel, University College, London, and was able to realize that here was a major pioneer break-through in the scientific study of man. At the same time, however, I was being trained in schools of philosophy and theology which put the major emphasis on the nature and significance of the personality as a 'whole', regarding the human being primarily as a 'person' and only secondarily as an 'organism'. The days of Victorian 'scientific materialism' had been left behind in *philosophy*. But Freud's emphasis on instincts and mechanisms, and the marked physiological colouring of his thought-forms, begot a scientific theory which Fairbairn later termed 'atomistic'. True to the general orientation of science, the method of study evolved was termed 'psycho-*analysis*'. All this seemed to me to miss the final key to human problems by not beginning with *the primary fact about human beings, namely their experience of themselves as that significant and meaningful 'whole' which we call a 'person'*.

Since those days, psychoanalysis has steadily been changing in this respect, but even at that time Freud's approach could not be evaded. There was no other kind of approach capable of discovering in depth and detail what really goes on in the human mind, as psychoanalysis does. For a long time the two above-mentioned points of view interacted in all my thinking. I did not feel that Adler with his ego emphasis on 'the will to power', or even Jung with his theory of 'individuation', provided the adequate reconciliation of the two different approaches to man. I felt that Freud had opened the right path, and only by pursuing this path further would the answer be found. Now it is apparent that a radical reorientation of theory has been silently and logically developing in such a way that the approach to man as a 'whole person', i.e. ego-psychology, has grown out of the original psychobiological approach of Freud, and that Freud himself provided the first impetus. The consequences of this development for psychotherapy, and also for philosophy and ethics, press for elucidation. This present book is an attempt to organize my own thoughts on this matter beyond the point reached in the last chapter of my previous book.

One matter of general concern is that we now have a definite means of differentiating between mental illness and moral failure pure and simple. Mental illness springs specifically from the ravages of early fear and basic weakness of the ego, with consequent inability to cope with life in any other than a dangerous state of anxiety. Ideally, immoral behaviour occurs in a reasonably stable individual whose early education has given him bad values and standards of behaviour, or whose later experiences in life have caused in him a deterioration of the sense of responsibility to others and a drift into merely self-regarding habits of mind. He is not necessarily a person undermined by deep-seated fears. Yet we have to recognize that, all too often, immaturity of development and deep-seated fears are hidden and defended against by the adoption of immoral, and even criminal ways of living. So the overlap of these two separate orders of fact is not eliminated; although, with the uncovering of the schizoid problem, we can see better what is involved. The difference between illness and immorality is made plain by Winnicott's view that it is useless to inculcate 'tenets to believe in', if the child has not grown 'the capacity to believe in', through trust in human love.

It remains for me to acknowledge the tremendous debt I owe to W. R. D. Fairbairn and D. W. Winnicott. Their work, interacting together and with the material presented by my patients, has been the main stimulus to my thinking, and this book is the result. If it does something to direct attention to the basic problem of psychotherapy, it will have achieved its aim. Hitherto, though psychoanalysis has produced more therapeutic results than its critics are disposed to allow, analysts have never been satisfied with these. They have never taught that psychoanalysis produced quick and easy results. Meanwhile, however, psychodynamic research has been working its way forward, inch by inch, to the heart of the problem, the failure of strong ego-formation in earliest infancy, the persistence of a fear-ridden and withdrawn (or regressed) infantile self in the depths of the unconscious, and even the fact of unrealized potentialities of personality that have never been evoked. *The rebirth and regrowth of the lost living heart of the personality is the ultimate problem psychotherapy now seeks to solve.*

The plan of this book is first, in Part I, to present a descriptive clinical picture of the schizoid personality and his problems, with a minimum of theoretical discussion. Part II may be considered as the continuation and completion of my 1961 book. It develops the theoretical implications of the schizoid problem. Part III seeks to understand the nature and causes of persistence of primary failure of ego-development, and leads on to Part IV, where I have aimed to study the bearing of all this on psychotherapy. That it is necessary to bring out very clearly the fact that psychodynamic theory has moved on beyond the original classic theory of superego control, guilt, and depression, is evidenced by the fact that recent books seem to be quite unaware of this fact. I have recently received notices of two books published in America. *Psychoanalytic Theory of Motivation* by Walter Toman (Associate Professor, Brandeis University) gives as the principal contents of his 'Conceptual Introduction' the following: 'Psychological forces; Control of Desires, Derivative Desires . . . Deprivation of Desires; Defence Mechanisms; Aggression; The Super-Ego.' Here is the old 'moral psychology', all of it important but with no hint at all that the basic anxiety-producing conflicts in human beings are not over the 'gratification of desires' but over the frightening struggle to maintain themselves in existence at all as genuine individual persons. *The Crisis in Psychiatry and Religion*, by O. Hobart Mowrer (Research Professor of Psychology, University of Illinois) is described by the publishers as follows:

> The author has made a searching study of the reasons for the failure of both religion and professional psychiatry in their attempts to deal with the problems of mental and emotional disturbances. He insists that guilt, which is the core of psychological distress, is real and must be accepted as such in order for any therapy to produce beneficial results.

Of course guilt is a real experience and must be accepted, and there is no therapeutic result unless feelings of guilt are cleared up, but I hope that this book will disprove conclusively the idea that guilt is 'the core of psychological distress'. *Pathological guilt* is, as we shall see, a struggle to maintain object-relations, a defence against ego-disintegration, and is a state of mind that is preferred to being undermined by irresistible fears. The core of psychological distress is simply elementary fear, however much it gets transformed into guilt: fear carrying with it the feeling of weakness and inability to cope with life; fear possessing the psyche to such an extent that 'ego-experience' cannot get started. As H. V. Dicks wrote, as far back as 1939,

> . . . every patient with mental illness was more afraid than he could tolerate when he was a baby, and the faults in his psychic structure represent the gallant attempts to allay this intolerable feeling by the inadequate means at his disposal. (*Clinical Studies in Psychopathology*, p. 234.)

I am happy to acknowledge here that it was Dicks who, coming to Leeds as the first Nuffield Professor of Psychiatry in 1946, introduced me to the work of Fairbairn, drew me deep into psychotherapy, gave me research facilities, and, by his own broad outlook on psychiatric problems, influenced the direction of my earlier thinking more than at the time I could realize. His stress on man's humanity as a 'person' reinforced my previous philosophical training in the 'human relations philosophy' of Professor John Macmurray, and prepared me for understanding the theoretical and clinical work of Fairbairn and Winnicott. The theoretical results of this are summarized on pp. 418–434 of *Personality Structure and Human Interaction*.

The present book, as mentioned above, is based on a series of papers in which I pursue the implications of those ideas for psychotherapy, with the aid of clinical material I had been gathering. The first of these papers was 'Ego-Weakness and the Hard Core of the Problem of Psychotherapy' (1960), followed by 'The Schizoid Problem, Regression and the Struggle to Preserve an Ego' (1961), 'The Manic-Depressive Problem in the Light of the Schizoid Process' (1962), 'The Schizoid Compromise and Psychotherapeutic Stalemate' (1962), and 'Psychodynamic Theory and the Problem of Psychotherapy' (1963). This represents the chronological rather than the logical development of ideas. Since one's thinking never stands still, I feel now that it would be better to reorganize this and further new material into an attempt at a logical presentation of the theme of the schizoid problem and psychotherapy. The material of the above papers will therefore be found in a revised form, scattered throughout the present volume in, I hope, the appropriate contexts. This makes for some amount of repetition which would not arise if one were starting to write a book *de novo*, and which I hope the reader will feel able to judge leniently. The final result will, I trust, prove more useful than simply a volume of collected papers.

This result convinced me that it was necessary now to clarify 'Object-Relations Theory' and the 'Concept of Psychodynamic Science' it implies, beyond the point of my 1961 volume, in the light of Winnicott's work of the last ten years; and also by making a close comparative study of the very different types of 'Ego-Theory' developed respectively by Heinz Hartmann and the 'Object-Relations' Theory. Though this is, in fact, a big enough subject for a book in itself, it could not be ignored here, and is responsible for Part 5.

Part I

CLINICAL DESCRIPTION OF THE SCHIZOID PERSONALITY

I

THE SCHIZOID PERSONALITY AND THE EXTERNAL WORLD[1]

My interest in the schizoid problem was first vitally aroused about 1948 by the coincidence of the acquisition of several markedly schizoid patients in the Leeds Department of Psychiatry with the fact of my having been studying, in the first post-war years, the stimulating papers of W. R. D. Fairbairn. I have commented more fully on that in Chapter IV. The first result was to lead me to undertake a study of Fairbairn's theory of schizoid reactions in the light of my own clinical material and to embark on a personal analysis with him. This study is the natural starting-point for this whole enquiry.

THE SCHIZOID CONDITION

The Picture of the Shut-in Individual

The psychotherapist must be greatly concerned with those states of mind in which patients become inaccessible emotionally, when the patient seems to be bodily present but mentally absent. One patient said, 'I don't seem to come here', as if she came in body but did not bring herself with her. She found herself in the same state of mind when she asked the young man next door to go for a walk with her. He did and she became tired, dull, unable to talk; she commented: 'It was the same as when I come here: I don't seem to be present.' Her reactions to food were similar. She would long for a nice meal and sit down to it and find her appetite gone, as if she had nothing to do with eating. One patient dreamed:

> My husband and I came to see you and he explained that I wasn't here because I'd gone to hospital.

Complaints of feeling cut off, shut off, out of touch, feeling apart or strange, of things being out of focus or unreal, of not feeling one with people, or of the point having gone out of

[1] This chapter is a revised version of 'A Study of Fairbairn's Theory of Schizoid Reactions', *Brit. J. med. Psychol.*, **25** (1952).

life, interest flagging, things seeming futile and meaningless, all describe in various ways this state of mind. Patients usually call it 'depression', but it lacks the heavy, black, inner sense of brooding, of anger and of guilt, which are not difficult to discover in classic depression. Depression is really a more extraverted state of mind, which, while the patient is turning his aggression inwards against himself, is part of a struggle not to break out into overt angry and aggressive behaviour. The states described above are rather the 'schizoid states'. They are definitely introverted. Depression is object-relational. The schizoid person has renounced objects, even though he still needs them.

External relationships seem to have been emptied by a massive withdrawal of the real libidinal self. Effective mental activity has disappeared into a hidden inner world; the patient's conscious ego is emptied of vital feeling and action, and seems to have become unreal. You may catch glimpses of intense activity going on in the inner world through dreams and fantasies, but the patient's conscious ego merely reports these as if it were a neutral observer not personally involved in the inner drama of which it is a detached spectator. The attitude to the outer world is the same: *non-involvement and observation at a distance without any feeling*, like that of a press reporter describing a social gathering of which he is not a part, in which he has no personal interest, and by which he is bored. Such activity as is carried on may appear to be mechanical. When a schizoid state supervenes, the conscious ego appears to be in a state of suspended animation in between two worlds, internal and external, and having no real relationships with either of them. It has decreed an emotional and impulsive standstill, on the basis of keeping out of effective range and being unmoved.

These schizoid states may alternate with depression, and at times can be confusingly mixed with it so that both schizoid and depressive signs appear. They are of all degrees of intensity ranging from transient moods that come and go during a session, to states that persist over a long period, when they show very distinctly the specific schizoid traits.

An example of a patient describing herself as depressed when she was really schizoid may be useful at this point. She opened the session by saying: 'I'm very depressed. I've been just sitting and couldn't get out of the chair. There seemed no purpose anywhere, the future blank. I'm very bored and want a big change. I feel hopeless, resigned, no way out, stuck. I'm wondering how I can manage somehow just to get around and put up with it.' (Analyst: 'Your solution is to damp everything down, don't feel anything, give up all real relationship to people on an emotional level, and just "do things" in a mechanical way, be a robot.') Her reaction brought out clearly the schizoid trait: 'Yes, I felt I didn't care, didn't register anything. Then I felt alarmed, felt this was dangerous. If I hadn't made myself do something I'd have just sat, not bothered, not interested.' (Analyst: 'That's your reaction in analysis to me: don't be influenced, don't be moved, don't be lured into reacting to me.') Her reply was: 'If I were moved at all, I'd feel very annoyed with you. I hate and detest you for making me feel like this. The more I'm inclined to be drawn towards you, the more I feel a fool, undermined.'

The mere fact of the analyst's presence as another human being with whom she needed to be emotionally real, i.e. express what she was actually feeling, created an emotional crisis in her with which she could only deal by *abolishing the relationship*. So her major defence against her anxieties was to keep herself emotionally out of reach, inaccessible, and keep everyone at arm's length. She once said: 'I'd rather hate you than love you', but this goes even further. She will neither love nor hate, she won't feel anything at all, and outwardly in sessions often appeared lazy, bored at coming, and with a *laissez faire* attitude. This then is the problem we seek to understand. *The schizoid condition consists in the first place in an attempt to cancel external object-relations and live in a detached and withdrawn way*. What is really happening to these patients and why? It is not just a problem in treatment. It pervades the whole of life.

Living in an Internal World

(*a*) *Need of the Object and of Internal Object Relations*

Fairbairn's object-relations theory arose out of his study of schizoid problems, and throws much light on the schizoid's 'life inside himself'. He laid it down that the goal of the individual's libido is not pleasure, or merely subjective gratification, but the object itself. He says: 'Pleasure is the sign-post to the object' (1952a, p. 33). The fundamental fact about human nature is our libidinal drive towards good object-relationships. The key biological formula is the adaptation of the organism to the environment. The key psychological formula is the relationship of the person to the human environment. *The significance of human living lies in object-relationships*, *and only in such terms can our life be said to have a meaning, for without object-relations the ego itself cannot develop.*

Quite specially in this region lie the schizoid's problems. He is driven by anxiety to cut himself off from all object-relations. Our needs, fears, frustrations, resentments and anxieties in our inevitable quest for good objects are the substance of psychopathology, because they are the real problem in life itself. When difficulties in achieving and maintaining good object-relations are too pronounced, and human relations are attended with too great anxiety and conflict, desperate efforts are often made to deny and eliminate this basic need. People go into their shell, bury themselves in work of an impersonal nature, abolish relations with actual people so far as they can, devote themselves to abstractions, ideals, theories, organizations, and so on. In the nature of the case these manœuvres cannot succeed and always end disastrously, since they are an attempt to deny our very nature itself. Clearly we cannot do that and remain healthy.

The more people cut themselves off from human relations in the outer world, the more they are driven back on emotionally charged fantasied object-relations in their inner mental world, till the psychotic lives only in his inner world. But it is still a world of object-relations. We are constitutionally incapable of living as isolated units. The real loss of all objects would be equivalent to psychic death. Thus a young woman of nineteen who was chronically agoraphobic and experienced serious attacks of depersonalization if she went out even with her own family, said, 'I get frighteningly claustrophobic in a big store and want to rush out.' It appeared that what actually happened was that she would feel overwhelmed and helpless in the midst of the big crowd of shoppers and before the fear could develop she would undergo an immediate and involuntary schizoid withdrawal. She said, 'I suddenly feel a lack of contact with everybody and everything around and I feel I'm disappearing in the midst of everything.' Hence her agoraphobia. She felt overwhelmed by the world outside home and would 'lose herself'. Karen Horney (1945) says: 'Neuroses are generated by disturbances in human relationships.' But Horney thinks only in terms of relations to external objects at the conscious level. Bad external relations in infancy lead to the development of a less obvious danger, an attempt to withdraw and carry on living in an inner mental world, a repressed world of internalized psychic objects, bad objects, and 'bad-object situations'. What is new in all this is the theory of internal objects as developed in more elaborate form by Melanie Klein and Fairbairn, and the fact that Fairbairn makes object-relations, not instinctive impulses, the primary and important thing. It is the object that is the real goal of the libidinal drive. We seek persons, not pleasures. Impulses are not psychic entities but reactions of an ego to objects. It is impossible to understand the schizoid problem without using Melanie Klein's theory of the inner world of internal objects and internal object-relations, and the consequences of that theory as worked out by Fairbairn. As this metapsychology is still not accepted or perhaps even understood by all analysts and psychotherapists, it may be useful here to express it as simply as possible.

What is meant by a world of internal objects may be put in this way: in some sense we retain all our experience in life and 'carry things in our minds'. If we did not, we would lose all continuity with our past, would only be able to live from moment to moment like butterflies alighting and flitting away, and no relationships or experiences could have any permanent values for us. Thus in some sense everything is mentally internalized, retained and inwardly possessed; that is our only defence against complete discontinuity in living, a distressing example of which we see in the man who loses his memory, and is consciously uprooted.

But things are mentally internalized and retained in two different ways which we call respectively *memory* and *internal objects*. This has recently been emphasized by Bion's work. Good objects are, in the first place, mentally internalized and retained only as memories. They are enjoyed at the time; the experience is satisfying and leaves no problems, it promotes good ego-development, and can later on be looked back to and reflected on with pleasure. In the case of a continuing good-object relationship of major importance as with a parent or marriage partner, we have a combination of memories of the happy past and confidence in the continuing possession of the good object in an externally real sense in the present and future. There is no reason here for setting up internalized objects. Outer experience suffices to meet our needs. On this point Fairbairn differs from Melanie Klein. He regards 'good objects' as not needing to be internalized in the first place, in any other form than 'memory', though this must involve the experience of secure possession of relationship.

Objects are only internalized in a more radical way when the relationship turns into a bad-object situation through, say, the object changing or dying. When someone we need and love ceases to love us, or behaves in such a way that we interpret it as cessation of love, or disappears, dies, i.e. deserts us, that person becomes, in an emotional, libidinal sense, a bad object. This happens to a child when his mother refuses the breast, weans the baby, or is cross, impatient and punitive, or is absent temporarily or for a longer period through illness, or permanently through death; it also happens when the person we need is emotionally detached, aloof, and unresponsive. All that is experienced as frustration of the most important of all needs, as rejection and desertion, or else as persecution and attack. Then the lost object, now become a bad object, is mentally internalized in a much more vital and fundamental sense than memory. In the language of Bion, bad experiences cannot be *digested* and absorbed; they are retained as foreign objects which the psyche seeks to project. Bereaved people dream vividly of the lost loved one, even years afterwards, as still actually alive. A patient, beset by a life-long fear of dying, was found in analysis to be persistently dreaming of dead men in coffins. In one dream, the coffined figure was behind a curtain and his mind was on it all the time while he was busy in the dream with cheerful social activities. A fatal inner attraction to, and attachment to, the dead man, threatened him and set up an actual fear of dying. The dead man was his father as he had seen him actually in his coffin. Another patient had a nightmare of his mother violently losing her temper with him, after she had been dead twelve years. *An inner psychic world* (see Riviere, 1952, p. 26 and Heimann, 1951,) *has been set up duplicating an original frustrating situation, an unhappy world in which one is tied to bad objects and feeling therefore always frustrated, hungry, angry, and guilty, and profoundly anxious, with constant temptation to seek transient inner relief by projecting it back into the external world.*

It is bad objects which are internalized, because we cannot accept their badness; we seek to withdraw from them in outer reality and yet cannot give them up, cannot leave them alone; we cannot master and control them in outer reality and so keep on struggling to possess them, alter them and compel them to change into good objects, in our inner psychic world. They never do change. In our inner unconscious world where we repress and lock away very early in life our original bad objects, they remain always rejecting, indifferent or hostile to us according to our actual outer experience. It must be emphasized that these internalized objects are not just fantasies. The child is emotionally identified with his objects, and when he mentally incorporates them he remains identified with them and they become part and parcel of the very psychic structure of his personality. The fantasies in which internal objects reveal their existence to consciousness are activities of the morbid psychic structures which constitute the internal objects. Objects are only internalized later in life in this radical way by fusion with already existing internal-object structures. In adult life, situations in outer reality are unconsciously interpreted in the light of these situations persisting in unconscious, inner, and purely psychic reality. We live in the outer world with the emotions generated in the inner one. A large part of the psychopathological problem is: how do people deal with their internalized bad objects, to what extent do they feel identified with them, and how do they complicate relations with external objects? It is the object all the time that matters, whether external or internal, not pleasure.

(*b*) *Psychodynamics of the Inner World*

From this point of view Fairbairn constructed a revised theory of the psychoses and psychoneuroses. In the orthodox Freud–Abraham view, these illnesses were due to arrests of libidinal development at fixation points in the first five years: schizophrenia at the oral sucking stage, manic-depression at the oral biting stage, paranoia at the early anal; obsessions at the late anal; and hysteria at the phallic or early genital stages. Fairbairn proposed a totally different view, based not on the fate of libidinal impulses, but on the nature of relationships with internal bad objects. Accepting Melanie Klein's theory of the depressive position, *he held that the schizoid and depressive states are the two fundamental types of reaction in internal bad-object relationships*, *the two basic or ultimate dangers to be escaped from*, and that they originate in the difficulties experienced in object-relationships in the oral stage of absolute infantile dependence; and he treats paranoia, obsessions, hysteria, and phobias as four different defensive techniques for dealing with internal bad objects so as to master them and ward off a relapse into the depressed or schizoid states of mind. This makes intelligible the fact that patients ring the changes actually on paranoid, obsessional, hysteric, and phobic reactions even if any particular patient predominantly favours one technique most of the time. The psychoneuroses are, basically, defences against internal bad-object situations which would otherwise set up depressive or schizoid states; though these situations are usually re-activated by a bad external situation.

Thus what has to be done in treatment is to help the patient to drop these unsatisfactory techniques which never solve the problem, and find courage to become conscious of what lies behind these symptom-producing struggles with internal bad objects; in other words, to risk going back into the basic bad-object situations in which they feel they are succumbing to one or other of the two ultimate psychic dangers, depression or schizoid loss of affect in their conscious self. Naturally, depressive and schizoid states constantly develop in consciousness, in varying degrees of severity, in spite of ego-defences.

(c) *Depressive and Schizoid Reactions*

The nature of the two ultimately dangerous situations may be simply described. When you want love from a person who will not give it and so becomes a bad object to you, you can react in either or both of two ways. You may become angry and enraged at the frustration and want to make an aggressive attack on the bad object to force it to become good and stop frustrating you—like a small child who cannot get what he wants from the mother and who flies into a temper-tantrum and hammers on her with his fists. This is the problem of *hate, or love made angry*. It is an attack on a hostile, rejecting, actively refusing bad object. It leads to *depression* for it rouses the fear that one's hate will destroy the very person one needs and loves, a fear that grows into guilt.

But there is an earlier and more basic reaction. When you cannot get what you want from the person you need, instead of getting angry you may simply go on getting more and more hungry, and full of a sense of painful craving, and a longing to get total and complete possession of your love-object so that you cannot be left to starve. Fairbairn arrived at the view (1941) that *love made hungry* is the *schizoid* problem and it rouses the terrible fear that one's love has become so devouring and incorporative that love itself has become destructive. Depression is the fear of loving lest one's hate should destroy. Schizoid aloofness is the fear of loving lest one's love or need of love should destroy, which is far worse. We shall find that this does not carry us far enough into the schizoid problem, though it is an important element in it, the best starting-point for studying it.

This difference of the two attitudes goes along with a difference in appearance, so to speak, of the object. The schizoid sees the object as a desirable deserter, or as Fairbairn calls it, an *exciting needed object* whom he must go after hungrily but then draw back from lest he should devour and destroy it in his desperately intense need to get total possession of it. The depressive sees the object as a hateful denier, or, in Fairbairn's terms, a *rejecting object* to be destroyed out of the way to make room for a good object. Thus one patient constantly dreams of wanting a woman who goes away and leaves him, while another dreams of furious, murderous anger against a sinister person who robs him or gets between him and what he wants. The schizoid is hungry for a desirable deserter, the depressive is murderous against a hateful robber.

Thus the two fundamental forms of internal bad objects are, in Fairbairn's terminology, the exciting object and the rejecting object. In the course of years, many externally real figures of both sexes may be absorbed, by layering and fusion, into these two internal bad objects, but at bottom they remain always two aspects of the breast-mother. They are always there, and parts of the ego (split off, disowned, secondary or subsidiary 'selves') are always having disturbing relationships with them, so that the depressive is always being goaded to anger, and the schizoid always being tantalized, made hungry, and driven into withdrawal. Whereas the depressed person turns his anger and aggression back against himself and feels guilty, the schizoid person seeks to withdraw from the intolerable situation and to feel nothing. If the schizoid starts feeling for real people, he reacts to them as if they were identical with his internal bad objects.

The depressive position is later and more developed than the schizoid, for it is ambivalent. The hateful robber is really an aspect of the same person who is needed and desired, as if the mother excites the child's longing for her, gives him just enough to tantalize and inflame his appetite, and then robs him by taking herself away. This was neatly expressed in a patient's dream:

> I was enjoying my favourite meal and saved the nicest bit to the end, and then mother snatched it [the breast, herself] away under my nose. I was furious but when I protested she said 'Don't be a baby'.

There is the guilt reaction, agreeing with the denier against oneself and giving up one's own needs. Fairbairn held that depression has occupied too exclusively the centre of the picture of psychopathological states as a result of Freud's concentration on obsessions with their ambivalence, guilt and superego problems. He believed the schizoid condition is the fundamental problem and is pre-ambivalent.

Melanie Klein (1932) stressed how ambivalence rises to its

maximum over the weaning crisis at a time when the infant has learned to bite and can react sadistically. Love and hate block each other. The infant attacks and also feels identified with, the object of his aggression, and so feels guilty and involves himself in the fate, factual or fantasied, of the object. Hate of the object involves hate of oneself: you suffer with the object you attack because you cannot give up the object and still feel one with it. Hence the familiar guilt and depression after a bereavement: you feel guilty as if you have killed the lost person and depressed as if you were dying with him or her. Three patients who all suffered marked guilt and depression recovered repressed and internalized death-bed scenes of a parent.

What is the meaning of hate? It is not the absolute opposite of love; that would be indifference, having no interest in a person, not wanting a relationship and so having no reason for either loving or hating, feeling nothing. Hate is love grown angry because of rejection. We can only really hate a person if we want their love. Hate is an expression of frustrated love needs, an attempt to destroy the bad rejecting side of a person in the hope of leaving their good responsive side available, a struggle to alter them. The anxiety is over the danger of hate destroying both sides, and the easiest way out is to find two objects, and love one and hate the other. But always hate is an object-relationship.

As we have seen, however, the individual can adopt an earlier simpler reaction. Instead of reacting with anger, he can react with an enormously exaggerated sense of need. Desire becomes hunger and hunger becomes greed, which is hunger grown frightened of losing what it wants. He feels so uncertain about possessing his love-object that he feels a desperate craving to make sure of it by getting it inside him, swallowing it and incorporating it. This is illustrated by a patient who fantasied standing with a vacuum cleaner (herself, empty and hungry), and everyone who came near she sucked into it. At a more normal and ordinarily conscious level this is expressed by a patient thus: 'I'm afraid I couldn't make moderate demands on people, so I don't make any demands at all.' Many people show openly this devouring possessiveness towards those they love. Many more repress it and keep out of real relations. This fantasy and comment illustrate Fairbairn's view of the psychodynamics of the schizoid state which, unlike depression, is a cancellation of object-relationship.

So much fear is felt of devouring everyone and so losing everyone in the process, that a general withdrawal from all external relationships is embarked on. Retreat into indifference is the true opposite of the love which is felt to be too dangerous to express. Want no one, make no demands, abolish all external relationships, and be aloof, cold, without any feeling, do not be moved by anything. The withdrawn libido is turned inwards, introverted. The patient goes into his shell and is busy only with internal objects, towards whom he feels the same devouring attitude. Outwardly and in consciousness everything seems futile and meaningless. Fairbairn considered that a sense of 'futility' is the specific schizoid affect. The depressive fears loss of his object. The schizoid, in addition, fears loss of his ego, of himself. We shall see later that other concepts besides Fairbairn's original one of 'love become destructive', are needed to account for the full range of schizoid phenomena. Reaction to deprivation involves anger, hunger, sheer fear and withdrawal, and to these are added reactions to real external menace.

THE SCHIZOID'S RELATION TO EXTERNAL OBJECTS (NEED AND FEAR OF OBJECT-RELATIONS)

Active. Fear of Loss of the Object

(*a*) *The Object as a desired Deserter or 'Needed Object' from whom the Schizoid Withdraws*

Theory only lives when it is seen as describing the actual reactions of real people, though the material revealing the schizoid position only becomes undisguisedly accessible at deep levels of analysis, and is often not reached when defences are reasonably effective. In the very unstable schizoid it breaks through with disconcerting ease, a bad sign.

A headmaster described himself as depressed, and went on to say, 'I don't feel so worried about the school or hopeless about the future.' He had said the same things the week before and regarded it as a sign of improvement, but the real meaning emerged when he remarked, 'Perhaps my interest in school has flagged', and it appeared that his loss of the sense of hopelessness about the future was due simply to his not thinking about the future. He had cut it off. He then reported a dream of visiting a camp school:

The resident Head walked away when I arrived and left me to fend for myself and there was no meal ready for me.

He remarked: 'I'm preoccupied with what I'm going to eat and when, yet I don't eat a lot. Also I want to get away from people and am more comfortable when eating alone. I'm concerned at my loss of interest in school. I don't feel comfortable with father and prefer to be in another room. I'm very introverted; I feel totally cut off.'

Here is a gradually emerging description, not of depression but of a schizoid state, loss of interest in present and future, loss of appetite for food, getting away from people, introverted, totally cut off. The situation that calls out the reaction is that of being faced with a desired but deserting object (the Head in the dream who prepares no meal for him, and leaves him to fend for himself when he is hungry). The Head is the father, of whom he complains that he can never get near him; also the analyst, to whom he says: 'You remain the analyst, you won't indulge me in a warm personal relationship, you won't be my friend. I want something more personal than analysis.' The schizoid is very sensitive and quickly feels unwanted, because he is always being deserted in his inner world.

Faced with these desired deserters he first feels exaggeratedly hungry, and then denies his hunger, eats little and turns away from people till he feels introverted and totally cut off. He has withdrawn his libido from the objects he cannot possess, and feels loss of interest and loss of appetite. There is little evidence of anger and guilt as there would be in true depression; his attitude is more that of fear and retreat. It is to be noted that the situation from which he withdraws in his outer world is duplicated in his inner world, as shown in his dream.

(*b*) *The Fear of Devouring the Object*

This entire problem is frequently worked out over food. The above patient is hungry but rejects both food and people. He can only eat alone. One patient says that whenever her husband comes in she at once feels hungry and must eat. Really she is hungry for him but dare not show it. The same turning away from what one feels too greedily and devouringly hungry for is shown very clearly by this same patient in other ways. Visiting friends, she was handed a glass of sherry, took a quick sip, put it down and did not touch it again. She had felt she wanted to swallow it at one gulp. Her general attitude to food was one of rejection. Appetite would disappear at the sight of food; she would nibble at a dish and push it away, or force it down and feel sick. But what lay behind this rejecting attitude was expressed in a dream in which she was eating an enormous meal and just went on and on endlessly. She is getting as much as she can inside her before it is taken away as in the dream where her mother whipped it away under her nose. Her attitude is incorporative, to get it inside where she cannot be robbed of it, because she has no confidence about being given enough. The breast one is sure of can be sucked at contentedly and let go when one feels satisfied; one knows it will be available when needed again. The breast that does not come when wanted, is not satisfying when one has it because it might be snatched away before need is met. It rouses a desperate hungry urge to make sure of it, not by merely sucking at it, but by swallowing it, getting it inside one altogether. The impulse changes from 'taking in from the breast' into an omnivorous urge to 'take in the whole breast itself'. The object is incorporated. The contented baby sucks, the angry and potentially depressive baby bites, the hungry and potentially schizoid baby wants to swallow, as in the case of the vacuum cleaner fantasy. A patient who at first made sucking noises in sessions, then changed to compulsive gulping and swallowing and nausea.

Fairbairn (1941, p. 252) writes:

> The paranoid, obsessional, and hysterical states—to which may be added the phobic state—essentially represent, not products of fixations at specific libidinal phases, but simply a variety of techniques employed to defend the ego against the effects of conflicts of oral origin.

Now, as Fairbairn says: 'You can't eat your cake and have it.' This hungry, greedy, devouring, swallowing up, incorporating attitude leads to deep fears lest the real external object be lost. This anxiety about destroying and losing the love-object through being so devouringly hungry is terribly real. Thus the patient who had become more conscious of her love-hunger with the result that on the one hand her appetite for food had increased enormously, and on the other her anxious attitude to her husband had become more acute, said: 'When he comes in I feel ravenously hungry, and eat, but towards him I'm afraid I'm a nuisance. If I make advances to him I keep saying "I'm not a nuisance am I, you don't 'not want me' do you?" I'm terribly anxious about it all, it's an appalling situation, I'm scared stiff, it's all so violent. I've an urge to get hold of him and hold him so tight that he can't breathe, shut him off from everything but me.' She has the same transference reaction to the analyst. She dreamed that

I came for treatment and you were going off to America with a lot of people. Someone dropped out so I went and you weren't pleased.

Her comment was: 'You didn't want me but I wasn't going to be thrown off. I was thinking today of your getting ill, suppose you died. Then I got in a furious temper. I'd like to strangle you, kill you.' That is, get a strangle-hold on the analyst so that he could not leave her, but then he might be killed. The schizoid person is afraid of wearing out, of draining, or exhausting and ultimately losing love-objects. As Fairbairn said, the terrible dilemma of the schizoid is that love itself is destructive, and he dare not love. Hence he withdraws into detachment and aloofness. All intimate relationships are felt in terms of eating, swallowing up, and are too dangerous to be risked. The above patient says: 'I lay half awake looking at my husband and thinking, "What a pity he's going to die." It seemed fixed. Then I felt lonely, no point of relationship with all I could see. I love him so much but I seem to have no choice about destroying him. I want something badly and then daren't move a finger to get it. I'm paralysed.' One patient said, 'Love is more dangerous than hate. I lose everyone I love, so now I don't risk it.'

At this point we may say that the ego of the schizoid person in consciousness and in the outer world is delibidinized and feels no interest in objects because an oral sadistic and incorporative hunger for objects sets up intolerable anxiety about their safety and is withdrawn. *The withdrawn oral sadistic ego then has to be kept repressed* and is found to be still active in the inner world.

(*c*) *Schizoid Reactions to Food and Eating*

From the foregoing we may summarize the schizoid's reactions to food and eating, for since his basic problems in relation to objects derive from his reactions to the breast, food and eating naturally play a large part in his struggles to solve these problems. His reactions to people and to food are basically the same. These may be described as a *need* to possess and incorporate, checkmated by a *fear* to take, accept, and devour. Thus a patient says: 'Two men friends make me excited but it's not even a taste, only a smell of a good meal. I'm always feeling I want to be with one or the other of them, but I can't do it or I'll lose them both. One of them kissed me and I gave him a hug and a kiss and enjoyed it and wanted more. Ought I? I've sought desperately for so long and now I feel I must run away from it. I don't want to eat these days. I couldn't sleep. I felt I'd lost him. What if he or I had an accident and got killed? It's ridiculous but I'm in a constant furore of anxiety; I must see him; nothing else matters. I knew I'd be like this if I didn't see him but I didn't go. It's funny, I don't think I'm in love with him, yet I need him desperately. I can't engage in any other activity. I felt the same with a fellow ten years ago. He went away for a day and I was in an agony of fear; what if he were killed? An awful dread. It feels it must happen. I don't even like mentioning it in case this present friend gets killed, and I feel I'll have an accident, too. I get desperately tired, and feel empty inside and have to buy sweet biscuits and gobble them up.'

Thus she has the kind of relation with this man (and with all objects) that compromises her stable existence as a separate person when she is not with him: she goes to bits. She wants to eat him up as it were, and feels swallowed up in her relation to him, and feels the destruction of both is inevitable whether she is with him or apart from him.

Another patient, before she started analysis, was having visual hallucinations of leopards leaping across in front of her with their mouths wide open. At an advanced stage of treatment these faded into fantasies and she had a fantasy of two leopards trying to swallow each other's heads. She would enjoy a hearty meal and then promptly be sick and reject it. *There is a constant oscillation between hungry eating and refusal to eat, longing for people and rejecting them.* We must note here that the phenomenon of 'fear of loving as destructive' is not an entirely simple concept. In fact, the terms 'love' and 'hate' are used somewhat undiscriminatingly as including natural, pathological, immature and mature meanings. The difficulty arises because *love* in a mature sense is a highly developed achievement with its first beginnings in simple infantile *need.* Infantile need is a natural imperative demand to 'get', food, bodily attention, and contact, and emotional object-relationship, first from the mother. The infant is so helpless that his natural needs are extremely urgent, and if they are not quickly met, panic and rage develop. The infant's 'need-relationship' to the mother then becomes frightening because it has become dangerously intense and even destructive.

There are important differences in the way this situation is conceptualized by Fairbairn and Winnicott. Both still use the term 'love' for this dangerous, because frustrating, sense of need. It seems to me confusing to use the same term for this primitive disturbed state and for a mature capacity for affectionately respecting the integrity and independence of the needed object.

Fairbairn regards the destructive element in infantile 'love' or 'need of the object' as a direct reaction to rejection. Winnicott regards a destructive element in infantile 'need' as normal and natural. Here again it seems to me equivocal to use the same term 'love' for such different things. Winnicott (1964) writes:

> If the word 'love' is used, the most primitive meanings of the word must be included, in which love is crude and ruthless and even destructive. Hate is not absent.

Sometimes Winnicott speaks of this 'destructive primitive love' as simply 'hate', but though it is experienced by the mother as wearing, exhausting, and ruthless, we can hardly say that the infant is intentionally 'ruthless'. He is rather energetic, vigorous, alive, one might almost say enthusiastic, and he presumably experiences a sense of 'shock' when he finds mother cannot indefinitely cope with his needs. He may then grow at first angry and demanding, then frightened and withdrawing. Finally, if no satisfactory solution of the problem is found, if the mother becomes hostile, intolerant, and rejective, then the combination of natural vigour, natural anger, and natural fear develops into the pathological form of 'need' or 'love' which is correctly called 'hate'. It seems to me to guard best against confusion to keep the term *hate* for pathologically destructive need which once brought into being may persist throughout life. It is confusing to use the same term for the unintentional destructive element in the infant's natural vigour of primary need.

Similarly I would keep the term love for the infant's feeling of happy satisfaction and the growing child's and adult's capacity to feel for the object. One can see then why the co-existence of hate causes depression and guilt. But it does not seem to me to be appropriate to use the term 'love' for destructively frustrated 'need'. A much more careful definition and accepted use of the term is required when 'love' and 'hate' have been used in loose ways for so long. Possibly the source of prevailing confusion is the fact that Freud used the same term 'love' for both primary *somatic needs* for the mother's body and the developed *personality needs* of the maturing person. Also he held that hate was not a pathological growth but our primary relation to the outer world, antedating love.

(*d*) *The Transference Situation*

The treatment of a schizoid patient brings out acutely the problem of the relationship between patient and analyst. Is it possible for it to be therapeutic if it is impersonal? The frustration of a patient's libidinal needs in the analytical situation is certain to bring out schizoid reactions, as we have already noted. The patient longs for the analyst's love, may recognize intellectually that a steady, consistent, genuine concern for the patient's well-being is a true form of love, yet, because it is not love in a full libidinal sense (Fairbairn reminds us that it is *agape*, not *eros*), the patient does not 'feel' it as love. He feels rather that the analyst is cold, indifferent, bored, not interested, not listening, busy with something else while the patient talks, rejecting. Patients will react to the analyst's silence by stopping talking to make him say something. The analyst excites by his presence but does not libidinally satisfy, and so constantly arouses a hungry craving.

The patient will then begin to feel he is bad for the analyst, that he is wasting his time, depressing him by pouring out a long story of troubles. He will want, and fear, to make requests lest he is imposing on the analyst and making illegitimate demands. He may say 'How on earth can you stand the constant strain of listening to this sort of thing day after day?' and in general feels he is draining and exhausting, i.e. devouring, the analyst.

He will oscillate between expressing his need and feeling frightened about it. One patient says: 'I felt I must get possession of something of yours. I thought I'd come early and enjoy your arm chair and read your books in the waiting room.' But then she switches over to: 'You can't possibly want to let me take up your time week after week.' Fear and anxiety then dictate a reversal of the original relationship. The patient must now be passive and begins to see the analyst as the active devourer. He drains the patient of resources by charging fees, he wants to dominate and subjugate the patient, he will rob him of his personality. A patient, after a long silence, says: 'I'm thinking I must be careful, you're going to get something out of me.' The analyst will absorb or rob the patient.

This terrible oscillation may make a patient feel confused

and not know where he is. Thus one young man says: 'I've been thinking I might lose your help, you'll make an excuse to get rid of me. I want more analysis but you don't bother with me. Analysis is only a very small part of a week. You don't understand me. There's a part of me I don't bring into analysis. I might be swallowed up in your personality and lose my individuality, so I adopt a condescending attitude to you. What you say isn't important, you're only a bourgeois therapist and don't understand the conditions of my life, your focus of analytical capacity is tiny, you're cabined within bourgeois ideas. But if I said what I felt, I'd make you depressed and lose your support. You ought to be able to give me specific advice to help me when I feel helpless and imprisoned. I feel much the same with my girl. In analysis I feel I should get out, and away from it, I feel I should be in. This week I feel in a "no man's land".'

Here the whole dilemma of 'craving for' yet 'not being able to accept' the needed person, comes out in transference on to the analyst. The swing over in transference to the opposite, from 'devouring' to 'being devoured', leads to the specific consideration of the passive aspect of the schizoid's relation to objects.

Passive. Fear of the Loss of Independence

(*a*) *The Object as Devouring the Ego*

The patients' fears of a devouring sense of need towards objects is paralleled by the fear that others have the same 'swallowing up' attitude to them. Thus a young woman says: 'I can't stand crowds, they swallow me up. With you I feel if I accept your help I'll be subjugated, lose my personality, be smothered. Now I feel withdrawn like a snail, but now you can't swallow me up. I get a shutting-myself-off attitude which lessens my anxiety.'

A very schizoid married woman of 30, had for a long time been talking out devouring fantasies of all kinds and slowly emerging from her schizoid condition. She was thin, white, cold, aloof, frigid. Often it was some time before she could start talking in the session, and she would arrive terrified but hiding it under an automatic laugh or bored expression. When she did start talking she would begin to look tense, tears would roll silently down, and she would say she felt frightened. Gradually she began to talk more freely, put on weight and colour, and became capable of sexual relationships with her husband. Her fantasies included those of his penis eating her and of her vagina biting off his penis. On one occasion she said: 'Last night I felt excited at coming here today, and then terrified and confused. I couldn't sleep for thinking of you. I felt drawn towards you and then shot back. Then I felt I was one big mouth all over and just wanting to get you inside. But sometimes I feel you'll eat me.'

A male patient of 40, living in a hostel, reported that he had begun to get friendly with another decent type of man there, and commented: 'I've begun to get frightened. I don't know why but I feel it's dangerous and I just cut myself off. When I see him coming I shoot off up to my bedroom.' Then he reported a nightmare from which he had awakened in great fear. A monster was coming after him and its huge mouth closed over him like a trap and he was engulfed. Then he burst out of its head and killed it. So the schizoid not only fears devouring and losing the love-object, but also that the other person will devour him. Then he becomes claustrophobic, and expresses this in such familiar ways as feeling restricted, tied, imprisoned, trapped, smothered, and must break away to be free and recover and safeguard his independence; so he retreats from object-relations. With people, he feels either bursting (if he is getting them into himself) or smothered (if he feels he is being absorbed and losing his personality in them). These anxieties are often expressed by starting up in the night feeling choking, and is one reason for the fear of going to sleep.

(*b*) *Relationships as a Mutual Devouring*

We are now in a position to appreciate the terrible dilemma in which the schizoid person is caught in object-relationships. Owing to his intensely hungry and unsatisfied need for love, and his consequent incorporating and monopolizing attitude towards those he needs, he cannot help seeing his objects in the light of his own desires towards them. The result is that any relationship into which some genuine feeling goes, immediately comes to be felt deep down, and unconsciously experienced, as a mutual devouring. Such intense anxiety results that there seems to be no alternative but to withdraw from relationships altogether, to prevent the loss of his independence, and even of his very self. *Relationships are felt to be too dangerous to enter into*. Thus, the worst object-relations problem arises when the ego is driven to seek security by doing without objects altogether, only to run into the most alarming and ultimate fears of disappearing in a vacuum.

THE SCHIZOID RETREAT FROM OBJECTS

The 'In and Out' Programme

The chronic dilemma in which the schizoid individual is placed, namely that he can neither be in a relationship with another person nor out of it, without in various ways risking the loss of both his object and himself, is due to the fact that he has not yet outgrown the particular kind of dependence on love-objects that is characteristic of infancy. This has two different but clearly related aspects: identification and a wish to incorporate. Identification is passive, incorporation is active. Identification can feel like being swallowed up in another person, incorporation is the wish to swallow the object into oneself. Identification suggests regression to a womb state, and incorporative urges belong to the post-natal, oral infant at the breast. The full significance of this double aspect will emerge later in our enquiry. *The whole problem antedates the oedipal development.*

Thus Fairbairn regarded infantile dependence, not the Oedipus complex, as the basic cause of psychopathological developments. The schizoid patient feels that he himself and those he needs and loves are part and parcel of one another, so that when separated he feels utterly insecure and lost, but when reunited he feels swallowed, absorbed, and loses his separate individuality by regression to infantile dependence. Thus he must always be rushing into a relationship for security and at once breaking out again for freedom and independence: an alternation between regression to the womb and the struggle to be born, between the merging of his ego in, and the differentiation of it from, the person he loves. The schizoid cannot stand alone, yet is always fighting desperately to defend his independence—like those film stars who spend their best years rushing into and out of one marriage after another.

This 'in and out' programme, always breaking away from what one is at the same time holding on to, is perhaps the most characteristic behavioural expression of the schizoid conflict. Thus a young man engaged to be married says: 'When I'm with Dorothy I'm quiet; I think I can't afford to let myself go and let her see that I want her. I must let her see I can get on without her. So I keep away from her and appear indifferent.' He experienced the same conflict about jobs. He fantasied getting a job in South America or China, but in fact turned down every job that would take him away from home. A girl in her twenties says: 'When I'm at home I want to get away and when I'm away I want to get back home.' A nurse residing in a hostel, says: 'The other night I decided I wanted to stay in the hostel and not go home, then I felt the hostel was a prison and I went home. As soon as I got there I wanted to go out again. Yesterday I rang mother to say I was coming home, and then immediately I felt exhausted and rang her again to say I was too tired to come. I'm always switching about; as soon as I'm with the person I want, I feel they restrict me. I have wondered if I did get one of my two men friends would I then want to be free again.' A bachelor of 40 who was engaged, says: 'If I kiss Mary my heart isn't in it. I hold my breath and count. I can only hug and kiss a dog because it doesn't want anything from me, there are no strings attached. I've always been like that, so I've got lots of acquaintances but no real close friends. I feel I want to stay in and go out, to read and not to read, to go to Church and not to go. I've actually gone into a Church and immediately come out again and then wanted to return in.'

So people find their lives slipping away changing houses, clothes, jobs, hobbies, friends, engagements and marriages, and unable to commit themselves to any one relationship in a stable and permanent way—always needing love yet always dreading being tied. This same conflict accounts for the tendency of engaged or married couples to fantasy about or feel attracted to someone else—as if they must preserve freedom of attachment at least in imagination. One patient remarked: 'I want to be loved but I mustn't be possessed.'

Giving up Emotional Relations to External Objects

The oscillation of 'in and out', 'rushing to and from', 'holding on and breaking away' is naturally profoundly disturbing and disruptive of all continuity in living, and at some point the anxiety aroused becomes so great that it cannot be sustained. It is then that a complete retreat from object-relations is embarked on, and the person becomes *overtly* schizoid, emotionally inaccessible, cut off.

This state of emotional apathy, of not suffering any feeling, excitement or enthusiasm, not experiencing either affection or anger, can be very successfully masked. If feeling is repressed, it is often possible to build up a kind of mechanized, robot personality. The ego that operates consciously becomes more a system than a person, a trained and disciplined instrument for 'doing the right and necessary thing' without any real feeling entering in. Fairbairn made the highly important distinction between 'helping people without feeling' and 'loving'. Duty rather than affection becomes the key word. The patient with a disruptive conflict over her men friends sought temporary relief by putting it away and making a list of all the things she ought to do, and systematically going through them one by one, routinizing her whole life—and that had been a life-long tendency. She had always had to 'do things in order'; even as a child she made a note-book list of games and had to play them in order. This obsessional trend aimed to control and subdue her emotions.

A man with strongly, in fact exclusively, religious interests, showed markedly this characteristic of helping people without really feeling for them. He said: 'I've no real emotional relations with people. I can't reciprocate tenderness. I can cry and suffer with people. I can help people, but when they stop suffering I'm finished. I can't enter into folks' joys and laughter. I can do things for people but shrink from them if they start thanking me.' His suffering with people was in fact his identifying himself as a suffering person with anyone else who suffered. Apart from that he allowed no emotional relationship to arise.

It is even possible to mask more effectively the real nature of the compulsive, unfeeling zeal in good works, by simulating a feeling of concern for others. Some shallow affect is helped out by behaviour expressive of deep care and consideration for other people; nevertheless, genuine feeling for other people is not really there. Such behaviour is not, of course, consciously insincere. It is a genuine effort to do the best that one can do in the absence of a capacity to release true feeling. What looks deceptively like genuine feeling for another person may break into consciousness, when in fact it is based on identification with the other person and is mainly a feeling of anxiety and pity for oneself.

Many practically useful types of personality are basically schizoid. Hard workers, compulsively unselfish folk, efficient organizers, highly intellectual people, may all accomplish valuable results, but it is often possible to detect an unfeeling callousness behind their good works, and a lack of sensitiveness to other people's feelings in the way they over-ride individuals in their devotion to causes.

The schizoid repression of feeling, and retreat from emotional relationships, may, however, go much further and produce a serious breakdown of constructive effort. Then the unhappy sufferer from incapacitating conflicts will succumb to real futility: nothing seems worth doing, interest dies, the world seems unreal, the ego feels depersonalized. Suicide may be attempted in a cold, calculated way to the accompaniment of such thoughts as 'I am useless, bad for everybody, I'll be best out of the way.' One patient who had never reached that point, said: 'I feel I love people in an impersonal way; it seems a false position, hypocritical. Perhaps I don't do any loving. I'm terrified when I see young people go off and being successful and I'm at a dead bottom, absolute dereliction, excommunicate.

THE NATURE OF THE SCHIZOID PROBLEM (RETREAT TO IDENTIFICATION)

Identification and Infantile Dependence

It has already been mentioned that schizoid problems involve identification, which is generally held to be the original infantile form of relation to, and dependence on, objects. The criticism is sometimes made that psycho-analysis invents a strange terminology that the layman cannot apply to real life. We may therefore illustrate the state of identification with the love-object in the words of Ngaio Marsh (1935), a successful writer of detective fiction. In *Enter a Murderer* she creates the character of Surbonadier, a bad actor who expresses his immaturity by being a drug addict and blackmailer. Stephanie Vaughan, the leading lady, says: 'He was passionately in love with me. That doesn't begin to express it. He was completely and utterly absorbed as though apart from me he had no reality.' In other words, the man was swallowed up in his love-object, had no true individuality of his own, and could not exist in a state of separation from her. It was as if he had not become born out of his mother's psyche and differentiated as a separate and real person in his own right, and identification with another person remained at bottom the basis of all his personal relationships. *The schizoid person enmeshed in the problems of the 'in and out' programme, and unable to sustain real object-relationships, succumbs to withdrawal and then only has identification as a means of maintaining his ego*. His difficulties in object-relations are due to his being basically bogged down in identification, to which he can always retreat, and to which, indeed, he is always being secretly drawn back.

A patient said: 'If I go away from home I feel I've lost something, but when I'm there I feel imprisoned. I feel my destiny is bound up with their's and I can't get away, yet I feel they imprison me and ruin my life.' Another patient dreamed of being 'grafted on to another person'. The 40-year-old male patient said: 'Why should I be on bad terms with my sister? After all I am my sister', and then started in some surprise at what he had heard himself say. A young married woman struggling to master a blind compulsive longing for a male relative she played with as a child, said: 'I've always felt he's me and I'm him. I felt a terrible need to fuss around him and do everything for him. I want him to be touching me all the time. I feel there is no difference between him and me.' Identification is the cause of the compulsiveness of such feelings as infatuation. Identification is betrayed in a variety of curious ways, such as the fear of being buried alive, i.e. absorbed into another person, *a return to the womb*. This is also expressed in the suicidal urge to put one's head in a gas oven; or, again, in dressing in the clothes of another person. One patient feeling in a state of panic one night when her husband was away, felt safe when she slept in his pyjamas.

Identification is a major problem in the schizoid patient's relations to the external world, because it leads to the danger of over-dependence on objects, creates the fear of absorption into them, and enforces the defence of mental detachment. Thus the original schizoid withdrawal from an unsatisfying outer world is reinforced by this further obstacle of detachment as a defence against risking dangerous relationships. One patient identified with her work as a means of maintaining her personality without risking any close personal attachment. Then she insisted that she would have to commit suicide when she retired because she would then be nobody.

Dissolving Identification: Separation-Anxiety and Psychic-Rebirth

The regressive urge to remain identified for the sake of comfort and security conflicts with the developmental need to dissolve identification and differentiate oneself as a separate personality. This conflict, as it sways back and forth, sets up the 'in and out' programme. Identification naturally varies in degree, but the markedly schizoid person, in whom it plays such a fundamental part, begins to lose all true independence of feeling, thought and action, as soon as a relationship with another person attains any degree of emotional reality. A single illuminating example will suffice.

A patient says: 'I feel I lack the capacity to go out. I can never leave the people I love. If I go out I'm emptied, I lose myself. I can't get beyond that. If I become dependent on you, I'd enjoy my dependence on you too much and want to prolong babyhood. Being shut in means being warm, safe, and not confronted with unforeseen events.' But this kind of security is also a prison, so the patient goes on to say: 'I feel I'm walking up and down inside an enclosed space. I dreamed of a baby being born out of a gas oven [i.e. reversal of the suicide idea]. I was struck with the danger of coming out, it was a long drop from the oven to the floor. I feel I'm disintegrating if I go out. The only feeling of being real comes with getting back in and being with someone. I don't feel alone inside even if there's no-one there. Sometimes I feel like someone falling out of an aeroplane, or falling through water and expecting to hit the bottom and there isn't one. I have strong impulses to throw myself out of the window.' This 'birth symbolism' shows that suicidal impulses may have opposite meanings. The gas oven means a return to the womb, a surrender to identification with mother. Falling out of the window or the gas oven means a struggle to separate and be born. The struggle to dissolve identification is long and severe, and in analysis it recapitulates the whole process of growing up to the normal mixture of voluntary dependence and independence characteristic of the mature adult person. One cause of anxiety is that separation may be felt to involve, not natural growth and development, but a violent, angry, destructive break-away, as if a baby, in being born, were bound to leave a dying mother behind. But the major cause of separation-anxiety is that it feels to involve loss of the ego.

SCHIZOID CHARACTERISTICS

There are various characteristics which specifically mark the schizoid personality, and the most general and all-embracing is:

(i) *Introversion.* By the very meaning of the term, the schizoid is described as cut off from the world of outer reality in an emotional sense. All his libidinal desire and striving is directed inwards towards internal objects and he lives an intense inner life, often revealed in an astonishing wealth and richness of fantasy and imaginative life whenever that becomes accessible to observation; though mostly this varied fantasy life is carried on in secret, hidden away often even from the schizoid's own conscious self. His ego is split. But the barrier between the conscious and the unconscious self may be very thin in a deeply schizoid person and the world of internal objects and relationships may flood into and dominate consciousness very easily. Deeper down than this level of 'internal objects' lies the ultimate 'return to the womb' state of the introverted regressed schizoid.

(ii) *Withdrawnness* detachment from the outer world, is the other side of introversion.

(iii) *Narcissism* is a characteristic that arises out of the predominantly interior life the schizoid lives. His love-objects are all inside him, and moreover he is greatly identified with them, so that his libidinal attachments appear to be to himself. This subtly deceptive situation was not apparent when Freud propounded his theory of autoeroticism and narcissism, and ego-libido as distinct from object-libido. Melanie Klein holds that a physically incorporative feeling towards love-objects is the bodily counterpart, or rather foundation, of a mentally incorporative attitude which leads to mental internalization of objects and the setting up of a world of internal psychic objects. The question, however, is whether the intense inner life of the schizoid is due to a desire for hungry incorporation of external objects, or to withdrawal from the outer to a presumed safer inner world. For these mentally internalized objects, especially when the patient feels strongly identified with them, can be discovered, contacted and enjoyed, or even attacked, in his own body, when the external object is not there. One patient, who cannot be directly angry with another person, always goes away alone when her temper is roused and punches herself. She is identified with the object of her aggression which leads to a depressive state, which occurs, however, on the basis of a schizoid set-up. The normally so-called autoerotic and narcissistic phenomena of thumb-sucking, masturbation, hugging oneself, and so on, are based on identification. Autoerotic phenomena are only secondarily autoerotic; autoerotism is a relationship with an external object who is identified with oneself, the baby's thumb deputizes for the mother's breast. Narcissism is a disguised internalized object-relation. Thus one patient felt depressed while bathing and cried silently, and then felt a strong urge to snuggle her head down on to her shoulder, i.e.

mother's shoulder in herself, and at once she felt better. Again, sitting with her husband one evening reading, she became aware that she was thinking of an intimate relation with him and found she had slipped her hand inside her frock and was caressing her own breast. These phenomena lead to a fourth schizoid characteristic:

(iv) *Self-sufficiency*. The above patient was actually taking no notice of her husband as an external person: her relation with him was all going on inside herself and she felt contented. This introverted, narcissistic, self-sufficiency which does without real external relationships while all emotional relations are carried on in the inner world, is a safeguard against anxiety breaking out in dealings with actual people. Self-sufficiency, or the attempt to get on without external relationships, comes out clearly in the case of a young wife. She had been talking of wanting a baby, and then dreamed that she had a baby by her mother. But since she had often shown that she identified herself very much with babies, it represented being the baby inside the mother. She was wanting to set up a self-sufficiency situation in which she was both the mother and the baby. She replied: 'Yes, I always think of it as a girl. It gives me a feeling of security. I've got it all here under control, there's no uncertainty.' In such a position she could do without her husband and be all-sufficient within herself.

(v) *A sense of superiority* naturally goes with self-sufficiency. One has no need of other people, they can be dispensed with. This over-compensates the deep-seated dependence on people which leads to feelings of inferiority, smallness and weakness. But there often goes with it a feeling of being different from other people, Thus a very obsessional patient reveals the schizoid background of her symptoms when she says: 'I'm always dissatisfied. As a child I would cry with boredom at the silly games the children played. It got worse in my teens, terrible boredom, futility, lack of interest. I would look at people and see them interested in things I thought silly. I felt I was different and had more brains. I was thinking deeply about the purpose of life.' She could think about life in the abstract but could not live it in real relationships with other people.

(vi) *Loss of affect* in external situations is an inevitable part of the total picture. A man in the late forties says: 'I find it difficult to be with mother. I ought to be more sympathetic to her than I can be. I always feel I'm not paying attention to what she says. I don't feel terribly drawn to anyone. I can feel cold about all the people who are near and dear to me. When my wife and I were having sexual relations she would say: "Do you love me?" I would answer: "Of course I do, but sex isn't love, it's only an experience." I could never see why that upset her.' Feeling was excluded even from sexual activity which was reduced to what one patient called 'an intermittent biological urge which seemed to have little connexion with "me"'. As a result of this lack of feeling, schizoid people can be cynical, callous, and cruel, having no sensitive appreciation of the way they hurt other people.

(vii) *Loneliness* is an inescapable result of schizoid introversion and abolition of external relationships. It reveals itself in the intense longing for friendships and love which repeatedly break through. Loneliness in the midst of a crowd is the experience of the schizoid cut off from affective rapport.

(viii) *Depersonalization*, loss of the sense of identity and individuality, loss of oneself, brings out clearly the serious dangers of the schizoid state. Derealization of the outer world is involved as well. Thus one patient maintains that the worst fright she ever had was an experience which she thought occurred at the age of two years: 'I couldn't get hold of the idea that I was me. I lost the sense for a little while of being a separate entity. I was afraid to look at anything; and afraid to touch anything as if I didn't register touch. I couldn't believe I was doing things except mechanically. I saw everything in an unrealistic way. Everything seemed highly dangerous. I was terrified while it lasted. All my life since I've been saying to myself at intervals "I am me".'

(ix) *Regression*. The tendency to regress is much more fully dealt with later and only mentioned here. It represents the fact that *the schizoid person at bottom feels overwhelmed by the external world* and is in flight from it both inwards, and, as it were, backwards, to the safety of the womb.

BEYOND THE OEDIPUS PROBLEM

When one surveys the material here set out, it becomes apparent that Fairbairn's theory of the schizoid problem represented (1938–1946) a radical revision of previous psychoanalytical thinking. Freud rested his theory of development and of the psychoneuroses on the centrality of the Oedipus situation in the last phase of infancy. Failure to solve the Oedipus conflict of incestuous love, and jealous hate of the parent of the same sex, led to fixation on pregenital levels of sexual and emotional life and a lasting burden of guilt. This must now be seen as the pioneer's map of the lower reaches of a great river to where it enters the sea, leaving its upper reaches and its source yet to be explored. It paved the way for the detailed map of infantile development which is based on the work of Klein, Winnicott, Bowlby, Spitz, and many others, on the mother–child relation, the depressive and schizoid positions, and the earliest stages of ego-development. *The Oedipus problem, as Freud saw it, was, in fact, the gateway opening back into the area of the psychopathology of infancy.* Fairbairn's position was essentially simple. Once stated it should be apparent that *man's need of a love-relationship is the fundamental thing in his life, and that the love-hunger and anger set up by frustration of this basic need must constitute the two primary problems of personality on the emotional level.* Freud's 'guilt over the incestuous tie to the mother' resolves itself ultimately into the primary necessity of overcoming infantile dependence on the parents, and on the mother in particular, in order to grow up to mature adulthood. The Oedipus conflict theory in a purely biological and sexual sense misrepresented the real problem. We must distinguish between an earlier pathological Oedipus complex and a later healthy oedipal phase of development. In the latter, a boy needs a mother he can fall in love with and a father who will be a friendly rival. This promotes realistic growth. In the earlier pathological complex mother and father have become unreal idealized good and bad internal objects. The primary emotional attitude of the child to both parents is the same, though in fact that to the mother is fundamental. It is determined, not by the sex of the parent but by the child's need for a secure, stable, loving personal environment in which he can achieve an ego-development out of primary identification towards maturing self-identity. In his quest for a libidinally good object the child will turn from the mother to the father, and go back and forth between them many times. The less satisfactory the object-relationships with his parents prove to be in the course of development, the more the child remains embedded in relationships by identification, and the more he creates, and remains tied to, an inner world of bad *internal objects* who will thereafter dwell in his unconscious as an abiding fifth column of secret persecutors, at once exciting desire and denying satisfaction. A deep-seated ever-unsatisfied hunger will be the foundation of the personality, exposing the infant to the fundamental danger of the development of a schizoid state.

CULTURAL EXPRESSIONS OF SCHIZOID FEARS

Psychoanalysts are often accused of dealing with abnormal minds, and drawing from them unjustified conclusions about normal minds. In fact psychoanalysis shows conclusively that this is an entirely misleading distinction. It would be easy to demonstrate every psychopathological process from the study of so-called normal minds alone. Nowadays many people seek analysis not for specific neurotic breakdowns but for character and personality problems, and many of them are people who continue to hold effectively positions of responsibility and who are judged by the world at large to be 'normal' people. Thus psychopathology should be capable of throwing an important light on many aspects of ordinary social and cultural life. This is far too large a theme to be more than touched on here. A few hints must suffice.

Common Mild Schizoid Traits. One has only to collect up some of the common phrases that describe an introvert reaction in human relationships to realize how common the 'schizoid type' of personality is. One constantly hears in the social intercourse of daily life, such comments as 'he's gone into his shell', 'he only half listens to what you say', 'he's always preoccupied', or 'absent-minded', 'he lives in a world of ideas', 'he doesn't live in this world', 'he's an unpractical type', 'he's difficult to get to know', 'he couldn't enthuse about anything', 'he's a cold fish', 'he's very efficient but rather inhuman', and one could multiply the list. All these comments may well describe people whose general stability in any reasonable environment is quite adequate, but who clearly lack the capacity for simple, spontaneous, warm and friendly responsiveness to their human kind. Not infrequently they are more emotionally expressive towards animals than towards the human beings with whom they live or work. They are undemonstrative: it is not merely that they are the opposite of emotionally effervescent, but rather that their relationships with people are actually emotionally shallow. It is well to recognize, from these schizoid types, that psychopathological phenomena cannot be set apart from the so-called 'normal'.

Politics. All through the ages politics has rung the changes, with monotonous regularity, on the themes of 'freedom' and 'authority'. Men have fought passionately for liberty and independence, freedom from foreign domination, freedom from state paternalism and bureaucratic control, freedom from social and economic class oppression, freedom from the shackles of an imposed religious orthodoxy. Yet at other times men have proved to be just as willing, and indeed eager, to be embraced in, and supported and directed by, some totalitarian organization of state or church. No doubt urgent practical necessity often drives men one way or the other at different periods of history and in different phases of social change. But if we seek the ultimate motivations of human action, it is impossible not to link up this social and political oscillation of aim, with the 'in and out' programme of the schizoid person. Man's deepest needs make him dependent on others, but there is nothing more productive of the feeling of being tied or restricted than being overdependent through basic emotional immaturity. Certainly human beings in the mass are far less emotionally mature than they suppose themselves to be, and this accounts for much of the aggressiveness, the oppositionism, and the compulsive assertion of a false, forced, independence that are such obvious social behaviour trends. The schizoid person frequently 'has a bee in his bonnet' about freedom. The love of liberty has been for so long the keynote of British national life that what Erich Fromm (1942) calls 'the fear of freedom' found in totalitarianism, and in political as well as religious authoritarianism seems to us a strange aberration. It is well to realize that both motives are deeply rooted in the psychic structure of human personality.

Ideology. Much has been said of 'depressed eras' in history, but when one considers the cold, calculating, mechanical, ruthless, and unfeeling nature of the planned cruelty of political intellectuals and ideologists, we may well think this to be a 'schizoid era'. The cold and inscrutable Himmler showed all the marks of a deeply schizoid personality and his suicide was consistent. The schizoid intellectual wielding unlimited political power is perhaps the most dangerous type of leader. He is a devourer of the human rights of all whom he can rule. The way some of the most ruthless Nazis could turn to the study of theology was significant of a schizoid splitting of personality. But if we turn to the purely intellectual and cultural sphere it is not difficult to recognize the impersonal atmosphere of schizoid thinking in Hegelianism where a purely intellectualized scheme expounds 'the World as Idea'. Still more apparent is the schizoid sense of futility, disillusionment, and underlying anxiety in Existentialism. These thinkers, from Kierkegaard to Heidegger and Sartre, find human existence to be rooted in anxiety and insecurity, a fundamental dread that ultimately we have no certainties and the only thing we can affirm is 'nothingness', 'unreality', a final sense of triviality and meaninglessness. This surely is schizoid despair and loss of contact with the verities of emotional reality, rationalized into a philosophy; yet existentialist thinkers, unlike the logical positivists, are calling us to face and deal with these real problems of our human situation. It is a sign of the mental state of our age.

SUMMARY

We may finally summarize the emotional dilemma of the schizoid thus: he feels a deep dread of entering into a real personal relationship, i.e. one into which genuine feeling enters, because, though his need for a love-object is so great, he can only sustain a relationship at a deep emotional level on the basis of infantile and absolute dependence. To the love-hungry schizoid faced internally with an exciting but deserting object all relationships are felt to be 'swallowing-up things' which trap and imprison and destroy. If your hate is destructive you are still free to love because you can find someone else to hate. But if you feel your love is destructive the situation is terrifying. You are always *impelled into* a relationship by your needs and at once *driven out* again by the fear either of exhausting your love-object by the demands you want to make or else losing your own individuality by over-dependence and identification. This 'in and out' oscillation is the *typical schizoid behaviour*, and to escape from it into detachment and loss of feeling is the *typical schizoid state*.

The schizoid feels faced with utter loss, and the destruction of both ego and object, whether in a relationship or out of it. In a relationship, identification involves loss of the ego, and incorporation involves a hungry devouring and losing of the object. In breaking away to independence, the object is destroyed as you fight a way out to freedom, or lost by separation, and the ego is destroyed or emptied by the loss of the object with whom it is identified. The only real solution is the dissolving of identification and the maturing of the personality, the differentiation of ego and object, and the growth of a capacity for cooperative independence and mutuality, i.e. psychic rebirth and development of a real ego.

II

THE SCHIZOID PROBLEM, REGRESSION, AND THE STRUGGLE TO PRESERVE AN EGO.[1]

In Chapter I we saw that the most easily recognizable characteristics of the schizoid person are his difficulties in external object-relationships. His need to achieve relations with real people is countered by his intense fear of this, so that after oscillating with great anxiety between 'in' and 'out' situations, he is driven to retreat into detachment and mental isolation. We have now to turn to the other side of the problem. *What happens to the ego when object-relationships in real life break down and are renounced?* Among the schizoid characteristics mentioned in the last chapter was 'regression' and this now calls for fuller consideration. The schizoid has withdrawn from the outer world and the future, and in doing so turns back, regresses to the inner world where the past is enshrined. How deep does this ego-regression go and what does it involve?

REGRESSIVE PHENOMENA

A number of years ago I had a patient, a professional man in the forties, who in his own view presented only one symptom. He was embarrassingly preoccupied with breasts and felt compelled to look at every woman he passed. He regarded his schizoid shy and introverted make-up as simply natural. 'I'm not naturally a good mixer, not one of the sociable sort.' He felt that his preoccupation had something to do with the fact that his wife was an extremely cold and unresponsive woman, as also had been his mother, whom he always thought of as 'buttoned up tight to the neck'. This preoccupation with breasts appeared to be a regressive symptom and went along with a number of childish feelings which he intensely disliked admitting. As analysis proceeded his dwelling on breasts diminished markedly, but its place was taken by a spate of fantasies, all of the same type, in which his interest was intense. They went on for a number of weeks, gathering force and competing

[1] This chapter is a revised version of an article in the *Brit. J. med. Psychol.*, **34** (1961), pp. 223–44.

seriously with his professional work in the daytime. The general theme, embroidered by endless variations, was that he would retire to an isolated part of the country on the sea coast, and there build a strong house and wall it off from the busy inland life. No one was allowed to enter his domain and those who tried to break in by force were miraculously kept at bay. As contrasted with his professional and social life, his inner mental life constituted a house of that kind inside which he lived apart, and into which no one from the outside was ever genuinely admitted.

The series came to a head with a tremendous fantasy of building an impregnable castle on top of a breast-shaped mountain, walling it round with impassable defences, and taking up residence inside. The authorities camped round about and tried to storm his citadel but were quite unable to break in. He clearly felt some uneasiness about this 'safe inside' position, did not wish to be a totally self-made prisoner, and arranged to emerge at times in disguise to inspect the outer world, but no one could get in to contact him. Finally he saw me coming up the mountain side, hurled great boulders at me and drove me off. The fantasy shows some evidence of a wish for a position of security at the breast, in conformity with his symptom, but, like the fantasies that led up to it, the real theme is retreat to a 'safe inside' situation. In this fantasy he oscillates between a breast he can leave and return to, and a womb he can get safe inside. A week or two later he suddenly broke off analysis, using a passing illness of his wife as a reason. The fantasies and the analysis had revealed the powerful regressive drive that underlay his general character of schizoid detachment and withdrawal from real personal relationships. At that time I regarded the fantasies as all of a piece with the interest in breasts, and as a further extension of regression into the depths of infantile experience, beyond the breast into the womb where he would be 'safe inside'. I have now come to regard that as an incomplete interpretation.

I am inclined to think that interpreting his preoccupation with breasts only as regression broke down what was in fact a defence against the final regression, and led him back into *the ultimate regressive impulse to return to the safety of the womb*. By comparison with adult life his attraction to the breast was a regressive phenomenon, but compared with a return to the womb we must see it as a struggle to stay in object-relationships. Breasts are the concern of the baby who has been born and is staying in and reacting to the world outside the womb. His compulsion to cling desperately to breasts and not give them up, was a constructive and forward-looking struggle to defeat his powerful longing to take flight from the post-natal world, return to the womb and be safe inside. Perhaps, if at that time I had credited his presenting symptom with this constructive motivation, we might both have uncovered his deep regressive drive back to a protected passive state, and also supported in the analysis his struggle to preserve an active, even if on that deep level as yet only an infantile, breast-seeking ego. Perhaps he withdrew from analysis through fear that it was betraying him into the power of his regressive flight from active living.

I did not at that time recognize the element of determined defence against schizoid withdrawal and regression which I now feel to be the essential purpose of a good many reactions which, considered from the adult point of view only, present the appearance of merely infantile phenomena. All post-natal phenomena, however infantile in themselves, as oral, anal and some genital phenomena are, belong to the sphere of active 'object-relations' of a differentiated kind, and so can serve as a defence against the impulse to withdraw into passive ante-natal security. This is a clue of far-reaching importance for the understanding of the whole range of psychopathological experiences. The facts about regression and fantasies of a return to the womb have long been familiar to analysts. Nevertheless, they have never been securely placed in the theoretical structure of psychoanalysis. Schizophrenic and depressive states were linked by Abraham to the oral-sucking and oral-biting phases of infancy, but fantasies of a return to the womb have simply been taken as part of the fantasy material of regression in general. *The withdrawn schizoid states* have been loosely linked with schizophrenia in much the same way as the 'depressive character' is related to 'depressive psychosis'. Much clinical material makes me feel that they have a more definite significance.

EXISTING THEORETICAL CONCEPTS

The history of psychoanalysis records one major attempt to take account of ante-natal life in a psychologically meaningful way, namely Otto Rank's 'birth trauma' theory of neurosis. This misfired because he founded it on the assumption that a physical trauma at birth was the origin of all anxiety. He sought a psychoanalytic means of securing a quick unmasking and reliving of this birth trauma in the fond hope that neurosis would then prove amenable to rapid cure. Treatment and cure appeared as a process of 'rebirth', implying that in some sense the neurotic personality was still 'in the womb'. Freud exposed the fallacy of this theory as a whole. In a letter to Abraham in February 1924, he wrote:

I do not hesitate to say that I regard this work [of Rank] as highly significant, that it has given me much to think about, and that I have not yet come to a definite judgement about it. . . . We have long been familiar with womb phantasies and recognized their importance, but in the prominence which Rank has given them they achieve a far higher significance and reveal in a flash the biological background of the Oedipus complex. To repeat it in my own language: some instinct must be associated with the birth trauma which aims at restoring the previous existence, one might call it the urge for happiness, understanding there that the concept 'happiness' is mostly used in an erotic meaning. Rank now goes further than psychopathology, and shows how men alter the outer world in the service of this instinct, whereas neurotics save themselves this trouble by taking the short-cut of phantasying a return to the womb. (Jones, 1957.)

Freud regarded this fantasy of a return to the womb as an erotic wish all of a piece with the oedipal incestuous desire for the mother, and as opposed by the father's prohibition arousing guilt. In March 1924 he wrote again to Abraham:

Let us take the most extreme case, that Ferenczi and Rank make a direct assertion that we have been wrong in pausing at the Oedipus complex. The real decision is to be found in the birth trauma, and whoever had not overcome that would come to shipwreck in the Oedipus situation. Then, instead of our actual aetiology of the neuroses, we should have one conditioned by physiological accidents, since those who became neurotic would be either the children who had suffered a specially severe birth trauma or had brought to the world an organization specially sensitive to trauma. (Jones, 1957.)

Freud rejected Rank's views on two grounds principally, that he found the cause of neurosis in a physical accident (thus failing to give a true psychodynamic aetiology) and even then there was no evidence that a quick unmasking of a birth trauma could produce a rapid cure. Freud's criticism was decisive and yet we are no nearer to seeing the true significance of these womb fantasies and of regressive phenomena in general. After the publication in 1926 of Freud's *Inhibitions, Symptoms and Anxiety*, Jones wrote to him:

You were wise enough to do what none of us others could do: namely to learn something from it all by allowing Rank's views to work on you in a stimulating and fruitful way. (Jones, 1957.)

We must continue to do that ourselves for the solution of the problem has not yet been arrived at.

Freud regarded fantasies of a return to the womb as having the same basic significance as the oedipal desire for the mother. The maternal genital, breast, and womb were all to be held alike as objects of the incest wish. Wishes for them, when activated in adult life, constitute a progressive return to ever earlier stages of the positive, active, infantile sexual drive. This, I now feel, overlooks an important fact. Further, Freud regards the 'instinctive drive' active in these regressions to 'restore the previous existence' as 'the urge for (erotic) happiness'. This also, I believe, misses the real point, and in such a way as to hide the motivational difference between fantasies of a return to the womb, and breast and incest fantasies. *Womb fantasies cancel post-natal object-relations; breast and incest fantasies do not. This fact makes an enormous difference to the ego, which is quite peculiarly dependent on object-relationships for its strength and its sense of its own reality. Return to the womb is a flight from life and implies a giving up of breast and incest fantasies which involve a struggle to go on living.*

The situation revealed by the case material with which I began shows that the patient felt quite simply that the entire external world into which he had emerged at birth was hostile and dangerous and he was afraid of it. If we are to use 'instinct' terminology, then his regressive longing to get back inside the safe place was caused, not by incestuous longing for erotic happiness with the mother, but by *fear*. It is true fear dictates a return to the mother, but for safety rather than for pleasure. He felt he had been born into a menacing outer world and fear stimulated the instinctive reaction of *flight*, escape, withdrawal back into the secure fortress from which he had emerged. From this point of view it would appear that fantasies of the breast, and of anal and incestuous genital relations with the mother of post-natal existence, are expressions of a struggle by a different part of the personality to 'stay born' and function in the world of differentiated object-relations as a separate ego. They are a defence against the danger of being drawn down into another part of the personality which has 'gone back inside' to save itself from being overwhelmed; for this 'going back inside' does very peculiar and frightening things to the ego. *What seems to promise security in one sense is feared as annihilating in another. The wish to return to the womb can also be felt as a wish to die.* That was why my patient provided for his emergence in disguise, at least to inspect, to keep up some contact with, the outer world. Rank was close to the ultimate problem in psychodynamics but hit on the wrong solution, in repudiating which Freud, in turn, failed to hit on the right one. The point of view from which the problem could be solved, a point of view arising out of the study of schizoid phenomena, had not then emerged. We saw in Chapter I that Fairbairn does (to quote Freud) 'make a direct assertion that we have been wrong in pausing at the Oedipus complex'. He traces trouble deeper, to a failure to outgrow *infantile dependence*. 'Regression to the womb' is the profoundest expression of infantile dependence, when a weak infantile ego cannot cope with an inadequate or traumatic environment. 'The real decision is to be found' (Freud) not in the birth trauma but in *the psychological significance of the ultimate regressive longing*. Is it mere escape or a secret hope of rebirth in greater strength?

Since 1924 much work has been done on the early years of infancy. Melanie Klein carried intensive analytical investigations back into Freud's pre-oedipal period. She showed that 'persecutory anxiety' antedates 'depressive anxiety', and that the infant of the first few months is capable of *fear* so intense that it can amount to fear of death in the absolute sense of annihilation. It is true that Klein regarded this fear of destruction as due ultimately to fear of the internal working of the hypothetical death instinct and therefore as a basically endopsychic phenomenon. However, Freud's speculative theory of a death instinct met with little acceptance among analysts, and was rendered unnecessary by the genuinely new development of Klein's '*internal objects theory*'. This, and her view of *the intense fear that can dominate the infant in the earliest period* are indispensable for solving the problem of the profoundest regression underlying schizoid states.

Three other contributions bear vitally on our problem, those of Winnicott and Balint from the clinical, and Fairbairn from the theoretical point of view. In this section we are concerned with theory and Fairbairn's revision of psychoanalytical theory appears to me to be a necessary framework within which this problem can be understood. He transferred emphasis from instincts to the self or ego which owns them, and from impulses to the object-relationships within which they become active. He did this under pressure from his clinical work with schizoid patients, and was led beyond depression to the schizoid state as the basis of all psychopathological developments. A 'personal' rather than a 'psychobiological' theory eventuated. *Freud's analysis of the ego* is a *conceptualization of depression*—a theory of endopsychic structure as essentially a matter of ego and superego control and/or repression of raw id-impulses of an anti-social order. Guilt, ultimately in an unconscious form, is the dynamic of the process and the real source of resistance to psychotherapy (Freud, 1923). By contrast, *Fairbairn's analysis of the ego is a conceptualization of the schizoid process*, and meets the demand that process makes for a theory of endopsychic structure which makes intelligible the 'ego-splitting' that schizoid withdrawal involves. Here the dynamic is not guilt but simple fear. Since schizoid withdrawal is, in the first place, from a bad frightening outer world, Fairbairn does not regard the infant's psychic life as almost wholly endopsychically determined in the way Klein did.

He regards the infant as from the start a whole, unitary, dynamic ego or psyche, however primitive, reacting to his object-world, development being determined by the kind of reception he meets. External object-relations determine the start and future course of endopsychic development in the structural sense. The pristine psyche of the infant is not an unintegrated collection of ego-nuclei, nor is it objectless and purely autoerotic. The work of Klein in fact outmoded both those elements of the original psychoanalytic theory, though she wavered on the first point. Fairbairn is explicit that the infant from the start is a whole, if primitive, dynamic ego[1] with a unitary striving, at first dim and blind, towards the object-relationships he needs for further ego-development. It is an infantile ego of this kind, already a whole human being in essence, in however elementary a way, that we must conceive of as capable of experiencing the intense 'persecutory anxiety', the sheer fear, that Klein found could characterize the very first few months of life. Jones wrote:

> Dr Fairbairn starts at the centre of the personality, the ego, and depicts its strivings and difficulties in its endeavour to reach an object where it may find support . . . a fresh approach in psycho-analysis. (Fairbairn, 1952a, preface.)

Fairbairn's theory of endopsychic structure enables us to conceptualize regression as withdrawal from a bad external world, in search of security in an inner world. It can be seen as the essence of the schizoid

[1] But see page 272 for a qualification of this view.

problem and as the deepest element in all psychopathological development.[1] He points out that the problem of the schizoid individual is that his withdrawal in fear results in an inability to effect genuine relationships with personal objects, a fear which is so great, and which leads to a consequent isolation which tends to become so absolute, that in the end he risks the total loss of all objects and therewith the loss of his own ego as well. It is a grave question whether schizoid withdrawal and regression will lead to rebirth or actual death. His attempt to save his ego from persecution by a flight inside to safety creates an even more serious danger of losing it in another way. This is the indispensable starting-point for the study of regression. It is illustrated with startling clarity by the dream of a University lecturer of a marked schizoid intellectual type:

I took off from the earth in a space ship. Floating about in empty space I at first thought it was marvellous. I thought 'There's not a single person here to interfere with me'. Then suddenly I panicked at the thought 'Suppose I can't get back'.

The schizoid person can withdraw so thoroughly into himself that he fears losing touch altogether with his external object world, which is possible. A young wife, who had become deeply schizoid in early childhood through sheer maternal neglect, was faced with the coming into the home of a loud voiced and domineering mother-in-law. She said simply: 'She scares me. I feel I am just going miles away. It's frightening. I fear I'll get so far away I can't get back. I fear I'll go insane.' She had to ring me several nights in succession to keep in touch and allay fear.

It is at that point that the schizoid person begins to face the danger of the depersonalization of his ego-of-everyday-life, along with the derealization of his environment, and he faces the appalling risk of the loss of definite selfhood, a psychological catastrophe that may lead to suicide, which may primarly be a longing for escape, but may end in death. The patient first cited had good reason to provide for his emergence in disguise to contact reality outside his castle. Yet this was not 'contact' but only 'observing from a detached standpoint'. He had no real relationship because he was afraid to let the outer world get in, to contact him. Apart from psychotherapy, regression and schizoid withdrawal are one and the same thing. Though

[1] In Chapters VIII and IX we shall consider what is an even more ultimate problem which Winnicott investigates, namely how does the infant arrive at a sense of 'being', and get a start in ego-development at all.

regression is a search for safety, it is only safe if there is a real person to regress with and to. Melanie Klein was influenced by Fairbairn's work on the schizoid problem and adopted his term 'schizoid' as an addition to her own term 'paranoid' to describe the earliest developmental 'position', antedating the later 'depressive' position. The combined term 'paranoid-schizoid' position is not, however, strictly accurate. Just as the 'depressive position' is guilt-burdened, so the 'paranoid position' is fear-ridden. The 'schizoid position' is still deeper, for an infantile ego has withdrawn, seeking safety inside away from persecution, or is resolutely seeking to achieve this.

'Paranoid' and 'schizoid' represent 'danger' and 'flight' respectively. Klein holds that failure to work through this total situation renders the child unable later to solve the problems of the depressive position, so that he may regress to and reactivate the earlier problems, as a defence against the pain of unresolvable depression. Klein regarded the 'depressive position' as the central one for development, the stage at which what Winnicott (1955b) calls 'ruth' or 'concern' for others arises, and the development of moral feeling in the civilized person. The earlier paranoid and schizoid or persecuted and withdrawn positions are pre-moral and allow of no concern for others. The question of defence, however, can work the other way round. The paranoid individual faces physical persecution (as in dreams of being attacked by murderous figures) and the depressed individual faces moral persecution (as, for example, in feeling surrounded by accusing eyes and pointing fingers), so that Klein regards both positions as setting up a primary form of anxiety. In fact, most individuals prefer to face either depressive anxiety (guilt) or persecutory anxiety (amoral fear), or an oscillation between them, rather than face the extreme schizoid loss of everything, both objects and ego. *Both persecutory anxiety and depressive anxiety are object-relations experiences, while the schizoid position cancels object-relations in the attempt to escape from anxiety of all kinds.*

Though *schizoid withdrawal and regression are fundamentally the same phenomenon*, they have different meanings for different parts of the total self. From the point of view of the central ego, i.e. the conscious self or everyday living, withdrawal means total loss. From the point of view of the part of the self that has withdrawn, it is not 'loss' but 'regression' or retreat backwards inside the small safe place, as represented in the extreme by the fantasy of a return to the womb. We must therefore allow for *three basic developmental positions, schizoid* (*or regressed*), *paranoid* (*or persecuted*) and *depressed* (or guilt-burdened); and the paranoid and depressed positions can both be used as a defence against the schizoid position. When an individual is inwardly menaced by an involuntary schizoid flight from reality and depersonalization (as when too deep fear is too intensely aroused) he will fight to preserve his ego by taking refuge in internal bad-object fantasies of a persecutory or accusatory kind. Then, unwittingly projecting these on to outer reality, he maintains touch with the world by feeling that people are either plotting his ruin or criticizing and blaming him for everything he does. Fairbairn classes the paranoid reaction with the psychoneurotic reactions as techniques for the manipulation of internal objects as a defence against the primary dangers of schizoid apathy and depression, and places the main emphasis on the underlying 'schizoid position' as determinative of all subsequent development. We may agree that the '*depressive position*' *is decisive for the moral, social and civilized development of the infant*, while the clinical material I present appears to me to confirm Fairbairn's view that *schizoid phenomena, and the flight from object-relations, are more significant for illness* than depression, are more frequently presented clinically, and that the schizoid position is the vital one for development and for psychopathology.

THE SCHIZOID QUEST FOR COMPROMISE IN HUMAN RELATIONS

Womb fantasies and/or the passive wish to die represent the extreme schizoid reaction, the ultimate regression, and it is the more common, mild characteristics which show the extraordinary prevalence of schizoid, i.e. detached or withdrawn, states of mind. Before we study these more common manifestations it may be well to look frankly at the extreme case. A girl of 11 began to find life simply too much for her and sought support in increasing dependence on her mother. She was taken to hospital and treated by discipline to correct this 'hysteric attempt to control the family'. After a few weeks she said to her mother, 'I can't go on. I wish I could faint and wake up inside your tummy.' She was taken home in an exhausted state and at once fell into a deep sleep from which she only partially roused at intervals for several days. Keeping this profound regression in mind, let us turn to its commoner forms. In Chapter I, I used the term 'in and out programme' to describe the dilemma in which schizoid people find themselves with respect to object-relationships. They are caught in a conflict between equally strong needs for, and fears of, close good personal contacts, and in practice often find themselves alternatively driven *into* a relationship by their needs and then driven *out* again by their fears. The schizoid person, because of his fears, cannot *give himself* fully or permanently to anyone or anything with feeling. His most persisting object-relationships are emotionally neutral, often simply intellectual. This plays havoc with consistency in living. He tends to be unreliable and changeable. He wants what he has not got, and begins to lose interest and wants to get away from it when he has it. This particularly undermines friendships and love relationships but can become a general discontent with most things. 'Absence makes the heart grow fonder' is true of schizoid people unless too much fear is roused, and then it turns love to hate. The schizoid individual can often feel strong longings for another person so long as he or she is not there, but the actual presence of the other person causes an emotional withdrawal which may range from coldness, loss of interest and inability to find anything to say, to hostility and revulsion: 'presence makes the heart grow less fond'. Many a patient complains that he carries on long conversations with the therapist 'in his head' but his mind goes blank when he is in the session. So the schizoid person is liable to be constantly 'in and out' of any and every kind of situation.

He usually has a rich and active fantasy life, but in real life is often tepid and weak in enthusiasm, is apt to suffer from inexplicable losses of interest, and feels little zest in living. Yet deep inside he has particularly intense needs. He can live in imagination but not in the world of material reality from which he is primarily withdrawn into himself. He wants to realize his dreams in real life but if he finds a dream coming true externally he seems to be unaccountably unable to accept and enjoy it, especially if it concerns a personal relationship. One spinster patient had longed for years to marry and at the age of forty was able to develop her first serious friendship with a male. He was an excellent man in general but a rather reserved bachelor and not very forthcoming as a lover. As long as she was not sure how much he cared for her, she impatiently and often angrily desired him to be more demonstrative. In fact she did draw him out and then it suddenly dawned on her that he really did want her, and she at once took fright, lost interest, and became critical and off-putting. A crisis developed in her which exploded in one session the moment she entered the consulting room. She stood in the middle of the floor and said in a tense voice: 'I can't come near you. Don't come near me. I'll have to go away, miles away, and live all alone.' I asked her what she was afraid of and she replied: 'If you get close to people you get swallowed up, you go inside.'

Here was a striking expression of the claustrophobic reaction to close relations that the schizoid person experiences, and which had kept her lonely all her life. She had earlier speculated as to which of two male acquaintances she would like to marry if she had the chance, and said: 'Whichever one I chose, I would immediately feel it ought to be the other one.' The schizoid person dreads that a close relationship will involve loss of freedom and independence. This predicament leads to many variations of reaction. To be 'in' with one person, it may be necessary to have someone else to keep at a distance. To remain 'in' with the marriage partner, may necessitate being 'out' with the children or parents; or to be 'in' with one child may involve being 'out' with another one. Sometimes it leads to deep-seated fluctuations of moods with the same person, varying from periods of warm emotion to other periods of coldness and distance. No consistent full free warmth of affection can be achieved. This claustrophobic reaction to any genuine close relationship is seen in the dream of a female patient that her sister was being very loving and affectionate to her and she was enjoying it; then suddenly she felt panicky and thought 'We're getting too close, it's dangerous, something dreadful will happen', and she broke away. This 'in and out' policy, alternately dictated by needs and fears, has serious effects on sexual relationships in marriage so that a man may only be able to risk sexual relationships with a woman he is not 'tied' to and does not really love, while he is unconsciously inhibited by deep fears of too close a bodily relationship to the woman he does love. He splits himself into a mental self and a bodily self, and if he is 'in' with the mind he must be 'out' with the body, and *vice versa*. He cannot commit the whole of himself to one person.

Schizoid persons are extremely liable to fear good and loving relationships more than bad and hostile ones, the reason why they face such exceptional difficulties in personal relationships. As soon as they feel they are getting close to someone they experience an automatic and sometimes catastrophically uncontrollable withdrawal of all positive feeling accompanied by great fear. This more commonly appears in the milder form of unaccountable loss of interest. Thus two male patients revealed a history of broken engagements. The engagements were made on the crest of a wave of strong emotion and almost immediately a state of panic and alarm supervened to make them rush to break it off. Their reaction was 'I feel trapped, doomed'. The fundamental fact, through all these varieties of behaviour, is that *however much the schizoid person tries to make contacts he is also always withdrawing.*

The fundamental schizoid fear, which is expressed by patients with monotonous regularity as the dread of being 'smothered', 'stifled', 'suffocated', 'possessed', 'tied', 'imprisoned', 'swallowed up', 'dominated', 'absorbed' if a close relationship is risked, is often experienced in vaguer general forms. Thus the safeguarding of independence, even to being unable to accept any suggestion or tolerate any advice, becomes quite an obsession. It begets a fear of committing oneself to anyone or anything in any way. People will change clothes, houses, jobs, interests, as well as chopping and changing in friendships and marriage. *Indecision* is a typical result. Sudden enthusiasms are followed by loss of interest. One patient reported what is in fact quite a common symptom. He said, 'I can't really settle myself to read a book. I think "I'd like to read that" and I start it. Just when I begin to enjoy it I lose interest and think "Oh! I don't want to go on with this. I'd rather read that other book." I've got six books all on the go together just now, and can't give myself properly to any one of them to finish it.' The bibliophilic Don Juan is likely to collect and possess books without reading them. This schizoid fear of full self-committal accounts for much inability to concentrate attention in study.

In Chapter I we considered the 'alternating in and out policy' as leading to drastic withdrawal, but this makes life extremely difficult, so we find that *a marked schizoid tendency is to effect a compromise in a half-way-house position, neither in nor out*. The famous Schopenhauer parable, adopted by Freud, of the porcupines, illustrates the position accurately even if its account of the motivation is too limited. A number of porcupines huddled together because they were cold, but found that they pricked each other with their quills and so drew apart again. They went on in this 'in and out' fashion till ultimately they established a mean distance where they were not quite so cold but also did not prick each other. One patient says: 'I live on the edge of life all the time, in a state of muted feelings, neither very miserable nor really happy. I don't enter into anything enough to enjoy it.' Another patient says: 'I'm a chronic non-joiner. I go to the meetings or lectures of some society and quite like them up to a point, but as soon as someone asks me to join I never go again.' A third patient, with extensive philosophical interests, says: 'I'm an adept at the art of brinkmanship. In group discussion I don't put forward a view of my own. I wait to hear what someone else will say and then I remark "Yes, I rather think something like that", but I'm thinking "I don't really agree with him". I won't belong to a recognized school of thought yet I have a dread of going out into the wilderness and standing alone, on some definite views of my own. I hover half-way. It has stopped me doing any creative work.'

Thus, the schizoid person's needs plus fears of good relationships drive him to ring the changes on being in and out with the same person or thing, being in with one and out with another, or compromising in a half-way position, neither in nor out. Unless skilled help is available to enable the person to grow out of his fears of good relationships, the compromise position is often the best remedy for it is more practically workable than disruptive oscillations. During the course of treatment the patient may have to fall back on this compromise, as it were for a breathing space, from time to time while the anxieties of close relationships are being faced. Yet in this compromise position people live far below their real potentialities and life seems dull and unsatisfying. If we could pursue this problem into a mass study of human beings in their everyday existence, we would probably be shocked at the enormous number of people who cannot live life to the full, and not through any lack of means or opportunity, but through lack of emotional capacity to give themselves to anything fully. Here is a cause of boredoms, discontents, dissatisfactions, which are often disguised as economic and social but which no economic or political means can cure. The person with schizoid tendencies usually feels that he is 'missing the bus' and life is passing him by, and it eases his mind superficially if he can find a scapegoat. One patient who lived an unnecessarily restricted life, partly because his withdrawnness involved him in travel phobias, fantasied that he was living at a small wayside country station on the moors, on the side of a main railway line, and all the mainline traffic rushed through and past but never stopped there.

It is far more common to find people exhibiting mild traits of introversion, and poor affective contact with their outer world, than exhibiting signs of true depression, and as Fairbairn pointed out (1952) most people, when they say they are depressed, really mean that they are apathetic and feel life to be futile—the schizoid state. The poor mixer, the poor conversationalist, the strong silent man, the person who lives in a narrow world of his own and fears all new ideas and ways, the diffident and shrinking and shy person, the mildly apathetic person who is not particularly interested in anything, the person of dull mechanical routine and robot-like activity into which little feeling enters, who never ventures on anything unfamiliar, are all in various degrees withdrawn and out of the full main stream of living. One patient dreamed that he was in a small boat in a backwater off a main rushing river. It was choked with weeds and he was struggling without success to get his boat out into the current. Such people have but little effective emotional rapport with their world. They are in the grip of fear deep down and remain drawn back out of reach of being hurt.

On the other hand, this fundamental detachment is often masked and hidden under a façade of compulsive sociability, incessant talking, and hectic activity. One gets the feeling that such people are acting a somewhat exhausting part. Patients will say 'I feel vaguely that I'm play-acting and that my life isn't real'. The jester or comedian or the person who is 'the life and soul of the party' in public is often 'depressed' in private. Schizoid shallowness of feeling in the part of the personality that deals with the outer world in everyday life is the cause of inability to find much real satisfaction in living. The emotional core of the personality is withdrawn from the self that lives in the external world. The outer self, like a skilled actor, can act even an emotional part mechanically while thinking of other things. A middle-aged woman patient discovered in the course of analysis that she did not need the spectacles she was wearing and discarded them. She said: 'I realize I've only worn them because I felt safer behind that screen. I could look through it at the world.' A somewhat common schizoid symptom is the feeling of a plateglass wall between the patient and the world. Another patient says: 'I feel I'm safe inside my body looking out at the world through my eyes.' One is reminded of the Greek idea of the body as the prison of the soul, one of many marks of a schizoid mentality in the Greek intellectualist view of life. Winnicott's account of the split between the psyche and the soma throws much light on this. The healthy personality does not feel to be in two parts, one hiding from the world within the other, but whole, all of a piece, and active as a unity.

Both the part of the personality which is deeply withdrawn and out of touch, and the part of the personality left to maintain some shallow and precarious contact with the outer world, depleted of emotional vitality, are withdrawn, but the former more profoundly so. The deeply withdrawn part of the whole self is profoundly 'schizoid', extensively 'cut off'. The ego of everyday life is not so fully cut off. It maintains a mechanical rather than an emotional contact, and tends to feel affectively devitalized, emptied even to the risk of depersonalization. Dreams in which the patient is only an observer of the activities of others are fairly common. An unmarried woman in the thirties dreamed that she stood at a little distance and watched a man and woman kiss, became terrified, and ran away and hid. In her first position she was considerably withdrawn but not entirely out of touch. In her second position she was completely cut off. In fact, patients maintain both positions at the same time in different parts of their total self, and *the process of withdrawal in successive stages through fear emerges as a major cause of what we have come to call 'ego-splitting', the loss of unity of the self.*

This state of affairs creates two problems. *The part of the self that struggles to keep touch with life feels intense fear of the deeper and more secret, withdrawn self, which appears to be endowed with a great capacity to attract and draw down more and more of the rest of the personality into itself. Hence extensive defences are operated against it.* If those defences fail, the ego of everyday consciousness experiences a progressively terrifying loss of interest, energy, zest, verging towards exhaustion, apathy, derealization of the environment, and depersonalization of the conscious ego. It becomes like an empty shell out of which the living individual has departed to some safer retreat. If that goes too far, the central ego, the ordinary outer world self, becomes incapable of carryin on its normal life, and the whole personality succumbs to a full-scale 'regressive breakdown'.

Fortunately, there are several ways in which life in the outer world can be kept going in spite of a considerable measure of withdrawal of the vital feeling-self. Ways of living can be devised which do not depend on immediate vitality of 'feeling for' the object-world. Three such ways are common. The schizoid intellectual lives on the basis of 'thinking', the obsessional moralist on the basis of 'duty' and the 'organization-man' on the basis of carrying on automatically in a fixed routine. If the emotionally withdrawn person can by such means ward off a great deal of the impact of real life, and prevent its pressures from playing on the secret inner fear-ridden feeling-life, then a relatively stabilized schizoid character may result, a human being who functions as an efficient robot within a restricted and safe conception of how life is to be lived. Life is the pursuit of truth, not love, the thinking out of an ideology; and ideas become more important than people. He tends to hold the Greek rather than the Christian view of life, and the scientific rather than the religious view. In religion theology is exalted above love of one's neighbour. In politics, a party creed is exalted above humane feeling, so that people have to be 'done good to' and forced to accept the right kind of social order for their own interest even if many of them have to be killed in cold blood to make the rest accept this nostrum.

This outlook can easily slip over into the unswerving performance of 'duty' in a rigidly conceived way, doing the 'right thing' according to one's own fixed conception without regard to human realities, or concern for the feelings of others; much as Graham Green's 'Quiet American' created havoc everywhere by the way he 'acted on principle'. Or again life may be reduced to simply carrying on the usual routine, doing the obvious thing, in a mechanical manner, seeking not even to think, being in a cold neutral state of mind that freezes everyone around but is safe for the person concerned. All degrees of this kind of stabilization of the schizoid personality occur, from mild tendency to fixed type.

The schizoid intellectual is a particularly important type, for he can become a serious social menace especially if he comes to political power. Highly abstract philosophy seems unwittingly designed to prove Descartes' dictum, 'Cogito, ergo sum', 'I think, therefore I am', the perfect formula for the schizoid intellectual's struggle to possess an ego. A natural human being would be more likely to start from 'I feel, therefore I am'. Even the schizoid person can become rapidly convinced of his own reality for the time being by feeling angry, whereas his thinking is usually a not very convincing struggle to hold on to a somewhat desiccated personal reality. This happens when a person cannot go to sleep but lies awake 'thinking'. Thus a patient suffering from a very traumatic bereavement felt 'emptied' and would ward off attacks of depersonalization in the night by lying awake for hours just thinking. She said it did not seem to matter what she thought about so long as she continued to think. When an elaborate ideology is fanatically defended it is usually a substitute for a true self.

Behind all these methods by which the schizoid person struggles to save himself from too far-reaching a withdrawal from outer reality with its consequences of loss of the ego, lies the hidden danger of a secret part of the personality which is devoted to a fixed attitude of retreat from life in the outer world. It is the part of the total self that most needs help and healing. Its two most extreme expressions are regressive breakdown and fantasies of a return to the womb or a passive wish to die. In face of this internal threat, the business of maintaining an ego is fraught with unceasing anxiety. The schizoid problem is an 'ego' problem. Like the British army at Dunkirk, the too-hard-pressed child retreats to save himself from annihilating defeat, so that back in a protected security he may recover strength, an analogy which suggests that the schizoid withdrawal, if we understand it aright, is a healthy phenomenon in the circumstances which initiate it. By retreating back 'inside the safe place', the British army gained the chance to recover and lived to fight another day. Winnicott holds that under stress the infant withdraws his real self from the fray to await a better chance of rebirth later on (1955a). Yet this retreat to save a 'hidden ego' also goes a long way to undermine the 'manifest ego' which experiences it as a threat of breakdown or death. This is the problem presented for solution by schizoid data.

CAUSES AND STAGES OF SCHIZOID WITHDRAWAL

(1) *Fear and Flight from External Reality.* The most pathological schizoid withdrawal takes place astonishingly early, in the first year of life. It can, of course, occur at any time of life as a generalized reaction, but the more it is found to be structurally embedded in the personality the earlier it originally occurred. It can then, certainly, be intensified and consolidated all through later childhood and evoked by pressures in real life at any time, but there is little doubt that in the beginning it is associated with what Melanie Klein called 'persecutory anxiety' and 'the infantile anxiety situations'. It is a 'fear and flight' reaction in the face of danger. In Chapter IX we must consider the fact that at first the infant cannot distinguish between subject and object, self and breast. In this chapter we start with the infant aware of an outer world, and trace the process by which he comes to live in two worlds at once, outer and inner.

The view of the later Freud and of Klein that the *ultimate* source of the danger is wholly internal, a 'death instinct', innate active aggression working inwardly, threatening destruction against the primary psyche, has found no general acceptance. It would be unscientific to fall back on such a speculative idea when satisfactory clinical analysis is available. The view of the earlier Freud that psychopathological development began, not with innate aggression but with the libidinal drives of the sexual instinct aiming at erotic pleasure and proving to be incompatible with social reality, at least implied that the source of the trouble was more in the environment than in the infant. The world into which the infant was born could not tolerate his nature and his needs and he came up against painful frustrations. However, this view does not cover all the facts.

Fairbairn takes a wider view of libidinal need as not limited to the sexual but embracing all that is involved in the need for personal relationships, on however simple and primitive a level at the beginning; the goal of libidinal need is not pleasure but the object (at first the breast and the mother). *The frustration of libidinal need for good object-relations both arouses aggression and intensifies libidinal needs till the infant fears his love-needs as destructive towards his objects.* In the later 'depressive position' which Winnicott calls the stage of 'ruth' or 'concern for the object' this would lead to guilt. But *at this earliest stage it leads to the schizoid withdrawal, a simple fear reaction, away from the danger of devouring and therefore losing the love-object.* Schizoid persons have given up the outward expression of needs, while also being haunted by the fear of losing love-objects. One patient says: 'I can't make moderate demands so I don't make any at all', and another insists 'I lose everyone I love'. *Yet the schizoid fear is not so much on behalf of the object as on behalf of the ego and the consequences to it of losing the object.* Here lies the difference between the moral and the pre-moral level of development. The schizoid personality is basically on a pre-moral level; hence the horrifying callousness schizoid people can manifest. It is not in accordance with Fairbairn's psychodynamic outlook to treat these libidinal needs as discrete entities demanding satisfaction in and for themselves. They are the needs of an ego. Since the need for an object arises from the fact that without object-relations no strong ego-development is possible, we must conclude that the satisfaction of libidinal needs is not an end in itself but is an experience of good-object relationships in which the infant discovers himself as a person, and his ego-development proceeds firmly and self-confidently. Fairbairn's view brings out the question of ego-growth in weakness or in strength as the background of all problems arising out of fears, conflicts and withdrawals over frustrated needs.

Deprivation of needs is, however, not the only cause of schizoid withdrawal, and Winnicott emphasizes what seems to be an equally primitive situation. Not only must the mother meet the infant's needs when he feels them, but she must not force herself on him in ways and at times that he does not want. That constitutes 'impingement' on the as yet weak, immature and sensitive ego of the infant. He cannot stand this and shrinks

away into himself. There are many other sources of 'impingement' in loveless, authoritarian and quarrelsome families and often sheer fear is aroused in the tiny child. Fairbairn also stressed in private conversation that trouble arises not only over the child's needs for the parents, but also over the parents' pressures on the child who is often exploited in the interests of the parents' needs, not the baby's. The startle-reaction to sudden loud noise is perhaps the simplest case of fear at impingement, and such impingement experiences, particularly at the hands of parents, begin the building up of basic impressions that the whole outer world is not supporting but hostile.

Judging by the reflexion of these early events in the psychopathology of adults, this factor of impingement and pressure of a hostile environment, bearing to an intolerable degree on the tender infant mind, is the true source of 'persecutory anxiety', of fear of annihilation, and of flight back inside, of withdrawal of the emotionally traumatized infant libidinal ego into itself out of reach of the dangerous outer world. What an adult may do consciously, as in the case of a wife who felt that her husband was inconsiderate and said 'I built a wall round myself so that I should not be hurt', the infant does instinctively. He takes flight inwards from the outer world. Fear of deprived and therefore dangerous active oral-sadistic libidinal needs belongs to a higher level, that of the struggle to remain in object-relationships. It precipitates withdrawal in two ways, however, through fear of devouring and losing the object, and through fear of retaliation and of being devoured by the object. This latter fear may develop into guilt and the fear of punishment. Withdrawal from direct frightening impingement by the object in the first place is more primitive. Deep fear-enforced withdrawal from object-relations is then to a regressed passive level of a womb-like state inside. *Severe schizoid states disclose a total fear of the entire outer world, and deprivation and impingement combine. The world is a frightening emptiness when it does not respond and meet the infant's needs, and a frightening persecutor when it actively and hurtfully impinges. The infant cannot develop a secure and strong ego-sense either in a vacuum or under intolerable pressure and he seeks to return to a vaguely remembered earlier safe place, even though in fact he can only withdraw into isolation within himself.*

With one patient, a doctor, suffering from apparent 'depression' which was really apathy, indifference, and loss of zest for work, the analytical uncovering of a clear-cut castration fear, led to an outbreak of apathy, loss of interest and energy so serious that for a time he could hardly carry on his daily work.

It was a herculean effort to get himself out of bed and one day he was quite unable to get up. He lay in bed all day, curled up and covered over with bed-clothes, refusing food and conversation and requiring only to be left alone in absolute peace. That night he dreamed that he went to a confinement case and found the baby sitting on the edge of the vagina wondering whether to come out or go back in, and he could not decide whether to bring it out or put it back. He was experiencing the most deeply regressed part of his personality where he felt and fantasied a return to the womb, an escape from sheer fear of castration, not by father but by mother and aunt. The whole family life had been one of anxiety, a nagging mother, a drinking father, quarrelling parents, pressure on the child to be 'no trouble' from babyhood, and then as he grew older a mother and aunt who made actual and literal castration threats, sometimes as a joke, sometimes semi-seriously: 'if you're not a good boy I'll cut it off', accompanied by half gestures towards the little boy with knife or scissors which terrified him. But that well-founded castration complex, which brought back a wealth of detailed memories, was but the end-product of all the child's memories of a mother whose basic hostility to him he had always sensed. His serious schizoid-regressive illness was the result of a withdrawal into himself which must have taken place first at an extremely early age to escape intolerable impingement by his family life.

Deprivation of libidinal needs and separation anxiety play their part along with impingement in provoking withdrawal, not only by intensifying needs till they seem too dangerous to express, but also by the threat of emptying the ego. One very schizoid agoraphobic patient reacted primarily to gross neglect and rejection by her mother in her first year. Outwardly the position improved at about one year when a neighbour said 'Excuse me, Mrs X, but you only take notice of your older child, you never take any notice of the baby.' The mother's guilt then made her subject the baby to oppressive attention, but the damage was done. Before the vacuum changed into a smothering environment the mother's emotional withdrawal from the child had been met by the child's emotional withdrawal from the mother. She developed so-called epileptic fits in the first year, which faded out into 'dizzy turns'. They must have represented the collapse of her conscious ego, as what Winnicott would call her 'true self' took flight from a world in which she could find nothing by which she could live. In after years, when the patient's husband was called up for military service, this represented at bottom her mother's desertion of her and she broke down in acute anxiety, could not be left alone, and remained house-bound, withdrawn from life and 'safe inside'. Late in analysis, when she felt she had got back to her early childhood, she reported a dream. 'I was small and I pointed a brush at mother like a magnet to draw her to me. She came but said "I can't be bothered with you, I'm going to help Mrs So-and-So." I felt a terrible shock, like an electric shock, inside—"So you didn't want me"—as if the bottom dropped out of me, life seeped away and I felt emptied.' Did that 'shock' represent her original 'epileptic fits'? During that same night she dreamed that she 'just fell, collapsed', and in fact she did do that next day. The importance of an object-relationship for the maintenance of the ego, both in real life and in psychotherapy, is clear from the dream in which this patient fell.

She dreamed that she met a woman and asked her the way; when the woman did not answer she 'just fell'. Then she was with me and I took her hand 'to warm her up', i.e. bring her back to life.

One seriously schizoid male patient who had to sit during sessions so that he could see me, at times would begin to fade away into unconsciousness, a process which was only arrested if I held his hand till he felt securely in touch again.

Impingement, rejection, and deprivation of needs for object-relationships must be bracketed together as defining the traumatic situation which drives the infant into a retreat within himself in search of a return to the womb. Probably deprivation in the sense of 'tantalizing refusal' leads to *active* oral phenomena while impingement, and deprivation as 'desertion', lead to shrinking away inside into a passive state.

(2) *A Two-stage Withdrawal, From External and Internal Bad Objects.* The previous section describes the origins of the first stage of what appears to be a two-stage retreat from bad-object relationships. This initial escape is from the outer material world into an inner mental one. But contact with the object-world cannot be given up, especially at this early stage, without threatening to lead to loss or emptying of the ego. Thus part of the total self must be left to function on the conscious level and keep in touch with the world of real external objects. If that were not done, and relationship with outer reality were wholly given up, the infant would presumably die. Thus a 'splitting' of the hitherto unitary, pristine ego occurs, into a part dealing with the outer world (Freud's 'reality-ego' and Fairbairn's

'central ego') and a part that has withdrawn into the inner mental world.

The withdrawn part of the total self must also, however, keep in object-relationships if it is to maintain its experience of itself as a definite ego. 'Psychic reality', instead of registering the active function of dealing with the outer world, becomes a 'place' to live in. As Melanie Klein has shown, the infant internalizes his objects and builds up an inner world of object-relations. Fairbairn regards the infant as internalizing his unsatisfying objects in an effort to master them in inner reality because he cannot master them in the outer world. In the result, however, they are felt to be as powerful and terrifying in inner reality as in outer, a 'fifth column' of internal persecutors or saboteurs who have infiltrated into the inner world where the infant has sought relief inside himself from pressure. A serious predicament has arisen. On the face of it no further retreat seems possible and a series of fresh manœuvres are made. Fairbairn has described these in terms of 'object-splitting' and 'ego-splitting' processes, which build up the structure of the inner world in terms of endopsychic object-relations. The internal unsatisfying object is split into its three main aspects, libidinally exciting, libidinally rejective, and emotionally neutral or good and undisturbing. The last or Ideal Object is  projected back into the real object and what has all the appearance of an external object-relationship is maintained with it by the central ego, the ordinary ego of everyday living. Nevertheless, this is not a properly objective relation, for the object is not fully realistically perceived but only experienced in the light of a partial image projected from inner reality. Thus, once some measure of schizoid withdrawal has been set up, such contact with the outer world as is maintained is defective and governed by the projection of partial and over-simplified images of the object: a fact constantly demonstrated by the poor judgment of others, the over- or under-estimation of either good or bad qualities, commonly displayed by people.

Then, while the real object (the actual parent) is unrealistically idealized, his or her exciting and rejective aspects remain as distinguishable and separate fantasied objects of the infant's need for relationships in the inner world. Thus, the unity of that part of the ego which has withdrawn inside away from outer reality becomes split into an ego attached to the exciting object and an ego attached to the rejecting object. Just as the exciting object arouses libidinal needs while the rejecting object denies them, so the attachment to the exciting object results in a *libidinal ego* characterized by ever-active and unsatisfied desires which come to be felt in angry and sadistic ways; and the attachment to the rejecting object results in an *antilibidinal ego* based on an identification which reproduces the hostility of the rejecting object to libidinal needs. Inevitably the libidinal ego is hated and persecuted by the antilibidinal ego as well as by the rejecting object, so that the infant has now become divided against himself. This is easy to recognize in the contempt and scorn shown by many patients of their own needs to depend for help on other people or on the analyst. It is seen also in the fear and hate of weakness that is embedded in our cultural attitudes. The internal persecution of the libidinal ego by the antilibidinal ego is vividly seen in the dream of a male patient.

> He was sitting in an armchair in my room wanting to relax, but at the same time he was also standing behind the chair looking down on the 'him' who was sitting in the chair, with an expression of hate and hostility and raising a dagger to kill the needy weak self.

At this stage, the part of the ego which has withdrawn from outer reality has now created for itself a complex inner world of objects both exciting and persecuting. *The existence of these internal objects enables the parts of the ego which maintain relations with them to retain ego-sense.* It seems evident that the real need which dictates the creation of Melanie Klein's world of internal objects, good and bad, and the resulting processes of ego-splitting described by Fairbairn, is not simply the urge to master the object but the vital need of the psyche to retain an ego-sense. This can only be done by maintaining object-relations at least in the inner mental world, after withdrawing in that part of one's personal life from the outer material one. So long as a continuing fantasy life can be kept going by the libidinal and antilibidinal egos, the ego is kept in being though cut off from outer reality. At one time the libidinal ego is sadistically fantasying the incorporation of its exciting object in inner reality; at another the antilibinal ego has possessed itself of the sadism, and along with the rejecting object fantasies crushing or slave-driving the masochistically suffering libidinal ego. According to Fairbairn, internal objects are psychic structures just as much as partial egos are. The total psychic self 'impersonates' objects to itself in the inner world so as to retain ego-identity in fantasied relations. Though this kind of inner life results in states of acute 'persecutory anxiety', the ego is still in being; it has not succumbed to depersonalization after breaking off emotional rapport with objects in real life. This is indeed *the rationale of the creation and maintenance of the Kleinian internal objects world: it is a defence against ego-loss, which shows why it is so hard for the patient to give it up.* In withdrawing from the outer world, the ego would lose itself in a vacuum of experience, if it could not create for itself an inner psychic world.

Yet the position of the withdrawn ego is little bettered, for its enemies have infiltrated into its safe retreat where they are even harder to get away from than before. Freud realized this when, in the early days of psychoanalysis, the sources of internal dangers were thought of as 'instinct-derivatives'. He stressed that the ego cannot escape from what is actually a part of internal reality. This, however, turns out not to be entirely true; or at least it is indubitably true that the ego makes one further attempt to escape from the intolerable internal pressures put upon it by its post-natal world of bad objects. It is the libidinal ego which is the part of the originally whole and now split ego in which the persecutory pressure is felt; and clinical facts have suggested to me that it repeats, in face of the *internal* bad-object world, the same manœuvre that was made by the whole ego when it sought to withdraw from the *external* bad-object world. It leaves part of itself to carry on such relations as are possible, in sadomasochistic terms, with the exciting and rejecting objects of the internal fantasy world, while the traumatized, sensitive and exhausted heart of it withdraws deeper still. The evidence provided by regressive behaviour, regressive symptoms and regressive dreams and fantasies, shows that this most deeply withdrawn ego feels and fantasies a return to the womb, safe inside the 'fortress' from which it probably still has some dim memory of having emerged. Only thus can we account for the distinct and separate functioning of an active oral infantile libidinal ego tied to a terrifying world of internal bad-object relations, and of a passive regressed libidinal ego concerned only with an imperative need to escape and be 'safe inside' and giving up all definite object-relations in favour of an enclosing protective environment. It is the irresistible pull of this regressed ego under certain circumstances that precipitates the schizoid breakdown in the most extreme cases, but its powerful pull manifested in the teeth of stubborn resistance and defence accounts for all the tensions and illnesses that arise out of this desperate struggle to possess and to retain an ego.

I first made this suggestion of a final split in the libidinal ego itself, in an article on 'Ego Weakness and the Hard Core of the Problem of Psychotherapy' (1960) (see Chapter VI) and traced out some of its consequences in the closing section of *Personality Structure and Human Interaction* (1961). Here I have sought to give fuller clinical evidence for this view. In addition to the two levels of ego-splitting which Fairbairn describes, namely, first, that between the central ego in touch with the outer world and a withdrawn ego in the inner world, and, second, the further splitting of this withdrawn ego into the libidinal ego and the antilibidinal ego, there is a third and *ultimate split in the libidinal ego itself. It divides into an active sado-masochistic oral ego which continues to maintain internal bad-object relations, and a passive regressed ego which seeks to return to the antenatal state of absolute passive dependent security.* Here, in quietude, repose, and immobility it may find the opportunity to recuperate and grow to a rebirth, as Winnicott (1955a) holds. This regressed ego may come to seem identical with what Winnicott calls the 'true self' put into cold storage to await the chance of rebirth in better conditions. But we may have to distinguish between potentialities never yet evoked and a frightened ego that has fled back. I do not feel sure whether the regressed ego feels itself to be 'frozen in cold storage' (frozen in fear perhaps) or whether it feels hidden in the deepest unconscious in the warmth of a hallucinated intrauterine condition. Some patients appear to feel one way and others the other. The dream of a University lecturer which shows how little his academic life had touched his deeper mentality, illustrates this two-stage retreat:

I was on a tropical South Sea Island and thought I was all alone. Then I found it was full of white people who were very hostile to me and surged at me. I found a little hut on the shore and rushed into it and barred the door and windows and got into bed.

He has retreated from civilization to his lonely island (his internal world) only to find that his bad objects, white people, are still with him. So he makes a second retreat which is a complete regression. In defence against this he had twice succumbed to a manic psychosis followed by a depressed, apathetic state. The fact that this manœuvre involves a splitting of the withdrawn libidinal ego into two is seen in another dream:

The patient was in the analyst's consulting room. There were two little boys in the room whom he wanted to send out, but the analyst was looking after them and wished them to remain. They sat together on chairs; one was unnaturally alert and watchful, keeping in touch with everything that went on, while the other had a dull

expressionless face and took no notice of anything at all, but was completely withdrawn.

Here are the active oral ego and the passive regressed ego, along with the central ego, i.e. the patient in his familiar every-day self, sitting apart in an armchair. But his antilibidinal ego was in concealed partnership with the central ego and hostile to the children, i.e. to both parts of the split libidinal ego.

We have, therefore, as we saw in the last section, at least three possible causes of very early arousal of an intense impulse to *withdraw* from immediate relationship with the outer world, into a mentally interior life, namely: (*a*) *Tantalizing refusal* by those responsible for the infant to satisfy his libidinal needs. This arouses hungry impulses so powerful as to be feared as devouring and destructive. Oral sadistic needs are then repressed and the external object is given up. Libido and aggression are withdrawn into the inner world. (*b*) *Impingement* of a hostile aggressive object or situation arouses direct fear of an overpowering outer world, and evokes withdrawal as a flight into the inner world. (*c*) *Rejection and neglect*, non-recognition or desertion, by the outer world, all that is implied in Winnicott's comment that 'schizophrenia is an environmental deficiency disease', leaves the infant facing, as it were, a vacuum in which it is impossible to live. He turns away from it into himself, withdraws into an inner world which must, however, itself be empty even of persecutory and tantalizing internal bad objects, owing to the poverty of initial real life experience. (I have stated on p. 66 that I do not accept the Kleinian view that bad objects originate in an inherited, innate factor, a death instinct.) In this case the danger of ego-loss and depersonalization is at its maximum; (*a*) and (*b*) precipitate the split of the libidinal ego into an active oral sadistic libidinal ego struggling on in an internal bad objects world, and a passive regressed libidinal ego in flight from it; (*c*) leads to the experience of emptiness inside and out, and probably leads to the most profound regression of all, which the patient can experience as dying and death. No doubt all three of these causes coalesce in different degrees in various types of schizoid state. Patients do undoubtedly maintain persecutory anxiety as a defence against the development of a feeling of 'fading out into nothingness'.

(3) *Regression to a Symbolic Womb.* Since this regressed ego is the basis of the most dangerous and undermining psychopathological developments, it is as well to reflect on the fact that it is in itself a necessary, reasonable, and healthy reaction to

danger. Something is wrong primarily not with the infant but with the environment. The problems arise from the fact, not that what the frightened and regressed infant seeks is psychopathological in itself, but that it is something that, however realistically needed, he ought not to be driven to want, and in any case is exceedingly difficult to obtain in any substitute form once the actual womb has been left. The primitive wholeness of the ego is now lost in a fourfold split, a depleted central ego coping with the outer world, a demanding libidinal ego inside persecuted by an angry antilibidinal ego (the Kleinian internal world), and finally a regressed ego which knows and accepts the fact that it is overwhelmed by fear and in a state of exhaustion, and that it will never be in any fit state to live unless it can, so to speak, escape into a mental convalescence where it can lie quiet, protected, and be given a chance to recuperate. This is exactly clinically manifested in the case of the 11-year-old girl cited on page 58.

I have heard Fairbairn's scheme of endopsychic structure criticized as too complicated (though we do not criticize physics on such grounds). The criticism is not valid. Of Freud's scheme Colby (1955) writes:

> There are ... theoretical disadvantages to the id-ego-superego model. Today its simplicity makes it insufficient to conceptualize specifically enough the manifold functions of psychic activity. ... In psycho-analysis our knowledge has increased in such a way that to subsume the complexities of psychic activity under three undivided categories is to stretch generalizations perhaps too far.

The complexity describes the terrible disintegration that can be forced on the tender and weak infantile ego if it is subjected to pressures it is too immature to bear. Freud wrote in his last book:

> The weak and immature ego of the first phase of childhood is permanently damaged by the strain put upon it in the effort to ward off the dangers that are peculiar to that period of life (1940).

He further states:

> The view which postulates that in all psychoses there is a *split in the ego* could not demand so much notice, if it were not for the fact that it turns out to apply also to other conditions more like the neuroses and, finally, to the neuroses themselves. (1940.)

Fairbairn's scheme reduces to order the tangled mass of self-contradictory reactions presented to us as clinical material, and reveals this permanent damage to the immature ego in the form of the 'ego-splitting' of which Freud speaks. The additional structural complexity that I have added is called for by clinical data that we have long failed to include properly in any structural scheme. It conceptualizes the ultimate desperate bid made by the overtaxed infant to save himself, a move which perpetuates thereafter what we may call a 'structural headquarters of fear' in the personality as a basis for the danger of regressive breakdown in later life. It may be well to say explicitly that these endopsychic structural differentiations are not to be regarded as separate entities into which the psychic whole is fragmented as if it were a material object. They are clearly recognizable different aspects of the functioning of the complex psychic whole, however much they at times shade off into each other. At times their distinctness is quite startling.

The *regressed ego* denotes, not a freely available generalized 'fear and flight' reaction but *the deepest structurally specific part of the complex personality, existing in a settled attitude of fear, weakness, withdrawal, and absolute dependence not in the active post-natal infantile sense but in a passive ante-natal sense. It represents the most profoundly traumatized part of the personality and is the hidden cause of all regressive phenomena* from conscious escapist fantasies to complete schizoid apathy, unless its need is understood and met; but there lies the greatest difficulty and challenge to therapy. In a letter to me dated 1 January 1960, Fairbairn accepted this extension of his structural theory. He wrote:

> I consider your concept of the splitting of the libidinal ego into two parts—an oral needy libidinal ego and a regressed libidinal ego—as an original contribution of considerable explanatory value. It solves a problem which I had not hitherto succeeded in solving.

Winnicott wrote on 31 October 1960:

> Your split in the libidinal ego seems to have a lot in common with my 'hidden true self' and the 'false self built upon a compliance basis' (a defence in illness, and in health simply the polite self that does not wear its heart on its sleeve). I do think that research can usefully be based on these ideas that are in the air and which you are developing in your own way.

It is a pleasure to quote these two writers to whose pioneering work in theory and therapy I owe most for stimulus. I would think that Winnicott's 'false compliant self in health' corresponds to the central ego of Fairbairn and his 'false compliant self as a defence in illness' corresponds to Fairbairn's anti-libidinal ego, especially in its function of hating weakness. This to me especially seems to warrant the term 'false self'.

How can the need of the exhausted regressed ego for recuperation in and rebirth from a reproduction of the womb-state be met at all, and how can it be met without the risk of undermining the central ego of everyday living? That seems to be the ultimate problem for psychotherapy. There is evidence that in some cases it can be done, though we have almost everything to learn about this process. At least it is safe to say that it cannot be done without the aid of a psychotherapist, i.e. the setting up of a therapeutic object-relationship. This is the significance of Winnicott's work on 'therapeutic regression'. The limitations of psychotherapy hitherto must be the result of this problem not having been recognized earlier. When the individual is left to himself, he can only do what he was driven to do as a child, struggle to repress his regressive trends by developing a hard and hostile attitude to any 'weakness' in himself, i.e. develop an anti-libidinal ego which is really the child's determined effort to keep himself going by being independent (see Chapter VI). If his regressed ego becomes irresistible he can only provide for it by a regressive illness. Perhaps, if he did not give in to that in time and compel his environment to take responsibility for him he would die of psychic self-exhaustion. The psychotherapist must help the patient to find a way of substituting a controlled and constructive regression for an uncontrolled and involuntary one in the form of an illness that might be an irretrievable disaster for the patient's real-life status. But I believe that this also cannot be done without the aid of a psychoanalytical psychotherapist; for the main obstacle to the patient's accepting a constructive regression in treatment is his own antilibidinal ego which needs the closest analytical uncovering. *The final aim of this therapy is to convert regression into rebirth and regrowth*. This must result from the regressed ego finding for the first time an object-relationship of understanding acceptance and safeguarding of its rights, with a therapist who does not seek to force on the patient his preconceived views of what must be done, but who realizes that deep down the patient knows his own business best, if we can understand his language. But before the problem of therapy can be solved we must understand how the patient's struggles to save himself form a resistance to the true therapy.

THE FIGHT AGAINST REGRESSION

(1) *The Determined Drive Backwards.* We have stated that, *left to himself*, the individual can only either provide for his regressed ego in the extreme case by illness, owing to the practical difficulties of providing for it in any other way, or else seek to suppress it as an internal danger threatening to undermine his adjustment to real life in the outer world. The vague influence of a regressed part of the total self is easy to recognize in many people as an attitude of getting through life with as little trouble as possible, getting out of things if they can, and having to push themselves to do what they must. One woman passing middle age, who had functioned adequately and brought up a family, experiencing anxiety all her life without any breakdown said: 'Now and again I feel I can't cope and will have to give in.' She had a recurring dream of drowning. Generally a sustained if automatic effort is made over the years to stave off regression in any more definite sense, though many people have a history of periodic breakdowns, say every four or five years, with minor signs of nervous strain and tension in between. In many cases, however, very vigorous defences of an antilibidinal nature (antilibidinal towards the self even when apparently libidinal towards others) are built into the personality and direct very energetic if over-tense drives into real life.

The individual from the beginning has had to cope with the problem himself. No one has really known or understood what was going on in the child, and so far as his deeper life was concerned he had to bring himself up and manage himself in secret. Hence the self-centredness and introversion of schizoid persons. Life becomes a long, hidden, tension-filled struggle against regressive trends. Tremendous tension can be masked by a calm exterior, but is often not masked, breaking out physically if not in other ways. Melanie Klein and Fairbairn treat the psychoneurotic states as defences against the psychotic dangers of schizoid apathy and depression. If, however, the deepest danger is regression to passivity, we must regard all states, psychotic as well as neurotic, in which an 'active' ego struggles and suffers, as defences.

The ultimate characteristic of the regressed ego is dependent passivity, the vegetative passivity of the intrauterine state which fostered original growth and can foster recuperation. Nature heals in a state of rest. That is the goal. Nevertheless, the regressed ego shows great energy and activity in pursuit of its goal, an activity in reverse that carries it not into life but out of it. There is a great deal of research to be done on various aspects of regression, for, clinically, the picture presented is confusing. One comes across states which suggest that there is a regressed ego which feels itself to be already 'in the womb' and oblivious to all else, or if not in a warm safe hiding place then completely withdrawn, immobilized in fear, and having never emerged since the first drastic schizoid retreat in infancy. Some patients, after long analysis, can find themselves suddenly totally 'cut off' and living in the deepest, most hidden schizoid part of their total self which they have at last contacted and must live in and with, till they regain emotional rapport with the outer world at that deep level. Again, a regressed ego, which in itself seems quite dissociated, exerts a powerful pull on the rest of the personality, drawing it down while it resists frantically. Yet again, at times the whole self seems to have become a regressing ego, showing great energy in a drive backwards towards the goal not as yet reached; and sometimes the regressed ego is fantasied as in the womb and resisting every effort to force it to a premature rebirth.

Thus a male patient in his thirties dreamed that

> he was working, doing business correspondence at a table, when he suddenly felt an invisible and irresistible pull emanating from a pale passive invalid in the bedroom.

Only after a tremendous struggle was he able to break the spell and save himself from being drawn in there. Here the regressed ego is 'pulling' the central ego down into itself and success would mean breakdown into illness such as this patient had already experienced once. But the other aspect of the situation was revealed in a dream of the same patient during his earlier illness:

> He was driving a peculiar car, which was closed in with no proper outlook on his side. In the passenger seat was another man with a definite personality who could see out more clearly. 'Driving blind', he felt that they ought to have been somewhere else, taking part in some activity that involved duties and responsibilities, but he was gleeful that they were not and he was driving away taking the other man with him.

Here the regressing ego is sweeping the central ego away out of the pressures of active life in a determined but blind drive into oblivion and passivity, i.e. breakdown. Just as the first dream represents a successful later effort to resist another breakdown into illness, the second one represents the original breakdown in full career.

Once the regressed ego feels itself to have reached its goal of retreat deep inside the hidden, womb-like state of the deepest unconscious, the central ego seems to have little success in drawing it out again. Thus an unmarried woman in middle life dreamed:

> She was watching a child-birth, but the baby could not be got out. Its head emerged but then it stuck fast, and even ropes tied on to it and passed through the window and fastened to horses who were driven to pull failed to drag it out.

This patient was telling herself that she could not force her regressed ego to a rebirth. In this state some patients manage to carry on routine living in a de-emotionalized, cold, mechanical way. This patient felt exhausted with the fight to keep her central ego functioning. Some patients exhibit more the determined drive backwards into regression or the pull of their regressed ego on the rest of their personality, others give the impression that a part of their personality has for long been inaccessible and hidden away quite out of touch with outer life. I am inclined to feel that in every case there is a deeper part of the original ego split off and hidden in a state of regression corresponding to what Winnicott calls the 'true self' hidden away in safe storage to await a favourable chance of rebirth. But his concept may include *both a regressed ego awaiting rebirth and unevoked potentialities which have never yet emerged.* The more active phenomena of the 'pull and drive' to regression may represent the conflicts set up in the psyche over the effects on the whole, of the existence of a profound regressed ego originating in very early life. This creates, from the point of view of external living, a struggle between longings for, fears of, and resistances against breakdown. *The 'struggle to preserve an ego' has two aspects: the struggle to preserve the central ego of everyday life from being undermined by regression, and the struggle to preserve the basic libidinal ego, the core of the personality, from being crushed by overpowering outer reality or lost irretrievably when it withdraws deep within out of reach of being hurt.*

This latter aspect of the problem emerges in tragic self-contradictoriness in the problem of schizoid suicide. The longing to die represents the schizoid need to withdraw the ego from a world that is too much for it to cope with. Whereas depressive suicide is the result of an angry destructive impulse, schizoid suicide is the result of apathy towards real life which cannot be accepted any longer. All available energy goes into a quiet but tenacious determination to fade out into oblivion, by means of gas, hypnotic pills or drowning. One patient expressed the longing to die at a time of great stress and I suggested that what she wanted was not destruction, non-existence, but escape into warmth, comfort, and being almost but not quite unconscious. She said 'That's it; just conscious enough to be aware of being warm and safe, like having gas at the dentist's to escape pain,' which appeared to her 'like a very pleasant way of dying'. Unfortunately, in practice, more is achieved than is intended and the patient may die and lose the chance of rebirth.

(2) *The Need to Save the Ego by Internal Object-relations.* Once the fear-dictated retreat from outer reality has been set up, the schizoid individual has two opposed needs both of which must be met unless death is to supervene: *the need to withdraw from intolerable reality and the need to remain in touch with it, to save the ego in both cases. This is what enforces the final ego-split into an active suffering and a passive regressed libidinal ego.* The flight into regression begets a counter-flight back into object-relations again. But this return to objects must still compromise with fear and the need to remain withdrawn. This leads to the creation of an object-world that enables the ego to be both withdrawn, yet not 'in the womb', the Kleinian world of 'internal objects', dream and fantasy, *a world of object-relationships which is also withdrawn 'inside' out of the external world. This, par excéllence, is the world of psychoneurotic and psychotic experience.* Sometimes the flight back from deep regression to objects in the sense of 'internal objects' appears to go further and become a return to the external world itself. But close inspection shows this to be illusory. It is not a return to the actual reality of external objects as such in their own right, but a projection on to them of the internal world of fantasy objects, which accounts for the unrealistic reactions of psychotic and psychoneurotic patients to real people. Nevertheless, it is evidence of a struggle to remain in touch with the outer world. Living in the *internal fantasy world* and the *projected fantasy world* both constitute a defence against loss of the ego by too complete regression and depersonalization, while remaining in varying degrees withdrawn from external reality which is still felt to be hostile.

This type of defence, however, has its own dangers. Over and above the ultimate danger of ego-loss by schizoid depersonalization, there are three further dangers of ego-loss that arise in this mid-region of defensive activities: (i) The flight back to objects is at first a return to the bad objects from whom escape was originally sought. Bad object-relations at first safeguard the separate identity of the ego by setting it in clear opposition to its object, a defence much used. The frightened person becomes quarrelsome, but this may go too far and get out of control, mounting up to *persecutory anxiety* in the inner world and the schizophrenic fear of being torn to pieces. There appear to be two ways of escape from this schizophrenic terror of disintegration of the ego under persecution by internal bad objects or under the pressures of real life experienced in the internal persecutory set-up. (ii) The flight to good objects gives rise to another perilous situation for the ego. The basic attitude to good objects is already fixed as a panic-stricken flight inside for safety. Even short of that, the relation to a good object is so much one of fear-enforced infantile dependence that it feels smothering, as already noted. Thus *claustrophobic anxiety* arises, to be distinguished from (iii) the schizoid fear of *ego-loss by depersonalization*, the typical state to which the central ego in touch with the outer world is reduced when all vitality has been drained out of it by too complete regression. This could lead to death and total ego-loss. The claustrophobic fear of being stifled by being shut in is the price to be paid for seeking safety through flight back inside. The active ego is in danger of being lost by reduction to a state of passivity in which no self-expression is now possible.

Thus *no objects* involve the fear of ego-loss by depersonalization, *bad objects* involve the fear of ego-loss by disintegration under destructive persecution, *good objects* involve the fear of the loss of the active ego by imprisonment in smothering passivity. (iv) One further possibility remains, a *compromise between bad and good objects*. If one hates good objects instead of bad ones, there will not be the same danger of retaliation by the object and also smothering is avoided. But now a fourth danger appears. If one hates a good object the ego feels fear, not only for itself but for the object. Guilt will arise and with it Klein's '*depressive anxiety*' in place of the more primitive 'persecutory anxiety'. *Ambivalent object-relations* involve fear of loss of the ego for all practical purposes through the paralysis of depression, in which state the ego dare not do anything at all for fear of doing wrong. The good object becomes an accusatory object and the ego feels morally persecuted. We may thus grade the dangers to which the ego feels exposed. The ultimate and worst danger is that of total ego-loss, represented in consciousness by depersonalization, and by such profound apathy through schizoid withdrawal and regression that death would ensue. Against this danger the defence of resort to bad object-relations tends to over-develop, and leads either to schizophrenic terror of disintegration under violent persecution, or depressive paralysis under merciless accusation and pathological guilt. Nevertheless these two psychotic dangers arise out of the operation of the defence of bad object-relations against the ultimate schizoid danger.

With the claustrophobic anxiety of being shut in and stifled in good object-relations we ascend to the level of what Melanie Klein and Fairbairn agree to regard as the defence of psychoneurosis against psychosis. Thus the claustrophobic fear of being stifled is the least virulent danger to which the ego is exposed. Its overcoming, so that good object-relations can be accepted without fear, even when in order to secure the rebirth of the deepest regressed ego they must involve a measure of passive dependence at first, is the obvious line of advance to the psychotherapeutic goal. This complex situation in its entirety is illustrated in the early sessions of a patient who, prior to analysis, had suffered a paranoid-schizophrenic illness. During the opening sessions she oscillated violently between hopes and fears concerning myself. 'You'll let me down, you'll walk out on me, you don't feel any real concern about me, you'll tell me my attitudes are all wrong'; or else, in defence against her fears, 'I hate you, I feel furious with you, I could murder you', and then at other times 'When I come here I'm numb, I can't feel anything.' It was a sign of progress when, after two months, she could say: 'The other night I felt you did care about me and I was near to tears.' This was soon followed by 'I feel I hate you and myself when I think I creep and crawl to you and depend on you.' Here are the serious difficulties of an utterly insecure ego rushing from one kind of relationship (in the transference situation) to another more in the hope of escaping dangers than of finding security. The inner situation is brought out plainly in her dreams at this time:

> People were pushing into my room and I was trying to keep them out. Then I rushed out into a church, flung myself at the feet of the Mother Superior and asked to enter a convent.

Here is a powerful regressive flight from bad objects (especially a persecuting father) into the maternal womb and the practical danger of an undermining flight from life. To counteract this she turns the good mother, who in being a refuge might swallow up her personality, into a bad object from whom, by antagonism, she can maintain her separateness. Thus in another dream:

I was with mother in the bedroom and got furious. She said 'You can go to bed'. I said 'I can do that any time'. Then she was on a bike coming at me. I pulled her on the ground and said 'There, enjoy your masochistic pleasures'.

But this hate of her good objects frightened her, for in a third dream she excluded herself altogether from the good protective situation:

There was a party at my Minister's house. I wanted to go but was not invited. I rushed in hoping not to be noticed but his wife saw me and said 'You've not been invited. You can't stay.' I was in despair.

But rather than have no objects at all, and having run into difficulties with both good and bad ones, she turned in a fourth and fifth dream to ambivalent morally persecutory situations:

I was bending over waiting to be caned: and, more explicitly, Mother and father were smiling and arranging for me to be beaten. I felt 'Oh! well, its belonging to home anyway'.

She mentioned that in a previous treatment with a psychiatrist she had attacked him to make him control her forcibly, 'like Daddy did'. This patient would say at various times: 'Whichever way I turn, I feel there's no way out.'

THE PSYCHOTHERAPY OF THE REGRESSED EGO

The problems of psychotherapy are reserved for Part IV. This chapter deals with diagnosis, not treatment, and only a brief word can be said about psychotherapy at this point. Usually, it is a very long time before the patient can consistently accept and bring to the analyst the regressed, passively dependent ego. The analysis of antilibidinal reactions against not only active but also passive needs, constitutes, I believe, the most important part of 'analysing'. I have seen real improvement appear and be retained when what Winnicott calls 'therapeutic regression' at last comes to be understood and accepted. I shall explore the difficulties of arriving at that constructive stage in Chapters VI and VII. This approach to therapeutic analysis shows that the cause of trouble is not to be found simply in the vicissitudes of separate instinctive drives which operate in antisocial ways, but in the basic weakness of the infantile ego perpetuated in a fear-ridden state. Infantile fear, regressive flight from reality, and resulting ego-weakness in the face of the real outer world are at the bottom of all personality disorders. Our natural impulse-life is not normally antisocial but becomes such through the forced self-assertion and even violence of an antilibidinal attempt to over-compensate weakness. The one important exception is the unwitting 'ruthlessness' of the healthy infant's need of mother, as Winnicott describes it. Our greatest need is to understand more about the earliest stages of strong ego-development and of the ways in which it is prevented, or promoted.

The hope and possibility of the rebirth of the regressed ego is the obvious final problem raised in the interests of psychotherapy. I cannot see that we know very much about it as yet. Winnicott has opened a pathway that many research workers will tread before the problem is mastered. I have found encouraging results with several patients who, each in his or her own different way, have been able to find security for their regressed ego in the psychotherapeutic relationship. There appear to be two aspects of the problem. The first is the slow growth out of their antilibidinal (Freudian sadistic superego) persecution of themselves; they need to unlearn their ruthless driving of themselves by ceaseless inner mental pressure to keep going as 'forced pseudo-adults' and to acquire the courage to adopt more of the understanding attitude of the therapist to the hard pressed and frightened child within. Simultaneously with this there goes a second process, the growth of a constructive faith that if the needs of the regressed ego are met, first in the relation to the therapist who protects it in its need for an initial passive dependence, this will mean not collapse and loss of active powers for good and all, but a steady recuperation from deep strain, diminishing of deep fears, revitalization of the personality, and rebirth of an active ego that is spontaneous and does not have to be forced and driven; what Balint calls 'primitive passive dependence' making possible 'the new beginning'. Finally we must stress that regression and illness are not the same thing. Regression is a flight backwards in search of security and a chance of a new start. But regression becomes illness in the absence of any therapeutic person to regress with and to.

III

THE REGRESSED EGO, THE LOST HEART OF THE SELF, AND THE INABILITY TO LOVE

Summary of Chapters I and II

THE first two chapters have sought to build up, from the outside inwards, a clinical description of the schizoid personality and character. Melanie Klein spoke of the 'anxiety-situations of early infancy' and it is these that start up the processes of schizoid development. We use the term 'fear' in general for a short, sharp, intense, and directly object-related reaction, an *ad hoc* reaction to a bad object or a bad-object situation. Similarly we use the term 'anxiety' in general for a persisting, pervasive fear state that arises out of a prolonged danger situation. *In pathological anxiety the danger situation is an internal one, ultimately the fear of ego-breakdown*, past fears having so determined the development of the personality structure that they both infect new object relationships, and also operate in an internal fantasy life, undermining the personality both inside and out. We have seen how too early and too intense fear and anxiety in an infant who is faced with an environment that he cannot cope with and does not feel nourished by, sets up a retreat from outer reality, and distorts ego-growth by a powerful drive to withdrawal and passivity.

We have seen how this leads to acute conflict between the struggling operative conscious ego of everyday living and the retreat backwards in search of protection and security; with the basic nature of the infant, the 'natural self' with its will to live hidden behind the conflict, unevoked, unborn. In an adult facing external danger, the flight to safety can be carried out realistically and physically. The infant cannot take literal flight, and can only take flight in a mental sense, into an attempt to create and possess an hallucinated or fantasied safety in a purely psychic world which is part of his own experience, an inner world split off from the realities of everyday living. We have seen how this enforced split in the ego through having to live in two worlds at once, inner and outer, drives the growing 'person' to seek compromise positions in an attempt to hold on to both worlds. These compromises are found in various ways of living half in and half out of object-relationships. We saw further that the creation of an internal fantasy world can itself be used as one of the most significant of these compromises, so that we have to distinguish between healthy and pathological fantasy. Healthy fantasy is basically a preparation for action in the outer world. In pathological fantasy the psychic self creates for itself a means of keeping touch with fantasy objects while remaining largely withdrawn from real ones. An unfeeling, and in extreme cases automatic, ego is left to take care of external situations. Since, however, anxiety situations cannot be kept out of even this private inner world, it precipitates *a final split in the infantile ego which permits a most secret hidden core of the self to regress completely into what is probably an unconscious hallucinated reproduction of the intrauterine condition.* At least, that is what is sought, though the result may be experienced as a fear of dying. Certainly severe hysteric, schizoid, and psychotic patients act out this condition. A regressed part of the total ego has gone back into the womb driven by an intensity of fear that is absolute, an ever-present threat. The most explicit dream expression of this I have come across was produced by a grandmother in her late fifties. For many years she had converted the most intense unconscious anxiety into hysterical bodily symptoms and remained outwardly remote, calm, and unfeeling. After a very long analysis she dreamed:

> I opened a steel drawer and inside was a tiny naked baby with wide staring expressionless eyes.

This is the problem we must now explore.

The Cause of Schizoidism

Hinsie, writing of 'The Schizophrenias' (1944) said:

> The mental deviation known as schizophrenia is an outgrowth of a special set of personality traits that is called schizoidism, which is but a name used to designate that type of person who lives essentially within himself, who shuns reality for reverie. He is an introvert, loosely connected with the members of his family. He is emotionally selfish, or, as we say, pre-eminently narcissistic, self-loving. He cannot abandon the centre of the infantile stage in favour of later, integrated behaviour.

This seems to imply some element of judgment and social disapproval. The schizoid person is 'selfish . . . narcissistic . . .

self-loving'. The term 'self-loving' is particularly unfortunate, first because those who hate themselves cannot love others, and second because the schizoid person usually thinks very poorly of himself in his inner thoughts and is in a state, not of complacent self-love, but of consuming anxiety for his very existence as a proper person. He may often produce superficial attitudes of superiority but only as a defence against feeling inferior. His narcissistic self-preoccupation is enforced by his fears for the stability of his ego. If this is not apparent, it is because he is managing to get along with so little feeling at all. He keeps detached from human relations in varying degrees while keeping his frightened sense of utter isolation repressed and unconscious. He is afraid equally of being with or without people. Hinsie's description, otherwise, from the point of view of external appearances, is true enough, but why is the schizoid person like this? Hinsie continues:

> Until we know differently, it is perhaps desirable to believe that there are certain basic character organizations that constitute the framework upon which patterns of living are erected. These fundamental character outlines appear at birth and it is not improbable that they stem from what are commonly called hereditary elements.

It is not, however, the province of psychodynamic research to accept that we are limited to two alternative explanations, moral disapproval or the fatalism of attribution to heredity. This would mean abandoning the task of analysing this pathological condition, and Hinsie does indeed hand the problem over to 'physical constitution and ethnological psychology' as playing here

> a more decisive role than ontogenetic experiences . . . or personal experiences (which) give a particular cast to personality-organization.

We must not evade the task of psychodynamic analysis by saying as Hinsie does, that it is:

> The original (i.e. inherited) structure of the personality (which) helps to determine whether the energies of the individual are to be essentially confined within himself, as in introversion, or principally directed outwards, as in extraversion.

If the analysis of schizoid withdrawal from the external world given in Chapters I and II is correct, ontogenetic analysis and the study of 'personal experiences (which) give a particular cast to personality organization' is urgently relevant to the understanding of this problem. The schizoid problem is perhaps simple in its ultimate conceptualization but it is extremely complex in its psychodynamic elaboration. Hinsie's[1] view (1944) was based on the earlier psychoanalytic orthodoxy, uninfluenced by the 'internal objects and internal object-relations' psychology of Melanie Klein and Fairbairn, or by all the work that has now been done on the mother-child relationship. But it is just this psychodynamic development, growing as it did, not from Freud's instinct theory but from his superego theory, which has opened up this most serious problem which *underlies* all other personality disorders. Hinsie's description, however, does suggest that *the central feature of the schizoid personality is the inability to effect personal relationships because of a radical immaturity of the ego, involving in severe cases a profound mental withdrawal.* One cannot easily get in touch with the heart of the schizoid person and he is usually aware of the fact that he does not have the capacity to feel with the emotional warmth and liveness of interest that other people show. As the title of this chapter suggests, the living heart of him has fled from the scene, has regressed deep within, and he has lost his true self without which he cannot form loving ties. It is this fact that we must study more deeply. Having surveyed in Chapter I the typical schizoid difficulties in object-relationships, and in Chapter II the stages of his retreat inwards from the external world, we now seek to understand the nature and results for ego-functioning of this fundamental withdrawnness.

The Lost Capacity to Love

Hinsie's description of the schizoid introvert 'loosely connected with the members of his family' gives only the defensive external mask of a profoundly undermined and weakened personality. The internal tragedy of it is simply described by this dream of a very schizoid married woman who felt that she could neither give love nor accept it with any real belief in its sincerity:

I was back in my childhood home with my parents, brothers and sisters. I had a lovely cake which I wanted to give them all, but they wouldn't have it and were not interested. I felt 'They don't want

[1] The short answer to Hinsie's invocation of heredity can be found in the title of Winnicott's 1965 volume: 'The Maturational Processes and the Facilitating Environment'.

what I have to give'. Then my eldest sister was making cakes and she wouldn't give me one of hers. I felt despairing. There was nothing to live for, and I went to my bedroom alone to lie down and die. My mother came in and said 'Don't be silly'. She didn't understand at all.

The schizoid person's capacity to love has been frozen by early experiences of rejection and the breakdown of real life relationships. This patient's dream at the time was a reaction to moving house. She shrank from having to meet and get to know new people, and professed to feel indifferent and did not want to meet anyone. Yet unconsciously she was feeling this tragic and *longstanding, unsatisfied hunger for love about which, however, she could only feel hopelessness and despair. This had long ago evoked in her a dangerously strong wish for an absolute escape from an irremediable situation.* The inevitable consequence was a withdrawn and schizoid personality. She felt there was no chance of making new friends in a new place and she broke down into an exhausted and sobbing state, at which time she had this dream. In some patients the wish to die, which emerged in this dream, covers a still deeper feeling that the vital heart of the self *did die* in some sense in early childhood, and only the empty shell of a person is left which goes through the motions of living in an automatic way. Thus the patient who dreamed of the baby in the steel drawer said: 'I feel half of me is dead and I'm terrified of losing the rest. I need to let go absolutely and trust you, but I fear I'll die if I do.' We shall come again on this tense feeling of the patient that he has to hold on to himself from minute to minute to keep himself alive, and dare not let up for a moment.

This schizoid condition can hardly be an ultimate, hereditary factor. It must be a post-natal development brought about by what Winnicott calls 'the failure of the environment' to support and nourish the infant personality. The deepest thing in any human being must be, to use Bergson's term, an *élan vital*, a life-force, a positive dynamic 'will to live' expressing itself in what psychoanalysis has called 'libido'. This 'libido' is too narrowly conceived if held to connote simply 'sexual libido' which is only one aspect of the living whole of the person. In Fairbairn's view 'libido' must be regarded, not as a thing-in-itself, but as the object-seeking drive of the primary natural ego or psychic self. *The basic drive to object relations is at the same time the drive to self-development and self-fulfilment as a person. The importance of object-relations lies in the fact that without them the ego cannot develop.* An ego without object-relations becomes meaningless. In this comprehensive sense the libidinal quest for objects is the source of the capacity to love, and the maintenance of loving relationships is the major self-expressive activity of the total self. In the seriously schizoid person, the vital heart of selfhood and the active quest of object-relations are alike paralysed, resulting in a condition out of which the individual cannot help himself.

For reasons given further on in Chapter V, I do not accept the idea of aggression or an aggressive instinct as an ultimate factor in the same sense as this libidinal drive. It is the frustration of the basic energetic need to live and love that arouses the double reaction of 'fight' and 'flight'. The first leads to aggression and so to the classic guilt-depression, while the second leads to schizoid regression, a withdrawal of the libidinal ego from the outer world so that its energy 'flows backwards' to infantile levels and 'downwards' into the depths of the unconscious. Hydraulic and spatial metaphors are a handy way of envisaging the invisible process of change from extraversion to introversion which, however, becomes visible enough when it is an accomplished fact. The 'will to live and love', on the outflowing and unimpeded activity of which the whole healthy development of the ego depends, is precisely what has been overlaid by fear, choked back and dammed in, in the schizoid personality. Spontaneous outflowing into object-relations has been given up, in part or in whole, on different levels of the personality, and its place taken in varying degrees by an early infantile fear-laden longing for absolute withdrawal from life, not into death as non-existence but into the living death of oblivion, an escape into passivity and inactivity. This, however, may be felt by the patient as a secret experience of psychic death. Consciously, the need for oblivion may drive the patient to alcohol or drugs. *Once created, this hidden regression becomes an even greater danger to the personality as a whole than the originally feared unsatisfactory outer world.*

Thus a woman of forty with an ill husband and two children, feeling the long-drawn-out strain of her heavy responsibilities, discovered that her schizoid reaction to the situation seemed to be as frightening as the situation itself, while at the same time it also carried with it a feeling of relief from the pressures she did not feel strong enough to cope with. At one point she said: 'I feel so exhausted that I just want to lie down flat and not move at all, go into a deep sleep and never wake up.' She was in fact alternating between periods of exhausted apathy and feverish excited activity (see Chapter V). She dreamed that one of her children, certainly representing herself, 'didn't like people and had gone right away alone', and commented, 'I'm interested in food, not in people, I don't want anyone near, not even you. I feel I'm in a plastic bag.' She visibly started when I said that her loving self was shut in, and she sobbed and said, 'There's nothing to live for, life's empty.' She then brought this dream:

> I had been turned inside. I don't know how, but I was just 'like that'. I could hear what was inside but I couldn't hear anything outside. I could vaguely see my husband and some other people but they didn't mean anything to me, they didn't seem real. But I felt safe.

Here is the clearest possible expression of a motivated withdrawal into herself, breaking off relations with real people in the outer world to find security in an enclosed retreat, a shut-in introverted state. No one reacts in this drastic way for the first time in adult life. The normal reaction even to severe difficulty is to be stimulated to greater effort. She withdrew into unreality as an adult because she had already been driven into a schizoid state as a child. The result was derealization of her outer world and depersonalization of herself. She found that in the evening, when the children were in bed, if her husband went out of the room she suddenly felt unreal. She needed the family present to give her pressing reasons to 'keep in touch' or she lost her own ego. Yet all the time she felt a powerful secret wish for this complete withdrawal because it enabled her to feel safe. She did not want to die but simply to escape into absolute inactivity and the oblivion of deep sleep, and never wake up. Other people must not withdraw from her, but she must feel free to withdraw from them. This reveals an extremely undermined and demoralized ego. She voiced a complex variety of motives for this almost irresistible regressive longing. 'I don't want anyone to know that I have feelings because then they can hurt me.' 'I am afraid to love because I feel so weak; it would exhaust me and I would lose myself.' 'I am afraid if I love I won't get a response. People don't think me nice. The family used to say I was ugly. I am afraid to risk showing that I want to be wanted.' *All these important motives for the schizoid retreat are aspects of a profound complex inhibition of the capacity to love and be loved in the outer world, which leaves the person all the more a helpless victim of the strength of the regressive pull back out of life.*

Until this determined wish for a total release from the pressures of having to have anything to do with people in real life is uncovered, made explicitly conscious, recognized for what it is and given sympathetic acceptance, it cannot be outgrown. It is the pathological equivalent of our nightly retreat from normal strains to normal regression in normal sleep. Pathological regression not infrequently takes the form of compulsive and prolonged sleep of a deep 'drugged' kind, in which even the patient's fantasy and dream life is dissociated as well as the outer world cut off. It seems likely that prolonged deep sedation in hospital would be more therapeutic if its emotional significance were interpreted to the patient. The purpose of regression of any kind is a much needed retreat from a 'here and now' life which the individual feels he cannot cope with. He goes back to life on a simpler earlier level, not involving so much strain. On this principle we all do such a normal thing as taking holidays. In pathological regression, the important strains have come far too early, have seriously disturbed the normal development of ego-strength, and have left the unfortunate individual inwardly undermined and inadequate to face adult responsibilities. In such a case, regression, supported and controlled by the treatment situation, is an urgently needed therapeutic process. It is dangerous simply to interpret this as hysterical malingering and manipulation of the environment. The intense demands that the 'hysteric' makes on those around have their cause in the combination of genuine infantile need of dependence, the strength of the drive to retreat mentally from a world he cannot stand up to and which he feels is loveless, and the fear that this will lead to his complete loss of contact with his outer world and therefore loss of his own ego.

The more intensely the patient experiences his need for a therapeutic regression, the more afraid of it he is and the more he resists it by means of internal struggles which fill him with most painful bodily and mental tensions. We must presently study more closely this determined *antilibidinal* opposition to any acceptance of a permitted therapeutic regression, an opposition that has to be so repeatedly analysed that often it seems this battle is never completely won. Patients will say 'I've been over all this before. Why do I still cling to it?' The double aspect of the problem, both need and fear of a breaking off of relationships with the frightening outer world, is neatly illustrated in the case of a severely agoraphobic young woman of 19 years. A school phobia began to develop after she passed the 'Eleven Plus' examination creditably. This had in fact been preceded by insomnia during the period of heavy school pressure prior to the exam. Causes of insecurity could be discerned going back into early childhood. During her teenage years she became more and more unable to face life without a markedly protective environment including private tuition, and attacks of depression occurred sufficiently serious for her to be given an antidepressant drug which would relieve her for the time being. Her basic condition was unaltered. From about fifteen years she became subject to sudden attacks of depersonalization if left alone at home, or when out shopping even if her parents were with her. One day in a shop her mother left her for a moment to step up to the counter, and she said 'Suddenly I couldn't see what was around me, everything went blurred, I grabbed mother's arm, and then it all went black and I felt myself falling. I kept saying to myself "Don't be silly" and kept saying my name to myself. I felt very wide awake inside and I didn't lose consciousness but I couldn't see. *I felt very frightened, then for a few moments quite safe, then very frightened again.* I'd been in an increasing state of tension ever since we'd been in the shop, and I wanted to get out quick back into the car (i.e. retreat into the small safe place). *As I blacked out I felt safe for a few seconds. Then I felt I'd shut myself away so much I feared I'd never get back and that frightened me again. I don't like going upstairs in the house now because I feel cut off, I feel I'll never get down again.*'

To diagnose this simply as an aggressive hysteric attempt to control everyone around her for her own comfort would be to miss the significance of the problem. Of course such a patient makes every effort to ensure that she shall never be left alone because she is terrified of having these 'attacks'. Fear of this mental state tends to bring it on, and no doubt this serves to maintain and intensify the symptoms, which become a means of getting the needed protection. But to put the emphasis on the secondary gain of symptoms, as the diagnosis of hysteria does, fails to explain their original cause, and throws no light on the intense struggle going on between an irresistible need to escape from a frightening world and an equally compelling fear of that need. The rapid alternation of *feeling frightened, feeling safe, feeling cut off and then feeling frightened again* lights up the endopsychic conflict in which she was caught, and points us back to some basic weakness of the ego.

Let us summarize thus far. In *The Penguin Dictionary of Psychology*, Drever defines 'schizoid' as 'a personality-type tending towards *dissociation* of the emotional from the intellectual life: a shut-in personality'. The use of the term 'dissociation' takes us back to the early studies in hysteria by Charcot, Janet and Freud. Janet held that the psyche, through some inherent weakness, could lack the strength to hold itself together and could 'fall apart' into dissociated fragments operating independently. *Freud's dynamic explanation* in terms of emotional conflict and repression led the way to the opposite view that *ego-weakness is the outcome, not the original cause, of a splitting of the primary unity of the psyche under severe early traumatic stress.* Fairbairn was one of the first to point out that hysteria runs back into a schizoid condition of the personality.

We shall no longer then speak of a 'dissociation of the intellectual from the emotional life', but rather of a fear-enforced retreat within, away from an injurious outer world, of the sensitive feeling heart of the infant psyche, leaving an unemotional, superficial, automatic ego in consciousness to deal with external reality. The intellectual life is then regarded as adult and consciously operated, while the emotional life is felt to be weak and childish and is kept repressed. This fear-induced flight within, to hide away in the depths of the unconscious out of reach of hurt, is the basis of pathological regression. We may consider regression or 'going backwards', giving up the state of activity and seeking relief from pressures in passivity and even oblivion, as having two opposite poles, healthy and pathological. Healthy regression is the natural urge to deal with fatigue by relaxation, rest, and sleep. It is a necessity for the maintenance of life, and it is modelled psychologically, and sometimes even physically, on a return to the womb, or a womb-like condition. Every night in sleep we return to a symbolic but material substitute for the womb. Just as the new-born baby is wrapped up in a cot as a womb-substitute, so we envelop our undressed bodies in the bed clothes where we lie in the darkness and stillness of the night. Waking and rising is a rebirth. This healthy regression, for which nature provides, has its instinctive basis in the impulse to flee or escape from further strain to where we can recuperate in safety. It alternates easily and naturally with activity.

Pathological regression, which defines the basic nature of the schizoid problem, has the same natural basis in the flight impulse. The difference is that the pressures from which the psyche takes flight occur so early in life, when the ego is undeveloped, that they are experienced as overwhelming. The intensity of the fear generated becomes itself severely traumatic, and the result is not a natural healthy rhythm of activity, fatigue, rest, recuperation and renewed activity, but a permanent damaging of the infant psyche, a splitting of the infant ego, so that thereafter the child grows up unable to make contact with the outer world with his whole self. The vital heart of the self is lost, and an inner 'deadness' is experienced. For practical purposes he is 'not all there', the living, feeling, loving heart of him seems absent; not absolutely, for it is hidden deep in the unconscious, but it can only later be drawn back into consciousness, resurrected or reborn, at the price often of the most severe mental disturbance. It is when the child feels a primitive *despair* of being able to *do* anything to cope with his environment, that drastic withdrawal is the only thing left, and *feelings of despair, loneliness, weakness, and incapacity to love always lie hidden behind the cold detached mask of the schizoid personality*, however stable he may appear to be. Some time ago a woman's body was found curled up dead inside a trunk. A verdict of suicide was passed, and the psychiatrist at the inquest stated that a psychotic patient might well take tablets and curl up in a trunk as a symbolic return to the womb which goes to show how significant and intelligible psychotic reactions can be.

We may select six descriptive aspects of this complex problem which are very clearly illustrated in clinical material: (i) depersonalization and derealization as a result of withdrawal, *the emptying of the ego of consciousness*; (ii) the feeling of emptiness and *nonentity in depth*, sensed as experienced *in the unconscious*, creating the feeling of not having an ego, only an amorphous experience of indefiniteness and weakness, (iii) *the fear of ego-collapse*, the feeling of disintegration or of facing a dark abyss into which one is about to plunge and be lost, a fear of psychic death; (iv) *the inhibition of the capacity to love* and the inability to experience meaningful relatedness to other persons; (v) *The need for regression* opposed by the fear of being 'dragged down' by an unconscious regressive drive; (vi) *the longing for and the fear of sleep and oblivion*, coupled with the inability to relax lest it involve an irrecoverable surrender to regression. (i) to (iv) give a negative picture of schizoid regression as 'flight from' the outer world; (v) and (vi) show the positive aspect of regression as 'flight to' a deeper security, a longing for a return which implies the possibility of a rebirth, even though this is countered by an intense fear of risking it, in case it should turn out to involve total breakdown. Some patients intuitively know that they must break down and regress to the level of their earliest insecurity, to turn the corner and get a new start.

Henry James, a Relatively 'Normal' Schizoid Personality

It will serve as a standard of comparison for the more disturbed clinical examples, if we examine a schizoid personality in a relatively stable state. The novelist, Henry James, provides an excellent example. He was the younger brother of the great American philosopher-psychologist, William James, and was, fortunately for himself, left financially independent by his father. His novels were never a source of much income, and if he had had to earn his living one wonders how his delicately poised mental stability would have stood up to the impingement of the outer world. As it was, he did not need to concern himself with the means of physical existence. He was free to live in the private inner life of his mind, and to travel and mix with people, to uproot and re-root and again uproot himself, without feeling irrevocably involved or tied anywhere. In a study of James by Michael Swan (1952) he is described as 'poised in mid-Atlantic, half-way between America and Europe', a striking example of the schizoid 'half-in and half-out' compromise. The heroine of *The Portrait of a Lady* rejects both an American and an English lover, and Swan comments

> Like James himself, she is between two worlds, in danger of being mentally deracinated. Her instinct is to 'find' herself in a world which she can feel is her own. (p. 49.)

For James this was the schizoid inner world of the mind. He was unable to settle permanently in his own country, and yet after moving around between America, England, France, and Italy, he became a naturalized Englishman only seven months before he died at the age of 73. All this is highly characteristic of schizoid non-involvement and evasion of permanent ties.

One of the remarkable characteristics often found in schizoid persons is profound psychological insight, on which James drew for his writing. As a young man he met Ruskin and wrote of him:

> He has been scared back by the grim face of reality into the world of unreason and illusion, and he wanders there without a compass and a guide—or any light save the fitful flashes of his own beautiful genius.

He could have been describing himself. Swan tells us that

> He said that marriage would make him pretend to think quite a little better of life than he really did. How much the frustration

which his novels always ultimately express can be related to this it is unwise to surmise. (p. 21.)

Both, however, spring from the same source, the deep fear of the outer world felt by the withdrawn individual. When Henry James was 46 his brother William wrote of him thus:

Harry lives hidden away in the midst of his strange, heavy, alien manners and customs; but they are all his 'protective resemblances' under which the same dear, old, good, innocent and at bottom very powerless-feeling Henry remains, caring for little but his writing.

Swan tells of 'his obsession with the problem of the relation of art to life', and we may regard this as his obsession with the problem, for him unsolvable, of the relation of his inner mental life to external reality. In *The Death of the Lion* James is saying:

The artist and the society of his time are irreconcilable. Criticism stumbles here, and it is at this point that all readers of James are obliged to make their decision, subjectively, about him: either that, in the words of F. R. Leavis, 'something went wrong' or that he is coming in sight of what he liked to call 'the great good place'. (Swan, pp. 27–8.)

We may conclude that this 'great good place' was a goal in fantasy, the womb of his inner world into which he was retreating ever deeper. Swan writes:

All who knew him were well aware that beneath the urbane exterior was a mind which existed fully only through the life of creation. By the end of the nineties he seemed to have entered a state of poetic vision. . . . The opposition camp believes that James retired into an escape world of Art on finding life too difficult. (p. 31.)

In the 1890's James had suffered some prolonged depressions, and when his brother William saw him again in 1899 they no longer understood each other. William read many pages of *The Wings of the Dove* over again to see 'what the dickens they could mean'.

Swan stresses the sense of loneliness, that profoundly schizoid characteristic, which became intensified in his later years.

To his friends he was the sociable, kindly, elderly gentleman who gave little impression . . . of being troubled by his isolation and neglect. 'My young friend', he once said to Logan Pearsall Smith, 'there is one word—let me impress upon you—which you must inscribe upon your banner, and that word is *loneliness*.' (pp. 36–7.)

With this goes *the sense of futility and lack of meaning in life*. Many of his stories are

> . . . about the unrealized dreams of writers, stories of men's souls torn by the realization that life has gone by and given them nothing. These stories are an important part of James's biography. (p. 25.)

The name of one of his writings, *The Figure in the Carpet*, represents the hidden meaning in the artist's work, which nobody knows and which we must infer he himself never found, since the artist dies with the secret unrevealed.

F. L. Pattee, in *American Literature Since 1870* (1915), wrote:

> He had been reared in a cloister-like atmosphere where he had dreamed of 'life' rather than lived it. . . . He stood aloof from life and observed it without being a part of it. With nothing was he in sympathy in the full meaning of the word.

Economic security left him free, without external strains, to use his great intellectual ability and artistic powers to construct for himself an internal life of the mind which did not in the end save him from serious attacks of depression in later years, but left him *alone within himself in an existence which failed to disclose any real meaning*. James illustrates the schizoid person who is stable enough under favourable circumstances to avoid serious breakdown and the wreckage of his personality, while possessing great gifts which enable him to make a real contribution to life for others, without solving his own personal problems or overcoming his own detachment. Henry James was one of the founders of the 'psychological novel'. Edel (1955) writes:

> Henry James extended the definition of experience and the province of fiction to include the subjective world.

The Complexities of the Schizoid Condition

Of the six most striking descriptive aspects of this complex state of the personality (cf. p. 97), which emerge ever more clearly as it develops towards specific illness, the first four, depersonalization and derealization, the feeling of nonentity or ego-emptiness, the fear of ego-collapse, and the inhibition of the capacity to love or enter into human relationships, must be taken together as representing the actual 'cut-off' schizoid condition, due to fear of and flight from the outer world. The other two, the fear of and struggle against the regressive drive, and the fear of sleep and relaxation, are aspects of the psyche's self-defence against its insidious internal danger of losing all contact with external reality. A still further problem arises at this point. *Fear of loss of contact with the external world constantly motivates efforts to regain contact with it, but this cannot be done by loving relationships, and therefore can only be done in terms of the other two basic emotional reactions, fear and aggression.* To relate in terms simply of fear sets up the paranoid state, which can pass over into the cold-blooded defence of mere destructive aggression. If the individual does not feel so utterly hopeless about loving, then the relationship in terms of aggression will lead to ambivalence and depression.

The first four characteristics mentioned are not separate 'entities'. They overlap and merge into one another, and are but varying descriptions of the same fundamental if complex psychopathological state. Depersonalization and derealization describe the emptying of the ego of ordinary consciousness in the world of everyday living, when the vital feeling-self withdraws deep within. No study of this problem can be made without referring to Fairbairn's description of schizoid withdrawal (pp. 49–52, 1952a). Depersonalization and derealization depend on breaking off relationships with the outer world, and in the section quoted on 'withdrawal of libido', he gathers all four characteristics together.

> In acute schizoid states withdrawal of libido from object-relationships may proceed to such lengths that libido is withdrawn from the realm of the conscious (that part of the psyche which is, so to speak, nearest to objects) into the realm of the unconscious. When this happens, the effect is as if the ego itself had withdrawn into the unconscious. . . . The withdrawal of libido from the conscious part of the ego has the effect of relieving emotional tension and mitigating the danger of violent outbursts of precipitate action. . . . Much of the schizoid individual's anxiety really represents a fear of such outbursts occurring. This fear commonly manifests itself as a fear of going insane or as a fear of imminent disaster. It is possible, therefore, that the massive withdrawal of libido has the significance of a desperate effort on the part of an ego threatened with disaster to avoid all emotional relationships with external objects by a repression of the libidinal tendencies which urge the individual on to make emotional contacts. . . . It is when this effort is within measurable distance of succeeding that the individual begins to tell us that he feels as if there were nothing of him, or as if he had lost his identity, or as if he were dead, or as if he ceased to exist. . . . *Loss of the ego* is the ultimate psychopathological disaster which the schizoid

individual is constantly struggling, with more or less of success, to avert. (1952a, p. 52.)

This quotation is from Fairbairn's first major published paper, and came before he had revised his terminology for endopsychic structure. It calls for some revision from his later point of view. He ceased to speak of 'libido' as a psychic 'entity' and regarded it as 'libidinal energy characterizing an ego'. Thus he would not later have spoken of a 'repression of the libido out of the ego' and into the unconscious, nor would he have said 'the effect is *as if* the ego itself has withdrawn into the unconscious'. Indeed, in the paper quoted, he wrote:

Whether such a mass-withdrawal of libido can properly be ascribed to repression is a debatable question. (1952a, p. 52.)

In conformity with his later terms, he would have written, not 'it is as if', but 'actually part of the ego itself has withdrawn into the unconscious'. Fairbairn's matured theory was of the splitting of the ego itself under extreme stress, and the drastic withdrawal of a split-off *libidinal ego* into unconsciousness, to avoid all emotional relations with objects, a process resulting not only in loss of the objects, but, therefore, and finally, in the feeling of loss of the ego itself. In fact the withdrawn libidinal ego leaves what he calls the conscious central ego denuded of energy, so that the personality can only function in relation to the outer world in a mechanical way; nothing feels real, and the capacity for love is lost. Further, we must notice that, under the influence of existing psychoanalytical ideas, Fairbairn attributed the schizoid withdrawal only to fear of losing control of aggressive impulses, or of libidinal impulses felt in an aggressive way. This is very important, especially in the form Winnicott stresses, namely, that when the mother cannot tolerate the infant's demandingness, he becomes afraid of his own love needs as ruthless and destructive. But we have to add to this that *withdrawal is basically due to the inability of the weak infantile ego to stand its ground and cope with outer reality* in the absence of adequate maternal support. It is because a consequence of this is that the ego is starved of satisfaction of libidinal needs, that it then further experiences an angry urge to hit back aggressively, at the rejective outer world that drove it into retreat.

This condition is perfectly described by one male patient, a professional man in the late forties, of marked ability and carrying heavy responsibilities, while feeling grave strain and exhaustion. He dreamed

I was living in a dugout. It was covered over completely at the top and there was a mechanical turret at ground level which revolved. It had two periscopes (eyes) which brought me information of what was going on outside, and two slits (ears) through which sounds could come to be recorded on tape for me, and an opening (mouth) through which I could send out messages from my tape-recorder.

This represents the way a capable schizoid person feels about himself while he is still able to function in the outer world, mechanically efficient but impersonal. To him it feels automatic. His heart is not in it but hidden away out of reach inside. If withdrawal becomes extreme break-down of functioning must occur, exhaustion and regressed illness. Before that stage is reached, the patient puts up a tremendous fight for life, a struggle which may be protracted over a long period of time, to keep his ego in existence.

A young woman in her twenties provides a striking example of how a clear-cut Oedipus complex can mask a serious schizoid condition. She was severely agoraphobic, having become progressively housebound from the onset of menstruation at about 12 years, and was consciously extremely detached, sleeping all day while people were about and only getting up at night when she could be alone. During these lonely hours she was a compulsive hand-washer and clothes-arranger, with chronic obsessional repetitiveness over everything she tried to do. At this stage she was brought to one session feeling in despair. After a long silence she said: 'I'm quite hopeless. I feel I've no personality at all. I don't know who or what I am, I'm nobody. I've no faith in anyone or anything, not even in you, not even in God, no trust or belief in anything at all to keep me alive.' Just prior to this we had succeeded in bringing to full consciousness a clear and intense incest wish and oedipal fantasy, of which she had for long been conscious in disconnected bits. A dream of some years previously had remained vivid to her. The earth was running with filth which she knew was semen, and she could not stop it getting into her. She had always had a fear of something getting from her father's clothes into her body, and she had long had a fear of germs which explained (though only in part) her obsessional washing. For a time she concentrated all her fears into a dread of having a baby, without being able to give any coherent account of what she was afraid of. She wanted love and marriage and sexual relations but not a baby. The feeling that she wouldn't be capable of looking after one was realistic, but not the unconscious reason. Then she said that she had always felt that if she got married it would be all right so long as she and her husband did not go to her parents' home. If they did, she would be pregnant and would not know if it was her husband's or her father's baby. There would be a terrific row with mother and she would have to have a miscarriage and get rid of the baby. One could hardly have a clearer conscious incest wish with great guilt and fear. In fact the analysis of this oedipal material did not clear anything up. It did not ease her handwashing compulsions which turned out to have other uses besides those of a protective cleansing and guilt-relieving ritual. It led on to the fact that her father had been very largely an absentee father most of her childhood, and when he did come home he paid more attention to her mother than to her. Her incest wish, and jealousy and fear of her mother, arose out of an intense loneliness in which she found it difficult to hold on to any feeling of being a positive person. As she had said to me, she had not sufficient faith and trust in anyone to keep her alive. The incest and oedipal fantasies were a means of keeping alive the feeling that she was in relationship and was an ego after all, even though a very disturbed ego, and only having relationships in imagination and with parents who were the source of her difficulties.

This oedipal fantasying was a defence which analysis removed and laid bare the fact that her obsessional symptoms were a direct expression of a frantic struggle to keep her ego in being. She said: 'I've got to concentrate on myself. I mustn't forget about being "me" or I'd lose myself. I fear I'll be cut off and lose contact with everything. I feel I have no real contact. I can't just do a thing and be done with it. If I want to make tea, I put a little water in the kettle and empty it out and go on doing that again and again. It's ages before I can get it filled and on the gas. In the same way I have to keep on washing my hands again and again and it takes ages to get to bed. When at last I stop washing I can't just throw my clothes off and drop into bed and be done with it. I might not wake up. I might die in my sleep. I can't go to bed at all now. I can't undress but just sleep in the chair downstairs.' She felt less afraid of complete loss of contact with her outer world if she went to sleep that way. *The obsessional repetitiveness of all her activity was a method of keeping on putting off the dread moment when something would be finished, ended, done with. As each activity threatened to come to an end, she felt she would collapse and come to an end with it; so she had to keep every activity going as long as she could, to keep alive her feeling of being a person.* Ultimately her analysis disposed of her psychic defences and laid bare a weak helpless little child afraid to grow up to adult responsibility. She could only grow then if the therapist supported her ego as a mother does her infant. Ultimately she made an excellent recovery. The breakdown of object-relations, the loss of the capacity to love, and the dread of ego-loss as a mental experience of nonentity involve the patient in great dependence on the therapist. Patients frequently say they feel 'cut off' in the treatment situation by an inability to get in touch with the therapist. One patient would say 'I'm miles away. You don't seem to be here. I can't get in touch with you. You must get in touch with me. If you can't find me, there's no help for me.' This sense of a gulf which the patient cannot cross but which perhaps the therapist can and does if he shows the patient that he knows about it, is of the highest importance in treatment. It is vividly illustrated by the case recorded on pages 232–5, and one contributory cause is touched on by a patient who said: 'I always felt I could never make mother understand what I wanted to get across to her. She would listen for a few sentences and then get restless and be too busy to hear me through.' She had grown up more isolated than she realized.

Thus the schizoid patient confronts us with the problem of a basically weak ego whose development has been gravely compromised in the earliest stages. Life for such a person is one long unremitting struggle to keep mentally alive; he feels he has to do it by his own efforts, and is always in danger of collapse. The experience of growing as a positive secure person can only be had by freedom to express oneself actively in a good relationship, receiving, giving, loving, creating in mutuality. With a good mother who evokes a positive loving response from the baby, the baby's ego grows strong in the spontaneous exercise of this good active responsiveness, both in taking happily the good that is given, and in developing a natural capacity to make a good response in return. If we take the term 'love' to stand for the quality of a good relationship, then we shall say that a stable ego can only grow in the atmosphere of loving relationships, and its most important characteristic is its capacity to give love, at first in return for love, and later in an absolute unconditional way. But the ego that lacks this primary security is always in doubt about its ability to keep itself in being from moment to moment. An unsatisfactory pathological ego can be kept going precariously by hating, when loving is impossible. But this motivation is negative and destructive, aiming either at the elimination of bad objects or of the bad-object element in good objects. It has no positive aim in itself and does not provide any experience of a positive self. We shall see later how hating is used, along with the guilt it engenders, in the manic-depressive personality, as a desperate method of keeping the ego in touch with objects so as to fend off a breakdown into a schizoid state; for in that condition the individual feels always on the brink of hopeless despair, with not enough of an ego to make any real contacts, unless the therapist can find him in his isolation.

The Fear of Ego-Breakdown and the Re-experiencing of Maternal Deprivation

In surveying the foregoing material it becomes clear that the last and deepest element to be reached and uncovered by analytical therapy is the patient's infantile experience of the failure, non-possession or absolute loss of an adequate mother. This is the final problem for psychotherapy to find an answer to: the fear of ego-breakdown over the re-experiencing of the original maternal deprivation. 'Maternal deprivation' is not a simple fact or a fixed quantity. It includes, at one end of the scale, the death or illness of the mother or the failure of breast-feeding without compensatory nursing. It graduates through the frankly rejective mother who does not want her baby, and the tantalizing mother who frustrates as much as she satisfies, to the mother whose primary maternalism fades out too soon and who weans the baby too traumatically. We are concerned here, not with the angry or over-authoritarian mother of a later period (i.e. possibly from the cleanliness training period onwards) who is experienced by the child as aggressive and becomes the source of a sadistic 'superego'; but with the depriving mother of the first year who fails to give the infant that kind of emotional rapport that would support the beginning of firm ego-development. It is on this problem that the work of Winnicott and Bowlby is of such great value.

How deep is the ego-weakness left by very early failure of a good mother–infant relationship, and how long it can take to grow out of it, may well emerge in a protracted analysis, long after specific 'illness' has been overcome. Analysis has to go very deep indeed to enable the patient to feel basically safe against the *fear of breakdown in an environment that feels empty of support.* When analysis has been begun because of specific illness, that illness can be overcome in due course, most of the patient's anxieties relieved, and his practical life rehabilitated. Yet there can still be dependent characteristics and vulnerabilities to anxiety, after the patient has held his gains for a number of years, to show that there remains a deep hidden core of infantile trauma, insecurity and need for the mother who failed the baby. This *deprivation trauma*, the loss of the good mother of the first year, sets up an unalleviated need for mother-substitutes and a liability to separation-anxiety and depressive despondency, which profoundly affects adult living.

The following case illustrates this with exceptional clarity. The patient was a professional man in early middle life, whose socially respectable early home life was essentially loveless because of a neurotic mother from whom the father escaped by going out, leaving the child deprived of both parents' love. He had always been markedly dependent on both father and mother substitutes, in the form of both people and drugs. He came to analysis in a state of severe breakdown and had to enter hospital to be weaned of drugs. His analysis continued all through his three months in hospital and afterwards, and he maintained steady improvement, coping adequately with his work. A major factor in his life and in his analysis had been his fear of his mother, both consciously and in his dreams. In the ensuing three years of analysis, this fear faded out, completely so far as his conscious reactions were concerned, and very markedly in his dreams. He reached a point where he and his friends were surprised how well he was. He worked normally, became a naturally interested father to his children and a more considerate and supportive husband to his wife, and moreover improved his physical health by taking adequate physical recreation.

At that point he appeared to mark time. He had given up sleeping tablets, but could not give up his antidepressant drug nor make a proper end of his analysis. A medical friend advised him to accept the position that he should depend permanently on the drug as a diabetic does on insulin, and he felt inclined to stop analysis and do just that. But in fact he had no free choice in the matter. There was a very deep problem that demanded solution, and despite the antidepressant drug he began to manifest a vulnerability to acute flare-ups of anxiety and depression, even though at the same time he had been for three years and was still remaining well, active and efficient in general, had never felt better, and got over these attacks quickly. Usually one session of analysis sufficed to clear them up, or even a telephone call, but still they continued to recur.

His analysis had to be continued at the rate of one session a week to solve this problem.

His attacks of either anxiety or depression clearly followed a fixed pattern. In spite of his great improvement, he was extremely emotionally dependent on his wife, and on a wide range of mother-substitutes. It was always over some threat to his security through the loss of a supportive mother-substitute in fact or symbol, that his anxiety and depression broke out. He had dealt successfully with the hostile, critical, castrating mother of his later childhood. (In fact he had had actual castration threats made against him by both his mother and a very aggressive aunt.) He still had to deal with the trauma of the loss of the good nursing mother at the beginning, and the serious infantile depression that this had evoked in him.

The substance of the final stages of his analysis can be gauged from the following summary. At the beginning of the period he said, 'I feel much more confident in my ability to work and enjoy life and I'm happier with people.' Yet in that same month he panicked after drinking a cup of tea in a house where someone was ill with cancer. He rushed home and said to his wife: 'I've had tea in that house and I feel I want a stomach pump.' She said, 'I've made coffee. Don't you want it?' He said, 'Oh yes,' and drank two cups, feeling it would dilute the bad tea. He commented, 'I was full of food fads at home with mother. As soon as I left home I could eat the same foods easily.' This need to take in a good mother to neutralize an internal bad mother was simply illustrated by three dreams:

I was back at the University and going home to stay with mother, and not looking forward to being alone with her. I kept being delayed and couldn't get there.

I was happy marrying my wife and hugged her and told her how I loved her.

Then the two themes came together in one dream:

I went home to see mother and sister and they were nagging at me as usual. I could only put up with it because I had taken a vague but very nice girl friend with me, who made a fuss of me,

an idealized mother fantasy which protected him in his inner world. This fantasy later became very important.

His psychic situation at that time was that his bad object was inside and he must have absolutely secure possession of a wide range of maternal good objects outside to ward off depression. These fell into two groups, *helpful women* (his wife, domestic helps, a good female colleague) and *symbolic objects* (food, sweets, multivite pills, and the specific antidepressant drug). Threats to all of these occurred in the ensuing months and every time evoked strong anxiety and then depression. When a good domestic help fell ill he was 'absolutely cast down'. In one session he recalled how an aunt he had been very fond of, who had lived with the family and done all the housework, died when he was 5 years old. He missed her very badly, being left at the mercy of mother and sister and a new domestic help who was a friend of mother's and sided with her against him and his father. When he had talked this out he observed, 'I am amazed how much better I feel. Once I was in bed a whole day when a domestic help left.' On that occasion he had dreamed that his wife was kidnapped and smuggled away and he was in a rage. Gradually everything began to point to an early severe traumatic loss of mother. His problem came to be less and less that of being afraid of a hostile woman, and more and more that of losing a supportive one. For a time he was very well and said he felt 'better for that last bit of trouble'.

He now began to think of reducing sessions to once a fortnight, and cutting down his drug from six to five-and-a-half tablets a day. One day at teatime he took one-and-a-half instead of two. Within half an hour he developed a raging hay fever. He took not the missing half but two extra whole ones and the hay fever died down. He had been told that to get him off drugs in the first place, the antidepressant drug had been necessary to stop manic-depressive effects. It was doing exactly that, defending him against the breakthrough into consciousness of a very early infantile depression, as ultimately became quite clear. His original drug addiction and his dependence on the antidepressant drug, like his dependence on his wife and supportive women, and on myself as analyst (at every crisis he would 'phone me and if necessary have an extra session) were all alike forms of a 'good mother addiction' as a defence against the deep depression of early deprivation of mother. The emergence of hay fever as a symptom, over his attempt to do without half a tablet, threatened to persist, and establish itself. Soon after this there arose a possibility of his wife having to stay away overnight to visit an ill member of her family. His hay fever flared up and he went back to eating sweets, which he had dropped. The threat did not materialize and the hay fever disappeared, only to return quickly when his female colleague went on holiday. A telephone session with me cut that short.

Then one evening, sneezing and nose running broke out violently. He took four antihistamine tablets that he had for his hay fever, twice the normal dose, and six more later, thus revealing a panic which called for the rushing up of reinforcements. He asked for a session next day, and I suggested that his attempt to do without his drug had evoked not only acute anxiety, but also a sense of intense, unsatisfied, hungry need, and that the hay fever was like salivating in his nose instead of his mouth, feeling hungry for more tablets and ultimately for mother. He replied, 'I salivated in my mouth too. I felt terrifically hungry and ate three plates full of flakes, milk and cream.' From that session the hay fever symptom died away.

By June 1964 he was, however, still tied to his antidepressant drug and multivite, and in the ensuing months dreamed constantly of his mother. These dreams were mostly short and to the point, as that he was telling his mother over and over again that she was responsible for his illness; that he was snowed up with work and his mother and father who should have been helping him were letting him down; that a senior colleague, who had been a supportive father-figure to him and had recently died, was alive again and with him in a hospital in nursing sister's uniform; that he was happy with a friendly girl whom he then lost, but found that now his wife was with him; that he met again a girl he had liked and lost touch with years ago and then to his horror found his mother-cum-(castrating) aunt behind the bar and he hid his face and got out with the girl; that he was on holiday with his mother and quarrelled with her because she was providing poor food. During this time he reported that he got very anxious if his wife went out in the evening, but otherwise he felt he was improving and felt better than at any time in the last three years. In fact he was mildly manic, got an 'incredible amount of work into each day', and realized that he tended to rush himself and then felt 'empty' and did better if he just plodded steadily along. This masked some anxiety, for he said, 'My recovery has lasted three years now and seems too good to be true. How long will it last?'

By January 1965 he tried again to do without his supports, drug, multivite, rests, and analysis. He had not been able to manage with fortnightly sessions but now once again said, 'I feel if I could reduce sessions to once a fortnight, I would gain confidence and be able to drop the drug and multivite.' He was trying to see if he could stand 'deprivation'. The most constant dream theme had been that of recovering contact with a good figure he had once possessed and lost. Now, with the hay fever eliminated, he felt he could try again, but it did not work. He dropped to fortnightly sessions, then one day omitted one of his twelve daily multivite tablets, felt bad and rushed to take not that one but twelve more. Here was evidence of real panic. To reassure himself he dreamed:

I put four extra tablets in my mouth, and flicked them round with my tongue. They tasted sweet, like Smarties. Should I take them out? I swallowed them.

How near to consciousness his deep-seated sensitivity to losing a supportive person was, appeared early in March when he was looking forward to seeing me on a T.V. programme. To his surprise, however, it made him feel 'queer. For the first time I saw you discussing something that wasn't to do with me. It was as if you were having nothing to do with me. It made me feel unreal as if I wasn't there.' His fantasy of exclusive possession of me had been shattered unexpectedly, but his need of the defence of this fantasy against separation-anxiety was explained by something he had said very early in his analysis. 'As a child I was always afraid of being left alone. Mother was always saying "I don't know what you'd do without me. One of these days I'll go out and not come back again."' That had bitten deep, the more so because he often came home from school to find the front door locked and had to wait about till mother returned home; but that was not the origin of his intense fear of losing the all-important person on whom he depended. The state he was reduced to by this fear was vividly expressed in a dream in April:

A small kitten gave birth to kittens who were terribly small, weak and helpless,

which was how he felt. That day he wanted more tablets, consciously because he felt hungry and had three helpings of pudding. (Cf. the analysis of the hay fever.) He commented, 'This is the first time I have associated the drug with hunger. Mother breast-fed me for quite a time.' I suggested that everything pointed to the probability that behind his symptoms there lay a severe weaning trauma, and that giving up the antidepressant drug would expose him to re-experiencing his post-weaning depression.

After this he developed discomfort in the throat for three weeks, and had a dream which left him with a strong need for the drug and the feeling that without it he would go into hospital and never get out.

I was made a chronic long-stay patient in the hospital I had been in (where he had felt supported). But it was dingy and unattractive and the food stodgy and awful.

I suggested that the dream described his post-weaning depression, imprisoned with a mother who had now gone bad on him, in a dingy world with stodgy food. The antidepressant prevented the return to consciousness of this infantile depression. He then remembered that in the dream there had been a doctor who had decided that he should be a long-stay patient, and his name had been his mother's maiden name. In May he suddenly brought out in two dreams how this early traumatic loss of the nursing mother had left him sexually over-stimulated and led to infantile masturbation. He dreamed simply that he had a nocturnal emission, and commented, 'I was proud that I could produce erections before I went to school. From 13 I had three or four nocturnal emissions a week and it frightened me.' Then a second dream:

I was masturbating and thought the semen looked like milk.

'I woke wondering if I had substituted masturbating for breast feeding.'

By June, his wife, who was pregnant, was nearing her term, and he began to get extremely anxious about her being away in hospital for a short time. He became both obsessed and distressed by a constant feeling that she had been unfaithful to him, and I was able to point out that this was in fact his feeling that his mother had been unfaithful to him, reactivated and attached to his wife by his growing separation-anxiety over the impending child-birth. I further suggested to him that it was probably not just the fact of weaning that had upset him so much, but his sensing a radical change in his mother's attitude to him. Her primary maternal feeling for him had probably faded out suddenly and led to her weaning him in a traumatic way. He said, 'It is a definite fact that if ever I was ill as a child, mother couldn't do enough for me for the first two or three days and then she would change suddenly, and if I needed anything she'd call out "Oh! You must wait. I'm busy." ' The next day he woke sobbing bitterly and could not stop. His wife rang me and I had a word with him, but it was two hours before the sobbing died down. Then he found he was singing to himself a song he had known years ago about a couple who had been in love in a previous life. He said to his wife, 'Ideally, I ought to have married a girl I had known from being a baby,' i.e. his mother.

At last his long repressed infantile depression had returned to consciousness, disclosing itself as the characteristic state of his isolated 'ego of infancy', which was the life-long cause of his marked dependence, feelings of weakness, inability to face life alone, panic at any threat of the loss of a supportive figure, and his ready addictions to food, sweets, and drugs. He had unearthed this trauma in its full emotional reality just in time, for his wife went to hospital a week later and he was able to cope well with the situation. The fear of ego-breakdown and of re-experiencing infantile maternal deprivation, were here associated not only with manic-depressive tendencies, but in the first place with a severe regressive illness involving a drastic withdrawal from real life and human contacts, and showed that an actual schizoid 'thinness' of object-relationships had been superficially overlaid by his intense needs for someone to depend on. We must later consider further clinical evidence for this basic problem of extreme ego-weakness bound up with severe and early failure of the object-relationships necessary to nourish the growth of the infantile ego.

But this patient's analysis proceeded from this point to develop into a quiet, uneventful, steady analytical uncovering and reintegration of his regressed infantile ego. The pattern was that some minor disturbance would occur and arouse enough anxiety for him to be aware of it, and to discover that he was having unconscious dream reactions to it, all of which he could then talk out with me. He came to see that the regressed secret heart of his personality could be manifested in two ways. First (i) it broke through as an uncontrollable eruption which undermined his adult personality, and drove him into the illness which brought him to me, and landed him in hospital in the first place. That stage had long since been got over, and his adult self was being more and more strongly established. Now (ii) it was re-emerging in a gradual process of internal self-discovery, carried on relatively quietly over a long period of analytical psychotherapy, without any serious threat to his adult life. In this process he was getting this lost heart of himself more and more into relationship with me and reunited with his conscious self. This would be the final phase of his treatment, which could and should go on quietly and reliably until he found that he no longer reacted with unrealistic anxiety to very minor threats to his security in life, and he ceased to be vulnerable at the point of over-dependence on mother-substitutes.

Typical of this last phase of analysis were three dreams:

I went on board the *Queen Mary*. It was rocking violently. Mother was there with some tiny children and both she and they were spilling things.

Here was a simple statement of the instability of life in the care of the unreliable mother.

I stood on the deck of a small motor-boat which was rocking violently, so I went down into the cabin. There it was warm and snug and safe. I did not feel any rocking at all.

Here is a simple statement of flight from the frightening instability of the unreliable mother, and regression back into the womb, a withdrawal in fact deep into his own unconscious, where the heart of him remained out of touch with life.

I was in a hotel and felt very secure there in bed. No one knew where I was, and no one could get at me to trouble me. Then there was a knock at the door. I opened it and there were some clients of a professional colleague of mine, seeking my help. I helped them and they went away.

Here was his discovery deep within himself that he now felt strong enough to stand the impact of the adult life of the external world and not be undermined by anxiety about it. In fact, he had been contemplating asking this professional colleague to do a job for him, but hesitated because the colleague never made such a request of him, and he wished he would. In the dream he had brought this about, and found that he could sustain the equal relationship involved.

Part II

THE REORIENTATION OF PSYCHODYNAMIC THEORY

IV

FOUR PHASES OF PSYCHODYNAMIC THEORY[1]

At the Sixth International Congress of Psychotherapy in 1964, Foulkes made this statement:

> Psychoanalysis is a biological theory which has only very reluctantly been pushed into being a social theory by the pressure of psychotherapy. Group therapy is not psychoanalysis.

This raises critical problems for theoretical thinking. The first sentence is undoubtedly right. Psychotherapy is a social, in the sense of a personal, relationship problem, and this is really as true of individual therapy as of group therapy. Is the second sentence correct? It means that psychoanalysis ceases to be psychoanalysis if it changes from its original biological orientation to meet the problems of psychotherapy. This is hardly a tenable position. Psychoanalytic theory arose out of the attempt Freud was making, as a practising physician, to find a therapy for the psychoneuroses. His first attempt was frankly neurological and he abandoned it because it had nothing to say to the psychological problems he was faced with. His second attempt was psychobiological and gave more scope for psychological thinking. But if psychoanalysis is to be theoretically fixed at that point for all time, it would be an unheard-of situation in science. Moreover Freud himself found this psychobiological theory inadequate as time went on, and moved into the more purely psychological problem of ego theory.

Theories that have no practical application can only be of academic interest. Our real concern is the 'cure' of mental 'illness' and the safeguarding of mental health, which has become, though it is as yet far from being recognized, as *the* major human concern. We do not do psychotherapy to demonstrate psychoanalytic theory. In fact, the theory has constantly been changed to meet the needs of therapy. We must therefore trace these developments in psychodynamic theory to

[1] This chapter is a revision of the first half of a paper which appeared in the *Brit. J. med. Psychol.*, **36** (1963), p. 161, under the title 'Psychodynamic Theory and the Problem of Psychotherapy'.

see how they bear on the as yet only partially solved problem of psychotherapy. This became a particular interest of mine from about 1950 as my clinical concern came to centre, of necessity, on a markedly schizoid group of patients, who called for particularly close study. The results of this work began to emerge by about 1960, and throughout I had found Fairbairn's formulations in the field of theory invaluable. Two concepts, *the ego* and *the schizoid process*, came to dominate the enquiry. They at once suggest a contrast to a psychodynamic theory based on the very different concepts of *instincts* and *depression*, as in the classic Freudian theory. Nevertheless, the fact that in the 1920's Freud himself turned his interest from instincts to the analysis of the ego, shows that what we have to consider is not two opposed views, but a development which has been going on in psychodynamic research for half a century. For this development Freud himself provided the initial impetus and it arose logically out of his own earlier work.

We may well at this point pause and reflect on the nature and place of theory in our work. All are agreed that we do not interpret to patients in theoretical terms, nor do we seek to fit the patient into a predetermined theoretical scheme. Were we to do so, we should learn nothing new from our clinical work. This error in technique is, probably, not in fact always avoided. We must use our theoretical concepts to guide our thinking in trying to understand the patient, and therapists obviously will not find it easy to let what the patient presents modify the concepts they are used to and have acquired a vested emotional interest in. Nevertheless, Winnicott (1963) has written:

> In a sense it is more difficult for an analyst to be original than for anyone else, because everything we say truly has been taught us yesterday (i.e. by patients).

Human problems are still so far from solution that we cannot afford to become theoretically static, and as Winnicott indicates, our patients do teach us and our concepts are always undergoing slow but subtle modification under the pressures of psychotherapy. *Concepts* are most useful at the stage at which they are being formed. They represent the intellectual effort to clarify and formulate new insights which are emerging in the thick of clinical work. For a time they act as signposts pointing the way in the right direction for the next advance: but the concepts are liable to date, sometimes in the very terms that connote them, sometimes in the content of an unchanged term. By the time new further experience has begun to gather, previous concepts have already come to represent, either a position permanently won which must now be moved beyond, or else the concepts have become stereotyped and too rigid, and act as a barrier to fresh thinking. This has happened to Freud's concepts. Thus 'depression' represents a position won in order to be moved beyond. Terms such as instinct, libido, aggression (as an innate drive), the id, the superego, defence *mechanisms*, the Oedipus complex, mark stages in advancing psychodynamic theory, some of which have certainly become too stereotyped and rigid. The term 'ego' in particular is a concept which is steadily enriching its content and changing in a profound way, to open up deeper levels of psychic experience where new insights and concepts are called for. To try to work on new material with nothing but the old conceptual tools retards deeper understanding.

We have no choice now but to focus our thinking more on the problems of ego-development in the first year than on the oedipal problems of later infancy though they are real problems. Klein's attempt to read back the three-person oedipal problems (dated at three to four years in classic theory) into the first year two-person problems, has not been generally accepted, but was eloquent proof that a change in basic theoretical standpoint was developing. The process of change has been at work ever since Freud turned definitely to ego-analysis in the 1920's, but of all the analysts who have contributed to the slow furthering of this change, so far only one, Fairbairn, has made a specific, systematic attempt to think out the nature of the fundamental reorientation of theory that is going on. He would have been the last person to wish that his contribution to theory should, in turn, become a fixed and stereotyped scheme blocking the way to further insights. Nevertheless, he formulated certain basic concepts which appear to be as necessary for the intelligible ordering of our field of knowledge at this stage, as were Freud's oedipal concepts and his structural terms at an earlier stage. Fairbairn's work is no more a mere proposed change in terminology, as one critic suggested, than was Freud's.

I hold no brief for any conceptual terminology as final. Terms are only useful tools to be discarded when we find better ones, a shorthand summary of what we know up to date. No doubt in fifty years,' time wholesale revision will have taken place. The term 'libidinal', though useful, is far from satisfactory as standing for the fundamental life-drive in the human being to become a 'person'. Its historical and linguistic associations are too narrowing for it to be adequate to this new orientation that we have now to take into account. If the term 'libidinal' is revised, all Fairbairn's terms will need revision. Meanwhile, till some-one suggests a better term than 'libidinal', I feel compelled to say that once mastered I have found Fairbairn's terminology, as far as it goes, closer to clinical realities than any other, and too valuable not to be used. Balint (1952) writes:

> How much unconscious gratification lies hidden behind the undisturbed use of accustomed ways of thinking . . . is best shown by the often quite irrational resistance that almost every analyst puts up at the suggestion that he might learn to use or even only to understand a frame of reference considerably different from his own. (p. 232.)

I shall seek in what follows to place Fairbairn's work in what seems to me to be its proper position and context in the march of psychodynamic theory, to show in what way I found it invaluable in my own particular study of schizoid problems, and to present it as a challenge to willingness to think, where necessary, in new terms as new insights develop. But at the same time, this book is primarily clinical, not theoretical, and we must seek to follow the clinical evidence wherever it leads. I feel now that Fairbairn's 'Revision of Theory' itself needs to be extended and revised or deepened in particular with regard to the meaning of the concept of 'ego' under the impact of work such as Winnicott's on the mother–infant relationship and the beginnings of ego-development (cf. Chapters VIII and IX). It is on that level now that we have most to learn. At the International Congress of Psychoanalysis in Edinburgh in 1961, one speaker objected to Winnicott asking us to use 'new terms such as "impingement" etc.' But progress will always be blocked if we persist in trying to pour new wine into old bottles which are too small.

My own interest in this matter was aroused when, around 1950, three patients, each in their own way, presented the same problem. The first was a middle-aged unmarried engineer running his own business, well educated, who sought analysis of his own accord for attacks of guilt-burdened depression. He had some six years of orthodox analysis whose content would be familiar to every analyst. He talked out his early loveless family life, his submissiveness to his egotistical mother and fear and hate of his violent father, sibling jealousies, and adolescent rebellion. He produced oedipal and castration dreams, sado-masochistic fantasies, genital, anal and oral, guilt and punishment reactions. A classic psychoanalytic textbook could have been written out of his material. Throughout he remained a conscientious hardworking obsessional personality, with all his emotions under tremendous internal control. His personality type did not change but he improved greatly as compared with his original crippling depression. His ego-defences, we may say, were modified and he felt much more free to work. He summed up his position thus: 'I'm very much better, I feel I've cleared all the outlying areas of my neurosis, but I feel I've come up against a circular wall with no doors or windows and too high to see over. I go round and round it and have no idea what is inside. I know there's something I'm doing that blocks further analysis and I don't know what it is. It's difficult to let anything more out. I've got to keep fit to run my business.' Here, apparently, was *a closely guarded hurt and hidden part of his inner self into which neither I, nor even his own conscious self, was allowed to intrude*. He once dreamed of going down into an underground passage and coming to a halt at a locked door marked 'hidden treasure'.

The second patient, an older, very ill professional woman whose doctor said she would never work again, had a similar background and normal oedipal analysis during which she returned to work, suffered no further breakdown, and was able to work till she qualified for a full pension. She then seemed to stick, and like the first patient held her gains but made no further progress. At that point she dreamed of walking along a road and coming up against a huge wall. There was no way of getting forward and she did not know what lay on the other side. Her comment was: 'I've got to go on if you can stand it.' She clearly felt that if she succeeded, it would mean a difficult time for both of us. Here again was *this clear-cut unconscious knowledge of an inaccessible cut-off part of the inner personal life into which the patient seemed unable and afraid to penetrate*, but which had to be opened up to secure a radical therapeutic result.

The third patient, a medical man in middle life, presented the same theme in a different way. This was the case with which I opened the 1961 paper on 'The Schizoid Problem and Regression' (cf. Chapter 2, p. 49). His presenting symptom, an embarrassing and active preoccupation with breasts, faded out under analysis only to be replaced by powerful fantasies of retirement from active living into some impregnable stronghold, isolated from the outer world. Like the other patients, he carried on his active professional life. This then must have indicated *the drastic withdrawal from the outer world of a specialized part of his personality existing passively inside the fortress, the impassable and the circular wall of the other patients*. They were all markedly schizoid, detached, shut-in, had great difficulty in human relationships, and would feel alone and out of touch in a group.

At this point I tried to write a paper on 'The Schizoid Citadel' but could not arrive at any satisfying conclusion. Therefore, as a starting point for enquiry I made a clinical study of 'Fairbairn's Theory of Schizoid Reactions' (1952, cf. Chapter 1, p. 17ff) in the light of material gathered from my own patients; and set out, secondly, to gather fresh clinical data on schizoid problems, and, thirdly, to survey the development of psychodynamic theory from Freud, through the American 'culture pattern' writers, to Melanie Klein and Fairbairn, to see what pointers were emerging for the solution of this problem. The result of that historical study I presented in the book *Personality Structure and Human Interaction* (1961) to which this is a clinical sequel. On the clinical side I owe everything to a group of schizoid patients whose variety was fascinating: a biologist, a communist, a hospital Sister, a university lecturer, a grandmother in her fifties, a young borderline-schizophrenic wife, a social worker who had had a paranoid schizophrenic breakdown, a young middle-aged mother who was also a language teacher, an outstandingly successful but most unhappy business man, and so on. Their treatment always seemed to move ultimately beyond the range of the classic psychoanalytic phenomena, the conflicts over sex, aggression, love and hate, guilt and depression. It was not that these classic phenomena were not there. All patients began by producing this kind of material and it could not be by-passed. Its analysis occupied the first years predominantly, though looking back I can see that deeper problems were peeping through, and in the end dominated the scene. For what came after, what emerged from behind the oedipal material, I did not find much help, except in the interpretation of details, in the literature on schizoid problems. It seemed to lack intrinsic connexion with the existing psychoanalytic theory of oedipal and depressive problems. I had to let impressions accumulate and only by about 1960 did these begin, as I feel, to disclose some definite pattern.

One strongly emerging theoretical trend provided the necessary standing-ground for thinking. In 1949 Balint called for *a transition from a physiological and biological bias to an object-relations bias in theory* (1952). That was exactly the major trend that stood out in the historical survey. It was visible in the work of Americans such as Horney, Fromm, and Sullivan, though more from the social and 'culture-pattern' point of view than in 'depth analysis'. As early as 1942–4 Fairbairn's fundamental revision of psychoanalytical theory had been on exactly the lines Balint later called for, from the endopsychic rather than the cultural viewpoint (Fairbairn, 1952). Here and elsewhere were the signs of a growing and widespread concensus which can be expressed in several different but parallel and related ways. Theory had been moving from (i) concentration on the parts to attention to the psychic whole, (ii) from the biological to the properly psychological, (iii) from instinct-vicissitudes to ego-development, (iv) from instinct-gratification to ego-maintenance, and (v) from the depressive level of impulse-management to the deeper schizoid level where the foundations of a *whole* personality are or are not laid. Throughout, the concepts of the *ego* and *the schizoid process* became ever more dominant.

Classic psychoanalytical theory is a moral psychology of the struggle to direct and control innate antisocial impulses, discrete and separate instinctive drives of sex and aggression, by means of guilt. This, when it produces too drastic repression instead of 'sublimation', leads to the mental paralysis of internalized aggression, self-punishment and depression. When Freud turned to ego-analysis, however, he started lines of enquiry which were destined to lead to a quite different orientation. Research went deeper than obsessional problems and the superego. The dissociations of hysteria began to assume new significance as ego-splittings. Schizoid problems came to view, not as problems of the gratification or control of instincts, but as problems of ego-splitting and the struggle to recover and preserve a whole adequate ego or self with which to face life. The term 'ego' began to denote something larger than just the conscious ego. This newer type of theory had much to say about the problems of my patients who were unconsciously guarding their secret schizoid citadel in which some vital part of their total self lay apparently buried, hidden and lost to view and use. Impulse-psychology had little enlightenment to offer on this.

Here I must record my agreement with Fairbairn that the term 'psychobiological' is an illegitimate hybrid which confuses two different disciplines. It is like that earlier hybrid 'physiological psychology' as set forth in McDougall's book (1905). It was just physiology and not psychology at all. We study the one whole of the human being on different levels of abstraction for scientific purposes. Biology is one level, psychology is another. Each deals with phenomena, organic or psychic, which the other cannot handle, but they are all the functions of one and the same whole or total self. When it comes to therapy, knowledge from all disciplines must be taken into account. We do not suppose ourselves to be dealing with two separate entities, one called body and the other mind. The language of 'id and ego' implies a dualistic philosophy. But neither can we study such a complex whole as if it were a kind of Irish stew with everything lumped together in one pot. We must abstract its main distinguishable aspects and stick consistently to what we select to study.

The business of psychodynamic research is with that aspect of the whole man which we call the motivated and meaningful life of the growing 'person', and his difficulties and developments in object-relationships with other persons. A dynamic psychology of the 'person' is not an instinct-theory but an ego-theory, in which instincts are not entities *per se* but functions of the ego. The way an instinctive capacity operates is an expression of the state of the ego. The trend of psychoanalytic theory moves steadily in that direction. Instinct-theory *per se* becomes more and more useless in clinical work, and ego-theory more and more relevant. Interpretations in biological terms would only make the patient feel helpless and answer: 'So what? That's how I'm made.' Outside the sphere of pure psychodynamics, I would think that the philosopher John Macmurray has given the *coup de grace* to instinct theory in the study of human persons, in his Gifford Lectures, Vol. 2, on 'Persons in Relation'. The most important single subject of investigation on all sides is the earliest stages of ego-growth, as in the work of Melanie Klein and her group, Fairbairn, Winnicott, Bowlby, Bion, and researches into the psychodynamics of schizophrenia. The classical oedipal, social, sexual, and aggressive conflicts are, of course, all there, but are disclosing themselves as aspects of the internal, sado-masochistic, self-exhausting struggle of *an already divided self* to maintain psychic defences against ego-collapse.

I have thus come to feel that the first great task which confronted Freud in his pioneer exploration was that of analysing the area of moral and pseudo-moral conflict (i.e. truly moral and pathologically moral). This had hitherto comprised man's whole traditional account of his nature and troubles: and it blocked the way to more radical understanding. Freud did analyse it so exhaustively that he opened the way to the deeper level hidden beneath it, the primitive premoral level of experience in which the foundations of ego-stability are or fail to be laid. The result of Freud's work is that unrealistic traditional ideas about children have been replaced by an ever deeper knowledge of the earliest infantile fears and ego-weakness. Freud actually took over the traditional and popular psychology of Plato and St Paul as his starting point (cf. Chapter V,

p. 132). Plato's charioteer of reason and St Paul's 'law of the mind' became the controlling ego with its scientific reason. Just as Plato's 'reason' made an ally of the lion (aggression), turning it against the beast (instincts) to enforce control, so Freud envisaged the ego working with the sadistic superego to turn aggression inwards against the id, and showed how pathological guilt produced depression.

Freud used the traditional philosophical moral psychology of impulse-control, but he used it in a wholly new way, to guide an original and factual clinical analysis of the detailed mental processes involved in man's experience of moral and pseudo-moral conflict. All this was analysed so exhaustively that it represents a reasonably completed scientific investigation of man's sadomasochistic struggle to civilize the recalcitrant impulse-life he finds within himself. There are no signs that Freud's basic analysis of moral conflict will need much revision *per se*, so far as it goes. But Freud did not answer, indeed failed to ask, the crucial question: since man is without doubt social by nature, how does it come about that he feels such antisocial impulses so often? Why do men have antisocial impulses? Freud, like all his predecessors, simply assumed that they were innate, that in man's nature there was an unresolvable contradiction of good and evil. This is the traditional view of man in our own and other cultures.

However, Freud's analysis of moral conflict unwittingly revealed the fact that this is not the whole of, nor even the deepest element in, the psychic experience of human beings. In fact, man's age old conviction that all his troubles come from his possession of mighty if nearly uncivilizable instincts of his animal nature, turns out to be our greatest rationalization and self-deception. We have preferred to boost our egos by the belief that even if we are bad, we are at any rate strong in the possession of 'mighty instincts'. Men have resisted recognition of the truth that we distort our instincts into antisocial drives in our struggle to suppress the fact that deep within our make-up we retain a weak, fear-ridden infantile ego that we never completely outgrow. Thus Fairbairn regarded 'infantile dependence', not the 'Oedipus complex', as the root cause of neurosis. The Oedipus complex is a problem of 'powerful impulses' (? instincts), Infantile dependence is a problem of 'ego-weakness'. Depression is the problem of our badness. The schizoid problem opens up the psychology of our fundamental weakness. I do not doubt that there is a strong resistance to recognizing this as the real basis of psychodynamic theory, for human beings would rather see themselves as bad than weak. One can see this in the very different attitudes that are often expressed to obsessionals and hysterics. Obsessionals get more respect than hysterics. Obsessionals are thought to be mastering bad impulses, while hysterics are held to be only trying to find someone to cling to in their weakness. Those professionally engaged in these matters will even admit: 'Well, you know, I think I am a bit obsessional', but you never hear them say: 'I'm a bit of a hysteric.' But it is hysteria that takes us closer to the fundamental problem. This shift in the centre of gravity in psychodynamic theory will enforce a radical reassessment of all philosophical, moral, educational, and religious views of human nature.

Psychoanalytic practice seems to be in advance of psychoanalytic theory in this matter. We shall see in the next chapter how, in the analysis of depression, it is coming to be recognized that this condition is more complex than at first seemed to be the case. Classic depression was explained by reference to ambivalent object-relations and guilt over sexual and aggressive drives. Yet there appears to be another aspect of it which is better characterized as regression, and which needs to be explained rather by ego-splitting, arrested ego-development, weakness, lack of self-fulfilment and apathy. We shall see that Zetzel holds that the significant new concept in the modern view of depression is that of the 'ego'. It is, however, hopeless to try to deal with ego-psychology in terms of instinct theory. The problems of ego-psychology are those of ego-weakness, loss of unity, depersonalization, the sense of unreality, lack of a proper sense of personal identity, of the terror some patients experience of feeling so 'far away' and 'shut in' that they feel they will never get back in touch again. These phenomena can only be dealt with by a theory based firmly on the analysis of the schizoid processes of withdrawal to the inner world under the impact of primary fears. It is in this region that the results of disturbed beginnings of ego-development are to be found.

So far only Fairbairn has sought *systematically* to reorientate theory from a depressive to a schizoid foundation. Nevertheless the whole drift of psychoanalysis today is in that direction. In a summary of the main points of his theory, Fairbairn states that the internal situation described in terms of object-splitting and ego-splitting

> represents a basic schizoid position which is more fundamental than the depressive position described by Melanie Klein. . . . A theory of

the personality conceived in terms of object-relations is in contrast to one conceived in terms of instincts and their vicissitudes. (1963.)

Freud's structural terms, id, superego, ego, give an account of classic depression and moral conflict. Fairbairn's structural terms, libidinal ego, antilibidinal ego, central ego, give an account of the schizoid process of the loss of the primary unity of the self.

As I see it, there have been four stages in the development of psychoanalytic theory. (i) *Freud's original instinct theory* which enabled a penetrating analysis of moral and pseudo-moral conflict to be made. This led to (ii) *Freud's ego-analysis*, which, because it remained tied to instinct theory, could not give more than a superficial account of the ego, as a utilitarian apparatus of impulse-control, an instrument of adaptation to external reality, a means of perceptual consciousness, etc. Before an adequate theory of *the ego as a real personal self* could be worked out, a third stage had to come about. (iii) *Melanie Klein had to explore the psychology of the object as psychically internalized to become a factor in ego-development.* She explored the psychology of internal object-relations as thoroughly as Freud had explored that of impulse-management. Klein's work is 'an object-relations theory with emphasis on the object', and it led to a fourth stage, (iv) *Fairbairn's 'object-relations theory with the emphasis on the ego'*. His primary interest had always been in the ego, as seen in his early paper (1931) on a patient's dream-personifications of herself. But he made no progress with this till Klein's work made its impact on him, as he explicitly acknowledged. Now, his work brings out clearly that the importance of the object is not primarily that of being 'a means of instinctual gratification'; this gives only a psychology of instinct-vicissitudes. The importance of the object lies in the fact that it is 'a necessity for ego-development'. This gives us a psychology of ego-vicissitudes, ego-differentiations, splittings and what not. He brought Klein's object-relations theory back full circle to ego-theory again, but this time not to Freud's superficial ego-theory, but to *a fundamental ego-theory which makes psychodynamics a genuine science of a real self or person, a unique centre of meaningful experience growing in the medium of personal relationships.*

Fairbairn is, of course, far from being the only analyst to see the need to orientate theory and therapy afresh to the true selfhood of the whole person. Winnicott writes that the goal of therapy is

the shift of the operational centre from the false self to the true self. . . . That which proceeds from the true self feels real. (1955a, p. 292.)

Again,

In favourable cases there follows at last a new sense of self in the patient and a sense of the progress that means true growth. (p. 289.)

Winnicott's theory of the true and false self is likewise a theory of ego-splitting and deals with phenomena that Freud's structural terms take no account of. Fairbairn, however, is the only analyst so far who has taken up the task of the *overall* revision of theory from this point of view. The result is an impressive intellectual achievement of practical clinical value.

In the summary quoted, Fairbairn regards *separation-anxiety* as the earliest and original anxiety, and as the basic cause of the schizoid process of flight or withdrawal of part of the now split ego from contact with the outer world. There are several causes of separation anxiety. (i) Fairbairn earlier stressed that unsatisfied love-needs become dangerous and the infant draws back, a very potent cause. Winnicott emphasizes (ii) the infant's direct fear of the 'impingement' of a bad-object, from whom he must escape because he cannot defend himself; and further (iii) the situation in which the infant finds himself simply neglected, deserted. The mother just fails the infant. He can draw no adequate response from her and must escape by mental withdrawal from an environment that seems not persecuting but empty. These three causes of withdrawal are pathological in themselves. But (iv) Winnicott also puts great emphasis on what may be termed a healthy origin of withdrawal. This is a quite distinct problem of the infant becoming afraid to love because he finds that his mother cannot tolerate the natural, healthy, robust vigour of his love-needs, so that he comes to feel he is a ruthless destroyer without intending to be so. The mother is not frustrating, angry or neglectful, but she is not able to stand up to the strain of her thoroughly alive baby and he becomes frightened of this situation and withdraws, and has to spend his energy on inhibiting his needs and all pleasurable tensions and excitements they may arouse, leading eventually to apathy. However caused, the danger of separation, whether by desertion or withdrawal, is that *the infant, starting life with a primitive and quite undeveloped psyche, just cannot stand the loss of his object. He cannot retain his primitive wholeness for more than a short period in the absence of mother, and cannot go on to develop a strong sense of identity and selfhood without an object-relation. Separation-anxiety then is a pointer to the last and worst fear, fear of the loss of the ego itself, of depersonalization, and the sense of unreality.* The reason why patients hold on with such tenacity to their Kleinian world of internal bad objects, and their Freudian inner world of oedipal conflicts over sex and aggression, is that their external object-relations have become so weakened by early schizoid withdrawal inside, that they are compelled to maintain a world of internal fantasied objects to keep their ego in being at all.

Conflicts over sex, aggression and guilt, in addition to having their own obvious significance on their own specific level, are also in the last resort frequently used as defences against withdrawal, regression, and depersonalization, and the patient is reluctant to give them up. He will constantly go back to these classic conflicts unless we keep them well analysed as to their ultimate motives, rather than face the terrors of realizing how radically small, weak and cut off, shut in and unreal he feels at bottom. A dream of a male patient of 50 illustrates this:

I was engaged with someone (undoubtedly his tyrannical father) in a tremendous fight for life. I defended myself so vigorously that he suddenly stopped fighting altogether. I then immediately felt let down, disappointed and quite at a loss, and thought 'Oh! I didn't bargain for this'.

His real life was conducted very much in terms of rationalized aggression, opposing authority, attacking abuses, defending his independence (often when it was not threatened), all really in the interests of keeping his insecure ego in being. He couldn't keep going without the help of a fight. Another patient said: 'If I don't get angry with my employees, I'm too timid to face them. I feel some energy when I'm angry. Otherwise I feel just a nobody.' That is *the basic problem in psychopathology, the schizoid problem of feeling a nobody, of never having grown an adequate feeling of a real self.* If we go far enough, it always emerges in some degree from behind the classic conflicts. I suspect this to be more true of all human beings than we like to know, and that *the chronic aggression which has always seemed to be the hallmark of 'man' is but a defence against and a veneer over basic ego-weakness.* We must now consider this reorientation of psychodynamic theory in greater detail.

V

THE CLINICAL-DIAGNOSTIC FRAMEWORK

(The Manic-Depressive Problem in the Light of the Schizoid Process)[1]

The Historical Approach

THE last chapter traced in brief outline the four phases through which psychodynamic theory appears to me to have developed, a movement beyond biology to psychology, beyond instincts to the ego or self that possesses them, and beyond depressive to schizoid problems. It is, of course, not at all implied that biology has no contribution to make to the understanding of man and the treatment of mental illhealth. Any such suggestion would be absurd. The matter was put in correct perspective by Carstairs in his 1963 Reith Lectures:

> It is not on logical grounds that medicine has so long resisted psychotherapy. I believe that here we have another instance of events (in this case the series of discoveries about the human mind which were initiated by Sigmund Freud) that outstripped the grasp of human imagination. We have been living in an era dominated by biology and the physical sciences. . . . Medicine has profited by these discoveries . . . but I believe that as a result it has become too exclusively preoccupied with material techniques . . . which are far from being the only valid means of studying the human mind. Even in the practical realm of treating the sick, it may be that the great upsurge of biological research has already made its major contribution. Meanwhile we are neglecting some of the greatest health problems of our contemporary society, the problems of faulty psychological and social adjustment. (1963.)

Psychoanalysis cannot be accused of neglecting psychological and social problems, but its theory has shown evidence of the drag of the heavy emphasis on physical and biological science. True, the entire problem of heredity and the provision of the raw material of personality belongs to biology, along with all

[1] First published in the *Int. J. Psycho-Anal.*, **43** (1962), p. 98, and is here revised.

the physiological aspects of bodily symptom formation and organic conditioning, especially in the very earliest stages. Biochemistry must provide the psychiatric drugs for symptom-control. The study of the organism must be the basis for the physical treatments which have to be used when no psychological treatment is available or practicable.

Nevertheless, we cannot understand the 'person' in biological terms. Jung said that 'human beings cannot stand a meaningless existence', and at this level of the 'personal life' lived in terms of intelligible motives arising out of meaningful purposes, we need a fully psychological analysis. Psychoanalysis needs to disentangle itself from the biological matrix out of which it arose, and realize itself as a fully psychological discipline. It cannot explain everything about human beings, but its proper task is to understand the development and functioning of human beings as persons living in relationship with other persons. The analysis of man's moral life of impulse-management, guilt, and depression, did not necessitate a clear transcendence of the biological frame of reference, since it appeared to rest on the theory of inherited antisocial instincts. It is the analysis of the schizoid problem, centering on the stages of ego-growth in the medium of personal relationships, which has necessitated a more fully psychodynamic type of theory. In this chapter on the manic-depressive problem I have sought to trace in greater detail the depressive and schizoid levels of conceptualization and analysis. This provides our diagnostic clinical framework.

The increasing emphasis of recent years on schizoid problems represents the emergence of a distinct point of view in psychodynamic studies, which also diverges markedly from the traditional centuries-old approach to human problems. Like all other phenomena, psychopathological phenomena disclose hitherto unrecognized aspects when looked at from a different viewpoint. For a long time, the priority for Freud was hardly the evolving of a theory, but rather the 'seeing of what was there to be seen' and theorized about. So long as advance depended at first mainly on the accumulation of data, Freud could adopt and use the traditional theory of human nature as a sufficient framework for his thinking: i.e. the theory of conflicts arising from the need to control bad impulses rooted in 'the flesh'. He could get on with the pressing task of observation and description of psychopathological phenomena, not so much from the outside like Kraepelin and Bleuler and psychiatrists in general, but from the inside as suggested by the work of Charcot on hypnotic experiences and the unconscious. Up to somewhere between 1910 and 1920 that was his main work, and so far as his results were conceptualized in theory in this first period, it did not affect the simple traditional framework or scheme, of natural instincts versus social controls. His great theoretical concepts evolved in this first stage were those of repression, resistance, the censor, transference, the meaning of dreams and symbolism, infantile sexuality, the 'family' or 'Oedipus' complex, and so on. The work of observation and description never ends, and since that period has been carried much deeper with the fuller investigation of schizoid phenomena, and the close study of the earliest mother–infant relationships.

By 1920, however, it was already apparent that the increasing range of facts pressing on Freud's notice were calling for examination from other points of view than that of the traditional theory of bad impulses rooted in the flesh and calling for drastic control. That was the view of the pre-scientific philosophical and religious psychology of Greece and Palestine, and had always been the universal common-sense view, as indeed it is today. The ancient Persian Zoroastrians thought of a warfare between matter as evil and mind as good. Plato's famous picture of human nature as a chariot with two horses and a charioteer is described by R. Livingstone thus:

> He described human nature by a simile. On the outside men look like human beings, but under their skin three creatures are concealed: a monster with many heads, some wild, some tame, . . . the desires and passions: a lion—the spirited quality which will fight. . . ! and a human being—the rational element. . . . Plato urges us to make the man supreme and see that, helped by the lion, he controls the many-headed beast. (*Greek Ideals and Modern Life*, pp. 140–1.)

St Paul's doctrine of unceasing warfare between the flesh and the spirit, the law of the members and the law of the mind, the Platonic simile, and the traditional trichotomy of body, mind, and spirit, all represent the same diagnosis of the human predicament. As a first hypothetical basis for his investigations Freud adopted this 'theory' and gave it a scientific dress. The 'many-headed beast of the desires and passions' and the 'law of the members' became the instincts of sex and aggression functioning anti-socially according to a 'pleasure principle' and leading to a Hobbesian world in which life would be 'nasty, brutish, and short'. (Cf. *The Future of an Illusion*.) The 'lion' becomes aggression taken up by the sadistic superego and turned against the id instinct-derivatives. The 'law of the mind' and 'charioteer of reason' (on whom Freud, like Plato, pinned all his hopes as he makes clear in the last chapter of *New Introductory Lectures*), becomes the ego seeking to operate by a 'reality principle'.

This basic way of looking at things Freud never changed, and indeed the kind of change called for has only slowly become apparent. But the terms id, ego, and superego, in which he came to embody it, stand also for something that was to prove of far greater importance than this traditional scheme. They represent the fact that Freud made a second reorientation of his thinking, from the psycho-biological to the endopsychic-structural point of view. Hartmann has stressed the tremendous importance of Freud's importation into psychodynamic science of the structural viewpoint. He writes (1960):

> It was above all Freud's introduction of the structural point of view that made the psychoanalytic approach . . . more subtle and more conclusive.

In fact it gave ego-analysis priority over instincts in psychoanalytic thinking. Ego-splitting, a concept which Freud presents quite explicity as fundamental to psychoneurosis as well as psychosis, in the last section of his unfinished posthumous *Outline of Psychoanalysis*, begins to take the place of impulse-control as the centre of interest. It is possible now to see that this actually implies a shift of emphasis from a *psychology of depression* to a *psychology of the schizoid process*. All psychopathological phenomena look different when viewed from the schizoid rather than from the depressive viewpoint.

The 'Depressive' and the 'Schizoid' Standpoints

In Chapter II, I compared Freud's structural analysis of the personality, the id-ego-superego scheme, as a conceptualization of depression, with Fairbairn's revised theory of endopsychic structure as a conceptualization of the schizoid process (pp. 55 and 127). This difference in fact registers and consolidates the shift of viewpoint already referred to, and it enforces a reassessment of all phenomena. Fairbairn was the first, and is as yet the only analyst, to attempt the explicit systematic revision of theory on this basis, but it is implied and aspects of it are to varying extents expounded in a great deal of contemporary psychoanalysis. At the outset, after a searching study of 'Schizoid Factors in the Personality' in 1940 (which unfortunately was not published till after his theoretical papers) (1952, Chap. 1), he introduced his 'Revised Psychopathology of the Psychoses and Psychoneuroses' in 1941 (1952, Chap. 2) with these words:

Within recent years I have become increasingly interested in the problems presented by patients displaying schizoid tendencies. . . . The result has been the emergence of a point of view which, if it proves to be well-founded, must necessarily have far-reaching implications both for psychiatry in general and for psycho-analysis in particular. My various findings and the conclusions to which they lead involve not only a considerable revision of prevailing ideas regarding the nature and aetiology of schizoid conditions, but also a considerable revision of ideas regarding the prevalence of schizoid processes and a corresponding change in current clinical conceptions of the various psychoneuroses and psychoses . . . a recasting and reorientation of the libido theory together with a modification of various classical psychoanalytical concepts. (1952, p. 28.)

It seems now, looking back over the quarter of a century since those words were written, a matter of considerable surprise that that prophecy has not stimulated a more explicit theoretical response, a realization that some fundamental change was in process of developing, and specific attempts made to think it out in detail. It is not a good thing that complete systematic revision should have been attempted by only one analyst. What has happened is that *schizoid phenomena have been investigated while in the main a psychology of depression has been adhered to*. This change of viewpoint from the depressive to the schizoid position in viewing human problems, appears to involve some quite special difficulties. It is so radical and ultimate that it encounters our deepest and most powerful resistances; and here the patient's resistance against experiencing what it is that needs to be cured, can be supported by an unrealized resistance in the analyst against having to see it. I feel driven to conclude that *the age-old 'depressive diagnosis' involves man's greatest and most consistent self-deception*. We have all been in unconscious collusion, suffering individuals, religious philosophical and educational thinkers, and now psychodynamic researchers, to keep attention diverted from the deepest and ultimate causal factors and concentrated on a middle region of defensive endopsychic activity mistakenly regarded as causal and ultimate. This, I believe, is the conclusion we must draw. The tremendous resistance to its recognition is based on *mankind's universal preference for feeling bad but strong rather than feeling weak and afraid. The 'depressive' diagnosis fixes our attention on our badness, the 'schizoid' diagnosis fixes it on our weakness*—in a frightening change of emphasis and the more we explore it, the more far-reaching it appears to be.

Freud's id–ego–superego theory we have seen had two aspects: it was the first great step in the adoption of the structural standpoint, but it was also an embodiment of the traditional theory, an analysis of human personality on the basis of depressive phenomena. The id was the psychobiological source of innate and in the end unsocializable instincts of sex and aggression. Culture has to be defended against nature. If the defence fails we get criminality, if it succeeds too drastically we get neurosis. As Freud stated in his essay, 'Analysis, Terminable and Interminable' (1937), psychotherapy is helping the ego in its struggle against powerful antisocial instincts. The only way of avoiding either criminality or neurosis is to achieve maturity, not in the sense of basic socialization but in the sense of sublimation, a hypothetical process of detaching enough energy from the original instinctive aims to be redirected to valuable cultural goals. The original instinctive aims can, however, always be found still being energetically pursued under repression in the unconscious. I do not think there is any real difference in principle here between Plato, St Paul, and Freud. For all three, human nature is the scene of an unending internal strife and there is no real possibility of 'cure', only of 'compromise and relative stability' so long as man remains 'in the flesh'. The views of all three involve the underlying dualistic philosophy of body and mind, id and ego, as original, separate, and opposed entities. This is not avoided by Freud's idea of the ego developing on the surface of the id, a metaphorical statement that has no real meaning.

The classical psychoanalytical theory is that antisocial impulses, biologically determined, which certainly might be better tolerated socially than they usually are, must be controlled by the ego and in the process such intense guilt and repression are developed that the whole psyche is liable to fall into a state of illness and depressive paralysis. Unconscious guilt was for Freud the great source of resistance to psychotherapy (*The Ego and The Id*, p. 72, footnote). The patient feels that he is bad and ought to accept the punishment of going on being ill. Official Christianity took the side of repression (though the Gospels, the later St Paul, and the Johannine tradition had wiser insights). Freud took the side of easing repression and showing more toleration of instincts while strengthening the ego for rational control. But both agree as to the basic nature of the problem.

This depressive pattern has always been the favoured diagnosis. It is expressed in psychoanalytical terms as the alliance of the superego and the ego to control the id, while psychotherapy seeks to moderate the harshness of the superego control and to strengthen the ego. The theory is simple, precise, understandable, and it implies the possibility of practical measures on the social level to deal with the situation. Police control, legal punishment, denunciatory public opinion, moral disapproval, religious preaching of sin, all conspire to discipline recalcitrant instincts. In *The Future of an Illusion* (1927) Freud wrote:

> Every individual is virtually an enemy of civilization, though civilization is supposed to be an object of universal human interest. It is remarkable that, little as men are able to exist in isolation, they should nevertheless feel as a heavy burden the sacrifices which civilization expects of them in order to make a communal life possible. Thus civilization has to be defended against the individual. (p. 6.)

> It seems rather that every civilization must be built up on coercion and renunciation of instinct. . . . One has, I think, to reckon with the fact that there are present in all men destructive, and therefore antisocial and anticultural trends.

> It is just as impossible to do without control of the mass by a minority as it is to dispense with coercion in the work of civilization. For masses are lazy and unintelligent: they have no love for instinctual renunciation, and they are not to be convinced by argument of its inevitability; and the individuals composing them support one another in giving free rein to their indiscipline. (p. 7.)

The only way Freud could see to better this situation was:

> to lessen the burden of the instinctual sacrifices imposed on men, and to reconcile men to those which must necessarily remain and to provide a compensation for them. (p. 7.)

The fact that psychoanalytical therapy and every other kind of therapy has always found this result so extremely difficult to secure with the individual, is surely all of a piece with the catastrophic failures of practically all civilizations to maintain peace, security, and reasonable human happiness for more than short periods.

Nevertheless, though it seems to be proved beyond all doubt that we are very bad, since who dare gainsay such a trio as Plato, St Paul, and Freud, we may console ourselves that we are not weak. We have *a mighty sexual instinct* (Freud, 1908) and *a powerful and destructive aggressive instinct* (Freud, 1927), and if we are incapable of living together peaceably for long except as controlled subordinates (and always supposing our powerful coercive controllers do not fall out among themselves and drag us into the fray), at least we can glorify aggression as heroism, and live like Sir Tristram and Sir Palomydes and others of King Arthur's knights who idealized the role of picking quarrels with all and sundry to prove what 'mighty men of valour' they were. (Cf. Malory.) The incompleteness of the 'depressive' diagnosis is, however, seen the moment we realize that human beings always prefer to feel bad and strong rather than weak. *The diagnosis of 'antisocial instincts' has always been man's most convincing rationalization of his plight, a subtle defence against the alarming truth that the real trouble is fear, flight from life at deep mental levels, and the failure of basic strong ego-formation, resulting in consequent inadequacy, both felt and factual, in coping with life.*

The fact that human beings prefer to feel 'bad somebodies' rather than 'weak nonentities' may be illustrated historically and socially. There is the story of the ancient Greek who burned down a temple because he could not get recognition in any other way. Much crime and delinquency must be motivated by a quest for power, and for notoriety for destructive behaviour, to cover the felt inability to achieve true value by constructive work. This comes out clearly in clinical work. One patient, a married woman in the thirties, who had been actually cruelly brought up and felt utterly useless and worthless, described how, at her first school, she felt a terrible need to be noticed by the teachers, and bent all her energies to pleasing them by good work and good behaviour. As a result she was simply taken for granted as a girl who would not cause any trouble. Being already very schizoid, this made her feel depersonalized. She could not stand this and when she changed schools, she felt she must compel the teacher to take notice of her or she would feel just worth nothing at all. So she became a 'bad' girl and a ringleader in mischief. She got plenty of notice then and felt much safer that way.

Another married woman, also in her thirties, had grown up to feel that she was regarded by her family as inferior. She had not got the good looks or lively talk of her sisters, was shy, and in fact experienced transient states of depersonalization at a very early age. She was ignored by a busy father and was the perpetual butt of the criticisms of a very unstable mother. She would sit away in a corner when visitors came, feeling that it was hopeless for her to make any mark by good qualities. She was taken for granted as 'the quiet one' of the family. But in her late teens she suddenly developed a serious mental breakdown and her parents were alarmed. Her father became sympathetic and devoted to her, her mother said she was mad. She would say: 'No, I'm not mad, I'm bad', because her most obvious symptom was a compulsion to curse God, her parents, and sisters, and 'bad words and bad thoughts', aggressive, murderous, and sexual (with a strong anal colouring) would be 'running in her head'. She insisted on telling her parents all these curses and bad thoughts, and quite consciously knew she was shocking them. She felt proud of herself for being so daring, though she felt she could not stop it. The reason was clear when she said: 'I felt strong, powerful, when I was cursing and swearing. If I wasn't being bad, I could only shrink away into a corner and feel I was nobody.'

A male patient, a large employer of labour, came to analysis because he was so aggressive with his employees that he was always having labour troubles. He had been brought up on a regime of demand that he should not be a nuisance to his parents, and felt quite unwanted, unappreciated, and no good. If he was anything at all, he felt he was 'just a rotter'. He commenced every session for a long time by saying 'I'm cross as usual.' When gradually he arrived at some insight into this, he said: 'I know why I'm so aggressive with employees. I must get angry or I'm just scared stiff of them. When I can get angry I feel plenty of energy and I can do things; otherwise I'm nervous, always tired, and feel I'm no good.'

Historically in ideolgy and psychologically in the individual, the area of bad impulses, control, guilt, and depression lay right across the path of psychodynamic investigation and blocked the way to deeper insight, as it was intended to do. Freud's great task was to analyse this area. That is the significance of his shift of interest from hysteria to obsessional neurosis, depression, and the superego phenomena. So successful was his analysis that he opened the way to what lay deeper and made a start with the structural analysis of the psyche and the recognition of the importance of ego-splitting. Here lies the significance of Fairbairn's call 'Back to Hysteria' and his radical development of Melanie Klein's structural object-analysis into a parallel structural ego-analysis. Until the 'depressive' area was analysed, the 'schizoid' area could not be thoroughly investigated. But it begins now to appear that only if the schizoid background is taken into account, can the depressive foreground be thoroughly understood. The 'depressive' area of conflict over bad impulses comes into being when the individual exploits his active powers in antisocial ways to counteract a deep compulsion to withdraw, break off object-relations, and risk losing his ego. He becomes bad in order to feel real. Moreover, it becomes clear that the deeper schizoid problems have always been thrusting through the more obvious depressive one. This we must now examine.

The Manic-Depressive Condition and its Complexity

Clinical depression needs now to be examined specifically from the point of view of the schizoid problem. Fairbairn stated that in his experience true depression is more rare in the consulting room than schizoid phenomena, and that is also my experience. This could be due to a change in the general cultural outlook, a decline in guilt-inducing forms of religion. We do not now have the 'Hell-fire' preaching and the violent denunciatory 'sin and repentance' sermons of an earlier age. Few people have even heard nowadays of 'the unforgivable sin against the Holy Ghost' which used to be a marked depressive symptom. The patients in whom I have most clearly found classic depression were all religious people who had been driven to use and distort their religious beliefs as a defence in terms of guilt-inducement against a basic schizoid state. Furthermore, the present cultural era has seen a considerable shift of emphasis from the ethical to the scientific attitude to life. It is more characteristic of this generation to adopt a superior attitude to morality and reject guilt and depression in favour of a 'couldn't care less' attitude. This is a clearly schizoid phenomenon in its detachment and irresponsibility towards people. This trend, which was noticed at the end of Chapter I, has probably weakened the 'depressive defence' and made it easier for the 'schizoid background' in personality to appear.

The manic-depressive condition is, in all its varying degrees of severity, a mixed condition, and denotes a very complex state of mind in which a basic problem is countered by defences which in turn call for further defences. This is clear in the papers in a 'Symposium on "Depressive" Illness' (Zetzel *et al.*, 1960) where the guilt factor seems to drop more and more into second place and the factor of regression comes more and more to the front. Guilt is the heart of the depressive problem proper in the classical usage in which this term came to be technically defined, whereas regression is a schizoid phenomenon. (Cf. Chapter II.) It seems that one can see the schizoid problem always pushing through the depressive defence. This would explain why patients say they are 'depressed' when they really mean 'apathetic', irrespective of whether the apathy is associated with guilt-feelings, conscious or unconscious, or with a withdrawn state with loss of interest.

(a) *The Mixed Condition*

In the symposium referred to (Zetzel *et al.*, 1960) the contribution of Nacht and Racamier presents the classic conception, while the developing change in the basic theoretical conception of this illness is most apparent in the contribution of Zetzel and Rosenfeld. But the earlier classic concept and the newly developing concepts are not yet clearly demarcated and related, so that the question 'What is manic-depressive illness?' has a somewhat confused answer. Both Zetzel and Rosenfeld present clearly enough *the change of emphasis from guilt and repression of sadistic instincts to the problems of frustrated ego-development, resultant ego-splitting and ego-weakness, and the dangers of regression and ego-loss. Yet these two quite different groups of psychopathological phenomena are still confusingly held together under the term 'depression'.*

Rosenfeld states the classic diagnosis of depressive illness as 'precipitated by an object-loss' (1960, pp. 512–13) in which

> the patients unconsciously believed that their aggression omnipotently produced the death or illness of the object.

To clarify the complexity of this illness as it presents itself clinically, we must at this stage limit the term 'depression' to this quite definite psychic state. Depression is then, as it has been classically treated, a guilt illness, pathological mourning, the paralysing effects of which are due to the repression of sadism and aggression. This distinction is preserved when Clifford Scott writes:

> Our literature contains less about the relationship of pathological mourning to more regressed states. . . . than one might expect with such a crucial metapsychological problem which stands midway between the schizophrenias and the neuroses. (1960, p. 497.)

Thus Zetzel says:

> Abraham's original formulations with regard to depressive illness appear to have become more rather than less compatible with the general body of psychoanalytical knowledge over the passage of time. In particular, the importance he attached to object-relations,

aggression, and mastery of ambivalence have been confirmed by psychoanalysts of every school of thought.

Of depression in this sense it is particularly true that there are 'infantile precursors of the illness in adult life'. Zetzel points out that the work of Abraham, Rado, Jacobson, Spitz, and particularly Melanie Klein is an

> attempt to understand adult depression by reconstruction of its infantile prototype. . . . The most far-reaching analogies between adult depressive illness and early developmental phases have been proposed by Mrs Klein and the English school. A universal infantile depressive position has been postulated, the general characteristic of which determines depressive responses in adult life.

In this connexion Zetzel mentions the 'primary importance attached to early object-relations', and Rosenfeld writes:

> It is characteristic of such situations (i.e. object-loss) that all earlier experiences of object-loss are mobilized leading back to the earliest anxieties of the infant–mother relationship, a fact which might be regarded as a confirmation of the central importance of the depressive position as outlined by Melanie Klein.

This conception links depression particularly closely with the Oedipus stage, as Melanie Klein stresses, with its ambivalence of love and hate and its guilt. We must return presently to this question. This is the classic concept of depression and it makes depression clear, specific, and identifiable. It is of depression in this sense that Fairbairn said that it is not presented clinically anything like as frequently as schizoid problems. Moreover, it becomes ever more clear that it does not by any means cover the whole clinical picture of what has, evidently too loosely, been termed depression.

There is another group of phenomena which, as clinically presented, is commonly to be found mixed up with depression as above defined, whenever that is present. These phenomena are not illuminated by the concepts of ambivalence, sadism, repression, and guilt. They are the phenomena that led to the increasing concentration on ego-psychology and the facts concerning ego-splitting and regression, i.e. the schizoid problem. The two sets of facts, depressive and regressive, antisocial impulses and ego-weakness, come face to face with competing claims to priority when Rosenfeld writes:

> the psycho-analysis of ego-disturbances, like the splitting of the ego, has an important contribution to make to the understanding of the depressive illness,

but then goes on to say that:

> The importance of the internal object-relationships has, however, still to be regarded as the most important aspect of the depressive illness.

Rosenfeld shows that, clinically, the classic view of depression does not cover all the facts in a very complicated illness, and recognizes the different nature of the phenomena now more and more attracting attention; but he does not say outright that *the classic view of depression, if applied to the total illness, is inadequate.* While it is no doubt true that ambivalent and guilt-burdened object-relations are the important element in classic depression, nevertheless depression in that narrowly defined sense is not the most important element in the actual total illness as we meet with it in the patient. I shall hope to show that *depression in the classic sense is set up by the failure of a certain type of defence against an acute threat of ego-loss and regressive breakdown* '*precipitated by an object-loss*' *as Rosenfeld stated. We have to turn our attention to ego-loss, ego-splitting, and regression.* This does not imply that guilt is nothing but a defence and has no reality of its own. There is a rational and a pathological guilt. We may say that rational guilt is felt realistically by a strong ego and faced, and reparation made for the wrong done. The guilt can then die away. Pathological guilt of the kind that leads to depression is usually unrealistic guilt, as when a child is afraid to face the fact that he is not loved by parents and finds it easier to conclude that it is he himself who is all wrong. Pathological guilt and the depression it leads to is a product of gross insecurity and there is always a powerful escape motive. Faced with an object-loss, the undermined ego cannot accept and deal with the situation and risks breakdown. To stave that off, hate of the lost object and fantasies of aggression develop to restore the ego, but that engenders pathological guilt and depression. If guilt can be born without succumbing to depression, it functions as an object-relations experience.

Rosenfeld puts alongside the classic concept of 'object-loss', as the precipitating factor in depressive illness, the parallel concept of 'ego-loss'. He writes:

> We might ask if it is only a disturbance in an object-relation which may mobilize depression. Freud had raised the question early on whether an injury to the ego or to *narcissism* may alone precipitate depression. I found in some of the patients breaking down with acute depression that they were confronted with a situation which

made them aware that they themselves or their lives had been incomplete in certain ways. The patients were overcome by an acute sense of failure. They felt they had not fulfilled the promise of their gifts or had not developed their personality sufficiently. They were suddenly overwhelmed by a conviction that it might now be too late for them to find themselves and their purpose in life . . . This depression may be regarded as an awareness that certain parts of the patient's personality had been split off and denied. . . . These parts include not only aggressive features but are related to a capacity of the ego to bear depression, pain, and suffering.

Rosenfeld goes on to say that the problem of depression

has to be understood not only from the point of view of object-relations but in terms of ego psychology.

We do not, however, adequately distinguish and properly relate together these two different levels of this complex illness, unless we emphasise that the *importance of object-relations lies in the fact that without them the ego cannot maintain itself*. It is not a question of object-loss and ego-loss being alternative precipitating factors, nor of the split-off and denied parts of the personality being either or both aggressive features and ego-capacity to bear pain. The situation I have found with patients is that in order to escape the terrors of ego-loss as a result of an object-loss in reality, throwing them back on their underlying schizoid detachment from object-relations (depersonalization), they have fled back into ambivalent object-relations only to find that their hate threatens them with object-loss again and now also guilt, and depression, and recurring fear of ego-loss once more. The depression arises out of a failure of a defence against an *underlying* schizoid condition. Thus a patient whose basic isolation stimulated intense fears and needs, became afraid of directing towards both analyst and family an intensity of need which seemed potentially destructive. She sent a message that she could not come for her session, she felt such a horrible person, and was so depressed. She had withdrawn from both analyst and family both in outer reality and in her thoughts. She did not come to the session and shut herself in her room, feeling that she was bad for the family. The logical result of this breaking-off of all object-relations would have been to throw her back on her deep inner feeling of being utterly alone, and led to a developing fear of losing her own ego. This she staved off by maintaining active self-hate and depression.

I would rather say therefore that '*depression* has to be understood . . . from the point of view of object-relations', i.e. the need and struggle to retain object-relations (guilt being an object-relation), but that the *deeper problem of regression* which it masks has to be understood 'in terms of ego psychology'. In the long run it is only ego-psychology that can supply the key to any and all psychological problems. Rosenfeld himself says:

In such depressions there is a regression to the phase of infancy where the original splitting of the ego has taken place.

This is on a much deeper level than that of the repression of 'aggressive features' which plays so obvious a part in depression proper. The repression of sadism is not the deepest 'splitting off or denial' of a part of the personality. I have suggested elsewhere (1961) that the deepest ego-split is that which occurs under either object-loss or persecutory anxiety in what Fairbairn called the infantile libidinal ego, a split into an *active oral ego* which remains in a sado-masochistic inner world, and a *passive regressed ego* which seeks a return to the womb for security away from an empty outer world or terrifying bad object-relations. Winnicott considers that this corresponds to what he calls 'the hidden true self' awaiting a chance of rebirth. I regard this as *the basis of all schizoid characteristics, the deep secret flight from life, in seeking a defence against which the rest of the personality lands itself in a variety of psychotic and psychoneurotic states, among which one of the most important is depression.*

It would clear up much confusion to restrict the term depression to its narrow and classical definition, to correlate depression with ambivalent and guilt-burdened object-loss. We can then regard it as arising through the failure of one type of defence against the dangers of regression and ego-loss as the final result of object-loss. We must recognize two strata of the complex illness which has hitherto gone by the name of depression. Rosenfeld speaks of 'a progressive and reparative drive, namely an attempt to regain these lost parts of the self'. This represents a swing back from schizoid withdrawal to a recovery of object-relations, good, bad, or ambivalent according to the chosen strategy of the patient. Among other things this will lead to the manic defence, which presumably can operate, if with different characteristics, against both the depressive and the regressive schizoid dangers. Against depression it will take the form of a repudiation of all moral feeling and guilt: against the dangers of regression to passivity and ego-breakdown resulting from basic withdrawal it will take the form of compulsive activity. This latter is, in my experience, much the commonest form of manic state, and exists more often than not in particularly secret and hidden mental forms as an inability to relax and stop thinking, and especially to sleep. The total illness is very inadequately called manic-depressive, and should at least be called manic-depressive-regressive, recognizing that the schizoid component is more dangerous and deeper than the depressive one.

We may here refer to the brief contribution to the symposium by Melanie Klein, entitled 'A Note on Depression in the Schizophrenic'. She writes:

> The often observed connexion between the groups of schizophrenic and manic-depressive illnesses can in my view be explained by the developmental link existing in infancy between the paranoid-schizoid and depressive positions. The persecutory anxieties and splitting processes characteristic of the paranoid-schizoid position continue, though changed in strength and form, into the depressive position. . . . The link between these two positions—with all the changes in the ego which they imply—is that they are both the outcome of the struggle between the life and death instincts. In the earlier stage (extending over the first three or four months of life) the anxieties arising from this struggle take on a paranoid form, and the still incoherent ego is driven to reinforce splitting processes. With the growing strength of the ego, the depressive position arises. During this stage paranoid anxieties and schizoid mechanisms diminish and depressive anxiety gains in strength. Here, too, we can see the working of the conflict between life and death instincts. The changes which have taken place are the result of alterations in the states of fusion between the two instincts. (1960, p. 509.)

The statement that 'The persecutory anxieties and splitting processes characteristic of the paranoid-schizoid position continue . . . into the depressive position', confirms my view that depression rests on a schizoid basis, and that the schizoid trends can always be seen pushing through the depressive overlay. But I do not find that clinical evidence supports Klein's contention that 'paranoid anxieties and schizoid mechanisms diminish in strength and depressive anxiety gains in strength'. I believe that to be a very deceptive appearance. It would be true of a process of healthy maturing, but clinical depression is due to a failure of healthy maturing. If true depression develops, it is a sign that a defence is having to be put up against 'paranoid anxieties and schizoid mechanisms' which are still weakening an already split ego. Whenever I have treated depression as a struggle to keep in object-relationships, employing bad-object relations of an accusatory or morally persecutory kind, as a defence against the dangers of schizoid withdrawal from all object-relations, I have found that with surprising rapidity the depressive reaction was pushed aside by an outbreak of markedly schizoid symptoms. These showed no sign of having been diminished by depression; rather it was clear that it was the hidden power of the schizoid lack of contact with outer reality, that was being counteracted by seeking refuge in ambivalent object-relations, only to find that these in turn led to depression.

The source of Klein's views on this matter seems to derive from the confusing use of the unscientific and unverified hypothesis, one ought perhaps to say the mythology, of the life and death instincts, instead of abiding by purely factual clinical analysis. This hypothetical death instinct, of the reality of which hardly any analysts have ever been convinced, was assumed to be an innate destructive drive aimed primarily against the organism itself, and regarded by Klein as projected by the infant on to his environment. Persecutory anxiety is therefore self-manufactured and unrealistic in the last resort. So far as I can see, clinical evidence establishes the exact opposite of this strange view. Fear, persecutory anxiety, arises in the first place as a result of an actually bad, persecutory environment, what Winnicott calls 'impingement'. Anger and aggression arise as an attempt to master fear by removing its cause, but in the infant they only lead to the discovery of helplessness, and therewith the turning in of aggression against his own weak ego. This powerfully reinforces the splitting processes tending to be set in motion by the fear with its natural consequence, flight from the bad outer world. This turning in of aggression, however, does not necessarily lead to fear of death, but more often to masochistic suffering in the inner world which the patient cannot easily be helped to give up. It is true that under certain circumstances this can mount up to schizophrenic terror of being torn to bits, but I have usually found that the fear of death related ultimately to an unconscious inner knowledge of the existence of an ego-undermining, powerful drive to a flight from life and reality, the dread of the collapse of a viable self into a depersonalized state of combined object-loss and ego-loss. If there is any meaning, then, to be found in the terms 'Life and Death Instincts' it will refer to the conflict between active and passive trends, progressive and regressive drives, in the personality. This can mount in intensity to a veritable struggle between living and dying, but little light is thrown on this by instinct terminology.

To return to Zetzel, her position is the same as that of Rosenfeld. She observes that 'our concepts of anxiety and depression ... have changed with the development of ego-psychology'. She quotes Bibring (1953) as saying:

> Anxiety and Depression represent diametrically opposed basic ego responses. Anxiety as a reaction to danger indicates the ego's desire to survive. The ego challenged by the danger mobilizes the signal of anxiety and prepares for fight or flight. In depression the opposite takes place; the ego is paralysed because it finds itself incapable to meet the danger.

Zetzel comments: 'The key word, of course, in this more recent formulation is "ego".'

It seems to me, however, useful to keep anxiety and depression closely associated by means of Melanie Klein's valuable formulation of two kinds of anxiety, persecutory and depressive. We can then use Bibring's reference to the fact that the endangered ego can react in either of two ways, by 'fight or flight'. If it reacts by flight, the infant ego can only fly in one way, inside itself. It is precipitated into schizoid withdrawal and ego-splitting. It usually does do this, and leaves an active outer-reality ego (in contrast to the now withdrawn and passive part of the ego) to 'fight' and so hold on to object-relations. This it may do on two levels. A frightened ego, struggling not to give way wholly to 'flight', has only bad object-relations to keep contact with. This is a decision then to face danger rather than withdraw altogether, i.e. to make use of bad object-relations to keep in touch with the object world. On a more primitive level this exposes the ego to persecutory paranoid anxieties which may mount to schizophrenic terrors. On a more developed level, it leads to guilt under moral persecution which may mount to depressive anxieties and even to the paralysis of severe depression in which the ego is inhibited from all activity by a sense of utter badness. The opposite possibilities of flight and fight lead on the one hand to regression and on the other to psychotic conflict-states and further to psychoneurotic defences, which are attempts to deal with ultimate internal bad object-relationships.

Zetzel confuses these different things when she says first that:

> Depression, like anxiety, is a subjective experience, integral to human development and mastery of conflict, frustration, disappointment, and loss,

but then adds,

It is also the main presenting symptom of a regressive clinical syndrome.

The first statement applies to the results of the 'fight' reaction, i.e. classic depression, while the second refers to the effects of the 'flight' reaction or regression. We are brought back to the necessity for distinguishing between regression as a schizoid phenomenon differing from and *underlying* depression as a guilt paralysis in ambivalent object-relationships. It is the difference between fear and anger, and between withdrawal and the repression of sadism. *Aggression is characteristic of the depressive set-up, while fear and flight are the keys to the regressive situation, against which the former is employed as a main defence.* It is, of course, true, as Melanie Klein has shown, that a further development is the use of either of these two opposites alternately as a defence against the other.

Just as Rosenfeld contrasts depression as due to object-loss with another type of depression (really regression) involving ego-loss, so Zetzel regards disturbed infantile prototypical object-relations as repeated in classic depression, but evidently correlates the regressive aspect of the illness with the propensity of early disturbances for causing developmental failure of the ego. In contrast to Abraham, Jacobson, Rado, and Spitz, she says that Bowlby, Rank, Mahler, and Rochlin

rather emphasize the primary importance of early experience in determining ego-development and the capacity for genuine object-relations. (pp. 477–8.)

From the point of view of ego-psychology we would say that biological events (such as childbirth, involution) are able to evoke 'depression-regression' when they play upon a basic ego-weakness and stimulate a 'fight and flight' reaction. Zetzel says:

It is essential to make a distinction between the total helplessness implied by Freud's definition of a traumatic situation, and the relative helplessness implicit in Bibring's conception of loss of self-esteem.

This seems to be a matter of the depth to which any trauma penetrates in activating basic ego-weakness and consequent flight from life, or of the extent to which a deeply repressed feeling of not having a proper ego breaks through into consciousness.

The fact is that in Zetzel's exposition, regression looms ever larger in the picture:

The ego of the seriously damaged patient has undergone qualitative regressive alterations with associated intrapsychic changes of a varied nature. (p. 479.)

Nevertheless, she still holds fast to 'the significance of the aggressive instinct' and 'the crucial importance of unmastered aggression in the theory of depressive illness', and she quotes Bibring as saying:

The blow to self-esteem is due to the unexpected awareness of the existence of latent aggressive tendencies within the self.

Certainly the discovery of 'latent aggressive tendencies' can damage self-esteem and lead to the ego-weakness of depressive paralysis, but that is not the ultimate analysis. The first trouble arises because both flight and aggression arise at a time when the infant is factually too weak to fight effectively and is overpowered by his environment. The deepest blow to self-esteem comes from the discovery of one's actual weakness. Zetzel has to come back to

the whole problem of the regressive implications. . . . It is here that current ego-analysis appears to differ most widely from the early formulations. (p. 480.)

The only way to clear up this confused oscillating is to separate classic depression as the defensive top layer of aggression and guilt, from regression as the bottom layer of fear, flight, and infantile ego-weakness.

The whole illness is a complex mixture of depression and schizoid factors. If the presenting picture is at first one of classic depression and guilt, it is best relieved in the long run, after initial analysis of the problems of aggression, by exposing it as a defence against still deeper withdrawal from any and all kinds of object-relations into a schizoid condition. In my experience one more often finds the schizoid patient whose regressive trends become unconsciously activated and intensified and who then intermittently struggles forward into guilt and depression. Classic depression can then be seen to arise out of failure of an attempted defence against ultimate regression by resort to 'fight' rather than 'flight'. Bad object-relations are better than no objects at all, until they run away with the patient in his inner world, get out of hand, and produce their own insoluble problems. In passing, it may be repeated that unless we allow for a universal resistance to the proper recognition of our basic fear and weakness, it is hard to explain why an 'instinct of aggression' has been given such prominence in psychoanalytic theory, while the equally obvious phenomena of 'instinctive fear and flight' have been so passed over. Classic psychoanalytic theory has always treated anxiety as secondary to the working of sexual and aggressive drives. We now have to recognize that *pathological* sexual and aggressive drives are not primary facts but are secondary to the working of elementary fear, anxiety, and flight.

(*b*) *Abraham's Picture of Classic Depression*

In their contribution to the same 'Symposium on Depressive Illness' S. Nacht and P. C. Racamier (1960) write:

> We define depression as *a pathological state of conscious psychic suffering and guilt, accompanied by a marked reduction in the sense of personal values, and a diminution of mental, psycho-motor, and even organic activity unrelated to actual deficiency.*

It may be said that the last half of the definition concerning 'marked reduction' is just as true of people suffering from plainly regressed states, though people suffering from guilt-depression usually show little diminution of mental activity so far as self-accusation is concerned. However, Nacht and Racamier's definition is based on the general theory of man that has prevailed in psychoanalysis. They write:

> The study of depressive states leads the psychoanalyst to the centre of the fundamental drama that troubles the heart of man, for man is possessed by two apparently equal and contradictory powers, pulling him in opposite directions. Yet sometimes these forces may be intimately blended and linked together, and even, occasionally, replace each other. Thus man is moved by an imperious need to love, to create and construct, and by an opposing and equally tyrannical desire to hate and destroy.

Earlier in this chapter I have already shown reasons for rejecting that view, as the psychoanalytical equivalent of the age-old doctrine of evil lusts and passions of the flesh opposed to the rational mind, and the doctrine of original sin. It appears to me that *the conflict of love and hate in human society is secondary to the conflict of love and fear, or the need for human relationships versus the fear-ridden flight from relationships, itself the product of our basic weakness, vulnerability, and struggle to maintain a viable ego.* This comes out clearly in Abraham's classic pioneer picture of depression in 1911, at a time long before any realistic ego-analysis had been initiated by the Freud of the 1920's; a time when the psyche could only be thought of in terms of an instinctive unconscious and a regulating ego of consciousness.

The case history Abraham describes as 'depressed' is that of a basically schizoid personality struggling to keep a precarious contact with the object-relations world by means of hostility, hatred, and aggression in sporadic outbursts, countered by guilt. 'He had an indefinite feeling that his state of depression was a punishment.' (1911, p. 141.) Certainly at that date the priority for analysis was this problem of guilt-depression. It was the success and thoroughness of the analytical exploration of this area of mental life that opened up the deeper schizoid level. But one can also see that when Abraham wrote: 'I do not wish to discuss states of depression occurring in dementia praecox' (p. 139) the sound policy of not trying to analyse everything at once but taking problems one by one, led here to a non-recognition of the schizoid factors in the case he did describe. The patient as a child was depreciated in comparison with his older brother while a delicate younger brother got most of the attention. He never felt satisfied at home, and got little with which to develop a soundly based ego. He grew up to hate both parents and brothers and feel jealousy to a degree that once led to a violent and injurious attack on the younger brother. That all this, bringing in its train feelings of moral unworthiness and guilt, was part of a desperate struggle to keep in effective relationship with his object world, is clear from the rest of the descriptive data.

Abraham observed that

> Every neurotic state of depression . . . contains a tendency to deny life. (p. 138.)

This boy's denial of life took the form of a manifest schizoid withdrawal from human relationships. He

> never made any real companions, kept to himself . . . had no friends. He was quite aware of his lack of real energy when he compared himself with others. (p. 140.)

That this withdrawal from human contacts as emotionally hurtful was adequately motivated, is clear. He had 'no encouragement at home. His father was contemptuous of him in his presence' (p. 140). His first attack of depression occurred in a specific way when his teacher once called him 'a physical and mental cripple' in front of the class (p. 140). The 'depression', it is to be noted, was called out by the accusation not of being 'bad', but of being 'weak', which was also implied in his father's 'contempt' of him. He himself added the accusation of being 'bad' and was no doubt confirmed in this by being blamed for his hostility to those who despised him.

> Even later he made no companions. He kept away from them intentionally too, because he was afraid of being thought an inferior sort of person. . . . His life was a solitary one. He was positively afraid of women. . . . He showed little energy in practical life; it was always difficult for him to form a resolution or to come to a decision in difficult situations.

This is a picture not of a primarily guilt-burdened but of a devitalized personality. Grief over the loss of a good object is normal-Devitalization as a result of *not having* any good object is schizoid. In that situation, guilt and depression will arise out of an attempt to fend off depersonalization by the internalization of accusing bad objects, and identifying with them as a basis for self-accusation.

The problem of divitalization is of crucial importance. In view of the chronic fatigue and exhaustion such patients frequently suffer, it is as important a descriptive term for this illness as depression and regression. Of the above patient Abraham notes:

> In every situation he suffers from feelings of inadequacy and stands helpless before the problems of life. (p. 139.)

> In his depressive phase the patient's frame of mind was 'depressed' or 'apathetic' (I reproduce his own words) according to the severity of his condition. He was inhibited, had to force himself to do the simplest things, and spoke slowly and softly. He wished he was dead and entertained thoughts of suicide. He would often say to himself 'I am an outcast' or 'I do not belong to the world'. He felt non-existent and would often imagine himself disappearing from the world without leaving a trace. During these states of mind he suffered from exhaustion. (p. 141.)

These are the characteristic ways in which schizoid patients describe their experience of feeling withdrawn and cut off from outer reality, and so losing 'self' also in a vacuum of experience, while the attenuated 'central ego' tries to keep touch with the real world though feeling utterly deprived of all energy.

The classic theory as stated by Abraham was that this loss of energy was the result of the repression of the sexual and aggressive instincts.

His sexual instinct, which at first had shown itself so strongly, had become paralysed through repression. (p. 140.)

He was weakened or deprived of his energy through the repression of his hatred or . . . of the originally overstrong sadistic component of his libido. (p. 139.)

Surely this puts the cart before the horse. *I see no reason to think that sexual and aggressive potentialities operate in disturbed and anti-social ways, except in the fear-ridden person, and then they represent the exploitation of two among other active capacities as a method of over-coming devitalization and passivity.* We need not postulate 'an originally overstrong sadistic component of the libido' in this patient. Those on whom he depended made him hate them, and the only way he could try to gain any position in life was to fight for it and be met with disapproval and contempt. Naturally his whole 'active' nature would become inhibited, sexually and aggressively, and even generally intellectually and physically. But there is more here than the direct repression of active processes. While one part of his split ego was putting up a fight only to succumb to the pressure of environmental hostility and guilt, another part of him had taken flight, had contracted out of object-relations; his energy was flowing in reverse away from real objects into his inner world, and powerful regressive drives would involve sexual impotence as part of a general devitalization. Abraham says 'Depression sets in when (the neurotic) has given up his sexual aim', but in fact it is the other way round. This, however, was only one item in a general devitalization of his private and social life and his school work. He was not only afraid to be active in case he should be destructive, but also an important part of him had withdrawn and given up the very will to be active. As he oscillated between flight and fight the will to activity would reappear again in outbursts of sexual and aggressive behaviour as parts of the manic defence of overactivity.

A study of the manic defence should serve to complete the reorientation of theory concerning this illness, and the whole field of psychopathology. It is usually held that manic elation is essentially an anti-moral revolt against the burden of guilt. The paralysing restraints of the sadistic superego are suddenly overthrown and the person feels omnipotently free to do as he likes. This, however, is a secondary characteristic of the manic defence. Abraham wrote of his patient:

(At 28 years) a condition of hypomania appeared and this now alternated with his depressive attacks. At the commencement of this manic phase, he would be roused out of his apathy and become mentally active and gradually even over-active. He used to do a great deal, knew no fatigue, woke early in the morning, and concerned himself with plans connected with his career. He became enterprising and believed himself capable of performing great things, was talkative and inclined to laugh and joke and make puns. . . . At the height of his manic phase his euphoria tended to pass over into irritability and impulsive violence. . . . In the periods of depression he slept well but during the manic phase he was very restless, especially during the second half of the night. Nearly every night a sexual excitement used to overtake him with sudden violence. (p. 142.)

It is clear from this that the basic characteristic of this state is not amoral violence, but simply *over-activity*. The manic state is not primarily a repudiation of the repression of active sex and aggression, though that can at times enter into it. It is a desperate attempt to force the whole psyche out of a state of *devitalized passivity*, surrender of the will to live, and regression. The harder the struggle to defeat the passive regressed ego, the more incapable of rest and relaxation the patient becomes. His mind must be kept going non-stop, night and day. Deep sleep is feared as regression and every effort is made either to prevent its occurrence by insomnia (which is then a manic symptom) or to keep up a constant interference with it by intense dreaming and repeated waking. When the battle becomes a losing one, it may well happen that, as Abraham observed, euphoria turns into aggression and violent sexuality. The pathological forms of sexual and aggressive impulse are aspects of the struggle, on the one hand to wring satisfaction out of a reluctant environment, but on the other to defeat regression and the flight from life on the part of a person who feels that, at the deepest mental level he hardly has an ego at all to be active with. There are also other 'active' capacities which can be used for this purpose besides sex and aggression, such as thinking, overworking, the hectic social round, and so on. Abraham writes:

The affect of depression is as widely spread among all forms of neuroses and psychoses as is that of anxiety. (p. 137.)

This will not surprise us when we realize that the deepest psychopathological problem is the struggle to keep active at all with a basic ego that is fear-ridden and undeveloped, and a central ego that is devitalized.

We may at this point seek to make a summary statement of

the overall clinical diagnostic framework within which we must think. When an infant finds himself in a 'bad' human environment, hostile and impinging, tantalizing and unsatisfying, or neglectful and deserting, he is in a serious predicament. How can he keep himself in being, let alone develop a personality in such a medium? What are his alternatives? He needs and wants good relationships if he is to achieve a sound ego-development, but they are unobtainable, or not sufficiently obtainable, and his world makes a bad, disturbing impact on him. He can, as it were, either fight or fly. He can try to put up with bad relationships and struggle angrily for their betterment, and discover that '*depression' is a tie to bad objects, the inevitable state of mind in relationships where one cannot love without hating*. There appear to be two main reasons for the development of this guilt-burdened state. In the first place, when one's basic nature and real need is for good relationships, one will come to feel, as adult patients say, 'a horrible person' for having bad, aggressive, destructive emotions and impulses aroused. In the second place, this is powerfully reinforced by the fact that, since an infant or small child is factually so dependent and helpless, it is simply too frightening to face the full reality of being at the mercy of a bad world. Traumatic experience cannot be dealt with outside oneself and has to be taken inside. It feels safer to think of yourself as bad, and try to see the bad world as justified in its bad treatment of you. Fairbairn expressed this in the symbolic language of religion by saying that it is safer living as a sinner in a world ruled by a good God, than to be a saint in a world ruled by devils, and this does show vividly the predicament of the child in an environment that does not meet his need. Everything conspires to drive him into a position where he feels guilty about his hate and aggression and eventually about allowing himself to be an active person in any sense.

The only other choice open to him, if he finds this 'bad object-relations' position intolerable, is to take flight mentally from his environment, and escape the provocation to hate by ceasing to feel anything consciously at all for his bad world, i.e. to become withdrawn and schizoid, and at a deep inner level to regress in unconscious fantasy, maybe even back to the womb for security. It then becomes increasingly difficult to maintain external life. It can only be done in a cold and mechanical way, which is a precarious compromise. In fact both alternatives are so uninviting that they push him on to the other one, his unconsolidated ego 'splits' under the strain, and he attempts both reactions in different parts of himself. This interpretation is based on the *meaning* of ego-object relations, which allows impulses to be understood as governed by the nature of our personal relationships. An 'impulse-psychology' which treats impulses as 'given', as innate and instinctive and there to begin with, helps to buttress depression by fostering the idea that our human nature is bad intrinsically, aggressive at heart. For that reason Fairbairn held that interpretations in terms of aggression increase guilt. The human predicament is that, since we are so at the mercy of our human environment as children, if it fails to evoke our trust and love, and arouses insecurity, aggression, and hate, it dooms us either to paranoid anxiety and subsequent depression or to schizoid detachment, both of which involve serious regressive dangers. Probably most human beings find a way of keeping going in some position in between these two extremes, having a few good relationships to keep their true nature alive, while for the rest they exist in some degree of vague general depression varied by some outbursts of aggressiveness; while behind all this and deep within their unconscious, their potentialities of a true self that can love and create, are locked in. In this condition so many people live far beneath their real capacity.

In psychopathology we can only really diagnose the total situation, the overall predicament of man, and then use our various diagnostic labels for the psychoses and psychoneuroses to indicate various aspects of this whole complex problem which are tending to predominate in different patients or at different times in the same patient. Even though some individuals as it were 'petrify' in some more or less fixed state, the majority of patients ring the changes on a variety of reactions all of which find their place in the complex total diagnosis. This may be briefly expressed as manic-depression-regression.

The Analysis of a Case of Manic-Depression

The foregoing conclusions may best be summarized by presenting a brief account of the analytical treatment of an actual case. A deeply religious man in the late forties, married, with one child, had been diagnosed twelve years earlier by a psychiatrist as constitutionally manic-depressive, and told that there was nothing to be done but control the condition by means of drugs. This 'control' proved in practice to be of little use to him and his life was a misery as he swung between periods of profound depression with sluggish inactivity and acute guilt over his uselessness, and periods of compulsive early rising and hectic overwork. He could at such times feel strong guilt over sexual fantasies and aggressive outbursts in real life which he found hard to control, especially with his wife and child. Apart from these extremes, in his general attitudes he was rigidly puritan, intolerant of many things 'on principle', a strict disciplinarian, and extremely independent. He said, 'I have St Augustine's "heart of steel towards myself".'

Analysis of his guilt brought out ever more clearly that it was aimed mainly against his feelings of weakness, and guilt was mixed with contempt of himself. It was weak to be depressed, to be inactive and unable to work, to indulge in sexual fantasies or to want sexual relationships. It was weak to be unable to control his temper and irritability, and also to need anyone's help. His 'ego-ideal' was that of the strong and rather silent man who had iron self-control, which he could relax at times for the child's amusement in nonsense talk and joking; behind this he remained a deadly serious person. With his university training and gifts of leadership he was, when at his best, a successful and valuable obsessional personality, but this was always breaking down into the manic-depressive mood swing.

It emerged that he could and did periodically use the defence of a conversion hysteria technique against his depression, and in one period of eighteen months during his analysis he had recurring bouts of four or five weeks of laryngitis or lumbago. Invariably as these faded out under analysis he would begin to feel consciously depressed again. These two physical conditions, however, so clearly symbolized a state of withdrawal from active life into weakness and incapacity, in which he could hardly talk, or hardly walk about, and had to be off work, that they proved to be a valuable means of directing his attention away from his 'bad' impulses, sexual and aggressive, and towards the more unwelcome insight that he felt weak. His life had been one long struggle to keep going at all, since he had really always felt inadequate and apprehensive. He said, 'It's hell, going through life having to screw yourself up all the time to face everything you have to do, even though you know you can do it.' Gradually analysis focussed less and less on guilt over sex and aggression, and more and more on his fears, timidities, shrinking from life, and the constant tension of forcing himself on, in the teeth of these drawbacks. His manic-depressive cycle appeared to him now as an oscillation between ruthless overdriving of his secretly frightened inner self, leading on to collapse into physical and mental exhaustion. He could see clearly enough how his parents had completely undermined or prevented the development of any natural spontaneous self-confidence in him, and how seriously beset he had been in his teens by a crippling feeling of inadequacy and inability to 'make good'.

For practical purposes his treatment began to focus on his inability at that time to relax and rest. He was afraid to 'let go' in sleep and could not still his overactive mind. The analysis of his hidden manic drive in terms of his dread that if he once stopped he would never get started again, enabled him to see its real significance. It was a desperate struggle to overcome the emotionally crippled and fear-ridden child inside, and to force himself to be adult—a well-intentioned but self-defeating method of working hard to keep his ego in being, to be alive, to be a real 'person' while a weak infantile ego in which he felt he was a 'nobody' was hidden in the depths of his unconscious. *My interpretation of his depressive guilt as all a part of his organized system of self-forcing, and as a defence against his secret and hidden 'frightened child' self who was in a state of constant retreat from life, led to the revelation of life-long but hitherto undisclosed schizoid characteristics.*

This occurred when, after three-and-a-half years of analysis, he entered on a period of five months which proved to be a fundamental working through of the hard core of his self-frustrating personality make-up. After that, with diminishing and minor ups and downs, he entered on a long period of quiet and steady improvement. He was able to feel much greater interest in his work, a marked betterment in his relations with his wife both emotionally and sexually, greater patience with his child, more tolerance with other people and with himself, much less fear of facing people and a marked improvement in capacity for tactful handling of people, and finally a more simple and straightforward, conflict-free relationship with me. I shall summarize briefly this critical break-through period. (The numbers in brackets represent the chronological order of only the most significant sessions during those five months.)

(1) 'I get a picture of myself in the dark behind a door, banging on it. Ah! It's a memory. We were shut up in a dark cupboard when naughty. . . . I shut myself in now and get panicky. I've got a fundamental fear. At times it gets near to undermining the adult and I fear collapse.'

(2) His father had died a few months previously at an advanced age, and he said: 'Consciously I don't bother about

father's death. He's just gone. It's impersonal. But I want to get down to my real feelings.'

(3) 'I never had a father who loved and cared for his children. I'm sensitive to the sufferings of children.' I commented, 'But you inflict suffering on your own childself.' He replied, 'I'm tired and would like you to put me to sleep, and wake and find all my troubles solved.' That was one of the first signs of real dependence on my help. (Cf. session 5.)

(4) 'It's warm and comfortable in your room but I feel I ought to be uncomfortable.' He reported a dream:

I saw a coffin open and a man in it talking. I was very concerned because the lid was to be put on and he'd be buried alive. Then he folded his arms and said, 'Maybe now I'll be able to relax.'

The patient added, 'I'm talking at a terrific rate now. I used to be terrified of being buried alive.' I pointed out that he was frightened of becoming quite withdrawn, of being buried alive and coffined inside himself, and was talking at a terrific rate to fend it off; that a part of him had been for long so buried, and he feared relaxation, sleep, and any dependence on me or his wife because he felt it would mean losing his active self and slipping down into this regressed one. Until he could see his regressed self as something more positive than just a menace and get over his fear of it, he could not begin to recuperate at a deep unconscious level. He said, 'I feel I ought not to want my wife's breast or any comfort. Sexual intercourse ought to be purely mechanical. I'm afraid to let go and let you help me.'

(5) The basic problem, should the weak and frightened child in him be allowed to depend and be helped, or should he be ruthlessly driven on in a forced pseudo-adult way, now became focussed in the transference. He had a long series of fantasies each week as he approached my rooms and saw my car outside. At first he would fantasy smashing it up; then later he would get in and drive off; then again I would be in it and he would get in and lean his head on my shoulder and put an arm round me, but then suddenly attack me and take over the driving. Later still he fantasied me driving and himself as in the passenger seat, and finally he saw himself getting in my car, curling up on the back seat and going fast asleep knowing that I would approve. His hostile resistances to me and fantasied aggressions against me earlier on were clearly a defence against his fear of helpless dependence on me, and masked a fantasy of a return to the womb. The whole series of fantasies gives a striking picture of how mental changes can go on under analysis.

(6) This was the most critical session. He felt 'in a queer mood. Can't concentrate. I just sit and stare and can't apply myself to the job in hand. I lose interest. I want to escape from all responsibility to people. I feel I haven't got a mind. I had to go to a business meeting and had no feeling, no interest, no anger, only sad. I had intercourse with my wife and had no particular feeling.' Here was a schizoid, detached, impersonal, apathetic state, something much deeper than his earlier depressive guilt. I interpreted this to him and he said: 'I've always been a keen cricketer. In 1946–7 England were touring Australia and I was apathetic and couldn't understand why men should bother to play cricket. It was when I was becoming friendly with the girl I married. I had months of this apathy. It was awful, empty, nothing to live for, everything futile.' I suggested that he had been withdrawing in deep fear from the challenge of a human relationship, his growing friendship with the girl, and now he was withdrawing again in deep fear from his growing disposition to trust and depend more frankly on both his wife and me. That session was a turning point.

(7) At the next session he felt better and from then on he increasingly frequently reported improvement. He mentioned a dream:

I went down into a tower and then had to go through a tunnel to get out. Though I had come in that way I was horrified.

A clear fantasy of a return to the womb, showing that he was in touch with his lost regressed ego in the deep unconscious, the cause of all his schizoid reactions. He said, 'I wish you'd attack me and give me a chance to fight. A love relationship is smothering. I used to have premature ejaculation but now I go on and on and can't react, holding back. I'll be swallowed up. It's equivalent to lying on this couch.' The couch had been for a few weeks the focus of his conflict between the dependent child and the compulsively independent adult. From the start he had compromised and never allowed the couch problem to be analysed till now. He did not want to sit in the patient's armchair; that seemed exclusively adult. He did not want to lie on the couch; that seemed exclusively infantile. So he sat on the couch with his feet on the floor, for the first three-and-three-quarter years of analysis. In this session, for the first time, he tentatively put one foot up on the couch, and at once began to say: 'Should I sit in the chair? Lying on this couch suggests going to sleep, surrender, losing independence to you. I've always been afraid of an anaesthetic. Now I sit on the couch with one foot on the ground, afraid to be absolutely in your power. I had a dream that you'd taken my penis off and I just put it back on and it stayed there.'

(8) At the next session he lay down at once and said, 'Now I'm lying on the couch properly, much more comfortable. The last two nights I've had satisfying intercourse with my wife. I've always wanted to get away from the real world. I had very little happiness in life and marriage till I came to you. Now I've got a lot and am very grateful.' Then he suddenly added, 'Now I want to get off the couch. I'm afraid of any close relationship.'

(9) He produced another fantasy of smashing my car and then said, 'It would be so nice to give up the struggle and sink back into warm human flesh, surrender, letting go.' I said, 'You're frightened of that as well as needing it. If you can let your passive exhausted self of early life recuperate here, you'll become better able to be active outside without driving yourself.' He replied: 'When you said that I felt a great sense of relief.'

(10) The four sessions 6 to 9 seemed to be the turning point of the analysis so far as his specific manic-depressive illness was concerned. That pattern had quite gone and did not return. It had changed into an understandable conflict over accepting his regressed ego in sessions so that he could maintain an active adult central ego in his outer life without forcing and exhausting himself. But the problem was not to be easily solved. In this session he was tense. He said, 'I've been wanting to come and was all for lying on the couch and relaxing, but then I lashed myself, accused myself of being lazy and drove myself to work by discipline. The only way I've ever known how to solve my problems was to drive myself.' This is, in fact, what Fairbairn called the antilibidinal ego, the struggling child trying to crush out his needs and particularly the passive ones.

(11) Not long after this he came in to one session and said, 'I've only two things to say.' He said them and added: 'Now I want to relax.' He lay on the couch and sank into a deep doze for about forty minutes.

(12) At the next session he said, 'Last session has changed something in me. I feel somehow calmer and stronger.' Following the critical five months in which these twelve sessions occurred, he was able to make steady progress, his variations of mood bearing no resemblance to his original cyclothymia. Fifteen months later he reported in one session: 'Generally I feel very fit these days, a positive attitude to life, things are going well. I'm more in love with my wife and sex relations are enjoyable. There are still some problems but life has a different

feel. It's a breaking free and getting out of prison.' One must admit that not all regressions can be contained within the analytic situation as this one was, but even then I believe them to be treatable by combined support and analysis, if one is prepared to do it. I have been able to do this for several patients for whom hospitalization was necessary.

Eighteen months after this account was written the patient had retained and improved on his gains, and diminished the frequency of his sessions. Minor ups and downs were analysed with the valuable result of preventing the re-accumulation of unresolved and repressed anxiety. He had learned to accept and live with the fact that human personality is complex, does not develop all on the same level throughout, but is structured as it were in layers, and that there is always a legacy of childhood weakness persisting in the deeper layers. *The concept of 'continuous development' replaced that of 'cure'. As with the case recorded at the end of Chapter III, the elimination of 'the illness' left an ultimate and very deep problem to be analysed in a more leisurely way, to reach a more fully established result.*

It may be well at this point to summarize briefly the statement of Fairbairn's structural terms as given on pages 71–2 of this present book, and to define carefully the term 'passive' as applied to what I have called the schizoid regressed ego. Fairbairn regarded the pristine unitary infantile ego as split, under the impact of bad experience, into three fairly easily distinguishable aspects, sufficiently distinguishable to be recognizable operating in effect as three sub-egos: *a central ego* seeking adjustment to the outer world (and therefore in the main a conformist ego); *a libidinal ego* in a state of frustration, denial and repression (embodying the infant's needs in so far as he could not get them met), and an *antilibidinal ego*, comparable with Freud's superego, which is directly concerned with hostile repression of the needy libidinal ego (and which embodies the infant's struggle to carry on without needs and without other people's help).

To avoid creating the impression of 'psychic entities', we will speak of the *central ego aspect of the psychic functioning* of the infant in distress who seeks to keep himself disencumbered from emotional conflicts, and to live largely by reducing needs to a minimum compatible with the demands of outer reality. This includes the phenomenon referred to by Winnicott as 'a false self on a conformist basis', though it is not restricted to that solely. The central ego is capable of developing and using many valuable abilities and cultivating realistic interests in everyday living, without having full possession of creative spontaneity. The *antilibidinal ego aspect of psychic functioning* is specifically and aggressively 'against needs' and on that basis can easily join forces with a conforming central ego which is subservient to authority, conferring on it a sadistic attitude to the libidinal infant who is regarded as socially unacceptable. These two developments in the personality clearly come into being in response to the infant's difficulties with an unsatisfying human environment. The *libidinal ego aspect of psychic functioning* represents, therefore, the infant's original nature, the possessor of his basic and unmet libidinal needs, in a state of rejection by the outer world and by the central ego, persecution by the antilibidinal ego, and repression by both of them combined.

I have suggested, and Fairbairn accepted, that in this predicament the libidinal ego aspect of psychic functioning itself undergoes a final split. This occurs on the basis of the 'fight or flight' pattern discussed in this chapter. The infant cannot give up his active libidinal needs entirely or he would die. He must in part carry on a fight for their satisfaction, and get what he can masochistically out of clinging to bad-object-relationships, in so far as good ones are unobtainable. This maintains him in a sado-masochistic inner world of fantasy and symptom-formation which is a pattern also often projected and imposed on his external world as well. At the same time he also in part shrinks away from this suffering and seeks to take flight from object-relations in a state of hopeless despair. Thus the libidinal infant is pulled in two opposite directions, not now by the fact that he faces a split of his object into a good and a bad object, but rather by the fact that he faces a contradictory situation in himself, feeling on the one hand unable to do without objects and on the other hand unable to do with them. The choice lies between bad objects and no objects at all. While the central ego on the conscious level gets along with relatively good objects considerably emotionally neutralized, at a deep unconscious level the final split in the libidinal ego occurs between an ego actively clinging to bad objects and a fear-ridden ego devoted to escape from all objects.

In the first of these I am using the term libidinal ego in Fairbairn's sense, to stand for the frustrated libidinal infant actively struggling to maintain himself in touch with an unsatisfying outer world and a persecutory inner one. This is an *active*, and on the deepest level, an oral sadistic ego. By contrast I have adopted the term *passive regressed libidinal ego*, to stand for the infant in that part of himself where he feels hopeless and despairing and longs only for a flight from reality; not at first into non-existence but into secure inactivity which makes possible a passive receptivity to healing influences. This would correspond largely to what Winnicott has termed the true self, hidden away in cold storage with a secret hope of a chance of rebirth into a more favourable environment. By '*passive*' I intend what the *Concise Oxford Dictionary* gives as the meaning of 'passive', i.e. 'suffering action, acted on, offering no opposition, submissive, not active, inert'. Yet in one respect the regressed ego can be extremely active, in its flight reaction, rushing away into a retreat, striving with great determination to find a safe hiding place, as we shall later see clinically illustrated. There is a positive meaning of passivity as receptivity, pleasure in submissive intake, trustful acceptance of help, which is healthy and far from inertness, but which only becomes characteristic of the regressed ego as it finds its way into a therapeutic relationship.

In its active flight, the regressed ego is striving after that goal, seeking a state of restful near-oblivion, a safe shut-in withdrawnness which is expressed externally by the house-bound agoraphobic, and internally by the silent aloofness of the extreme schizoid character, and especially in fantasies of a return to the womb. The passive goal can be very actively sought, but when found it becomes a complete contracting out of life, which can only be described as hallucinated return to the womb for recuperation in quiescence. Yet for that very reason, the rest of the personality fears it as simply a breakdown and a point of no return. *A regressed illness is usually a conflict between a struggle to keep going at all costs, and a longing to give up, in which the latter drive is of dire necessity winning over the former.* One last fact has to be taken account of. When the suffering of the persecuted libidinal ego becomes too great, and the secret hope of the regressed ego fades into hoplessness, a simple wish to die, to escape once for all, to give up finally, can develop.

Part III

THE NATURE OF BASIC EGO-WEAKNESS

VI

EGO-WEAKNESS, THE CORE OF THE PROBLEM OF PSYCHOTHERAPY[1]

THE position we have so far reached is that the two ultimate mental disasters are the development of the two feelings: (i) 'I am bad, a horrible person, guilty'; (ii) 'I am nobody, a nonentity.' The first is the state of *depression and ego-paralysis*. The second is the state of *depersonalization and ego-loss*, the final result of the schizoid processes which were surveyed in Chapters I to III. The end-product of these schizoid processes is the result of primitive fear, and out of the struggle to ward it off emerge schizophrenic and paranoid disorders. The end product of the depressive process is the result of pathological guilt. Melanie Klein has described the developmental basis of psychotic states in what she terms the 'paranoid-schizoid position' and the 'depressive position'. The schizoid psychopath and the seriously paranoid person have presumably failed to develop beyond the earlier paranoid-schizoid position, and are arrested on an amoral, pre-depressive level of experience. They do not genuinely feel for other people, do not form transference relationships, feel only for themselves, and may well be unreachable by psychotherapeutic influences. They do not see the outer world as it is and do not question that it is identical with their isolated internal fantasy world, in which they are simply cut off from external reality.

Most individuals manage, even through a disturbed infancy, to grow at least sufficiently through the paranoid-schizoid position and on to the depressive one, so that they can feel for their objects, though not with fully healthy emotion. The 'splitting' of their psychic wholeness is shown in the fact that they are in part still in the paranoid-schizoid position, even though in part they have also moved on into the depressive one. A number of writers feel that 'depressive' is not a good term for this developmental stage, and indeed it would seem wiser to reserve the term 'depressive' for specific illness. Winnicott therefore speaks of the infant reaching, not the 'depressive stage' but the stage

[1] This chapter, with Chapter VII, was first published in the *Brit. J.med. Psychol.*, **33** (1960), p. 163, and is here revised.

of being capable of feeling 'ruth' or 'concern' for others. By contrast, the infant at an earlier stage is 'ruthless' though he does not know it. He pursues his personal ends without as yet any capacity to understand the effects he has on mother, until presently he is made frighteningly aware of this, and begins to fear his own vigorous needs as destructive, the one natural and normal starting point of 'depression'. Especially if this combines with objectively real bad experiences, he cannot grow sufficiently out of the earlier schizoid anxieties. His undeveloped ego is not strong enough to develop 'concern' and make 'reparation', but succumbs to guilt, and with that 'depression', and he cannot grow properly beyond that stage either. The result then is the one we so commonly find. There is an intermingling and overlapping of schizoid and depressive anxieties. In adult analysis, whichever state emerges first clearly, the other is sure to have to be analysed afterwards; not merely as a result of minor oscillations between the two, but in a radical way. Both problems must be cleared before the patient can become adequately stable. In the last chapter I gave an account of a clearly manic-depressive patient in whom the schizoid problem emerged in a very definite way. After that was analysed, he then returned, not to his earlier manic-depressive state, but to a more realistic, uncomplicated depression and guilt about his mother who had had, in fact, a cruelly hard life. Thereafter we slowly analysed, not manic-depression, but infantile dependence and basic ego-weakness.

For comparison, I will briefly summarize a case in which analysis worked the other way round. Here an extremely schizoid and hallucinated patient emerged, after a long analysis to a point where she could 'feel' for people and have needs of her own, only to find that she generated so much guilt and depression that, till this was dealt with, she could make no real improvements. Her moods with her husband constantly changed between anxiety, depression, and aloofness, and she remarked, 'I get so anxious about loving. It isn't safe.' Then suddenly she reported that she still had the letters and photos of her first boy friend, and could not read them. She had mentioned this boy early in her analysis but nothing very important had ever emerged about him. She was only 16 at the time and he was 25 and in the Army during the last war. Their friendship had lasted only about six months when he was sent abroad on war service, and after a few months caught an infection and died. His letters were simple, sincere, and genuinely affectionate, and there was no doubt but that he intended to marry her.

She had been astonished that he had even noticed her, let alone wanted her. She was the youngest of a family without affection and felt that he was the very first person who had ever loved her. The shock of his death was great and she became and remained deeply depressed for two years, crying alone in her room at bedtime most nights and hiding it all from her family, whose attitude was 'Don't be silly. You'll get over it.' She put his letters and photos in a box and never dared look at them again. I suggested that she bring them to her session and read them with me, which she did. This was over twenty years after the events, and she was now married with two children. Nevertheless, reading the letters called forth the depression she suffered on his death with unmistakable force. She was able, however, to get over this fairly quickly, and in talking of how that friendship had been the very first thing in her life that had brought her real enjoyment, she began to come alive in a new way. She realized that she had never really enjoyed anything since then. She had come to analysis in a very ill state, hallucinating representations of intense hungry needs, but in real life being affectless and shut in.

She now began to experience acute anxiety about me and about her husband, and the point of her remark that 'I get anxious about loving. It isn't safe' became clear. I put it to her that she was unconsciously convinced that if she loved anyone that person would die and she was bound to lose him; moreover she also felt that she dare not enjoy anything at all and could hardly let herself be alive. It was as if her mother was always saying 'Stop laughing or you'll be crying in a minute.' She replied, 'That is exactly what they were always saying to me', and in fact she rarely laughed, and felt it was wrong to enjoy oneself. Her mother began to come into this in a big way. The mother had become a widow only a couple of years after the patient's birth, had had a hard life, and was an awkward, hardworking, undemonstrative woman who endured life joylessly, provided for the family's material needs, and was unaware of their emotional needs. Earlier in analysis the patient had dreamed that

> she entered a room where a group of women (her mother and sisters) were talking together and entirely ignoring a baby lying on the table. She got on the table and lay down on the baby and became one with it.

She grew up in the position that, in order to escape depersonalization through a sheer lack of any genuine relationships she had to cling to mother with some sort of a relationship which would be, as it were, manufactured from her side because it was not given by the mother. She could not get a loving relationship so she tied herself to mother by 'duty'. She felt she must not ever leave her mother, must stay at home and look after her, and in the process became a passive, shy, silent, self-effacing girl. The one and only major revolt was when at sixteen she responded to the call of love. The young man's death aroused intense guilt. She should never have let herself be drawn away from mother into the prospect of marriage, and his death was her punishment. She felt guilt towards both mother and the man, and was overwhelmed by depression, of a severity that would have made life impossible but for the fact that gradually a friendship grew up with another young man whom she later married. This enabled her to bury the trauma and depression of her first tragic love. The man's letters were put away and never looked at, i.e. repressed, but the safety of her marriage was ensured by the fact that she was quite unable to enjoy it or anything else. To have enjoyed life would have been to release a flood of guilt and depression. Now, after a lengthy analysis, she was beginning to 'feel' once more and escape from her schizoid, affectless condition, only to find that she was compelled to revive and relive her repressed depression and guilt. Every time her husband was out she was a prey to anxiety about his safety till he returned. The unconscious conviction was active in her that her marriage was disloyalty to mother; she ought not to have made it and she would be punished for it. Thus her analysis recapitulated the development from the schizoid to the depressive position, and opened the way for growth beyond that to normal relationships, though not till her depression was analysed, was she able to go deeper with the analysis of her schizoid troubles.

This case brings us back to the fact that ego-weakness underlies pathological depression. The 'stage of concern' (Winnicott) may not be reached at all by the infantile ego that is too profoundly disturbed and remains stuck in a paranoid-schizoid state, a state of sheer fear of the outer world and drastic withdrawal from it. A return to object-relations can then *only* be made in the form of a paranoid fear and suspicion of all objects. But lesser degrees of disturbance permit a weakened ego to move on to a capacity to feel 'concern' for objects, and to experience anxiety and depression at the possibility of harming or losing or destroying them. But *the 'concern' for others felt by a weakened ego is not a fully healthy objective concern arising out of appreciation of the worth and the interests of the object. Fear in the ego for itself plays a big part. Panic at the loss of a supportive object and guilt over the loss of a love-object are mixed together. It takes a strongly developed ego to love disinterestedly and care for another person basically for that person's sake*, even though in practice no one is ever as mature as that. So we are brought back again to the problem of ego-weakness as a legacy of disturbed development in the earliest formative years, a problem which makes it obvious that psychotherapy in any radical sense cannot but be a gradual and lengthy process of re-growing.

Ego-Psychology

In 1913 Freud wrote:

> To shorten analytic treatment is a justifiable wish, and its fulfilment . . . is being attempted along various lines. Unfortunately it is opposed by a very important factor, namely, the slowness with which . . . changes in the mind are accomplished. (1913, p. 130.)

Nothing has happened since those words were written to modify that judgment. Psychotherapy remains a slow and difficult process. Nevertheless, we cannot remain scientifically content with this. Even if profound mental change can never be other than slow and difficult, we want to know why this is so, and there is always the chance that greater understanding may enable us to make psychotherapy more effective. If change were too easy and mental structure too fluid, the result would not be quicker psychotherapy but general instability. Relative stability at any point in the scale between immaturity and maturity involves that once an individual has developed a certain organizational pattern of personality, he is able to retain it with a high degree of persistence. Disturbed patterns persist as stubbornly as more harmonious ones. Yet, some personality patterns are so disadvantageous to their owners that we would gladly know whether and how they can be changed quickly enough to give the person a chance to live normally. The whole situation is a challenge to deeper investigation, and perhaps also to a rethinking of things that we are familiar with. It could be that the slowness of psychotherapy is not *only* due to the inherent difficulty of the problem, but also the possibility that our psychodynamic interpretations have been missing something vital. Everything in a given field cannot be seen from one point of view, and often a change of viewpoint leads to deeper understanding.

Psychoanalytic therapy was at first based on interpretations designed to uncover repressed libidinal needs and aggressive impulses. The phrases 'releasing the patient's libido' and 'releasing the patient's aggression' were characteristic of that approach. It led to the creation of a popular ideal of 'the uninhibited person'. But it was found that in so far as this was achieved, it made only a very doubtful contribution to the deep maturing of the personality as a whole. It may relieve the patient of some practical disabilities that spring from inhibitions. He may be better able to ask for what he wants and better able to stand up for himself superficially. Yet, when he has done so, he all too often recognizes that the impulses he has released are very immature ones, and he is liable to incur not only social criticism but also an increase of guilt in self-condemnation. In fact he is having to defy unconscious guilt to act more uninhibitedly, and if the guilt does not become conscious, he will not progress any further. To aim simply at the release of repressed immature and anxiety-driven impulses as if that were equivalent to the freeing of the healthy instinctive drives of a mature person, was seen to be naïve and a therapeutic delusion. Neither do impulses automatically mature by becoming conscious and being expressed. It is useless releasing impulses unless they are considered all the time as expressions of an *ego*, and indicative of the state in which that ego exists. This was what led Fairbairn to abandon impulse-psychology in favour of more radical ego-analysis.

The striking feature of the development of psychodynamic theory in the last thirty years is that, through the work of Melanie Klein in which the emphasis was shifting from the impulse to the object, there has now begun to emerge a steady trend towards concentration on the ego, as we saw in Chapter IV. Adler raised the problem of the ego in his theory of the inferiority-complex and the will-to-power; but he raised it superficially, prematurely, and mostly at the social level. It was from Freud himself that the real impetus to ego-analysis came in the 1920's. His structural scheme, id, ego, and superego, in spite of its ultimate inadequacies, was a tremendous first step towards *putting the ego in the centre of the picture* where hitherto psychobiological impulse had reigned supreme. This is clear from Anna Freud's statement (1936):

There have been periods in the development of psychoanalytical science when the theoretical study of the individual ego was distinctly unpopular . . . Whenever interest was transferred from the deeper to the more superficial strata—whenever, that is to say, research was deflected from the id to the ego—it was felt that here was the beginning of apostacy.

However, it is also clear from this that the dynamic depths of the psyche were still regarded as an impersonal 'id' while the 'ego' belonged to 'the more superficial strata'. So long as that relic of the earlier 'impulse psychology' remained, no satisfactory ego-theory could develop.

Freud stated clearly (1937) that:

We shall achieve our therapeutic purpose only when we give a greater measure of analytic help to the patient's ego.

Earlier he had written of 'the therapeutic efforts of psychoanalysis' that

Their object is to strengthen the ego, to make it more independent of the superego [present writer's italics], to widen its field of vision, and so to extend its organization that it can take over more portions of the id. (1933.)

With some re-interpretation of terms, nothing could be nearer the truth about psychotherapy. *It is our psychotherapeutic charter.* Its great importance, however, was obscured by the fact that the Freudian theory of an ego limited to the 'superficial strata', could give no meaning to 'ego' adequate to the implications of this statement. Freud's theory remained one of ego and superego control of psychobiological impulse. The ego remained a superficially developed control apparatus 'on the surface of the id' and not a true self, not the real heart of the personality. *We require the term 'ego' to stand for the 'whole' of the individual's nature and self-knowledge as a 'person', an 'I' in personal relations with other 'I's, whose wholeness can be 'split' by too disturbing experiences.* Fairbairn wrote: 'All inner problems resolve themselves ultimately into ego-problems.' Winnicott writes of 'therapeutic regression' in search of the 'true self' which has early been repressed and lies hidden behind a 'false self' which functions socially on a conformist basis. This is a point of view which classical psychoanalytical theory cannot explain intelligibly. In fact, psychodynamic theory is changing its orientation from 'release and/or control of instinctive impulses' to the 'maturing of the ego into an adult personality'. Perhaps we should put it in an even more elementary way as 'the individual's struggle to achieve and preserve a stable ego'. We must rethink all the familiar problems from this point of view.

Moreover this is really the patient's point of view. A patient of mine who had never heard of Winnicott said to me years ago: 'I have grown up an outer shell of conformities inside which I have lost touch with the real "me".' *She felt she had not got a proper ego and yet in some sense she felt it was potentially there.* Fairbairn presented the view that we must go beyond the repression of memories, emotions, and impulses and consider the repression of the object, making use of Melanie Klein's theory of 'internal objects' (Fairbairn, 1952). His work, however, went on to direct attention to the other half of the object-relationship, namely the ego. Our need for object-relationships lies in the fact that without them it is impossible to develop an ego that is sound, strong, and stable: and that is what all human beings fundamentally need. Fairbairn quotes a patient as saying: 'You're always talking about my wanting this or that desire satisfied; but what I really want is a father' (1952). Now, however, we have to go a step beyond that and say the reason why the patient wants a father (and needs an analyst) is that without a satisfactory relationship with another person he cannot become a developing ego, he cannot find himself. That is why patients are so often found complaining 'I don't know who or what I am; I don't seem to have a mind of my own; I don't feel to be a real person at all.' Their early object-relationships were such that they were unable to 'find themselves' in any definite way.

The primary drive in every human being is to become a 'person', to achieve a solid ego formation, to develop a personality in order to live. This can only be done in the medium of personal object-relationships. If these are good, the infant undergoes a natural and unselfconscious good ego-development. If these are bad, good ego-development is seriously compromised from the start, as the work of Bion is showing in a new way. *There are no fears worse or deeper than those which arise out of having to cope with life when one feels that one is just not a real person, that one's ego is basically weak, perhaps that one is hardly an ego at all.* These are the ultimate fears in our patients. Thus one patient who was often driven to make the kind of complaints cited above, burst out with: 'I'm afraid of life, of everything. Fear's the key.' Psychotherapy, defined as a process whereby the patient is helped to achieve a mature ego and overcome his deep fear of life, is the logical goal of Winnicott's work in the clinical and therapeutic field and Fairbairn's revision of theory. It is the discovery of the 'true self' which Winnicott regards as buried behind the defensive operations of the years, and it is the overcoming of the 'infantile dependence' which Fairbairn regarded as the root cause of psychoneurosis (the Oedipus complex being an example of infantile dependence). These two points of view seem to be the starting points for research on psychotherapy today. 'Infantile dependence' could not be more clearly illustrated as the cause of trouble than in the remark of a patient: 'I'm sick to death of dragging round with me wherever I go a timid small child inside me', the weak, over-burdened basic ego that just could not stand up to life. This baby has then to be repudiated, at the demand of the outer world, later internalized as an inner demand, as in this dream:

I was eating my favourite meal when my mother came into the room and snatched it away from me. As I protested she said, 'Don't be a baby.'

These two instances define for us in the patient's own terms the nature of the problem they bring to us. *An infantile ego has been rejected and repressed. It remains therefore undeveloped and weak, and deep maturing of personality comes to a standstill.*

The Fear of Ego-Weakness

If we now, for a moment, forget the complex theories of psychiatric, psychoanalytic, and psychological learning, and watch human beings at first hand as they struggle with life in and through their dealings with the people round them, we may ask ourselves the simple question, 'What are people most afraid of?' The multifarious ways in which people are on the defensive against one another, in business, social life, marriage, and parenthood, and even leisure activities, suggests that the one omnipresent fear is the fear of being and appearing weak, inadequate, less of a person than others or less than equal to the demands of the situation, a failure: the fear of letting oneself down and looking a fool in face of an unsupportive and even hostile world. This fear lies behind all the rationalized self-assertiveness, the subtle exhibitionism, the disguised boasting, the competitiveness or avoidance of competition, the need of praise, reassurance and approval, the safety-first tactics and security-seeking, and a multitude of other defensive reactions to life that lie open and on the surface for all to see.

If we now turn back to our patients with this in mind, we find the same fear of appearing weak, often in the manifest form of a sense of shame and humiliation in having to seek this sort of treatment at all. In this context, fear of the hostile world appears as fear of being despised if it is known that they have such treatment. 'People will think I'm a "nuts" case.' But behind this fear, without exception, we come upon the fact that patients suffer from very serious feelings of actual weakness and inadequacy as a result of which they are in a state of perpetual anxiety. Their fear of appearing weak has a foundation in fact, and likewise their fear of a hostile world also has a foundation in fact. It is true that feelings of weakness have no direct relationship to the patient's actual ability. They are found in the most able people, professional folk with good qualifications, men successfully running their own businesses, and so on. One of the most undermined personalities I have known, so far as basic lack of self-confidence was concerned, was a surgeon who had practised excellently for twenty years. But he said that no one knew the torture it had been. Every time the telephone rang he was in a state of utter anxiety, feeling certain he would be asked to perform an operation he could not do, or that he would fail in it. *The feeling of weakness arises out of a lack of a reliable feeling of one's own reality and identity as an ego*. 'I'm not sure of myself; sometimes I feel I'm just a nobody.'

With many patients, however, this deep down fundamental weakness of the ego is not obvious to them. We may be able to recognize its signs, but the patient's energies are strenuously devoted to hiding, denying, disproving, disguising or mastering and crushing out if possible whatever degree of these feelings of weakness, fear, timidity, and inability to cope with life that they find in them. The famous 'resistance' to psychotherapy which was one of Freud's most important discoveries is, in the first instance, mainly an attempt to deny the need for treatment. Patients will either play down their problems, minimize their symptoms, state frankly that they feel psychotherapy is humiliating and that they ought to be able to manage these difficulties themselves, resent the most carefully and tactfully made interpretations as criticism, and are very anxious that no one should know that they are consulting a psychotherapist; or else they may set forth their problems as unfair or inexplicable inflictions, with an attitude implying: 'There's nothing really wrong with me but somehow these misfortunes have befallen me', and feel they can rightly claim help for such things (a claim in which, in fact, they are justified in the end). Most patients, apart from the few who have had the opportunity of gaining some insight, seek the removal of their symptoms, without realizing the necessity of undergoing some basic changes in themselves, for they do not recognize their symptoms as evidences of basic weakness in their personality. If they do, they all the more regard treatment as a humiliation, and are on the defensive from the start. These patients are often right in their feeling that they will be looked down upon, judging by the rather thinly-veiled contempt with which hysterics are usually referred to by psychiatrists. In any case the patients look down upon themselves. One of my patients dreamed that she went past my rooms on top of a tram, but looking down she also saw herself entering in, and thought, 'Look at that silly creature going in there.'

The more one reflects on things from this point of view, the more impressive the facts become. The resistance to psychotherapy is strictly on a par with the defensiveness of people against one another in everyday life. If we study this question in the light of the mass of psychopathological data at our disposal today (which did not yet exist in the early days of psychoanalysis) we shall come near the heart of the matter. There is a greater or lesser degree of immaturity in the personality-structure of all human beings, and this immaturity is experienced as definite weakness and inadequacy of the ego in face of the adult tasks of life. The unremitting and strenuous efforts to overcome or hide this weakness, which they do not know how, genuinely, to grow out of, constitutes, together with the weakness itself, the mass of psychopathological experience and behaviour, as seen not only in patients but also in the general low level of mental health in the community. *The struggle to force a weak ego to face life, or, even more fundamentally, the struggle to preserve an ego at all, is the root cause of psychotic, psychosomatic and psychoneurotic tensions and illness.*

It is not inevitable or accidental that so many human beings are in a state of constant anxiety because they feel weak and inadequate at the very core of their inner self. Maybe we are barely emerging from the psychological Dark Ages so far as the mass of the population is concerned, in the matter of bringing up children. There are one or two primitive tribes whose simple culture is totally ignorant of our scientific civilization, yet their pattern of 'permissiveness' and parental affection embodies far more psychological wisdom than any forms of capitalist or communist society known to our anxiety-ridden world. Some other primitive tribes have been described as having a paranoid culture pattern, a term equally applicable to Nazism. The struggles to achieve democracy illustrate the enormous difficulties modern man encounters in trying to create a society in which human beings are valued as, and helped to be, persons in their own right. In fact, throughout our modern civilization, East and West, right and left wing, religious and scientific, a mass production of basically insecure and psychologically weakened human beings goes on, outstripping our ability to find a method to cope with them. Masses of children grow up frightened at heart, at the mercy of parents who work off their own fears and tensions on the children. Moreover our patients constantly meet a critical and unsympathetic reaction from friends. 'Oh, we could all give in like that if we let ourselves; you must pull yourself together. You should think less of yourself and more of other people.' So the cultural attitudes drive them to feel ashamed of weakness and to simulate strength. Ian Suttie, many years ago now, spoke of the 'taboo on tenderness' in our culture. But the matter goes deeper. The reason why there is a taboo on tenderness is that tenderness is regarded as weakness in all but the most private relations of life, and many people regard it as weakness even there and introduce patterns of domination into love-life itself. The real taboo is on weakness; the one great crime is to be weak; the thing to which none dare confess is feeling weak, however much the real weakness was brought into being when they were so young that they knew nothing of the import of what was happening to them. You cannot afford to be weak in a competitive world which you feel is mostly hostile to you, and if anyone is so unfortunate as to discover that his infancy has left him with too great a measure of arrested emotional development and a failure of ego-growth in the important early stages, then he soon learns to bend all his energies to hiding or mastering the infant within.

The Basic Emotional Predicament

The problem of ego-weakness has been slowly thrusting itself to the forefront of psychodynamic research. Perhaps the terrific resistance to admitting and facing 'basic ego-weakness rooted in fear' that all human beings show both in social life and as patients, is reflected in the slowness with which psychiatric and psychoanalytic research has come to face this problem. It may be that we ourselves would rather not be forced to see it too clearly lest we should find a text-book in our own hearts. It is less disturbing even to theorists to think in terms of mastering instinctive drives or reconditioning behaviour patterns rather than of helping a frightened infant inside to grow up. For one thing, if this latter emphasis is correct, the therapeutic problem cannot be solved only by analysis. Analysis must be seen as 'exposing' a developmentally arrested psyche to the support and new stimulus of an understanding relationship in which the therapist, like the parent, must wait while the child grows. The history of psychodynamic theory can be seen as the story of our long struggle to overcome our scientifically rationalized resistance to this fact. That this point of view is coming to dominate psychoanalysis today, may be illustrated by the following quotation from Zetzel (1965):

> Successful emergence and resolution of the transference neurosis in clinical psychoanalysis is contingent on the establishment and maintenance of the therapeutic alliance at all times. The qualities, moreover, in the analyst which best foster the therapeutic alliance correspond in many ways to those intuitive responses in the mother which lead to successful early ego development in the baby.

We must beware of becoming overweighted with complex analyses and, nowadays, statistical studies of secondary phenomena, of interesting psychodynamic morbidities, while missing 'The Basic Human Dilemma' in which our patients are caught, namely, that they were born into a situation in which they were unable to lay the foundations of a strong ego development, and have grown up feeling at bottom inadequate to the demands of living, even though they may not be conscious of this, full of fear and struggling with considerable though varying degrees of success, to keep going and shoulder their responsibilities. This fact of basic ego-weakness is the hard core of all personality disturbance and of the problem of psychotherapy. The one line of research most relevant to all forms of mental illness other than the purely organic in origin, is that which goes to the tap root, the failure or inability of the child in the environment it is born into, to lay the foundations of an adequate, strong, well-developed, self-confident, and capable personality equal to the adult tasks in life.

From the point of view of psychotherapy two problems arise. (i) How and why does the initial ego-failure occur? We defer the answer to this question to Chapters VIII and IX. (ii) *Why and how, or in what structuralized form, does this early arrest of ego-development persist? Once initial failure has occurred in laying the foundations of a non-anxious and active self in infancy, a mental organization evidently comes into being which effectively blocks the possibility of any further deep-level emotional growth.* Life then turns into an unceasing fight to force oneself to be equal to adult living without ever feeling to be so. (Cf. the case history given in Chapter V.) It is this psychic situation on its inner side that proliferates into all the psychic disorders and we must examine it in detail before we proceed further. The one fact which overrides everything else is that the baby must grow up to become a capable adult, strong enough to look after himself and make his own contribution to life among other people. Probably a majority of human beings never do feel thus adequate to living and are involved in the process of 'screwing themselves up' to face life. Freud pictured this state of things when, in his own terms, he spoke of the poor ego being so hard pressed by three taskmasters—the id, the superego, and the outer world. Fears of ego-breakdown and ego-loss within, come to be even greater than the original fears of outer reality. Freud's ego is only the 'ego of everyday life', in a purely controlling sense, and not the dynamic centre of the whole personality. Freud called it the reality ego, the ego in touch with the outer world, what Fairbairn called the central ego and what Winnicott, in at any rate one of its aspects, calls the false self. It is not of this familiar ego, not of this part of the total psychic self, that basic ego-weakness is characteristic. True, a profound sense of weakness and inadequacy does break through into this familiar conscious ego of daily living, but it does not originate there. When this breakthrough occurs, it is because the normal central ego defences have cracked. Usually this ego functions as a defence against the underlying sense of weakness, to prevent its invasion of consciousness. The obsessional character gives us a striking example of a central ego organized on a rigid and unyielding pattern of absolute self-control with no weakness shown; though in fact the central ego may here be said to have been captured by the Freudian sadistic super-ego, to slave-drive the weak needy infant within.

At this point it seems necessary to refer again to the structural terminology available. (Cf. pp. 71–2, 162–3.) We need terms by means of which we can identify and refer to the various aspects of psychic functioning, in order to discuss the problems that here face us. There does not exist as yet a generally agreed and thoroughly satisfactory set of terms, largely because the analytical distinguishing of different aspects of the inner complex conflict-state has grown so much more subtle since Freud first opened up this area of investigation with his distinctions of id, ego, and superego. We have to conceptualize three main aspects of psychic functioning, each of which has its own complexities: (i) the conscious self of everyday living, reacting, and adjusting to the outer world; (ii) the primary nature or innate potential self with which the infant is born, and which becomes in varying degrees developed or inhibited by post-natal experiences; (iii) a very complex set of functions in which the psyche interferes with itself, either under pressure from the outer world or else at the same time under pressure of its own fears of breakdown—the phenomena Fairbairn referred to as 'internal sabotage'. We have three suggested terminologies, which are not in any sense mutually exclusive, put forward by Freud, Fairbairn, and Winnicott.

The terms reality ego, central ego, and false self must be considered as denoting the conscious self of our ordinary daily life. None of them is wholly satisfactory. 'Reality ego' to be precise would have to be expanded into 'outer reality ego', for the outer world has no monopoly of the characteristic of 'reality'. The psyche has its own reality. But 'outer reality ego' is too cumbersome for regular use. 'Central ego', as Fairbairn used the term, stands for what is left in touch with the outer world after the libidinal and antilibidinal egos have been repressed. It is the 'remainder' of the pristine infantile ego which at first was in simple contact with its outer world, even though not conscious of it as such. However, in view of the fact that this 'outer reality ego' usually develops so many conformist characteristics as to warrant Winnicott's calling it a 'false self', it seems hardly adequate to refer to it as the 'central ego'. The dynamic centre of new growth so often seems to be outside of this socially adaptive ego. Yet, on the other hand, we can only promote the release of spontaneous energies dammed up in the unconscious by working *through* this ego of consciousness and it does possess and use much that must be regarded as belonging to the permanent possessions of the 'whole self' in any event, such as knowledge, skills, and interests which are not in any sense false. Without feeling that the terminology is fully satisfactory, I shall use the term 'central ego' to stand for the conscious self of our daily living, and use the term 'false self' to stand for that aspect of it which is most rigid and stereotyped on the basis of 'conformity for safety's sake', and which acts therefore as a barrier inhibiting the spontaneous flow of genuine self-expression. 'Central ego' is thus an extremely complex concept.

The primary natural potential self of the infant is not in any sense satisfactorily denoted by the term 'id' for this is not strictly speaking a psychological term at all. It can only convey the bare notion of impersonal biological instinctive energy, and that is something we never meet with in clinical experience. We meet only with energies that represent the functioning of a personal aspect of the total psychic self, mature or immature. The term 'id' can only suggest that our psychic energies have an ultimate biological source, what H. S. Sullivan called the 'biological substrate' of the personal self. That alone is an inadequate concept. Winnicott's term 'true self' stands for all that the child is, potentially, and all that he can and will become, if a sufficiently favourable environment facilitates his normal development. The term is valuable in making us realize that all human beings are potentially much more than in practice they ever succeed in becoming. Fairbairn preferred the term 'natural self' to 'true self', but there seems no compelling reason for preferring one to the other. His term 'libidinal ego' does seem to me to be valuable as in line with familiar psychoanalytical usage. He meant by it the primary nature of the infant as we can see it actively expressed in his urgent libidinal needs. 'Libidinal' in this sense means not just sexual libido, though that will be one aspect of it, but rather the total 'life-drive', the dynamic urge to be, and develop as a person specifically by seeking and entering into object-relationships. Fairbairn did not regard 'aggression' as a specific innate factor, a kind of 'entity *per se*', but as a reaction to thwarting of libidinal need, and therefore as secondary to the libidinal factor. *The term 'libidinal ego' cannot therefore be criticized as omitting aggression, for it is the libidinal ego itself which owns the capacity to fight to achieve its ends if it is frustrated.* On the whole, libidinal ego seems to me the best term we have, on a par with Freud's superego, to denote the pristine natural self of the infant which, when smothered in the course of development, is only the potentiality of the individual's true self. The true self does not yet exist: it is what psychotherapy must help the libidinal ego to become.

Freud's term 'superego' and Fairbairn's term 'antilibidinal ego' are valuable alternative terms, each useful in different contexts since they denote the same broad area of psychic functioning (that of internalized parental and social controls which have become self-controls), though they are not exactly identical. 'Superego' covers a wider range of phenomena than does 'antilibidinal ego'. Roughly we may say that 'superego' includes both 'sadism turned against the self' and 'mature morality'. It expresses well the fact that no human being can live as if he were entirely his own master. The world outside us has legitimate claims on us which the maturely developed person accepts. There is, as it were, a 'superego' larger than our own individual ego, which should be represented inside our psychic organization, not as a harsh tyrant but as a supportive and friendly authority. However, to whatever degree anxiety and illness pervades our inner being this internal authority is a cruel dictator in which all our rage and hate of a bad outer world has become concentrated into self-suppression and in particular aimed at the suppression of our own libidinal needs. For this particular aspect of the Freudian 'superego' the term proposed by Fairbairn, 'antilibidinal ego', though somewhat clumsy is entirely accurate, and emphasizes the clear-cut way in which the infant can be turned into sadistically hostile antagonism to his own needs. The 'antilibidinal ego' is specifically 'against needs' and is basically an internalization of the outer world's intolerance of the needy infant who is regarded as a nuisance to be kept quiet. For the narrower purposes of the following analysis, the terms central ego, libidinal ego, and antilibidinal ego seem most useful, while the wider terms, outer reality ego, true self, and superego, are valuable in larger contexts of discussion.

We seek to understand *how and why basic ego-weakness is perpetuated structurally in the life of the psyche. Ego-weakness in the ultimate sense in which it is basic and causal for all kinds of personality disorder is primarily a property of the infantile libidinal ego, whose development has been and remains arrested.* The primary nature of the infant is endowed with innate libidinal needs and energies in virtue of which, in a good environment, it will grow into a strong, active, and definitely individual personality. This is neatly expressed in the title of Winnicott's 1965 book, *The Maturational Processes and the Facilitating Environment*. But where personality disorder exists, this has not happened. The libidinal ego then represents the structural differentiation of that primary aspect of the total psyche in a state of deprivation, frustration, and distress, and hence of impotent rage, fear, and awareness of its own weakness. *It is this infantile frustrated and fear-ridden libidinal ego that is the seat of 'basic ego-weakness' and this is a deeper problem than that portion of the feeling of weakness that seeps through at various times into the ego of everyday consciousness.* Here is an ego-weakness, the greater part of which is kept hidden and repressed, dammed in behind all the antilibidinal defences that enable the central ego to function even if with anxiety on the adult plane. Resistance in analysis is directed with tremendous determination to the task of keeping this weak and panicky infantile ego under heavy repression. *Ego-weakness consists not in lack of energy or innate ability, but in this unremitting state of basic fear and distress and lack of self-confidence of which the individual feels ashamed, and of which he develops considerable secondary fears.* The main practical problem for psychotherapy is 'Can this patient stand the return to consciousness of his basic ego-weakness?'

When it does return, he is most likely to feel 'I can't stand it, I only want to die.'

The most obvious ways in which the person with a basically weak and immature ego seeks to protect himself in face of outer world pressures and inner world fears, is to hide the part of himself that is a child facing a life that feels too big for him, behind central ego detachment, or conformity, or aggressiveness, or conversion of tensions into bodily illnesses, or obsessional self-mastery, sheltering from realities behind technical professional knowledge, compulsive addiction to duty, or unselfish serviceableness to others, and so on. All the psychoneurotic defences come into play. The more serious pathological states of depression and schizoid apathy, depersonalization, suicidal trends, and schizophrenic disintegration of the ego, undoubtedly represent complex conditions in which the infantile libidinal ego feels driven towards the ultimate psychic dangers. The psychoneurotic defensive states represent rather the struggle to force a pseudo-adult pattern which masks the frightened child inside. This basically weak infantile libidinal ego has, as it were, been split off and repudiated in an attempt to live without conscious fears. This represents the hate and fear of weakness of which we have spoken. Our fear and intolerance of weakness is naturally great, and is so embedded in our culture pattern, and is so additionally stimulated in the infant by the adults who handle him, that he is driven to a premature repudiation of his weak infantile ego and to an attempt to force an equally premature pseudo-adult self. *In seeking to overcome his weakness, the child employs a method which ensures its perpetuation, creating an endopsychic situation in which natural development is impossible.* We must try to set this forth in more scientific terms, but it represents what we may well call 'The Basic Emotional Predicament' for human beings in growing up, the human dilemma; though there appear to have existed a few simple cultures in which this dilemma did not necessarily arise.

All the psychoanalytical investigation that has been devoted to the ramifications of the disease processes once they are in being in the personality, has now begun to lay bare the tap root of it all. We must be careful not to miss the basic shape and meaning of the illness in studying the variety of its manifestations. That this is being generally understood seems to be suggested by the fact that in *The International Journal of Psycho-Analysis* for 1948 and 1949 the word 'ego' did not appear in the title of any paper; in 1955 it appeared in two titles; in 1964 it appeared in seven titles in such striking phrases as 'splitting of the ego', 'structuration of the ego', 'ego distortion', 'ego restrictions', 'ego core'. Such casual statistics may not prove much but they probably do indicate an important trend. Human infants, so long biologically and psychologically dependent on their parents, are not in the mass very successful in growing up to mature adulthood. What keeps the child alive inside so long? Why is he not normally and naturally outgrown as the years go by, along with increasing physical and intellectual maturity. A person in a good state of mental health as a result of a good early emotional development does not feel himself to be an inadequate and frightened child inside. One does not have to have outstanding powers or exceptional endowments to feel quite sufficiently self-confident for normal purposes. It is much more a matter of the emotional attitude in which one lives with oneself in one's inner mental make-up, primarily at a deep unconscious level. An enormous number of people are unable to achieve an emotional development to mature, unafraid, self-reliant, and affectionate adulthood. *Why, however, is it not easier for human beings to make a belated growth in ego-strength after childhood is left behind?*

On a purely conscious central ego level many people, in fact, do. But it is startling to find through deep analysis how little this has affected the situation in the profoundly repressed unconscious. We may therefore state in this way the problem of the psychodynamic hard core of resistance to psychotherapy: when once the infantile ego has become disturbed and arrested in its development in the earliest stages, so that it comes to feel its weakness and to exist in a state of fear, what is it that keeps it thereafter fixed so stubbornly in that position of basic ego-weakness? What is it that leads to the perpetuation of a weak, undeveloped, fearful, and therefore infantile dependent ego? It remains buried in the deep unconscious and makes no progress to maturity, in spite of the individual's strenuous efforts in the 'self of everyday living' to grow and function as an adult. Why is this endopsychic situation so hard to change? And in what form does it persist so statically? This is the basic emotional predicament.

VII

RESISTANCE, THE SELF-INDUCED BLOCKAGE OF THE MATURING PROCESS

In the last chapter the question was raised as to why the infantile weak dependent ego persists so stubbornly in the deep unconscious. We are now so used to saying that the causes of neuroses lie back in childhood that we may miss the vital point of this problem. It is true that the origins of the trouble were in early childhood, but the actual emotional cause of instability and weakness in the personality in later life is something that is going on in the personality right here and now. It is a peculiar feature of the mental organization of the person (his endopsychic structure) which keeps him in that original state of basic fear and weakness, and perpetuates it and even intensifies it as time goes on. We have stated this in non-technical language as the fear and hate of weakness in the face of the necessities of living, and in comparison with other people. But we need to show how this fear and hate come to be permanently embodied in the organizational structure of the psyche.

Antilibidinal Resistance to Psychotheraphy

The situation must arise in this way: an inadequate environment, and particularly an inadequate mother, exposes the infant to steadily increasing awareness of his smallness, weakness, and helplessness. He will be what Winnicott calls 'a collection of reactions to impingement' but somewhere in the midst of that chaos the psyche, the basic subject of experience, who is potentially a whole self and owns these reactions, is unable to grow a secure sense of his wholeness, but can feel acute states of fear. The specific feeling of being little, helpless, and frightened can emerge with great definiteness in deep analyses. Gradually the child must grow to feel, if he could put it into words, that it is too frightening to be weak in an unfriendly and menacing world, and also that one cannot afford to have needs that one cannot get satisfied. As he grows steadily out of earliest infancy and becomes more acquainted with his outer world, he must realize that such needs make one dependent, and if you cannot change your world, you can try to change yourself. Thus he comes to fear and hate his own weakness and neediness; and now he faces the task of growing up with an intolerance of his immaturity. This is bound up with and reflects the impatience and intolerance that grown-ups have of the dependence of the infant and the childishness of the child. One patient described how his crying as a child drew on him such contempt and ragging that he managed suddenly to repress it, only to find the crying fits replaced by temper attacks. Another patient described how his attitude to his small son changed during the course of his analysis. At first when the boy cried, the father would feel in an absolute fury of intolerance and shout at the boy to stop it at once, which only made him worse. Then later on he managed to moderate this and would say: 'Come on now, stop this crying. You're a big boy now.' The patient explained that as a boy he was himself often very frightened of his father but never dared to cry, though he often felt like it. But his son was not 'a big boy now' and the father was trying to force him to a premature assumption of an attitude older than his years, because this was what had happened in his own case. Finally, however, he worked through to a third position, and said: 'Now, when the lad cries I don't feel that old fury. I can accept his childishness better and I say "I'm sorry old chap you're so upset. I know how you feel, but never mind. You have your cry and you'll feel a lot better soon."' That, he says, works far better, and in a short time the tears are dried and the boy has forgotten it all. But all too often the child is educated into the same intolerance of his childishness that the parents felt towards their own. A self-frustrating situation of deep internal self-hate arises, along with a concentrated attempt to drive and force oneself to the conscious feeling and behaviour that is regarded as adult, in the light of the pseudo-mature patterns of the grown-ups around.

This pseudo-adult pattern may be conventional, practical, moral, critical, intellectual, or even aggressive, angry, cruel, but it always masks an inward self-hate and self-persecution which, for intermittent self-relief, is turned outwards on to other people as occasion offers. The child models his own fear and hate of his immaturity on the parental attitudes of intolerance and rejection of it, so that he comes to treat his own primary needy dependent but now disturbed self as if it were a part of his whole self that he could disown, split off, hide and repress, and even crush out of existence, while his 'ego of everyday living' is compelled to develop tougher or at least more socially approved characteristics. This 'ego of everyday living', hiding the child's primary disturbed self, is based on adaptation to the demands of the outer world. Some measure of such adaptation is, naturally, always necessary, but when it covers over a denial of the spontaneous nature which is in a disturbed state, then it becomes what Winnicott calls the 'false self on a conformity basis'. The simple, elementary wholeness or unity of the child's nature is disrupted and we need terms by which we can identify the various persisting ways in which the psyche now functions in a state of internal disunity. I have examined in foregoing pages terms proposed for this purpose by Freud, Fairbairn, and Winnicott, and defined their usefulness in various contexts. I should make it clear that I regard such terms as having only a utilitarian value until better ones are found. I do not regard them as having any kind of final truth. Meanwhile, for the purpose of identifying and discussing the three main differentiated aspects of this condition of disunited psychic functioning, I have found Fairbairn's terms accurate and valuable.

The child's ego has been disrupted and now functions in three fairly clearly marked aspects. These are not 'bits' or 'entities', even though we use the metaphor of 'ego-splitting'. They are overlapping ways of one and the same psyche's functioning. Nevertheless, they are broadly distinguishable and at times have quite startling sharpness and distinctness. *The original needy, object-seeking, and ego-developing infant psyche remains the basis of all psychic functioning*, but in a rejected state of fear and unsatisfied need which Fairbairn called the *libidinal ego* to indicate that it is not an impersonal biological 'id' but the primary aspect of the potentially personal 'whole' psychosomatic self, an ego, however primitive and undeveloped. Over against this, a newly developing persecuting ego-function develops in which the psyche directs its energies to hating its infantile weakness and striving to subdue it rather than protect it. This Fairbairn at first called the internal saboteur, and then *the antilibidinal ego*. It produces a psychical condition in which *natural maturing* becomes impossible. It is Freud's 'sadistic superego', which can only be the basis of a pseudo- or pathological morality, and of illness. Over against these functionings which become mainly repressed and unconscious, and are most easily recognized in sado-masochistic dreams, fantasies, and symptoms, there is an ego-function in which the psyche is seeking to cope with the outer world and the demand of everyday living, often seeking security by conforming to approved standards. This Fairbairn called the *central ego* which is in principle conscious. Central ego is a familiar term in psychoanalysis, but I am not sure of its appropriateness here. In what sense is this ego-of-outer-world-living 'central'? Fairbairn regarded it as the core of the original psychic whole in touch with the outer world, from which the libidinal and antilibidinal egos are 'split off'. It seems to me that in this sense the libidinal ego would have more right to be called the central ego, the primary needy nature of the child over against which the total self has to develop defences and the capacity to conform to the outer world. Perhaps we may call it the central ego in view of its being the conscious self through which the psychotherapist must work towards the reintegration of the whole self. This illustrates the difficulties of finding a satisfactory terminology. For the time being I shall continue to use Fairbairn's terms, and speak of the central ego as in principle conscious, being the ego of external living, while the conflict between the antilibidinal and the libidinal egos is repressed and kept unconscious so far as possible, to disencumber consciousness in its dealings with the external object world; though its effects can and do seep through into consciousness as immature needs, fears, loves and hates, and symptoms. In the hysteric, the central ego is much influenced by the suffering libidinal ego and is dependent and help-seeking. ('Attention-seeking' is a most inadequate description.) In depressed and obsessional persons the central ego may be all but captured by the antilibidinal ego. In these patients, hostile self-attack and punishing self-mastery are quite visible. All sado-masochistic phenomena are expressions of the deep-down persecution of the libidinal ego by the antilibidinal ego.

Here is an accurate analysis of the fact that Freud made quite explicit, that *very early in life a human being tends to become cruelly divided against himself and becomes a self-frustrating and at times even a self-destroying creature*. Such an individual falls ill eventually because his secret sadistic attack upon himself, his despising of his immaturity, his hating of his weakness, and his attempts to crush out his unsatisfied libidinal needs for spontaneous and creative living, become a much greater danger and menace to him than the outer world normally and usually is. *This extraordinary condition of the psyche makes all the normal processes of maturing impossible and is the source of resistance to psychotherapy*. The libidinal ego's fear of the antilibidinal ego comes to be even greater than the fear of the external world, which is often felt to reflect it. Difficulties in real life that could actually be met and coped with, are repeatedly felt to be intolerable because of the weakening effect of the self-persecution and the incessant fear and hate kept going inside; the basis on which later morbid guilt is developed.

While the primary failure of ego-development, which we must consider in the next two chapters, is the ultimate source of all personality 'difficulties', we must regard the hard core of personality 'illness' as this persisting structuralized version of intolerance and rejection, through fear and later guilt, of the originally disturbed child, now existing as the deepest repressed immature level of the personality, debarred from the opportunity of further maturing. This is compensated for by the forcing of a pseudo-patterned adult ego on the level of everyday consciousness, an artifact, not a natural growth from the depths of the primary nature. The degree of self-hate and self-persecution going on in the unconscious determines the degree of the illness, and in severe cases the person can become hopeless, panic-stricken, and be driven to suicide as a way out. An estimate of the intensity of this can sometimes be got from the patient's reactions to actual difficult children and to immaturity in grown-ups, and also from their sado-masochistic dreams, and the painfulness of their physical psychogenic symptoms. A patient in a panic over extreme environmental pressure which she was in no condition internally to cope with, said, 'I wish I could have a baby and give it hell for years and years like I have had.' The central ego is partly a struggle to cope with the outer world, and partly a defensive system against the dangers of the inner world. It perhaps deserves a better label than Winnicott's term 'false self'. It is the result of an often heroic struggle to stay alive and discover a *modus vivendi*, and in this process the individual has had to make use of his actual abilities and has often achieved important results. The central ego possesses knowledge and has developed skills that must remain a part of the whole matured self. Yet it is a 'False Self' in so far as it is a conformist self in which creativity and originality have had to be sacrificed to safety and the need for external support. The pattern that is conformed to will vary with the cultural environment and may be tough, hard, competitive, submissive to authority, self-sacrificing, intellectual, obsessively moral, and so on. But it is not really the patient's true and proper self for it finds no room for his uniqueness and individuality. 'False self' might more truly describe the antilibidinal ego; yet even that must be respected as the patient's desperate struggle to keep himself functioning in the absence of genuine help. *The sado-masochistic deadlock between the cruel antilibidinal ego attacking the weak and suffering libidinal ego in the deep unconscious is the hard core of the illness, against which the central ego, so far as its internal functions are concerned, is a defence.* That ego-weakness is not due to lack of energy is evident from the tremendous energy shown by the antilibidinal ego in psychic self-attack. The libidinal ego feels weak because the focus of energy has shifted to the antilibidinal self-persecuting function. *Ego-weakness can exist along with psychic strength.*

One patient, a single woman in her early forties, in whom 'the illness' so seriously sabotaged her capacity to carry on normal relationships that it was only with great difficulty that she could keep a job, revealed this internal self-persecutory situation naïvely and without disguise. She would rave against girl children and in fantasy would describe how she would crush a girl child if she had one, and would then fall to punching herself (which perpetuated the beatings her mother gave her). One day I said to her, 'You must feel terrified being hit like that.' She stopped and stared and said, 'I'm not being hit. I'm the one that's doing the hitting.' Another patient, much older, exhibited the same self-persecutory set-up verbally. Whenever she made any slight mistake, she would begin shouting at herself at the top of her voice: 'You stupid thing! Why don't you think! You ought to have known better!' and so on, which were in fact the very words her mother used against her in daily nagging. We see in an unmistakable way the antilibidinal ego as an identification with the angry parent in a vicious attack on the libidinal ego which is denied comfort, understanding, and support, treated as a bad selfish child, and even more deeply feared and hated as a weak child. The first of these patients said she was always crying as a child and despised herself for it. Ultimately she managed to suppress this symptom of childhood misery and depression and its place was taken by these furious outbursts of self-hate.

In these two examples the central ego has been captured by the antilibidinal ego, which is openly and undisguisedly a self-hater. In the following example, the whole pattern of threefold splitting is revealed, though the antilibidinal ego is kept under strong controlling repression. The patient, a man in his forties, had a most unhappy early home-life and was a badly depressed child. He grew to despise himself as a 'cry-baby' and a 'little worm'. He repressed this tearful little boy and built up a rigidly controlled, capable, unemotional, and aloof central ego to deal with the outer world. But he suffered from recurring bouts of depression and his emotional life in the inner world was expressed in violent sado-masochistic fantasies and dreams.

After a long analysis during which his depressed childhood self was drawn nearer to consciousness in recognizable form, he came to his session one day saying: 'Just before I set out I felt apprehensive, as if I could burst into tears; a reaction I suppose to coming here.' When I asked him why he should feel depressed at coming to see me, he replied: 'I see a picture of a little boy shut up alone in a room, crying. If one were in a house where there was such a child, it would depend on how interesting one's work was whether you were aware of him. Sometimes I am aware of him and at other times when very busy I can forget him.' I said, 'Your fantasy is really that you as a grown-up person are working in one room and wanting to forget a crying little boy shut up in another room. What about that?' He answered, 'The obvious thing is to go to the child and find out why he's crying and comfort him. Why didn't I think of that at first? That strikes me as very odd.' When I replied by asking who shut the little boy in that room and why, he said, 'He's a nuisance. You can't get on with your work with a crying child around.' That answered his question. He did not think of going to help the child, because he regarded him as a nuisance, and he was the person who had shut him away there so as to forget him, or some part of him that did not appear in the fantasy had shut the child away. I suggested that a part of him that aggressively hated the child was being kept hidden, itself repressed, but that it guarded the door in the unconscious and tried not to let the child out or let me in to help. He said that he saw that that must be true but he was not conscious of feeling any such self-hate. I was able to remind him that in the previous session he had said: 'I like to think that I can be tolerant to a problem child and to the problem child in myself, but I can't. I am intolerant and aggressive to myself, and though I disagree with the way my parents brought me up, I operate *en bloc* all their standards against myself.' (Transference implications in this material have not been touched on, as it is used specifically to cast light on endopsychic structure.)

Here is a clear picture of the threefold differentiation of the ego: the central ego of everyday living working in one room and wanting to forget what is going on elsewhere; the distressed, weak and helpless child shut away in the unconscious as a disowned and hated libidinal ego in an immature state; and the implied, if repressed, antilibidinal ego hating the child and regarding him as a nuisance to be got rid of. *It is as if once the child is badly disturbed, and developed enough to realize that he is too weak to alter his environment, he feels driven to attempt the only other thing possible, namely to alter himself in such a way that he no longer feels so frightened and weak, or at least seeks to prevent himself from being conscious of it.* Unless there is someone to understand and help, this will be his only way of avoiding complete withdrawal into himself and the development of a schizophrenic ego. He comes to dislike himself intensely in the state he is in and, so to speak, detaches this hostile part of himself and sends it on a mission to crush out the frightened, needy, and therefore dependent child, so as to leave the rest of himself free to cope with the outer world with something more of the feeling of being a personality. He cannot know that his outer-world self will thereafter suffer a perpetual fear of the inner weakness. It is the struggle for an ego all the time. The more superficially successful this trick is (and parents so often help and educate the child to perform it), the more self-destructive it becomes, because the crushed child is the primary, natural self and his repression progressively leads to self-exhaustion. We have to think of this threefold 'splitting' of the ego as the pattern of a total strategy for facing life in an attempt to 'negotiate from strength, not weakness'. Again we must remind ourselves that this terminology of 'three egos' simply represents the fact that the same psyche can function in different ways at the same time, sometimes quite consciously so, and these three particular ways are so persistent and important that we need terms to identify and refer to them. *The one thing that the child cannot do for himself is to give himself a basic sense of security, since that is a function of object-relationship.* All that can be done is for the central ego to seek to become independent of needs for other people. The patient can become self-blinded and deluded into believing that hating is the only way to carry on, including hate of himself in so far as he wants to be different; and some aspects of the outer world support that view. In fact, *justice must be done to the antilibidinal ego because it is the child's struggle to keep himself going when he feels afraid and has no real help.*

We may now refer back to Freud's statement about psychotherapy as 'aiming to strengthen the ego and make it more independent of the superego'. This view embodies prophetic insight and gives us a basic truth about psychotherapy, but the terms now need reinterpretation. The ego that needs to be strengthened is not just the central ego or 'outer-reality ego' of everyday living in consciousness, but the patient's primary nature which is repressed and arrested in development in a state of frustrated, weak, frightened, and suffering immaturity. A problem of theory forces itself upon us here. Freud thought of the primary nature as consisting of separate and distinct biological instincts apart altogether from the ego, which he regarded as a superficial 'structure' invaded by primitive impulses arising from the instincts, the 'id'. Winnicott appears to retain this concept of 'impulses originating outside the ego' with one hand while he lets it go with the other. He writes:

I think it will be generally agreed that id-impulse is only significant if it is contained in ego-living. An id-impulse either disrupts a weak ego or else strengthens a strong one. (1965b, p. 33.)

This way of writing implies more than that the psyche has a biological substrate or basis. It implies that 'ego' is limited to Freud's superficial ego which is only one aspect of the psychic whole, so that impulse originates outside the ego which it invades. But this use of 'ego' is no longer adequate. *We need the term 'ego' to denote a state or developmental condition of the psychic whole, the entire self. 'Ego' expresses the psyche's self-realization and every psychic process has 'ego-quality'*, be it that of a weak ego or a strong one, a barely more than potential primitive ego in the new-born infant or a fully developed ego in an adult. We must say rather that a psyche with a too weak ego-sense is disrupted by its own impulses. The whole history of the psyche is that of ego-development towards the goal of self-realization, self-awareness, and self-responsibility, not by integration of disparate elements but by differentiation within a growing whole. The psyche begins as a potential primitive ego at an absolute starting-point, and should end as a fully matured ego, and from beginning to end its impulses are its own. Id and ego, energy and structure, as separate elements, is not a possible concept today. What orthodox theory has called 'id-impulse' is not only not significant if it is not contained in ego-living; impulse can only be thought of as contained in either weak or strong ego-living, for 'ego' *means* the growing potentiality of the psyche for realizing itself as a 'person'. In the absence of an ego, however undeveloped, there would be no psychic subject of which impulse could be predicated, except at the very earliest dim beginnings of an individual's psychic existence.

When Winnicott writes: 'an id-impulse disrupts a weak ego', he is describing the condition I described in the words 'Ego-weakness can exist along with psychic strength' (p. 209). The psyche's energies are innate factors, and the psyche's potential ego-quality is also an innate factor that awaits development. The infant psyche whose ego-development is as yet elementary needs the help of the mother's closest support for containing and finding satisfaction for its energetic needs, as Winnicott convincingly shows. If he is left inadequately supported, he rapidly loses the simple wholeness that is the starting-point of ego-growth. He becomes what Winnicott calls 'a collection of reactions to impingement'. Splitting processes have begun. The use of the term 'id-impulse' as if it stood for some entity originating outside the simple infant ego or psychic whole, invading and disrupting it, seems to me inconsistent with Winnicott's fundamentally 'ego-psychology'. I would not say that 'id-impulse strengthens a strong ego' but rather that 'strong impulse is here part and parcel of a strong ego'. 'Impulse' cannot even be thought except as part of ego-living, otherwise there is no one whose impulse it is. This is involved and implied when Winnicott (1965a) writes: 'From the beginning it is possible for the observer to see that an infant is already a human being, a unit' (1965a). Thus whereas Freud thought of the superego as a tyrant ordering the hard-pressed ego to master powerful id-impulses that were not part of itself, we must think of the central ego repressing and the antilibidinal ego persecuting an infantile libidinal ego which is both too weak and undeveloped and too weakened by early ego-splitting to be able to manage its own vital energetic needs. As I have already stated, the id-ego theory lands us in the philosophical dualism of 'matter and mind'. I shall, therefore, express Freud's insight into psychotherapy by saying that it 'aims to strengthen the infantile libidinal ego and make it more independent of the sadistic superego, the antilibidinal ego'. In truth, this means helping the patient to become reconciled to accepting help for his weakness, so that the libidinal ego may become re-endowed with the energies that had been turned to antilibidinal ends.

If the primary natural self, containing the individual's true potentialities, can be reached, protected, supported, and freed from the internal persecutor, it is capable of rapid development and integration with all that is valuable and realistic in the central ego. The total psyche, having regained its proper wholeness, will be restored to full emotional capacity, spontaneity, and creativeness. Resistance to this therapeutic process is long kept up by the antilibidinal ego which dedicates all the patient's anger, hate, and aggression to crushing his needs and fears. The antilibidinal ego is not re-integrated *qua* antilibidinal. Its aggression is taken back into the service of the libidinal ego and matured. The patient, in his antilibidinal functioning, to quote Fairbairn (1952) 'uses a maximum of his aggression to subdue a maximum of his libidinal need'. The reason is that libidinal need is held to be the main characteristic of the dependent infant, and all dependence is hated as weakness. The antilibidinal ego seeks to maintain a personality without needs for other people, self-sufficient, ultra-independent, hard and rejective. It always fails to recognize that its patterning by identification with the rejective parent, and its 'power-cult' in relationships of domination over others are actually only thinly disguised dependence. That is why persons of this conscious type of personality usually break down when they lose those they have tyrannized over.

The hostility, however, of the antilibidinal ego to direct dependence on anyone for help, and its hating to admit needs, is the most stubborn source of resistance to psychotherapy, and of resistance to the psychotherapist. It hates the needy child inside and hates the therapist to whom he desires to turn for help. Its opposition is so unyielding that it is the great barrier to psychotherapy. It keeps the basic self weak by active persecution and by denying it any relationship in which it could grow strong. This is illustrated remarkably clearly in two dreams of a patient:

I was a little girl, standing at the door of a large room, trembling with fear. I saw you inside and thought, 'If only I could get to him I'd be safe.' I ran across the room but another girl strode up and pushed me back to the door.

Some two years later, when the patient was trusting me much more fully, she dreamed this same dream again. This time she got to within an inch of being able to touch me when the other girl emerged, as it were, from nowhere at the last moment, smacked her viciously across the face and drove her away again. This is the field of detailed psychopathology where close psychodynamic analysis is so necessary if one is to find out exactly what is happening in the patient. I have had a number of dreams from a variety of patients in which one or other of their parents sought to interfere with or stop the analysis. One woman dreamed that her mother followed her into my room and tried to shoot her as she was entering. Another woman patient felt that her mother was hovering outside the window trying to break up the session. A male patient dreamed that his mother burst into the room and planted herself between him and me, saying to him, 'What have you been saying about me?' and to me, 'What ideas are you putting into my son's head?'

Such dreams represent a process of opposition that is developing in the patient's mind against the analyst and hostile to the treatment, and the process belongs to the Antilibidinal Ego with its identifications with rejective parents. The identification is not usually so obvious and undisguised as in these instances.

Moreover, it is not necessarily clear to the patient that his rejection and hate of the analyst and of his own infantile libidinal self go together. He may voice one or the other, but only rarely both together. One patient expressed a serious degree of ego-weakness followed by equally virulent self-rejection, thus: 'I feel inferior, I'm not sure of my identity, I've made a mess of life, I'm feeble, poor, and don't feel worth anything. Away from mother it all feels messy inside me, not solid, like a jelly fish. I'm nothing definite and substantial, only frightened, waffling, and clinging to anything for safety, it's an indescribable feeling.' Then she went on: 'I hate myself, I wish I wasn't me, I'd like to get rid of myself.' Here is her self-rejection, her antilibidinal concentration on running herself down, but on another occasion her antilibidinal reaction turns to rob her of my help. She said: 'I felt very small all this week and dependent on you. Then I felt I ought to be more independent of you and stop coming to you. Mother thinks I ought to be able to do without treatment now. I feel guilty about it, but I'm not strong enough yet not to have your support.' Often the antilibidinal reaction against the analyst is more serious. One patient, at a time of great strain over an event which greatly disturbed her, oscillated between an intensified need for my help and, on one occasion, an outburst, motivated by very serious fear of her panicky feelings of weakness, in which she said with great tension: 'You want me to come creeping and crawling to you, but I'll show you.'

Nevertheless, the more difficult antilibidinal reactions to treatment are those which are subtly disguised and only develop slowly in the unconscious. It is certain that *whenever a patient begins to turn to the analyst with any deeper and more genuine measure of trust and dependence and acceptance of help, at once a hidden process of opposition starts up*, and will sooner or later gather strength and lead to a subtle change of mood that makes the patient no longer able to co-operate as fully as he consciously wishes to. These antilibidinal reactions to anyone from whom help or affection is needed and sought are not confined to analysis, and they conspicuously sabotage marital and sexual relations. In fact the patient's mood can turn against anything and everything that is good, valuable, and helpful in life, as if in secret he were playing to himself the part of the mother in the dream of the patient who was eating her favourite meal, when the mother snatched it away and said, 'Don't be a baby.' The antilibidinal ego will snatch everything away if it can: analysis, friends, religious comforts, creative activities, marriage, and we need to be able to determine the exact source of its power, remembering that it is not an entity *per se* but one aspect of the patient's total, if divided, self, and withal to be respected as his genuine struggle to keep his ego in being, originally in the absence of all help.

The Static Internal Closed System

We may now recognize the antilibidinal factor in the personality, which is the source of resistance to psychotherapy, as the same factor which has all along *obstructed any natural basic maturing of the ego*, once it has become disturbed. This antilibidinal factor arises out of the child's necessity, as it seems to him, to make himself independent of all help, since the kind of help he requires does not seem obtainable. He must make his own internal arrangements to maintain his personality and stand by them. These arrangements consist of his own version of an antilibidinal ego sadistically mastering the weak and frightened libidinal ego. Bound up with this is the world of internal objects which Kleinian analysis has laid bare. With regard to this set-up in its entirety, Fairbairn (1958) spoke of:

> A further defensive aim which I have now come to regard as the greatest of all sources of resistance—*viz.* the maintenance of the patient's internal world as a closed system.

He describes the dreams of one patient as reflecting

> a movement in the direction of maintaining relationships with objects in the inner world at the expense of a realistic and therapeutic relationship with the analyst, *viz.* a movement having the aim of preserving inner reality as a closed system. Such an aim on the patient's part seems to me to constitute the most formidable resistance encountered in psychoanalytical treatment.

He also regards this 'closed system' as a 'static internal situation'.

Thus, one of my patients, writing to me from a residential Conference, explained why she had not written earlier although she had felt extremely anxious, saying: 'It was important to me to be able at least to *contain it* without having to come flying to you for help. I would just be too humiliated.' The same patient once said: 'Sometimes I feel I can only keep myself going by hating, I can't stop fighting, I won't give it up, I can't give in. I feel I'll lose everything if I do', a desperate antilibidinal struggle for an ego by means of independence. This desperate state of mind had come into being because she had had to fight all through her childhood to maintain a personality of her own in face of an over-powering, frightening father. But to resist his dominion, she had to fight not only against him but against her fear of him. The frightened child had to force herself to defy the angry father, even though that could only mean increasing fear and emotional exhaustion. Her mother told her that at the age of three, she had stood screaming at her father 'I hate you, I hate you.' In having to fight him with his own weapons she reproduced some of his attitudes, such as the view that all human beings are selfish and only fight for their own ends, and that love is weakness, a truly antilibidinal attitude embodying a cynical view of life. This cynical antilibidinal ego was a mental reproduction of her father so far as her attitude to her needy and frightened child-self was concerned. That had to be crushed out for the purposes of the 'fight', so that her libidinal ego was in the terrifying position of being faced with an internal version of the intolerant father as another part of herself from which there was no escape. This can drive a personality into a state of disintegration as a defence.

The antilibidinal ego, being considerably based on identification with the external bad object, involves resisting that bad object by a method that opens the gates of the fortress and lets him inside. By the time the patient had left home, she was more persecuted by her paternal antilibidinal ego inside than by her actual difficult father outside. Yet in this predicament, every patient agrees in saying: 'I can't change. I feel hopeless.' Whatever his more realistic central ego desires, the closed self-persecutory system of his inner world will only admit the analyst if it can fit him into its own pattern. It will not admit him as someone seeking to change the state of affairs and rescue the suffering libidinal ego from its plight. This 'closed system' situation is illustrated by a painting done by the above-quoted patient. It was a closed picture frame, the inside edge of which was an unbroken array of sharp teeth all pointing in at the patient. She lay as a helpless masochistic figure in the bottom righthand corner, faced with two menacing swords and a great hammer crashing down on her. Detached, but also inside the frame, were two praying hands stretched out appealing for help, but in vain because there was no one inside that set-up who represented a helper; the hands could not get outside to make their appeal, and no one could get in to bring aid. This is how the unconscious sado-masochistic inner world, inside which the distressed child is imprisoned, is felt by the patient, and it will not surprise us that this patient had suffered a paranoid-schizophrenic breakdown; yet it was she herself who maintained this 'static internal situation' as a 'closed system' while feeling hopeless about her inability to change it. The meaning of this we must consider later. I have found this inner prison often dreamed of as a concentration camp, and at least one such patient dreamed that he had decided to stay in because he might be worse off outside. So it is not only that the antilibidinal ego blocks psychotherapy by shutting the libidinal ego in the torture house and shutting the helpful analyst out. There is a further factor to take into account. The libidinal ego does not seem to be able to give up its persecutor. Clearly the motivation of this function is more complex than we have yet considered.

The problem of the analyst is, on the one hand, how to prevent himself being merely fitted into the pattern of this inner world as either a persecutor hated by the libidinal ego, or the libidinal object hated by the antilibidinal ego, two types of negative transference; and, on the other hand, how to break into this closed system as a helper to initiate change. The system cannot be absolutely closed or no progress would ever be made at all, but every little breach that is made in it at once evokes a powerful antilibidinal reaction aimed at closing it again. Every time the patient seeks help and protection through relying on the analyst in a positive transference, a negative transference immediately begins to develop unconsciously and presently breaks out. Thus a naïve enthusiasm on the part of the analyst in taking sides with the libidinal ego, and an over-anxious pressing desire to 'save' the patient is most likely to provoke a fierce antilibidinal reaction and be self-defeating.

Freud wrote concerning the 'negative therapeutic reaction':

> There is something in these people that sets itself against their recovery and dreads its approach as though it were a danger. . . . In the end we come to see that we are dealing with what may be called a 'moral' factor, a sense of guilt, which is finding atonement in the illness and is refusing to give up the penalty of suffering. We

are justified in regarding this rather disheartening explanation as conclusive. But as far as the patient is concerned this sense of guilt is dumb; it does not tell him he is guilty; he does not feel guilty, he simply feels ill. This sense of guilt expresses itself only as a resistance to recovery which it is extremely difficult to overcome. It is also particularly difficult to convince the patient that this motive lies behind his continuing to be ill; he holds fast to the more obvious explanation that treatment by analysis is not the right remedy for his case. (Freud, 1923.)

There can be no doubt that guilt does block psychotherapy in this way. In its most profound form it can be a feeling of guilt about going on existing at all. I have found more than one patient with a definite sense that he ought not to have been born at all, he was not the right sort of child and was not wanted, and was the cause of his parents' unhappiness and troubles; and if he does go on existing he must pay an unceasing penalty. One such patient, whose parents quarrelled a great deal, would always search back till she came upon something she had done which she was sure was the cause of their quarrel; it was all her fault.

Nevertheless this kind of guilt is not a simple reaction to events, and though it is a powerful factor in the 'negative therapeutic reaction', it calls for deeper understanding. Guilt is felt not only over destructive impulses, but also over weakness; but further than that, guilt is itself an object-relation, and pathological guilt is the maintenance of a guilt-relation to an internalized bad parent whom the patient feels quite unable to give up. Any kind of object-relation, even if it cause suffering, is a defence against more primitive terrors which we shall explore in the next chapter. Meanwhile we are back in the static internal closed system in which the patient suffers without hope. Freud adds a footnote to the passage in which he says:

The battle with the obstacle of an unconscious sense of guilt is not made easy for the analyst. Nothing can be done against it directly, and nothing indirectly but the slow procedure of unmasking its unconscious repressed roots, and of thus gradually changing it into a conscious sense of guilt.

This is even more true when we seek to go deeper than the guilt motive. Freud is drawing attention to the need for more rigorous analysis and the making conscious of all the motives that sustain what now appears as the closed system of the inner world of internal bad objects and the antilibidinal ego, in which is concentrated all the patient's secret and repressed hatred of his infantile dependent libidinal ego, the source of his basic weakness; but also his fear that if he were to give up or escape from his bad objects, he could be left with no objects at all and be facing the ultimate, and what Winnicott (1965b) calls the *unthinkable*, anxieties. If direct assault on this inner redoubt only intensifies resistance, perhaps an analysis that goes deep enough can infiltrate and get behind it.

Analysis of Motives Sustaining the Antilibidinal Ego

We seek to know how a patient can escape from his self-hate and his destructive relationship to internalized bad objects, so as to be free to enter into a constructive therapeutic relationship with the analyst. The closed system itself must have constructive implications or the patient would not maintain it with such desperate determination when it involves him in so much suffering. The factors that sustain it are certainly complex.

(*a*) *The Antilibidinal Ego represents an Object-Relationship with Parents*

Whether we view the libidinal ego as in bondage to guilt or fear, that is imposed by an antilibidinal ego which in part represents the frightening or accusing parents who have themselves disturbed the child. Fear and guilt are both object-relations, and undoubtedly in the end human beings prefer bad relationships to none at all. The infant in the first place was in distress because he could not get a good relationship. Thus his need of his parents was intensified, and had to be met both by suffering under them and identifying with them as bad objects. It is a long-standing psychoanalytical view that identification is a substitute for a lost object-relation. The infant comes to possess his disturbing parents in himself, in developing an antilibidinal ego, and its dissolution will therefore feel to him to be the equivalent of loss of parents. An inability to separate from parents with whom the relationship is mainly bad is illustrated by a patient sent for treatment during the war. She stated that she knew what was the matter with her. She had to live with her parents and they hated her and she hated them, but she could not get away. It was wartime and she could not get another job with as good a wage, and digs were hard to get. But it emerged that, a few weeks before seeing me, she had been offered promotion with an increased wage, with accommodation provided in another town, and she had refused it. She was too insecure to venture and therefore too attached to break away. She had made her external life an exact replica of her internal closed system and could not escape. Nor could she let me help, for when she had given me this information she abruptly stopped coming. Though the internal bad-object situation is felt to be persecution and a prison, the infantile libidinal ego is afraid to leave it. Thus a male patient dreamed of being in prison and being offered a chance to escape, and pointing out of the window and saying, 'But how would I get on if I found myself out there all alone?' Another patient dreamed of wondering why he did not try to escape from a concentration camp; but thought that though it was a bad place to be in, it was probably worse outside, and he was used to the camp, familiar with its life, and knew how to 'get by'; and he decided to stay in.

This clinging to the closed inner world seems based on the fear that, since one must have parents at all costs, bad parents are better than none, and if you break away you will be out of the frying pan into the fire. That attachment is also at work is shown in the patient who operated all his parents' standards against himself even though he disagreed with them. There is deep loyalty to the parental mores. The antilibidinal ego goes on 'bringing the patient up' in the same way as the parents did. Furthermore the disturbed child feels a need to be controlled, even though it be by the very parents who upset him.

Out of this, a clash in the patient's mind between parents and analyst often becomes visible in dreams. Thus a female patient who had had physically cruel treatment by her mother as a child, dreamed that she was being hurried along a road by her father who was cross and nagging her, when she saw me on the other side of the street, pulled her hand out of his and dashed across the road to me, refusing to return when he shouted at her. On another occasion she reported a dream that her mother had been beating her when I arrived and drove her mother away. Then later I had to go off on business (the end of the session) and she burst into tears and ran after her mother who began beating her again. A bad object is better than none, she could not be alone and her relation to a cruel mother was her most deeply rooted object-relationship. A striking dream of a female patient was to the effect that she met a terrifying lion and lionesss and fled up a nearby tree for safety. But the tree was a young one and bent under her weight, putting her nearly but not quite back within reach of the animals. She said, 'Of course, the lion and lioness are my parents, and I think you are the young tree. I've known them all my life but I've only known you a year or two, and that's too young a relationship to protect me from their influence. When I'm here I'm sure you know best but when I'm at home I feel they must be right.' One sees here the little-developed libidinal ego which has no convictions of its own.

Patients, however, easily miss the real implication of these dreams, as if it were now still a question of relationships with their actual parents. They do not easily grasp the fact that the parents in their dreams are parts of themselves, processes going on in their own minds, and represent now not so much their real parents as their own parent influenced self, the antilibidinal ego in which they possess their parents by identifying themselves with them. It is necessary to make this clear, not only in the interests of solving their internal problems, but also in the interests of allowing for improved realistic relations with the actual parents where they are still alive.

(b) *The Antilibidinal Ego further represents the Struggle to Possess an Ego*

The more ill a patient is, the more certain it is that analysis will in the end bring to light extremely frightening feelings of having no proper or satisfactory ego of his own. Here is the basic ego-weakness of which we have spoken. We have seen how, in the struggle to achieve an ego strong enough to live by, the child turns against his own actual ego as infantile, weak, and all too prone to betray him into the power of disturbing adults through his dependent needs. The ferocity with which this internal 'turning against the self' can persist for years into subsequent adult life is seen in this dream of a man of forty.

I saw a small dog in the house. It looked weak and was falling over on its side and lay there as if injured. I tried to shoo it away but it did not move. I suddenly felt an intense fury against it and wanted to kick it out. I felt I shouldn't treat it like that, but if I pushed it with my hands even that little dog might bite. Then it wasn't there. Then it was there again.

The little dog, like the fantasy of the crying little boy quoted earlier, was the infantile libidinal ego, the small hurt little child of years ago still alive within, hated, ignored but thrusting itself again into notice.

In proportion as the repression of this original libidinally needy self is successful, it leaves the child with little ego of his own: or perhaps we should say that in order to achieve this repression of his original self, the child must borrow an ego from elsewhere to do it with. However we put it, an identification is made with parents, and this comes to take the place of any further natural development in the child of an ego that is genuinely his own. The identification with bad objects serves as a substitute for proper ego-growth. Thus the dissolving of this identification is likely to be felt by the patient as the loss of his own personality, as well as the loss of parents. Since he has not been able to grow a mature ego of his own with deep roots in his primary nature, if he gives up the antilibidinal ego he has nothing to fall back on but his infantile dependent self. This amounts to a loss of object-relationships in his inner world, and he feels threatened with a regression or a collapse, the extent of which he cannot foresee. We must remind ourselves that the antilibidinal ego represents the inner retention of a bad object-relationship as a means of carrying on the struggle to retain an active ego to live by in spite of fears. Thus, since it represents both an object-relationship and an ego, in a situation where the patient does not possess either in a satisfactory form, it is apparent that he will have the greatest difficulty in growing out of this unnatural growth in personality structure.

(c) *The Antilibidinal Ego confers a Sense of Power, even if only over the Self*

This is involved in the two previous situations. The child feels weak because he cannot master his environment to better his situation. If he identifies with the persecutory adults in order to repress his infantile self, he is taking on the personality of those who appear as the powerful figures in his little world. Undoubtedly, patients experience a sinister sense of power and satisfaction in exercising a cruel and destructive repression of their own anxious child self. This is apparent when one patient fantasied scenes of angry and aggressive treatment of a child: 'Wouldn't I love to make it squirm. I'd break every bone in its vile little body, I'd crush it.' This cruelty to the child in fantasy is cruelty to the child within and is the root of all cruel treatment of real children. One regularly finds patients who are parents dreaming of their inward treatment of their own immature ego under the symbol of similar treatment of their own children. One such dream is particularly clear. The patient, a male, dreamed:

I and my father and my little boy were walking in the park by the lake. Suddenly my son broke away, dashed to the rowing boats, jumped into one and pulled off. He wanted to do things on his own. My father and I looked at each other. The lad had to be taught a lesson and I got into a boat and rowed after him, tipped him into the water to teach him and then pulled him out and brought him back to where my father was.

Here is the original father–son relationship repeating itself, by means of an obvious identification, in the next generation. But the sense of power over the child is itself an ego-booster. The child whose self-confidence has been undermined seeks to restore it by the exercise of power over himself, a dangerous antilibidinal situation that effectively puts an end to all normal development, especially of the power to love. Enjoying a feeling of power in self-hate easily alternates with feeling a sense of power over others by hating them. The cultivation of a fictitious sense of strength in the hating, antilibidinal ego, i.e. an embittered personality, has to substitute for genuine ego-strength.

Thus, in and through his antilibidinal ego, the patient enjoys a feeling of object-relationship and the security of being under control, the sense of the possession of an ego, and the feeling of power, even though it is all in a fundamentally self-destructive way. He is not likely to be able to sacrifice all this easily, unless he feels very sure of getting something far better in exchange. His problem is that he must risk dropping all pretences with himself that he is more adult and tough than he really feels to be deep down, in order that he may come back to the anxious child that he once was and still feels to be inside; and begin again from there, and this time in the security of a parental personal relationship, to treat this injured part of himself in a more constructive manner that promotes genuine growth instead of an artificial toughness as a mask for hidden fear.

The Analytical Outflanking of the Internal Closed System

We have seen that Freud, faced with the negative therapeutic reaction, came to the conclusion that nothing could be done against it directly. In fact, the analysis of the antilibidinal resistance to psychotherapy in terms of the motives described in the last section, does not by any means dissolve the resistance, though it paves the way for it. If it did, analytical psychotherapy would be a speedier process. My impression is that continued analysis of the internal bad-object world in terms of its contents only, perpetuates anxiety and confirms the patient in its maintenance. He becomes bogged down in an 'interminable analysis' of what is actually a 'security system' in spite of its psychopathological effects. If we cannot break up the closed system by a direct attack, perhaps we can outflank it by dealing with what it is a defence against. If laying bare its motivations piece-meal, motivations of both object-relations and ego-maintenance, does not of itself enable the patient to relinquish it, then we must take it as a whole and seek to know more of what lies behind its existence as a total structure. Why do human beings maintain an internal object-relations world at all, especially when it is a bad one? What greater danger is being avoided in electing to face the dangers of internal bad-object experience, which in the extreme may go as far as schizophrenic terrors of a paranoid variety and depressive paralysis?

The answer to this question must provide a still deeper understanding of the basic ego-weakness that is the tap-root of all later problems. So far we have only considered the *repression* of the weak, though still actively needy and demanding libidinal ego, in the interests of the central ego of outer-world living. There is another range of phenomena of a quite different kind consisting of *withdrawal*. What is repressed is thrust into unconsciousness because it is felt to be a danger to our conscious life and activity in the social world. But withdrawal is a retreat from the dangers which in the first place come from the outer world. Part I was devoted to a descriptive clinical study of this schizoid retreat from the outer to the inner world, which of recent years has attracted increasing attention. Fairbairn's view was examined that withdrawal is due to the outer world arousing needs of destructive intensity, so that the fear of destroying love-objects precipitates a breaking-off of object-relations. Winnicott stresses impingement or pressure of an intolerable kind by external reality on the tender infantile psyche, causing it to shrink back into itself out of reach of harm. Perhaps most fundamentally he stresses the failure of supportive mothering, into which we must enquire more closely in the next chapter. Whatever the occasion, very early and elementary fear is the motivating force behind the withdrawal of an essential part of the whole self from object-relations in real life.

Both repression of, and withdrawal by, the infantile libidinal ego prevent further normal development of the basic natural self. But schizoid withdrawal into an inner world seems ultimately a more important cause of ego-weakness than repression, especially when we consider how far it may go. It is a more radical process than repression, which I suggest is a secondary phenomenon arising when attempts to counteract withdrawal lead to the generation of dangerous anti-social impulses. These arise out of the maintenance of an internal world of bad-object relations, which suggests that the function of this world as a whole is to prevent a too drastic schizoid withdrawal from the condition of an active ego in object-relations. It halts the retreat from reality half-way, and saves the ego from a total breaking off of object-relationships. The destructive love-needs Fairbairn describes call for both repression of antisocial impulse (oral sadism) and the withdrawal of the oral sadistic libidinal ego from the outer world to operate only in an internal fantasy world. The fear-dictated retreat from impingement of which Winnicott speaks must be continued into an attempt even to escape from *internal* bad objects, a withdrawal of a more radical kind such as constitutes regression. Much clinical material seems to me to demonstrate that we are here dealing with two different levels of inner reality. Only when we reach and deal with the patient's deepest 'withdrawnness', are we getting at the real roots of his trouble. Here all the problems of regression will be encountered, the most difficult of all problems for psychotherapy.

Some degree of withdrawnness from full contact with outer reality can be found in the background of all psychopathological phenomena, as the result of fear. Thus a patient in his forties recovered sufficiently under psychoanalytic treatment to be able not only to resume work, but to pass some accountancy exams he had never before been able to study for effectively. At that stage he said: 'I find I don't take much notice of the weather. I'm too busy inside watching myself and I don't take a lot of notice of what goes on outside me. Mother said I used to "swoon" and I'm afraid of fainting. It's like losing myself, it feels like going down inside myself and losing consciousness. At times I've been afraid to go to sleep. As a boy I was afraid to lie down in bed in case I got smothered, and could only sleep propped up on pillows. I remember when small thinking "I wonder who I am? Why am I here" I suspected I didn't belong to the family and would feel thousands of miles away.' Here are all the marks of an early schizoid withdrawal into himself, and it carries with it the threat of depersonalization of the conscious self. He begins not to know himself. He then dreamed:

I suddenly found I still had the little dog I possessed as a boy. I'd had it shut up in a box and forgotten all these years and thought 'Why is it in there? It's time I let it out.' To my surprise it wasn't angry at being shut in but pleased now to be let out.

The dog represented a specifically withdrawn 'ego of childhood' recognizable as structurally distinct. Only now could he feel that it might come out again. This appears to be what Winnicott means by a 'true self' put in cold storage and awaiting a chance of rebirth.

The difference between repression and withdrawal was brought home to me forcibly by a patient who worked through an hysteric phase to reveal a basic schizoid condition. In the hysteric phase she dreamed of being undermined in her adult life by a hungry baby whom she kept hidden under her apron, and who needed feeding though she could not attend to it. Here was her needy, demanding, internally active oral libidinal ego, and energy had to be drawn off from her outer world life to keep it repressed. Gradually she worked through the hysteric phase and lost the physical symptoms associated with it, only to find herself frighteningly detached and out of touch with everything, living in a mechanical way, and markedly schizoid. Against this danger, her hysteria had been a defence. She would then begin every session with the quiet remark, 'You're miles away, you've gone away from me', projecting on to me her own withdrawnness. She then reported a lump in her tummy. She was sure it was in her womb and was terrified that if she told the doctor he would 'take it away' and that would be the end of her; she would be only an empty shell. Clearly she felt this lump symbolized the vital heart of her self. She thought of it as a baby but never as an active hungry baby, only as a dead baby, or buried alive, lying still, never moving, growing bigger perhaps but it could never get out. She would say, 'I can't come out. I'll only be rejected.' She had been an unwanted baby, parked out on her mother's sister who did not want to be burdened with her. Faced with her frightening withdrawnness, she had reverted again to the hysteric defence of a conversion symptom, but now the bodily substitute represented not a hungry oral ego but a withdrawn frightened regressed ego buried in the womb of the unconscious.

In this part of the personality one finds that what is important is not sex or aggression but fear simply. Thus an elderly spinster lost by death a valued friend, and felt empty, lifeless, and would wake at night with 'airy fairy feelings like a little nothing floating in the void'. This depersonalization by loss of a good object, she began to counteract by taking refuge in bad object-relations in the form of quarrelling with neighbours. Then insomnia developed as a defence against the felt risk of losing herself in sleep, and she lay awake 'thinking'. She said, 'It doesn't matter what I think about so long as I keep thinking about something', a struggle to keep her adult ego in being. (Cf. p. 65.) She became exhausted and could hardly drag herself out of bed in the morning. I suggested that she was afraid of facing the world without her friend, and felt an intense need to withdraw and bury herself in bed for safety, and yet she was fighting against that. She replied: 'I've got a peculiar thought. When you said that, I associated myself with an egg-cell in a womb. Yesterday I listened to a radio talk on that and it fascinated me. The man said the fertilized egg finds a soft place in the lining of the uterus and hides away there and grows. I got a mental picture of it and it's come back now.' Then after a pause she became tense and said: 'Oh! a terror of adults has suddenly welled up in me. I feel overwhelmed by the feeling of grown-up people who are so masterful and over-bearing. It's awful, they grip the life out of me. (That was an accurate picture of both her parents.) I couldn't tell this fear to neighbours or friends, only you would understand.' The bereavement has laid bare her withdrawn libidinal ego of an infancy in a hard home. It was no longer either sexual or aggressive, but weak, afraid and longing to remain shut in. Its exposure rearoused her old intense fear of the adult world, and she was only reassured by feeling safe with me.

The deepest root of psychopathological phenomena then is not sexual and/or aggressive instincts. These are the natural energies of the whole psyche and will be experienced primitively in a primitive ego, maturely in a mature ego and pathologically in a pathological ego. In this last case, these instinctive energies belong very much to the struggle to stay in object-relationships and are mobilized in an attempt to counteract a too drastic retreat from reality. They will then flourish in the inner world of dreams and fantasies, where internal object-relations are maintained to serve a double purpose. They satisfy the need to remain withdrawn from the outer world, while they halt the headlong retreat inside short of complete regression to a womb-like state. For regressive trends always tend to fantasies of a return to the womb, intensified needs for bed and sleep, inability to get up in the morning, longings to escape from responsibility and activity, to retire and to feel exhausted, rather than to feel healthy impulse-tension. Impulse-tension is then felt as counterbalancing flight to some safe-inside position.

The more specific is the regressed ego in the personality, the more deep dreamless sleep seems to be equated with re-entry into the safety of the womb, or, from the central ego point of view, profound regression. Then dreaming becomes, not a healthy equivalent of a child's play, but a defence against ego-loss by regression. Sleep will be intensely desired by one part of the personality and intensely feared by another. The dream-world is then half-way between the womb and the outer world. Dreams allow of simultaneous withdrawal from outer reality and the maintenance of an active ego. Daydreams show clearly the withdrawnness from external reality. Night dreams show in addition a resistance to passive dependence in sleep. Insomnia, or refusal to quit the central ego level, is an even more drastic attempted defence against regression. All this is part of the struggle to maintain an active ego in face of a powerful fear-driven urge to withdraw, the struggle to counteract the 'shut-in' self. When this state of being 'locked up inside' is converted into physical symptoms, we are then confronted with constipation, retention of urine, sexual impotence, sinus blocking, the tight band round the head; and the patient's secondary fears of not being able to escape from this self-imprisonment, a claustrophobic reaction, lead to the use of 'opening medicine', nasal inhalers and sprays, and the development of diarrhoea and frequency of micturition. The real trouble is that the patient cannot respond to the outer world with any true feeling except fear. One male patient who gave all the signs of being a hearty extravert, a successful energetic business man, complained of being 'stopped up' physically, and reported all the symptoms I have just mentioned. In fact, he was a bad relaxer, and hard-driven activity betrayed a characteristic drive to maintain perpetual motion. He had to 'keep going'. At his second session he reported a simple vivid dream which startled him:

I walked out of my business, and left my home, wife, and family. I just went away, I don't know where.

—a revelation of the regression and withdrawnness against which he was putting up such a fight. In the deepest withdrawn regressed libidinal ego we do not find active sexual and aggressive impulses, but fear and the desperate need to be quiet, still, safe, warm, and protected while recovery takes place. If we are to speak of instincts, then the deepest cause of psychopathological phenomena is not sex or aggression, but fear and the instinctive reaction of flight from the outer world of real bad objects in infancy. Everything else in psychopathology is defence: the struggle to counteract and over-compensate the retreat of the withdrawn regressed ego.

The distinction I have already suggested (in Chapters II and III), based on a split in the libidinal ego itself, between an active oral libidinal ego and a passive regressed libidinal ego, enables us to carry the analysis of ego-weakness to the deepest level. We have seen how the child struggles to cope with the outer world and its demands on him, while he seeks to master his weakness by turning his aggression against his own libidinal needs; and how this leads to the formation of an internal 'closed system' of self-persecution, the internal world of bad object-relationships, the sado-masochistic inner world of psychoneurosis and psychosis. This was illustrated by the painting of the patient inside a closed framework of teeth; not only, however, was she lying in one corner helplessly suffering under murderous attack, but she was also represented by a detached pair of praying hands. These seemed helpless to secure for her any aid, but also they were not themselves directly threatened. I take that pair of hands to symbolize the part of herself in which she had become able to detach herself from the sado-masochistic inner world and, as it were, turn her back on it and treat it as if it were not there. Part of her went on suffering, but part of her in the praying hands pleaded for and apparently achieved an escape into a regressive detachment from even inner reality. The regressed ego withdraws still deeper into the unconscious, breaking off all object-relationships except the most elementary one of a return to the womb and a flight into identification. The active oral masochistic libidinal ego is the ego of psychosis and psychoneurosis; the passive regressed libidinal ego is the ego of profound schizoid, fear-driven retreat from life, carrying with it the threat of radical depersonalization.

We may now see why the 'closed system' of internal bad object-relations, and of antilibidinal self-persecution is such a 'static internal situation' and so hard to change. In its entirety it represents a desperate attempt to fend off regression and depersonalization in any degree. Its method for the most part is to use fantasied and at times 'acted out' bad relationships to keep the distinct and separate identity of the ego in being. Bad relationships are often better than good relationships in the short run for that purpose, since good relationships are so often felt to be smothering, especially when deep infantile dependence is involved. *Psychotherapy and the internal bad-objects world represent rival policies for the saving of the ego.* The antilibidinal policy is to maintain unchanged the internal closed system of self-persecution of the traumatized child within, in an attempt to force an adult ego in consciousness. Psychoanalytical therapy is really an invitation into an open system in touch with outer reality, an opportunity to grow out of deep down fears in a good object relationship with the therapist. But this will only succeed in a radical way if the therapist can reach the profoundly withdrawn regressed ego, relieve its fears, and start it on the road to rebirth and regrowth, and the discovery and development of all its potentialities. The deeply regressed ego feels unable to get in touch with anyone. The masochistic libidinal ego cannot give up bad objects without succumbing to depersonalization. Unless the therapist can intuitively sense the manifestations of the patient's predicament in this respect, and by the needed interpretation at the right moment get through to that part of the patient which is cut off from all communication, the patient cannot undergo any change. If this contact is established, then what Winnicott (1955a) calls 'therapeutic regression' can take place. Whether the recognition of this makes psychotherapy any easier is another matter. Perhaps there is no way of making it easy. Here lies our greatest need for research, but at least it is better to know what we have to deal with, and to deal with the primary factor in illness rather than treat secondary and defensive factors as ultimate causes.

VIII

THE NATURE OF PRIMARY FAILURE IN EGO-DEVELOPMENT

THE foregoing chapters have gathered together clinical evidence for the existence, deep within every disturbed personality, of a specific centre of experience of what, in general, we call 'ego-weakness'. To arrive at more exact understanding of what this means would enormously clarify our aims in psychotherapy. Ego-weakness cannot be thought of as something clear-cut that either does or does not exist to provide an absolute means of distinguishing between mental illness and health. It is all a matter of degree. In psychosis it dominates the psyche almost completely and fades out to whatever extent stability and maturity is reached. Different people experience this underlying factor with many variations of definition and intensity. The patient's intense fear of experiencing his basic ego-weakness immediately in consciousness is certainly the main focus of tension in living and of resistance to psychotherapy. We saw in the last chapter how unremitting effort is kept up to master and repress this weakness, and to force the self to cope with outer reality and meet the demands of adult living in spite of it. The other side of that situation is encountered in psychotherapy, when the patient shows the most surprising tenacity of resistance to every attempt to help him to experience consciously in undisguised form that very part of his personality where he most urgently needs help. Having had to grow up, not on the basis of feeling safely in touch and secure in a reliable good relationship with mother, but on the basis of feeling that his inner self is not understood by anyone and he must work hard to organize himself to keep himself mentally alive and functioning, it seems impossible to the patient to reverse this situation. To give up operating onc's own ego-maintenance system seems like inviting collapse and extinction. Yet it appears to involve taking just that risk, to begin to put one's trust in the analyst and the relation to him, instead of in one's own struggles, as the necessary basis of feeling real and secure; and what if the therapist should prove in the end to be of no more use than mother was?

The Regressed Ego and Schizoid Suicide

The ultimate unconscious infantile weak ego is very clearly experienced consciously as *a fear of dying*, when its threat to the stability of the personality is being felt. Thus a mother in her forties reports: 'When I'm alone, and especially if I wake in the night, I get a sudden sinking feeling. I get scared and panicky and feel that I might suddenly drop dead.' This patient, as a girl, had been subject to fainting attacks when out with her mother, but did not seem to have had them at any other times. A doctor who had undoubtedly experienced a severe weaning trauma and had been very badly mothered all his childhood, had been working out in analysis a deeply rooted depression. One evening, the last patient in his surgery had been very depressed ever since her mother had died nine months previously. She had said, 'My world fell apart when my mother died.' That remark made a particularly deep impression on him, and that same night he dreamed:

> I was about to die and was interested to see what my reaction was. I felt very frightened and very sad, and wondered if dying was like going to sleep.

In less extreme form this becomes a fear of breaking down into a regressed illness, or, more mildly, still feeling unable to cope and worrying over everything. On the other hand, when exhaustion begins to develop, as it periodically does, out of the struggle to master this internal breakdown threat, then it is experienced as *a wish to die*. This is felt in less uncompromising terms as a longing to regress, to escape from life, to go to sleep for an indefinite period, or, more mildly still, as loss of interest and active impulse, a wish to get out of things and evade responsibility.

For these reasons I have called this structural aspect of the weakened personality, which is so clearly the tap-root of mental illness, the 'regressed ego'. I do not, however, feel satisfied with this as a descriptive term, for clearly it denotes the 'behaviour' rather than the actual 'nature' of this inner core of neurosis, psychosis, and all other forms of personality disturbance. We can recognize its manifestations most easily in all kinds of regressive phenomena, but these always challenge us to deeper understanding in terms of their actual meaning. Why in fact does this patient feel like that? What makes him want to run away from life instead of enjoying it? Why is there a regressed ego? What is its actual nature and condition? In fact it is more complex than the term 'regressed' indicates. The deep-seated source of underlying central or fundamental weakness in the total personality, the primary failure of strong basic ego-development, has at least three contributory causes in descending order of psychic depth: (i) *repression* of the frightened infant as an unwanted handicap in growing up to face life on the adult level (i.e., antilibidinal phenomena, cf. Chapter VII); (ii) *withdrawal* of the frightened infant from a world he cannot cope with, and also from internal antilibidinal self-persecution, thus precipitating specific regression or flight from life (cf. Chapter II, pp. 66ff); (iii) *unevoked potential* in the primary natural psyche which has never yet been 'brought to birth' (i.e. 'maturational processes' which have never got a start at all) because of the blocking effect of both repression and withdrawal, and lack of a good object to evoke a healthy response (i.e. an 'unfacilitating environment'). This is a matter we have still to examine in Chapter IX. For the moment we return to 'regression'.

We meet the regressed ego most undisguisedly in tendencies to *schizoid suicide*, and, less extremely, in states of exhaustion, fatigue, and loss of energy. These phenomena emerge if one succeeds in getting the patient to lay off his fanatical antilibidinal self-driving to activity; but they also repeatedly break through the manic compulsion to constant over-activity with its unrelieved tension, when a depressed or, more accurately, an apathetic state supervenes. One of the distressing states found in many patients is that of the 'bad relaxer' who longs to sleep, rest, and recuperate, and get back to work again, but whose body and mind just will not 'knock off', so that he lies tired out and physically restless and mentally active, being unable either to lie still or stop thinking. During the night he is as wide-awake as he would like to be by day, and in the day when he wants to be active he feels jaded and half dead. He is caught between the opposite fears of exhausting compulsive over-activity, and of giving up, breaking down, regressing.

A married man who had endured many years of exceptional strain owing to the illness and death of his first wife and the mental illness of his second, and whose underlying legacy of disturbances from his own childhood had been thereby reactivated, said at one session: 'I must have ten minutes at the end in absolute quiet. I know of several kinds of tiredness: physical tiredness, intellectual tiredness when I've studied too long without a break, emotional tiredness when things are difficult at home or at work. But behind all those I feel a deeper sort of tiredness, *life-tiredness*. I want just to be able to stop living for a period. I don't want to die, but I need to be able to escape from the strain of keeping on living for a time.' This striking double motivation of 'needing to stop living but not wishing to die', indeed fearing dying, emerges very clearly in some patients who experience definite schizoid suicidal tendencies. Thus one patient, a wife and mother in her late thirties, said: 'I've often felt it would be lovely to put my head in the gas oven and go unconscious. But I couldn't do it, because I couldn't be sure of being able to turn the gas off at the right time, before it killed me.'

Another patient, an extremely ill young woman in her early twenties, on several occasions went downstairs soon after she had gone to bed and lay down *beside* the gas oven and turned on the gas. Then she felt quite unable to stir herself to turn it off, but was longing for one of the family to wonder why she'd gone down and come and turn it off for her, which fortunately they always did. It would be quite incorrect to interpret that as simply a 'hysterical' exhibitionistic act designed to get the family worrying over her. It was the product of a genuine feeling of being too exhausted to carry on any longer, and needing to escape into unconsciousness, but not wanting to die. In fact, when she did not go downstairs and do that in a mood of desperation, she would be lying in bed unable to get to sleep because of a 'counting obsession' which she could not stop till she found the right number to stop at (which, of course, was never to be found), or an obsession about words in which she was frantically trying to cancel out words that suggested death and dying, by thinking up words that suggested life and living: an obvious conflict between the longing to regress, the fear of dying, and the ultimate wish to live. Sometimes she would fall asleep exhausted by this process; at others she would be driven to the gas oven for what she wanted to be only the temporary relief of an escape into unconsciousness. This is a clear motivation for the use of sleeping pills. She was in fact engaged in a frantic struggle to keep herself mentally alive and in being as a functioning person. Some aspects of her case, presented on pages 103–5 are very relevant here.

Schizoid suicide is not really a wish for death as such, except in cases where the patient has utterly lost all hope of being understood and helped. Even then there is a deep unconscious secret wish that death should prove to be a pathway to rebirth.

One patient in the middle of a paranoid-schizophrenic episode had a vivid compelling fantasy of slipping into the local river and drifting downstream to re-emerge at some point out of the waters as a new creature; and she was in fact stopped just in time from putting this fantasy into action. Whereas in depressive suicide the driving force is anger, aggression, hate, and a destructive impulse aimed at the self to divert it from the hated love-object, i.e. self-murder, schizoid suicide is at bottom a longing to escape from a situation that one just does not feel strong enough to cope with, so as in some sense to return to the womb and be reborn later with a second chance to live. Here is a dramatic version of that basic ego-weakness, into the nature of which we are enquiring. What is the mental condition which drives a human being into such a dilemma as needing to stop living while not wanting to die?

The Patient's Sense of Ultimate Absolute Isolation

As I have watched the analysis of such patients go deeper and deeper, I have become ever more impressed with their narrowing concentration on one unvarying central feature of their inner experience. Somewhere deep within them they come upon the feeling of being absolutely and utterly alone, or of being about to fall into such a condition. This may be expressed in varying imagery, sometimes suggestive of memory, at other times of the fantasy representation of a subjective psychic state. This is not just a feeling of loneliness, of being detached and solitary, of wishing they could make friends more easily and so on. It is something *sui generis*, final, absolute, and when felt in extreme form is accompanied by a sense of horror. Thus a woman of forty reported that for a week she had been vividly seeing an image of herself as a baby sitting in a high chair, with nothing to do, no one to talk to and no one to talk to her, in an empty room, and she was just sitting there immobile except that she was slowly shaking her head from side to side. Her infantile life at that point was reduced to nothing more than a feeble movement symbolic of an attempt to deny the terrifying isolation in which she felt herself to be.

Another female patient, a grandmother in her late fifties, of deeply schizoid personality, at a very advanced stage of her analysis awoke one night in a state of terror, feeling that she was looking into a black abyss yawning at her feet, into which she could not escape falling. A week or two later she woke in deep fear, feeling that she was blind, deaf, and dumb, and did not know where she was, lost without any means of communication. Still later, she dreamt of

looking at a baby whom she knew to be herself, in a baby chair. It was in a deep sleep or coma with eyes tight shut, but it also seemed to be swollen, in distress, but with everything shut up inside. Her mother and older sister came and looked at the baby briefly and turned away doing nothing for it. Then she was looking at an older woman sitting helplessly and looking extremely ill.

She knew that that woman was ill because she had that ill baby in her, and also that the woman was herself. This dream occurred at a time when she was in fact feeling very ill, and finding it barely possible to struggle on from day to day. This ill state began to clear up when she revived a much earlier picture of herself as a baby sitting on a chair in a dingy kitchen, with a man lying drunk on a sofa and a girl present but taking no notice of her. She then saw me come into the room and pick her up and carry her out, and from that point she began to give up a self-isolating stubborn resistance to me and a quiet argumentative negating of anything I said, became much more responsive to me, and felt markedly better. I interpreted to her that she felt I had made contact with her completely isolated, lost, and ill infantile self, and she could now drop her struggle to keep herself in being entirely by her own efforts while keeping me and everyone at bay. This was an important turning point in a very long analysis, and we must later consider more closely this fact of *the therapist contacting the hidden isolated core of the patient's self*. She had often said before, 'I feel I can't get in touch with you. You must get in touch with me.'

The following case of a young married man, a scientist working on technical problems of communication devices, shows how this sense of isolation and the accompanying feeling of emptiness of personality, can suffuse waking consciousness. After some fifty sessions, he said: 'This last two weeks I've been drained of any initiative, frightened. I feel in an empty hole, nothing there. In dreams I feel to be drawn into a vacuum. There's no real foundation for my personality. I'm living on the surface. I think I don't feel real. As a child I used to cry: "Nobody cares for me." ' Then he had to go to London on business and reported. 'I felt lonely there, couldn't make any contacts. I felt inferior, not qualified. I feel I couldn't attempt sexual intercourse. I haven't the status of an adult. I feel hollow, empty, and don't know what kind of person I am. I've no roots, no personality to stand on. I even feel frightened of you and am always alone in a crowd. I feel we've got down to bedrock in this.' In the next session he said: 'I've felt rotten all the week. I've been aware of you though, but I felt I didn't know you. I've never thought of the possibility of you understanding me. I thought I'd got to understand myself, no one else would.' His mother was a masculine woman who disliked men and had not wanted any children. In his dreams he was constantly fantasying her taking his possessions away from him, as he put it, 'robbing me of my personality'. So when he dreamed simply, 'I was asking my mother to go to bed with me', I interpreted that he was wanting his mother to give him a contact with which he could begin to feel real in himself, something she had never done. He replied, 'Yes, I feel there's nothing in me to get in touch with you with. And yet I don't feel so nightmarish now. I have got you.' He was beginning to feel that I was getting in touch with his isolated inner self, perhaps at first simply by understanding that it was there, that he felt like that.

In every human being there is probably, to some extent, a lonely person at heart, but in the very ill, it is an utterly isolated being, too denuded of experience to be able to feel like a person, unable to communicate with others and never reached by others. So long as that remains, all the rest of the psychopathological phenomena is camouflage, the day-to-day struggle to keep going, to try to deny the isolation, to sustain a secretly despairing effort to maintain physical existence and social activity, always liable to recurring minor or even major breakdowns. The isolated, developmentally arrested heart of the self has been there since early childhood. What the patient feels is, 'I can't get in touch with you. If you can't get in touch with me, I'm lost. But I've no confidence that you can get in touch with me, because you don't know anything about that part of me. No one has ever known and that's why I'm hopeless. I feel I'll never get better and you can't cure me.' This is the basic problem that confronts us in psychotherapy.

Winnicott's View of 'the Start of Ego-Development'

I shall turn at this point to the work of Winnicott on the earliest mother–child relationship for the clues needed to understand this problem of the inner core of the schizoid condition. In a paper on 'The Capacity to Be Alone' (1958) Winnicott uses the concept of *ego-relatedness* in a particularly fundamental way to denote the main positive result in the infant of good mothering from the start. *Ego-relatedness as a fundamental quality of experience developed in the infant ego* during the earliest stages of its growth, seems to me the most valuable idea we have for illuminating our problem. I have constantly emphasized, in writing about 'object-relations' theory, that the importance of object-relations lies in the fact that without them human beings cannot develop an ego. This is a statement in theoretical form, but it is expressed in a concrete, experiential, clinical way by Winnicott's concept of *ego-relatedness*. This needs elaboration to bring out its full force. He conceives it as a positive and persisting quality of the experience of a well-mothered infant, that he develops a growing sense of his own ego-wholeness and ego-identity, as a part of his overall experience of being in a reliable, secure, supportive relation to his mother. As this experience grows and becomes a permanent characteristic of his 'self-feeling', he becomes able for longer and longer periods to be alone, i.e. to accept the physical absence of mother and of other people without anxiety or panic. He has grown to be an intrinsically ego-related child. His feeling about his environing world is positive and trustful, and when he is *alone* he does not feel *isolated* or *mentally out of touch*. One might say in sophisticated language that he grows up with a natural, unquestioned, symbiotic quality in his experience of himself and his world. He feels a profound sense of *belonging* and of *being at one with* his world which is not intellectually 'thought out', but is the persisting *atmosphere of security* in which he exists within himself.

How basic this is can be illustrated from a highly interesting passage in Martin Buber's *I and Thou* (p. 25):

> The ante-natal life of the child is one of purely natural combination, bodily interaction and flowing from the one to the other. . . . (There is) a mythical saying of the Jews, 'in the mother's body man knows the universe, in birth he forgets it.' . . . It remains indeed in man as a secret image of desire . . . the yearning is for the cosmic connexion. Every child that is coming into being rests, like all life that is coming into being, in the womb of the great mother, the undivided primal world that precedes form. From her, too, we are separated, and enter into personal life, slipping free only in the dark hours to be close to her again; night by night this happens to the healthy man. But this separation does not occur catastrophically like the separation from the bodily mother; time is granted to the child to exchange a spirital connexion, that is, *relation*, for the natural connexion with the world that he gradually loses.

Buber is here describing the way in which unconscious ante-natal symbiosis has to develop into conscious post-natal personal relationship, a new type of meaningful symbiosis in which mere organic co-existence is exchanged for differentiation of individualities, separate egos coming together again in ultimately consciously significant mutuality. *Birth is mere separation, and will speedily result in isolation, in the snuffing out of the nascent personal ego, unless good mothering at once restores 'connexion' of such a kind that it can lead to the evolution or realization of the potential ego of the infant, and therewith of personal relationships.* It is impossible for a human being to exist as a human being in isolation. Unless the mother starts the infant off in the process of becoming 'an ego in relation', he cannot become a true human being, a person; at worst he will be psychotic or commit suicide. So fundamental is *ego-relatedness* as a quality of our whole experience. Only that enables us to be alone without being isolated and becoming a 'lost soul'. In the paper referred to, Winnicott writes:

> The capacity of the individual to be alone . . . is one of the most important signs of maturity in emotional development.

Our patients do not possess this.

Before we consider Winnicott's views in greater detail, it may be said that this concept of 'ego-relatedness' represents a deepening understanding of long familiar things. For many years 'separation-anxiety' has been a key concept in psychodynamic thinking. It acknowledges the fact that human beings are not made for isolation, and find their security in the undisturbed possession of their familiar supports. These supports were, no doubt, conceived as basically 'persons'; but it was recognized that many impersonal material objects, possessions, house, the neighbourhood or city long lived in, would acquire the values of the 'supportive person', so that people, and especially children and mentally disturbed adults, would react with severe separation-anxiety to being parted from possessions or home as well as family or friends. Winnicott himself stressed this in pointing out how children acquire 'transitional objects' such as cuddly toys to help on their capacity to grow more independent of mother.

Fairbairn (1963) stated explicitly that he held that

> The earliest and original form of anxiety, as experienced by the child, is separation anxiety.

This was of course implied in 'Object-Relations Theory' where object-relations are treated as the medium in which all psychodynamic growth of the person takes place. Nevertheless separation-anxiety is a negative concept. It states what happens when relationships fail, but it does not of itself define the positive quality of experience that is built up when relationships do not fail. It is this that is pin-pointed by Winnicott's term 'ego-relatedness', and we may expand that by saying that *vulnerability to separation-anxiety exists when the human being is not basically ego-related, is in fact in a state of 'ego-unrelatedness'*. This does not depend simply on external object-loss. The individual who has been securely ego-related from earliest infancy can bear the loss of his external supports, either personal or impersonal. The individual who from earliest infancy has remained ego-unrelated is wide open to the worst and most terrifying fears when his outer supports fail him. In a variety of ways what he will experience is the threat of the loss of his familiar conscious self by an uncontrollable process of deep-seated emptying or undermining (cf. withdrawal and regression); and this threat may not even wait for some external object-loss before it invades consciousness. *Primary ego-unrelatedness is the substance of ego-weakness*, and any degree of ego-development maintained over the top of it is only precariously held (by means of antilibidinal repression of the weak ego, and compulsive, forced activity). For the fuller understanding of this we will turn to the work of Winnicott on the nature of the mother–infant relation.

In a paper entitled 'The Relation of a Mother to her Baby at the Beginning' (1965a) he writes:

> We notice in the expectant mother an increasing identification with the infant . . . a willingness as well as an ability on the part of the mother to drain interest from her own self onto the baby. I have referred to this as 'primary maternal preoccupation'. In my view, this is what gives the mother her special ability to do the right thing. She knows what the baby could be feeling like. No one else knows. (p. 15.)

He distinguishes this from *pathological* preoccupation.

> It is part of the normal process that the mother recovers her self-interest, and does so at the rate at which her infant can allow her to do so. . . . The normal mother's recovery from her preoccupation with her infant provides a kind of weaning.

He points out that the ill mother cannot *wean* her baby, i.e. cannot let him grow to an increasing strength and security so that he can become independent of her, because either she has not been able to give him the primary necessity for his security, the state of identification and intuitive understanding—'her infant has never had her and so weaning has no meaning'—or else she weans him too suddenly to free herself from him 'without regard for the gradually developing need of the infant to be weaned'. (pp. 15–16.)

Looking at this again from the infant's side, Winnicott writes:

Only if there is a good-enough mother does the infant start on a process of development that is personal and real. If the mothering is not good enough, then the infant becomes a collection of reactions to impingement, and *the true self of the infant fails to form* or becomes hidden behind a false self which complies with and generally wards off the world's knocks. (p. 17.)

Here we meet with the third factor over and above repression and withdrawal, i.e. unevoked potentiality. Of the infant 'that has had a good-enough mother and that does really start' he writes:

I would say the ego is both weak and strong. All depends on the capacity of the mother to give ego-support. . . . Where the mother's ego-support is absent or weak or patchy, the infant cannot develop along personal lines. . . . It is the well-cared for babies who quickly establish themselves as persons. (p. 17.)

Here then are the facts we need to give content to the concept of 'ego-relatedness' and to endow with fuller meaning such terms as 'ego-weakness' and 'separation-anxiety'. These facts are the basis of Winnicott's paper on 'The Capacity to be Alone'. He writes:

The capacity to be alone . . . is a phenomenon of early life which deserves special study, because it is the foundation on which sophisticated aloneness is built. Although many types of experience . . . go to the establishment of the capacity to be alone, there is one that is basic, and without a sufficiency of it, the capacity to be alone does not come about; *this experience is that of being alone as an infant and small child, in the presence of mother*. Thus the capacity to be alone is a paradox; it is the experience of being alone while someone else is present. (p. 30.)

I take this to mean feeling so secure with mother that the infant can afford to forget her while she is there, and finds he does not lose her.

If the infant can begin with 'the experience of being alone while someone else is present', then he can go on to the experience of being able to be alone while that someone else is physically absent, because he does not feel alone essentially in himself. He is basically ego-related. We must differentiate between several terms that might roughly appear to be synonymous, such as being alone, being lonely, feeling isolated, and enjoying privacy. I have been accustomed to drawing a distinction with patients between being alone and being isolated, and I take *isolation* to mean a total absence of all object-relationship internally, for one can be isolated in the physical presence of other people. *Feeling lonely* is a less absolute concept. Many people feel this when they are in company, and it expresses a sense of precariousness and insecurity in object-relationships rather than their total loss. People feel lonely when their mental contact with others is uncertain and unsatisfying, and they do not fully 'get through' to one another. Feeling isolated and feeling lonely are not really related to the physical presence or absence of other people, and can be felt equally whether others are or are not there. The concept of *being alone* can mean either of two opposite things. If one is basically ego-related, one can 'be alone' either with or without other people, in the sense of *enjoying privacy*, and this is essential to maturity. If one is basically ego-unrelated, 'being alone' means the extreme experience of isolation, and even if other people are present they seem to be unreal, and the isolated person himself feels unreal. Thus the very schizoid patient whose case was summarized on pages 168–70, including the dream of being merged with a baby who was being ignored by a group of women, at a subsequent session felt quite out of touch with me. She said, 'I feel there's a gap in the middle of my body. There seems to be nothing between my legs and my arms and head.' She felt that the vital heart of her was missing and she was unreal, and she commented, 'It's not like that dream of the women ignoring the baby. It feels as if there isn't even anyone there at all to ignore me.' The earlier dream expressed loneliness, the later sensation of an empty gap in her personality expressed *isolation and unreality*, the loss of her ego, of her sense of selfhood, in experiencing object-loss through feeling out of touch with me. This is the negative of Winnicott's ego-relatedness; it is *the fundamental ego-unrelatedness of the seriously unmothered infant*.

The 'capacity to be alone' of which Winnicott writes, is the capacity to enjoy privacy and a sense of reality within oneself, either with or without the presence of other people, without succumbing to separation-anxiety, panic, and the sense of isolation and unreality. It clearly depends on the fact that the basically ego-related individual never feels mentally alone within himself, even if he is with people with whom he has nothing in common, or when there is nobody with him at all. Winnicott sees this 'special type of relationship' as first coming into being

> ... between the infant and small child who is alone, and the mother or mother-substitute who is in fact reliably present, even if represented for the moment by a cot or a pram or the general atmosphere of the immediate environment. (p. 30.)

> Ego-relatedness refers to the relationship between two people, one of whom at any rate is alone; perhaps both are alone, yet the presence of each is important to the other. (p. 31.)

Thus we may say that one can only stand being alone in outer reality if one is never alone in inner reality. Winnicott writes:

> The ability to be truly alone has as its basis the early experience of being alone in the presence of someone ... (This) can take place at a very early age, when *the ego-immaturity is naturally balanced by ego-support from the mother*. In the course of time the individual introjects the ego-supportive mother, and in this way becomes able to be alone without frequent reference to the mother or mother-symbol. (p. 32.)

The Essence of Ego-Relatedness

How are we to think of this 'not being alone in inner mental reality'? Two further quotations from Winnicott will serve as our starting-point.

> Maturity and the capacity to be alone implies that the individual has had the chance through good-enough mothering to build up a belief in a benign environment. (p. 32.)

> Gradually the ego-supportive environment is introjected and built into the individual's personality, so that there comes about a capacity actually to be alone. Even so, theoretically, there is always someone present, someone who is equated ultimately and unconsciously with the mother, the person who in the early days and weeks, was temporarily identified with the infant, and for the time being was interested in nothing else but the care of her own infant.

He here describes a process by which an infant achieves what in an adult we would call a *conviction* (in feeling, not in idea), through sufficient experience, *of the reality and reliability for him of good objects in his outer world. This is not the same as a capacity to fantasy good objects*. We must distinguish between *enjoyable remembering* on the basis of actual good experience, and *compulsive anxious fantasying and thinking* as an effort to deny actual bad experience.

Thus a male patient complained that when he was alone in his office, or in a train, he would begin to feel anxious and then mentally 'empty'. He explained that then he had to keep on thinking, evidently to stave off an unreality state. He would try to find pleasant things to think about, and he remembered that as a child he would lie in bed having to think of something good before he could go to sleep. Since in fact he often lay in bed listening to his parents quarrelling downstairs, and in general he had little experience of secure and supportive personal relations in the family life, it is clear that if he could not think of good happy things or imagine them, he would have to think of his actual bad experiences rather than risk the onset of the feeling of 'emptiness'. This, as we have already noted, is a characteristic of all obsessional thinking. It is a defence against the feelings of ego-loss. This patient said: 'I have to have my mind full of problems to worry about them so as not to feel empty. It's not really the problems, it's the "feeling empty" that is the trouble.' Thinking of bad things can, in the emergency of a panic and in a short-term sense, be an even more powerful method of retaining the feeling of reality and of being in touch, than thinking of good things. Thinking of good things may then be developed as a further defence against thinking of bad things.

This *threefold structure of fears and defences* is strikingly illustrated in the case of a married woman in her early thirties with two children. She grew up with a very anxious mother, and her insecurity in the face of life became apparent in her early teens, when she grew shy and timid, afraid to join a girl's club, and kept herself within the safe bounds of home, mother and father, and one girl friend who was shy like herself. Later engagement and marriage, and at first living on with her parents, was supportive and she seemed to be doing well. Then came removal to a home of her own, then the first baby, then removal to another town, then the second baby. She was by then phoning her mother every day, and was becoming ever more meticulously hard-working in the home, hardly ever going out, and getting obsessed with concerns about dirt and cleanliness. If she wasn't working hard all the time, she felt she couldn't keep things clean according to her perfectionist standards. Here were the signs of a progressive underlying feeling of not being able to cope with adult responsibility. Then her mother died and by the time she came for analysis after a short hospitalization, a full-scale obsessional neurosis was making life impossible for both herself and her husband. Her dependence on him for reassurance that things were clean was absolute, and she dare not go out for fear she should see dog mess on the pavement. Even to think of it seemed to contaminate her, and set her washing her hands.

I had told her that I thought her underlying teenage timidity and shyness, and her compulsive driving of herself to cope with life with a family and no mother, were more important than her obsession about dirt and cleanliness, which would turn out to be defensive symptoms and part of her struggle to master her fears. At the twenty-eighth session she suddenly came out with the following: 'When I'm upset I feel I'm not on the ground. I'm floating in space, not in touch with realities, my mind's floating off miles away, not really there. I go off like that and have to have someone to reassure me and bring me back to reality. I have to keep very calm to cope with real life. As soon as there's any pressure I panic, and float off and become quite unreal. I'm not in possession of my own person. I'm not there at all. If my husband's in a hurry or a lot of people are talking, I panic and find I'm going off. If I'm washing something and someone knocks at the door, I panic and then I feel, "Now this washing isn't right, it's not clean, I must start again at the beginning and do it all over again." I'm doing that all day and can't get on with things, unless my husband is there to reassure me they are all right. Any little thing throws me off balance. I have to keep myself in a little private compartment that's away from all that's going on around me and calm. The slightest distraction knocks me off balance. I need my husband to talk to me of pleasant things or my mind runs on unpleasant things, a subconscious voice goes on all the time saying unpleasant things. The bad things are always there, going on all the time like a film in my mind. If anything disturbs my conscious thoughts, my unconscious unpleasant things take charge of me. Why do I use these bad thoughts about dirt and uncleanness and disgusting things? I was always fussy about cleanliness and now I'm afraid of dirt.'

Here is an example of a woman who cannot stand separation from mother and home and stand alone, because she feels unreal in her basic experience of herself, 'ego-unrelated' or in her own words 'floating off miles away, not really there'. The more unable a growing child is to leave mother in outer reality, the more certain it is that she has no basic ego-relatedness to mother in inner reality. Yet nearly all this patient's dreams were about being with mother. She was having to fill the emptiness inside where mother should have been the centre of a built-in feeling of secure relationship, by compulsive thinking and fantasying about mother; dreaming of her mother in the night and talking to her in her mind during the day.

It is clear from this that the reason for much dreaming is that in the night, when asleep and with the rest of the world asleep around, the inwardly isolated person feels he will fall into the emptiness of his fundamentally ego-unrelated condition. He must either stay awake thinking, or as one patient said, 'Wake up every hour to make sure I'm still there', or else get busy fantasying complicated dream stories to have a world to feel in touch with, thus keeping his 'self' in being. This type of dreaming is a night-time equivalent of daytime obsessional thinking, and it is certainly a wish-fulfilment always to have objects present to feel real with, and mental activity going on to prove that one is in being, and to ward off the experience of unreality and isolation. Wish-fulfilment, however, seems too tepid a description for what is part of the struggle to maintain oneself as a viable reality when, as one more sophisticated patient put it, 'I feel that at bottom I haven't got an ego at all. I'm nothing.' There is another type of dreaming quite unlike this, which is to be understood more as the equivalent of play and enjoyment.

It is the state of primary ego-unrelatedness which makes it impossible for people to be alone without panic. Then 'compulsive fantasying and thinking', whether by day or night, whether bizarre or realistic and rational, is part of the struggle to keep oneself mentally alive. In the case of this obsessional patient, she felt so basically out of touch that any momentary fear made her feel that she had 'floated off', and become dangerously withdrawn and detached. Her initial obsessive hard work to keep the house clean was an unremitting struggle to fill every moment with activity to keep herself anchored to the realities of her daily life. As this became ever harder, she, as it were, sought to frighten herself into an even more strenuous fight against dirt by developing a fear of it, and an obsessional preoccupation with it. Everywhere she turned, she felt she was up against dirt to drive her to go over and over the same tasks to make sure. She could only dispense with this if she had her husband there to reassure her, i.e. to feel real with and in touch with, though she still needed her 'dirt obsession' to keep him there. The extent to which she had to use this 'fantasying of bad things' was shown when she spoke of these thoughts going on all the time like a voice or a film at the back of her mind. Then she needed her husband to talk to her of pleasant things. Here is the threefold structure of good fantasies as a defence against bad fantasies, which are themselves a defence against unreality, depersonalization, emptiness, the loss of the ego.

Thus, 'not being alone in inner reality' is not the same thing as fantasying good objects or any kind of objects. We have to distinguish between 'compulsive anxious defensive thinking' and simple 'enjoyable remembering of good experience'. Presumably a baby who is alone for a time can 'hallucinate the breast' or 'remember mother' with pleasure and not feel alone, so long as he is not left alone in reality for too long. If that happens, 'pleasurable remembering' must gradually deteriorate into 'compulsive stop-gap fantasying' to lay the foundations of future obsessional and other neuroses. If the baby is not left too long and mother comes and confirms his 'pleasurable remembering' by renewed good experience, and if the length of her absences are graduated to his capacity to feel securely with her when she is not there, then a permanent characteristic grows of feeling fundamentally 'in touch and secure' and confident about the outer world as a 'benign environment'. Fairbairn expressed this by saying that good ego-experience leads naturally to good ego-development, and not to a need to internalize objects. Every analyst will be familiar with this problem of the 'length of absences' cropping up in the form of the patient feeling he has lost the analyst between sessions. This may in fact be an actual, if unwitting, remembering of mother's absences in infancy.

The important thing about 'enjoyable remembering of good experience' is that it is spontaneous, and not a compulsion born of anxiety. If a secure ego is not actually engaged on some specific activity, it is free to relax and feel pleasure in the recollection of good experience, or else if healthily tired simply to rest or sleep. This is possible on the basis of a fundamental confidence in life which has not been destroyed by later experience of its dangers. The infant's initial and quite unconscious trust in the mother was not broken and betrayed, and he never had the devastating traumatic experience of feeling isolated, cut off, alone without help and afraid of dying. Perhaps few people are as absolutely secure as that, but there is a great difference between the inner condition of the person who can be alone without insecurity, and the person who really needs constant supportive attention to protect him against relapse into a terrifying state of unreality.

Ego-Weakness and Psychotherapeutic Relationship

At this point we come, once more, upon the inner contradiction in the schizoid condition, which we can never for long avoid dealing with unless or until it is resolved. *The schizoid condition is basically that of ego-weakness due to a fundamental state of ego-unrelatedness. The weak schizoid ego is in urgent need of a relationship, a therapeutic relationship capable of filling the gap left by inadequate mothering. Only that can rescue the patient from succumbing to the terrors of ultimate isolation. Yet when it comes to it, the weak ego is afraid of the very relationship that it needs.* The isolated infantile ego not only needs to be discovered and put in touch, but is also deeply afraid to be found, and at the very moment when 'rescue' seems imminent it will rush away again into the wastes of isolation. The possession of secure 'individuality' is as essential to human beings as 'object-relationship'. In fact, the two are inseparable, but it does not seem like that to the deeply schizoid person. *Without the medium of relationship to grow in, no potential human ego can develop a significant individuality of its own. But the weakened ego always fears it will be swamped by the other person in a relationship.* The psychotherapy of such a patient usually involves a prolonged process of drawing near to and then taking flight from the therapist, over and over again, while slowly and secretly the capacity to 'trust' is growing.

The following two cases show this conflict over accepting a therapeutic relationship very clearly. The first is that of the obsessional patient whose basic problems were described on pages 103–5 and 217. At one point she showed a marked improvement over a good period, following the analytical working through of a very severe traumatic rejection at the hands of her grandfather, of whom she had always been very fond, at the age of 6. Her panic fear at what she felt was a betrayal of trust, making it impossible for her ever to trust anyone again, emerged as a central feature of the depression that came out over this incident. I linked all this with her relationship to me, pointing out that she was afraid I would let her down as her grandfather did, and she was needing to prove me to the uttermost. From then on, she became markedly more responsive and came punctually to sessions and began to feel much better. Then suddenly she arrived fifteen minutes late for a session, said she had not wanted to come, and had hoped I would be a long time coming to the waiting room for her so that she could walk out before I came. She was plainly taking flight from me, and I said that I felt this was a reaction to the fact that she had begun to trust me so much more lately that she had suddenly become afraid of the situation. She sat silent, pale, cold, uncommunicative, and then said that she had told her mother that she felt her heart was a frozen lump inside her, and she was frightened that she would never all her life be able to feel warm and responsive and loving to any one. She added that she was afraid to get too close to people, they were too much for her, and she revived a fear that had died away some time earlier, of becoming pregnant and having a baby, a fear which would make marriage impossible. I said I thought that really it was some risk she felt in any close relationship, that made her revive this fear of childbirth to protect her from the risk of the close relationship of marriage and motherhood. She agreed that that was probably the truth of the matter because she felt overwhelmed as a personality at the bare thought of being close to anyone in any way. She could only feel safe at a distance from people.

I pointed out that she was feeling this fear now about me, just because she had been risking a closer relationship to me for some time and had been much more forthcoming and trustful, but had begun to fear that she could not maintain a personality of her own, if she went on depending on me. I suggested that she suddenly cut herself off from me because she needed to find that I could understand this, could leave her free to withdraw, could respect her independence, while at the same time I did not get angry and abandon her. I reminded her that at the previous session she had said, 'You wouldn't ever get angry with me, would you?' and this was the proper context of that remark. She needed to know that I could let her go without myself losing touch with her, without trying to force her back, and that I would be reliably and understandingly here for her to come back to when she needed. Then it became safe for her to withdraw, to experiment in being alone to retain some individuality of her own, and find that she was not so isolated as before and could now enjoy both relationship and independence. This made a marked impression on her. Her haunted expression died away, her face relaxed into a smile, she became easily communicative for the rest of the session, and went away at the end without anxiety.

The second case is that of a married woman of 40 with two children. Her childhood background was one of all-round insecurity, material and emotional. In early childhood, her father, whose health had been slowly declining, ceased to be the breadwinner and her mother went into business to support the family. Relationship between the father and mother was not good; the father, while being quite nice to the patient, conspicuously favoured her older sister; the mother, who was not really averse from being the breadwinner and being in business, was not truly maternal, and would rush in and out of the home always busy. The only way to get mother's attention was to have a tummy-ache; and mother was herself only nice, i.e. emotionally gentler and more approachable, when she herself had a headache and was lying down. In this family set up, the patient found so little emotional support at home, that she was happiest at school out of it. Though even then, for two years around the age of 11, she had queer sensations in the head which already, at that time, she thought must be what a baby feels like inside the womb. The first sign that she could break down under pressure began to emerge in her first two professional jobs, where she experienced so much exhaustion when off duty that she had to spend most of her leisure time lying on the bed. After marriage, though she wanted children, she found the pressures of motherhood similarly exhausting. When after some ten years, one of the children began to lose grip, became over-dependent and broke down into a severe regressed illness, this forced a crisis situation for the mother. At first she fought her inner weakness and strove to deny it, developing a bright, brittle, hard, superficial self, until suddenly she herself broke down into a regression in many ways similar to the child's. The child, who had by then improved greatly, announced that she would only be able to get completely well when Mummy was well, and Mummy's illness had to be faced.

It emerged now in analysis that she had for years experienced occasional nightmares. She would scream out in her sleep 'Mummy, Mummy' and wake up feeling that she was dying. She never heard herself scream and would not have known this but for her husband, but the feeling of dying was consciously very intense. These nightmares now became more frequent. Then she brought a dream:

I was alone on a seashore, frightened, and I saw your [the analyst's] house away up the shore. I was struggling to get to it when suddenly I found I was cut off by the tide, and panicked. Then I saw a little boat tied to your gate and I thought, 'It's all right. I can't get to him but he can get to me.'

I suggested that this gave the background of her nightmare. She felt utterly alone, isolated, and cut off from all help and could not help herself, since this, basically, was the situation when she was only a child. That was why in the night, when this fear stirred, she screamed out for her mother. She felt she was alone, because she felt that her mother was not in touch with her. (She was fundamentally 'ego-unrelated'.) But now she was becoming able to feel that I could fill the empty gap left by her mother and give her a basis of security. The nightmares diminished somewhat in intensity. Then she dreamed again of being

> on a lonely seashore. But now she suddenly saw a beautifully painted lifeboat on the water near by, and became aware that the lifeboatman was standing near her. He was not talking to her, or taking any obvious notice of her, but she knew that he had her in mind, and he was myself, and she felt safe. Then suddenly a small girl appeared on a rock nearby and fell off into the sea. The lifeboatman stepped up and caught her coat and pulled her out and she was quite all right.

Clearly she was growing an unconscious conviction that I was the answer to the utter isolation in which her mother had left her, and in which she felt she was dying. After that dream, she woke one night without having screamed, with a mild feeling that she was dying, but also that I was standing nearby in the darkness and it was all right. She went off to sleep again, which she had not previously done after the nightmares. For a time she felt better, more realistic, and more consciously 'in touch' with me.

Just then she and her husband were deeply disturbed by a tragic motor accident in which two close friends were killed, and she began to feel 'collapsy' again. But instead of being able to turn frankly to me for support, she must have felt that it was dangerous to depend on anyone. At the next session she reported that she had had the nightmare again, and for the first time actually heard herself screaming out 'Mummy'. She had, evidently, cut herself off from 'the lifeboatman' in her deeper feelings, and this was confirmed by the fact that she immediately challenged me to a stubbornly maintained argument in which she was taking occasion to differ markedly from what she knew I would think. She said that she must bring up a religious question, that I could not help her because I was not a Church of England clergyman and did not speak with the authority of the Church behind me. I accepted her need at this time to be independent of me, and so stated plainly that I disagreed with her, that I disagreed with her views of 'authority'. I hinted in passing that she probably felt a need for an authoritative church, a 'rock of ages', because she felt that a single individual could not be a basis for security—he might get killed; but stressed that we could disagree, and she could 'run away from me' (and find herself back in the nightmare situation) but that I did not desert her nor change my attitude to her. At the next session she brought a dream that

> she was at a hotel; the head waiter was going away and she felt very distressed. Then he decided that he would not go away but would stay for her sake. She then realized that she had a baby and that she had left her in the cellar, forgotten to feed her, and couldn't feed her because she had no milk, and thought, 'I must eat a lot so as to have milk, and fetch the baby.'

Clearly the head waiter was myself and she had become alarmed at the possibility of losing me. I pointed out that at the same time as she was doing without me, she had repressed the baby in herself and become unable to feel any care for her. This had returned when she once more accepted her need of me. I summed up the whole situation by saying that I felt there was more in all this than the shock and insecurity caused by her friends' death; that she had in fact begun to feel anxious because she had been for some time depending on me with increasing security, and had suddenly become alarmed lest she should lose her independence. But her dependence on me did not aim at robbing her of independence but at helping her to develop a more genuine capacity for real independence based on inner strength, and I could accept her independence as well as her dependence. Her argumentative and resistant reaction had now become unnecessary and she was feeling secure once more.

This case affords a very clear picture of the way in which psychotherapy is a slow patient process of 'growth in basic ego-relatedness', in which the patient is often driven to attempts to seize a premature independence, and needs to find that this is understood before therapeutic dependence can be continued till the deep underlying ego-weakness of 'primary ego-unrelatedness' is outgrown. This problem usually needs to be worked through repeatedly at different stages. The *fear of the loss of independent individuality, which is the basis of the schizoid 'half-in-and-half-out' policy*, calls finally to be studied in the light of another of Winnicott's concepts, namely 'the frightening fantasy of being infinitely exploited . . . of being eaten or swallowed up

. . . *the fantasy of being found*', a concept discussed in his paper on 'Communicating and Not Communicating' (1963). The subject is of fundamental importance for the understanding of all that we mean by 'a person'. I find myself able to accept the facts but not the whole of the interpretation that Winnicott puts on them.

He writes:

I suggest that in health there is a core to the personality that corresponds to the true self of the split personality; I suggest that this core never communicates with the world of perceived objects, and that the individual person knows that it must never be communicated with or influenced by external reality. . . . Although healthy persons communicate and enjoy communicating, the other fact is equally true, that *each individual is an isolate, permanently non-communicating, permanently unknown, in fact unfound*. . . . Rape and being eaten by cannibals, these are mere bagatelles as compared with the violation of the self's core, the alteration of the self's central elements by communication seeping through the defences. For me this would be the sin against the self. We can understand the hatred people have of psycho-analysis which has penetrated a long way into the human personality, and which provides a threat to the human individual in his need to be secretly isolated. The question is: how to be isolated without having to be insulated? (1963, p. 187.)

This raises certainly a final issue, but as it stands appears to me a dubious proposition. If isolation be absolute, I do not see how it is possible to distinguish between isolation and insulation. Nevertheless there is an issue of the greatest importance here, which I would rather formulate as: how to have *privacy and self-possession without isolation or insulation*. The phenomenon of preserving a central core of the psychic self secretly isolated, cut off and defended against all intrusion of the outer world, is exactly the main theme of this book. Winnicott may now be said to raise the question: 'Granted this does occur in a pathological form in the schizoid split ego, is it not true that it must also occur in a healthy form, as the ultimate source of the individuality and strength of the mature person?' Winnicott holds this to be the case. I do not feel convinced of this.

'Isolation' in the ultimate sense, Winnicott further defines as follows:

At the centre of each person is an incommunicado element, and this is sacred and most worthy of preservation. . . . The traumatic experiences that lead to the organization of primitive defences belong to the threat to the isolated core, the threat of its being found, altered, communicated with. The defence consists of a further hiding of the secret self. (*op. cit.*, p. 187.)

In this case, the 'isolated, permanently non-communicating, incommunicado' state of the core of the self is a primitive fear phenomenon, such as we could envisage in an infant who is not adequately protected and ego-supported by his mother and thus exposed to a fear of annihilation because of his own extreme weakness. The fear of annihilation Winnicott speaks of as one of the primitive 'unthinkable anxieties'. The defence of reserving an isolated core of the self, appears to me to correspond to what I have called the 'schizoid citadel' or the 'regressed ego', i.e. withdrawnness or 'a further hiding of the secret self'. Winnicott says that 'in health . . . this core of the personality corresponds to the true self of the split personality'. In that case, what does 'in health' mean? He describes the differentiation of this isolated core as produced by the very conditions that bring about the initial split in the personality. Winnicott equates 'the fantasy of being infinitely exploited' and the 'fantasy of being found'. In my experience the first is always a *fear*, the second is basically a *need* which, when bad infancy experience turns it into a fear, develops as withdrawal and the schizoid condition. If, even in health, or relative health, the secret core of the self remains permanently withdrawn, cut off and out of touch, then the total psychic self is never any other than split, and split by the earliest 'traumatic experiences that lead to the organization of primitive defences'. Any meaningful difference between health and illness is lost, if the core of the healthy personality is so isolate.

Empirically, I can well believe that this state of affairs is in fact and in varying degrees universal. It is what I have sought to describe clinically as *always* the ultimate underlying problem, the essence of the schizoid problem of *a secret withdrawal of the innermost self as a result of fear.* No human being ever has perfect mental health. Instead of saying that there is in health a situation of this kind, analogous to that found in pathological conditions, it would seem that this radical ego-split is actually a universal phenomenon, present in all of us without exception, not intrinsically or theoretically inevitable, but practically inescapable; that psychic health and illness are, in our experience, relative terms, and it is all a matter of degree. This, in fact, is the position I would think psychoanalysts in general hold, though it has not yet become generally recognized that the schizoid problem in the above sense *is* the *ultimate problem*. This, I feel, is what Winnicott's contention does now compel us to accept.

I have no doubt about his facts. I have become convinced that all individuals, however mature for practical purposes, do reserve an inner core of the self in some degree of isolation. The entire problem of psychotherapy revolves round the patient's difficulty of trusting the therapist to contact this schizoid central self. In the last chapter I explored various meanings of the antilibidinal resistance to psychotherapy, but I have reserved for this chapter what is probably the most important, the fear-dictated need to preserve one's ultimate individuality at all costs (even at the cost of not being 'cured') from being overwhelmed by 'the other person', a fear-dictated defence against the entire outer world as such. None of us can have had such perfect parenthood as to have escaped some degree of such primitive fear, ego-splitting, and consequent development of a basically defensively structured personality. Some will feel this as an ultimate fear of being 'infinitely exploited', used, drained empty; others as a fear of being simply 'steamrollered' by an overwhelming environment, others again as being simply abandoned, lost. It is these primitive fears which in their worst form occur as what Winnicott calls the 'unthinkable anxieties' of going to pieces, falling for ever, having no relationship to the body, having no orientation (*op. cit.*, p. 58). *Of all the ultimate terrors, my clinical experience suggests that the last and worst is the one that is set up precisely by too drastic use of this defence by self-isolation, namely the feeling of being 'a psyche in a vacuum', out of all touch, out of all relationship, empty of all experience, and so to speak collapsing in on itself, lost in a sense of complete unreality, and unable to be an 'ego'.*

This, however, would seem to me to be the fate of a permanently isolated, non-communicating core of the self, which Winnicott feels must be a basis of health. Here I am unable to follow him, for it seems to me that this is the same thing as the basic 'ego-unrelatedness' that is the true nature of ego-weakness. I do not see how a core of the self that is an absolute isolate and incommunicado can be a self at all. A self can only experience itself in the act of experiencing something else. If it is totally empty of experience it cannot be a self. I cannot distinguish between absolute isolation and insulation. Both appear to me to involve ego-loss.

The fear of being found, infinitely exploited, or eaten up,

must derive from our being not strong enough to retain our full and proper individuality *in a relationship*, and not strong enough to choose for ourselves which relationships with actual other persons we will accept, or decide when we wish to withdraw into our *privacy*, a privacy which would consist not in being an isolate and incommunicado, but in the ability to be alone outwardly because one is fundamentally ego-related inwardly. The account Winnicott gives of the earliest stages of ego development and of object-relations development, enables us to understand this. His contention seems to be a statement of the fact that, owing to the extreme dependence and weakness of the human infant at birth, and the extreme difficulty of providing enough security in practice, *fear* is bound to arise as the earliest disrupting factor, and remains always the deepest problem; fear, not of a hypothetical death instinct or destructive instinct working within, but fear of traumatic factors coming from without; though this is not in itself part of the necessary potential healthy personality, but 'a reaction to impingement'.

To clarify this we must examine Winnicott's views about the transition involved in what he calls 'The object, being at first a subjective phenomenon' and then 'becoming an object objectively perceived'. All statements about human experience at the beginning are obviously inferences from later experience. We have no means of knowing directly what is the experience of a new-born baby. Perhaps the most difficult of all experiences to conceptualize here is that of the emergence of *objective* experience. We are concerned with this problem at this point, not for its own sake, but because it bears on the problem of the earliest fears and ego-splits. However objective experience first emerges, this occurs when the infant is at his weakest and most vulnerable, and his only protection is the quality of mothering he meets. At first he has no defences of his own, and his only defence against the rapidity of the first fear-reactions, is the closeness of maternal ego-support. Is the object at first a purely subjective experience? Must there not be some element in very early experience that represents incipient objectivity, out of which later clearly recognized objectivity grows? The capacity to experience what is outside himself is laid down in the entire biological and psychological constitution of the child. It would seem that even the very earliest sensory experience of objects must contain some elementary factor of objectivity, awaiting clarification and development.

Following on from this, a number of concepts used to describe early infantile experience seem to me to call for close scrutiny, such as that before the experience of objectivity is clearly established, the infant has an *experience of omnipotence* as if he felt that he *created the good object* that meets his need when in fact he 'finds it presented to him'. Omnipotence and creation are extremely sophisticated concepts to apply to the experience of an infant, and I cannot think they do more than suggest a useful way of thinking about something that we cannot get direct evidence about. It is true that there are later clinical facts that suggest the usefulness of these concepts, but they are already contaminated by later and more developed experiences, in an ego that has already become split and also oscillates between defensive identifications and growing differentiations with regard to its objects. There is also the view that bad object experience promotes the growth of objective experience more rapidly than good object experience. Is this necessarily correct? Will it not be likely that good object experience and bad object experience differ in quality, but that the infant mind is equally capable of detecting the element of objectivity in the experience in both cases? What seems to me to be likely is that the infant's extreme weakness and vulnerability and absolute dependence on the closest maternal support, are the all-important factors in the way his experience of objectivity develops from being a latent or implicit factor to being an evoked and explicit one. If it were possible to have an experience of mothering that was absolutely and completely good, the result, one would suppose, would be an extremely strong experience of basic ego-relatedness, that ideally could be thought of as proof against ego-splitting, and in such a case I cannot think there would be any *fear of being found* or communicated with. This is in practice impossible, however, and the infant's experience is mixed. He has objective experiences that are both good and bad. His good experience relates him securely to a benign environment, and if that were his whole experience, I cannot see how he should need an inner core of personality that is an isolate, needing a permanent defence against the outer world. But he also has bad experience that compels him to develop defences at the earliest stages, and ego-splitting arises. It is probably true in fact that *every personality has to some degree a schizoid core of the self, but that surely must be the basis of whatever degree of insecurity and mental ill-health is experienced. For all practical purposes, mental health must consist in having enough basic ego-relatedness and therefore ego-strength, to be capable of controlling one's 'communications situation', so as to be able either to withdraw into a privacy that is not empty or venture forth into relationships without fear.* Winnicott's final comment (*op. cit.*, p. 192) is that in the

. . . con-communicating central self, for ever immune from the reality principle, for ever silent. . . .

there is a kind of

communication that is non-verbal; it is, like the music of the spheres, absolutely personal. It belongs to being alive. And in health, it is out of this that communication naturally arises.

This is profoundly true, but in that case the 'central self' is not 'non-communicating and incommunicado'. The most profound communication is non-verbal, pre-verbal. To quote Marjorie Brierley,

One thing I feel pretty sure about is that we feel before we think, even in images, that feeling is therefore our means of discrimination as to what happens to us well before we become capable of strictly cognitive discrimination. . . . (Private communication.)

or therefore, I would add, of verbal communication. I cannot conceive of any part of a personality existing in utter isolation and yet retaining the characteristics of a self. But if, as I am sure is true, there is in the 'central self' a 'communication that is non-verbal. . . . It belongs to being alive', then the central self is not after all an 'isolate' and 'incommunicado'. The fundamental importance of this concept of 'being alive and in relationship' must be explored further in Chapter IX where the whole issue is re-examined in a new context.

I am not sure whether Winnicott distinguishes between the self and the ego, treating the latter as a more superficial phenomenon, so that he could think both of the core of the self as an isolate, and of ego-relatedness as essential to health. But I feel we need to use the term 'ego' in a more fundamental sense than that in which psychoanalysis has traditionally used it, as representing the evolution and realization of the intrinsic nature of the self, and ego and self are the same thing. There are, as I see it, two final fears. The first, the fear of the loss of the ego in a vacuum of experience, is the worst fear of all; it drives the individual to seek help, to depend on the therapist, and to accept the psychotherapeutic relationship as a medium in which he can find himself. The other fear is in actual fact practically as strong as the first, the fear, in Winnicott's words, of

the alteration of the self's central elements by communication seeping through the defences, the fear of losing one's proper individuality, of becoming something different from what one is. This leads the individual to shy away from help and resist psychotherapy, and hold on to his ill self because it is the self he is familiar with and he cannot appreciate what his 'true self' could be. One male patient expressed both fears in his very first remark at his first session, 'I am a non-person and I fear involvement.' Only if the therapist can help the patient to grow out of the second fear, can he rescue him from the first one, and help him to find his 'true self'. A patient who had had fifty years of severe strains following on good early mothering, dreamed

I was in a cold place, like life itself, but somehow mother was peeping into it in the back-ground.

His own comment was, 'The deeper you go, the better it gets. I feel I won't break down again now.' Analysis had helped him to find his basic ego-relatedness.

IX

THE ULTIMATE FOUNDATIONS OF EGO-IDENTITY

The Ego the Core of Reality in the Person

It is clear that psychodynamic research has been pushing us back inexorably to the absolute beginnings, the very start of the human personality. Our interest must in fact go back even into the intra-uterine state, but of recent years psychoanalysts have shown an active concern with the infant from the moment of birth. We have seen how, ever since the 1920's, when Freud began to formulate the emerging concepts of his most important theoretical advance, *an ever-widening research into ego-psychology, into the deepest depths of the unconscious and the earliest stages of infantile growth has become the outstanding feature of psychoanalysis.* It goes without saying that this research into the very beginnings of psychic life is not a study of conditioned reflexes, but of the emotional dynamics of the infant's growth in experiencing himself as 'becoming a person' in meaningful relationships, first with the mother, then the family, and finally with the ever-enlarging world outside.

Meaningful relationships are those which enable the infant to find himself as a person through experiencing his own significance for other people and their significance for him, thus endowing his existence with those values of human relationship which make life purposeful and worth living. Psychoanalytic research, naturally, was compelled to work the other way round, beginning with the end result of the socialized adult, and tracing the paths backwards till they all converged finally at their starting-point, the neonate, alive, physically separated from the mother, but not yet capable of distinguishing him self and mother as separate objects; not even as yet able to experience himself as an object, and only vaguely as a subject; perhaps at the very beginning only able to experience transitions between states of comfort and discomfort in what he will soon discover to be the infant–mother relationship. This at first is both his whole world and also his whole being. *How, out of this obscure beginning, does a human being come to be a person?* How does he come to have a well-defined ego, and become able to enter into personal relationships? Clearly, the process can go badly wrong from the start, and *psychoanalysis has become the search for the ego as the core of reality in the person.* It has been an exploration from the psycho-social circumference to the psycho-dynamic centre of the circle of our psychic life.[1]

What is the ultimate centre of our psychic reality? The work of Melanie Klein and Fairbairn do not take us quite there. Klein lands us in the mythology of an innate conflict between hypothetical life and death instincts. Fairbairn traced the patterns of the psyche's development into a multiple split ego but he assumed rather than explored the psyche's first steps in ego-growth. Of the first draft of my paper on 'Ego-Weakness' (1960) Fairbairn said, in 1959, 'I'm glad you have written this. If I could write now, this is the problem I would be writing about.' His health failed him before he could probe into the final meaning of what a patient of his once said: 'I've gone to rock-bottom where I feel I have not got an ego at all.' The concept of a 'regressed ego' implies an already 'formed ego' of which a part splits off and returns to the starting-point. Winnicott's concept of 'basic ego-relatedness' implies the prior differentiation of subject and object. His concept of a 'true self', masked by a 'false self', and hidden away in cold storage awaiting rebirth in a better environment, answers our question by raising another one. What is this 'true self'? It could be a potentiality that has never yet begun to be realized. To understand the whole problem of 'ego-weakness' we must go as deep as that.

What do we really mean by such terms as ego, self, identity, personality: how does it start, how does it grow, what is its essential nature, how can we help an individual, in whom the process of ego-growth has failed, to become an ego? What does it mean to have, or not have, an ego? How does a person who feels he has not an ego, come by one? The problem is particularly acute if we ask, 'What are we trying to do in psychotherapy?' Formulated answers easily have more form than content. One could say in object-relationship terms that since bad relationships made the person ill from infancy onwards, psychotherapy must provide a good-object relationship in which he can get well. That is formally correct, but what does it mean in practice? What is the content, the actual nature of this vital kind of relationship that makes it therapeutic? Fairbairn's last paper, 'On The Nature and Aims of Psychoanalytical Treatment' (1958), made me feel that this was only

[1] The relation of this to the work of Heinz Hartmann will be considered in Chapter XV.

the beginning of an object-relations theory of treatment. It had not begun to take account of the problem of regression, or of the even deeper problem of 'not having an ego at all'. I have already made use of Winnicott's work on 'therapeutic regression in search of a True Self' as a valuable exploration into this most difficult area of our experience, and I propose to use some further ideas of his, in an unpublished paper of February 1966, to pursue the exploration. This paper, 'The Split-Off Male and Female Elements to be Found Clinically in Men and Women', is about the meaning of 'bisexuality' in the human constitution. The relevance of this will be clarified by first placing Winnicott's work in what appears to me to be its true position in the development of psychoanalytic theory. Psychoanalytic theory had for a long time the appearance of the exploration of a circle which had no obvious centre until ego-psychology got under way. Exploration had to begin with peripheral phenomena—behaviour, moods, symptoms, conflicts, mental 'mechanisms', erotic drives, aggression, fears, guilts, psychotic and psychoneurotic states, instincts and impulses, erotogenic zones, maturational stages, and so on. All this is naturally important and must find its place in the total theory, but actually it is all secondary to some absolutely fundamental factor which is the 'core' of the 'person' as such.

Stages of Psychoanalytic Theory

Winnicott quotes a case of a male patient for whom interpretations in terms of any of these secondary phenomena were not 'mutative'. He could see a real point in them, but they set nothing moving. *Interpretations, however, which bore on the ego's need and struggle to come by a sense of reality, of reliable on-going 'being' at once evoked a response.* The psychoanalytic circle was finding its centre. Here we are dealing with the truly universal problem, varying in degree, of all human beings. The theme of bisexuality, that there are normally both male and female elements in both men and women, each needing their appropriate development and integration with each other, along with the particular meaning Winnicott gives to these elements, has to do with *the very constitution and nature of the individual person, the basic 'ego' as such*, and what goes to its making. In the case quoted a crucial interpretation had taken the analysis into this region. Winnicott says:

We could now explain why my interpretations, made on good grounds, in respect of use of object, oral erotic satisfactions in the transference, oral sadistic ideas. . . ., why such interpretations were never mutative. They were accepted, but; so what? Now the new position had been reached the patient felt a sense of relationship with me, and this was extremely vivid. *It had to do with identity.* [My italics.]

This points to the very centre of the concentric circles of psycho-analytic theory and therapy: a series of five concentric circles with a common centre. The outermost circle is the life of the individual as a member of his social world. From there, investigation proceeds into his capacities for human relationships, as shaped by his experiences in childhood, raising the problems of personality illness on first neurotic and then psychotic levels. This brings us to the heart of the acute difficulties the human infant has in struggling to establish his personality in the earliest years, and thence to the centre of all these circles, the absolute beginnings of ego-identity in infancy. The five concentric circles with their centre may be set forth as six stages beginning with the latest and working down to the earliest.

FREUD

(1) *The Individual in Society*, object-relations in real life, with variable degrees of adjustment and maladjustment, and not too serious character neurosis and psychoneurotic symptoms. Human life in general as we see it and take it at face value, coping practically with it, rather than looking too deeply into its anxieties and tensions.

(2) *Oedipal Problems*, looking below the surface of the day-to-day dealings of human beings with each other, to the emotional capacities of the individual for object-relationships, as fashioned within and limited by the family set-up and ties to parents and siblings; healthy normal oedipal developments; pathological oedipal patterns grown-in to the structure of the emotional personality, and operative in the outer world.

(3) *Personality Illness, the Failing Struggle to Function Socially*, and maintain good-enough object-relations, and stand up to real life pressures when they play upon pathological patterns of grown-in tensions in the unconscious.

(*a*) *Psychoneurotic Anxiety States* over sexual and aggressive antisocial impulses, with their somatic resonances.

(*b*) *Ambivalence, Love-hate Conflicts, Guilt and Depression*, primitive ruthlessness, fear of destructiveness and the need to make reparation, manic-depressive mood swings, not yet of psychotic intensity. The transference neuroses, hysteria, obsessions, phobias, paranoid attitudes in neurosis.

(1), (2), and (3) are pre-eminently the sphere of Freud, taking into account the fact that, increasingly from 1920 his thinking revolved around *ego-analysis*, the aspect of his theory that Hartmann developed so fully. In (3), however, the work of Melanie Klein begins to go beyond Freud.

MELANIE KLEIN

(4) *Deeper Level Illness, the Struggle to Keep Possession of an Ego.*

(*a*) *Exploration of the earliest stages of ego-development*, the early infantile anxiety-positions, and infantile origins of psychosis. The depressive and paranoid positions in development, *internal objects and object-splittings*, and the fantasy 'inner world'.

This embraces the main original Kleinian contribution.

FAIRBAIRN

(*b*) *Schizoid Problems*, detachment from real object-relations, and withdrawal to living in the secret inner fantasy world. *Ego-splittings* matching object-splittings. Regressed illnesses.

This is particularly the sphere of Fairbairn.

The isolation of the schizoid ego in the unconscious, Winnicott's 'true self in cold storage', my development of Fairbairn's theory to include a split in the infantile libidinal ego, leading to a regressed ego.

At this point we must note that the work of Melanie Klein grew out of the analysis of young children in general, and the work of Fairbairn grew out of the analysis of schizoid adults in the light of Melanie Klein's findings. In all this, research was delving further and further back into earliest infancy. There were many workers in this field, but for the further stages I have designated (5) and (6), *the work of Winnicott on the earliest mother–child relationship* seems to me to yield the ideas that become the key concepts for understanding these deepest levels of psychic life.

(5) *The Beginnings of the Ego*. The differentiation of subject and object out of the state of primary identification, stimulating the beginnings of specific ego-development. The growth of the experience of *basic ego-relatedness*, and therewith of the capacity both to enter into objection-relations and also to be alone, without anxiety and insecurity. Difficulties at this stage, before the ego is strongly consolidated, will then lead to object-splitting and ego-splitting, as studied by Klein and Fairbairn.

WINNICOTT

(6) *Before the Differentiated Ego, the Absolute Start of the Ego*, factually in an object-relation which the infant cannot yet experience as an object-relation but can experience (in sophisticated adult language) as *symbiosis, identity* with (in favourable cases) a stable object, the good enough mother; making possible the beginnings of the experience of 'being', or 'security' and of 'self-identity'. With the good mother all this takes place in a condition of maximum protection against anxiety. It is sometimes said that bad-object experience provides the first powerful stimulus to the differentiation of a separate ego. If that were so, the ego could never have any other than an anxious base. *To be capable of development to full maturity, the ego must begin to differentiate out of a basic experience of full security in the mutual identification of mother and infant.* Primary identification is a relationship with a subjective object, an experience in which, for the baby, subject and object are as yet all one (in his experience). This, (stage (6), the centre of the five concentric circles discriminated in theory) allows of the emergence (stage (5), the first clearly definable phase of development) of the 'objective object' and the 'objective subject', i.e. the specific Ego.

Section 5 is covered in Winnicott's writings by Chapters 1, 2, and 3 in *The Family and Individual Development* (especially in Chapter 2, 'The Relationship of a Mother to her Baby at the Beginning'), and by Chapters 2, 3, 4, and 17 in *The Maturational Processes and The Facilitating Environment* (especially Chapter 2, 'The Capacity to be Alone'). Three quotations will suffice:

Ego immaturity is naturally balanced by ego-support from the mother (p. 32). The maternal ego implementing the infant ego and so making it powerful and stable. (p. 41.)

Is the (infant) ego strong or weak? The answer depends on the actual mother and her ability to meet the absolute dependence of the actual infant at the beginning, at the stage before the infant has separated out the mother from the self. (p. 57.)

This last quotation takes us back to stage (6); and his chapter on 'Communicating and Not Communicating' implies the need to go back to *the absolute start of the ego* where we find 'primary maternal preoccupation', and 'primary identification' of infant with mother. Winnicott's paper on bisexuality also takes us back to this starting-point, and especially his view of the nature of 'the female element', to which we now turn.

Psyche, Ego and the Experience of Being

Accepting the view that human nature is constitutionally bisexual, he seeks to ascertain what this means by trying to isolate the 'pure male element' and the 'pure female element' in our make-up. He suggests that the nature of the male element is expressed in 'doing' and the nature of the female element in the experience of 'being', which he regards as transmitted always by the mother. These terms 'doing' and 'being' call for exact and careful definition, but clearly the capacity for 'doing' should rest on a prior capacity for 'being', a basic experience of secure, non-anxious 'inbeingness'. We can observe clinically in our patients that the struggle to maintain activity and 'doing' when one is in the grip of a basic feeling of 'non-being', and of far-reaching lack of confidence in oneself as a person, is a receipt for gross anxiety and dangerous tension. A good enough relationship with a stable mother is the basis of the possibility, through primary identification, of the first nascent experiences of security, selfhood, identity, the definitive start of the ego, making possible in turn a growth in object-relationships, as *the differentiation of subject and object proceeds and the baby acquires a 'not-me' world and feels to be a 'me' over against it. Before that, the ego is there as a potentiality, latent in the psyche since the infant starts off as 'a whole human being' (Winnicott). That is really what Fairbairn meant in speaking of 'a pristine unitary ego'*. But it is only through this kind of experience with the mother that the ego can begin as a specific development, an increasingly conscious fact of experience (not the same as the later developed specific 'self-consciousness'). In the absence of this kind of mother–infant relation, a viable ego does not get started, and the resulting sense of profound underlying inner emptiness, nothingness, 'non-being as a person', is the gravest of all problems for psychotherapy; a problem that can only be solved if the analysts' understanding of it succeeds in relating the patient to himself, so as to make a belated start in ego-growth possible.

In the light of this, Fairbairn's term 'pristine unitary ego' should perhaps be understood to mean 'pristine unitary psyche' with latent ego-quality, for, as development proceeds, ego and psyche may not be identical, though in a theoretically perfect development they would be. Every aspect of the psyche that finds expression has ego quality, but the primary wholeness of the psyche is obscured and lost beneath the fragmentation of a split ego. The ego is always a latent possibility in, and indeed belongs to the essential nature of the *human* psyche. *The human psyche is an incipient ego and if it were not, it would not be human.* That is what Fairbairn was concerned to stress in speaking of a 'pristine unitary ego'. All psychic experience, however un-integrated or disintegrated, must have some degree of ego-quality as the experience of a 'subject'. There has to be a 'subject' to *have* the experience even of depersonalization and derealization. On the other hand, the human psyche does not always develop a very definite ego, and always, even in the most mature, there is some degree of ego -splitting and failure to achieve basic unity and wholeness of psychic development. 'Pysche' is the hereditarily constituted psychic existence of the human being as a subject of experience, there from the ante-natal start before the time when the term 'ego' could be meaningfully applied. It includes all his innate energies, latent capacities, and potential powers (intelligence, gifts, etc.). Even if no very specific ego forms, the human being struggles along 'in existence', feeling that his experience has no proper centre and no coherent ground; trying to become a 'person' by 'doing', by using his energies and abilities in spite of a lack of a proper sense of being, of whole stable selfhood. In the worst case he may be psychotic, struggling to achieve and maintain some semblance of selfhood in his internal fantasy world, by methods that most people will not recognize for what they are. Where there should be a feeling of 'ego', there is only the experience of uncertainty, of 'not counting', of being 'nobody in particular'.

The ego in its earliest beginnings is the psychic subject experiencing itself as 'satisfactorily in being', perhaps a realization of what Freud called the 'pleasure principle', though curiously enough this is the only possible basis for the growth of a sense of 'ego-reality'. It starts at some point in the feeling of security and the enjoyment of it, as part of the overall experience of 'being with mother' prior to differentiation of subject and object. *The ego is the psyche growing to self-realization and identity, in the initial experience of identification and shared emotional experience with the mother.* This will be found in its most complete form in the infant's relationship to the breast. Returning to Winnicott's use of 'bisexuality', i.e. that it involves the existence of both male and female elements in both females and males, he refers to a 'female element breast' which presumably above all makes possible for the infant *the sense of 'being' prior to 'doing'*. By contrast, the not very maternal, busy, bustling, organizing, dominating mother, who is determined that the baby shall 'get on with his feed' at the rate her time-table dictates, will present him with a 'pseudo-male-element breast' which seeks to 'do things' to him. The maternal mother, who understands her baby's emotional needs, especially in the earliest stages, can let him feed and enjoy it at his own pace, and can then (most important) let him go to sleep peacefully and restfully at the breast. She gives him a 'female element breast' *par excéllence*, at which he can experience utter peace of tranquil existence, simple 'being'. This must represent the most complete experience of security possible in human life. If it is sufficiently adequate and repeated for long enough, it must lay the psychic foundations of basic inner strength of ego-development as that proceeds and proliferates. It is an experience that we could only express in sophisticated verbal form by the simple statement 'I am', or possibly 'I am because I *feel* secure and real', (not 'I do' or even 'I think', for 'thinking' is only a psychic form of 'doing') though it must be a long time before it can arrive at such clarity. This is the sixth stage as outlined above, *the absolute start of the ego.*

Bisexuality as 'Being' and 'Doing'

We must now consider more closely Winnicott's use of 'being' and 'doing' to define the 'female' and 'male' elements in human nature. Questions of terminology and conceptualization confront us. He raises these with reference to the case of a male patient in whom he was faced with the

> complete dissociation between the man and the aspect of the personality that has the opposite sex. In the case of this man patient the dissociation was nearly complete.

Such dissociation can occur in either a male or a female patient and he regards this deep level of the personality as not easily reached by analysis. It is about

> matters that concern the deepest or most central features of the personality

and only

> . . . at long length [is] the patient able to bring [such] deeply buried matters into the content of the transference.

The evolution of two sexes, male and female, out of an originally sexless form of life, certainly involved not only a differentiation of physical functions but also to some extent of basic emotional capacities. Some years ago a case of physical change of sex was reported in a married man who was already a father; he became a woman and found that the outstanding turning point in the development of a new womanly self-awareness was the sudden emergence of a new strong maternal feeling for babies. True, fathers can share this feeling but we hardly claim that they feel it as powerfully as mothers do. The capacities of both sexes are present, if not developed identically, in both sexes.

In the case Winnicott examines he says:

> There was a dissociation [of the opposite sexual element] that was on the point of breaking down. The dissociation defence was giving way to an acceptance of bisexuality as a quality of the unit or total self. . . . I was dealing with what could be called *a pure female element* [i.e. in a male].

He adds:

> In our theory it is necessary to allow for both a male and a female element in boys and men and girls and women. These elements may be split off to a high degree . . . I wish to compare and contrast the unalloyed male and female elements in the contexts of object-relating.

Winnicott recognizes that the meaning of these terms is not yet finalized. He says:

> I shall continue to use this terminology [male and female elements] for the time being, since I know of no other suitable descriptive terms. Certainly 'active' and 'passive' are not correct terms, and I must continue with the argument using the terms that are available.

Repression, Withdrawal, and Dissociation

One other question of terminology is important, the meaning of 'dissociation'. In Janet's sense of the falling apart of elements in a psyche that was not strong enough to hold itself together, it was replaced by Freud's dynamic concept of 'repression', the active rejection into the unconscious of memories or impulses that were not acceptable to the conscious ego. The repression of antisocial impulses at the instance of guilt as a depressive phenomenon is a case in point, and may be contrasted with 'Withdrawal', the flight inside of a part of the ego that feels too weak to cope with outer reality. Both repression and withdrawal imply an ego already formed and capable of being split. Should we use 'dissociation' to denote 'withdrawal' as distinct from repression (much as a man may 'dissociate' himself from a movement he has fallen out of sympathy with, i.e. withdraw from membership): or does 'dissociation' denote a more primitive phenomenon, some constitutional potentiality that has been left out at the beginning of the process of growth, something apart, unevoked, blocked off from the start, never integrated or given a chance to develop. In this case the constitutional male and female elements in the psyche will have failed to become associated together in the early stages of development so that an incomplete self comes about. Winnicott regards the 'dissociated' as something in the patient's make-up that he himself cannot know; it is outside the range of his ego-experience, conscious or unconscious. It is something the analyst must discern for the patient. This applies radically to the unevoked and undeveloped potential in the psyche. The 'withdrawn' or 'regressed' libidinal ego is also kept repressed. The 'true self in cold storage' could, it seems to me, mean either the repressed regressed ego or the dissociated unevoked psychic potential. In both cases the patient has lost touch with his own potentialities, and we have to help him to find himself. With the patient under discussion, it was only Winnicott's 'seeing' his split-off female element as something the patient was expressing in the session without realizing it, that enabled him to know himself in that respect. He writes:

> The pure female split-off element found a primary unity with me as analyst, and this gave the man a feeling of having started to live.

We may see the withdrawn ego and the undeveloped potential as two different levels of the 'dissociated', and be prepared to find both present and the first barring the way to the second.

Then, accepting Winnicott's usage that the female element yields the experience of 'being' and the male element that of 'doing', it appears to me that clinically *it is always the female element that we find dissociated, in both men and women, and that the fundamental dissociation is of the female element.* If 'being' exists, 'doing' will follow naturally from it. If it is not there but dissociated, then a forced kind of 'doing' will have to do duty for both, but where the capacity for 'doing' fails completely, it must be because the sense of 'being' is totally absent. A speaker in a television programme on 'The Sense of Belonging' stated, 'I plunged into marriage and motherhood and tried to substitute doing for being.' It was the sense of 'being', the female element, that had either never been evoked in her, left out from the start of her development, or else had been lost through the withdrawal and regression into the unconscious depths, of the heart of her libidinal nature. It remained a dissociated potentiality in the absence of which any amount of busy 'doing' was like a superstructure of a house with no foundation to rest on. Her 'doing' was not dissociated except as spontaneous activity. It was forced and tensely obvious. *The female element is best exemplified in the maternal feeling that evokes and fosters an experience of 'being' in the infant as a starting-point of all personality growth; the capacity to feel with, and then to feel for, the capacity to feel oneself as 'in relationship', the basic permanent experience of ego-relatedness, of which the sense of 'being' is the core, and without which the psyche loses all sense of its own reality as an ego*. One cannot 'be' anything in a vacuum. Having developed this capacity to 'be' by experiencing the primary relationship with a good enough mother, this will lead spontaneously to the arising of a healthy unforced capacity to 'do', to carry on the activities necessary for maintaining and fulfilling the relationship in practical ways. The experience of 'being' would be stultified if it did not lead on to the practical expression of 'doing'. The experience of 'doing' in the absence of a secure sense of 'being' degenerates into a meaningless succession of mere activities (as in the obsessional's meaningless repetition of the same thought, word or act), not performed for their own proper purpose but as a futile effort to 'keep oneself in being', to 'manufacture' a sense of 'being' one does not possess.

An absence, non-realization, or dissociation of the experience of 'being' and of the possibility of it, and, along with that, incapacity for healthy natural spontaneous 'doing' is the most radical clinical phenomenon in analysis. Patients realize that they have been working hard all their lives busily 'doing', not in a natural but a forced way, to create an illusory sense of reality as a person, a substitute for the experience of 'inbeingness' in a solid and self-assured way that is the only basis of the self-confidence nearly all patients complain of lacking. The experience of 'being' is more than the mere awareness of 'existence'. It involves the sense of reliable security in existence, realized both in knowing oneself as a real person and as able to make good relationships. *The experience of 'being' is the beginning and basis for the realization of the potentialities in our raw human nature for developing as a 'person' in personal relationships*. These potentialities are given in our psychobiological inheritance, but can only be developed in what Winnicott calls a 'facilitating environment' of adequate mothering at the start: so that the experience of 'being' and of 'being in relationship' are inseparable from the start. When the sense of 'being' develops, 'doing' follows as easy and natural self-expression along lines of genuine interest.

If it is not there 'doing' in that natural sense does not occur. Activity is forced, tense, strained, an attempt to compel an insecure personality to carry on as a 'going concern'. This may become a manic or obsessional compulsive activity, for the 'mind' cannot stop, relax or rest because of a secret fear of collapsing into non-existence. *It is the individual's capacity for experiencing a sense of 'being' that is primarily dissociated, left unrealized at the start of development. He cannot get at his capacity to feel real*, because at the start of life no one evoked it, his mother gave him so little genuine relationship that he actually came to feel unreal. This emerges with startling clarity in those patients who feel so undermined that they feel they will never be strong enough to cope with living.

Pathological 'Being' and 'Doing' as Pseudo-female and Pseudo-male

Winnicott's equation of 'being and doing' with 'pure female and male elements' is illuminated if we consider its pathological forms. He regards 'passive and active' as not correct terms for these elements, but they have an important bearing on them. I shall speak rather of 'passivity and *forced* activity'. We find patients oscillating between these opposite states when hard-driven over-activity breaks down into passive, i.e. suffering, exhaustion. We may treat them as pathological forms of male and female elements, for they are, in fact, frequently thought of in that way by patients who feel that 'feminine' signifies 'weakness' and 'masculine' signifies 'aggressive pseudo-strength'. Thus a bachelor patient in his forties said: 'I used to rush about doing things as a "man about town" copying my mother's social role, my façade for not feeling sure of being anything, not being sure what sort of a person I was.' He had a steady, capable, but unassuming and unassertive father, and a dominant, socially successful manic-depressive mother who 'wore the trousers'. His parents presented him with an inverted pattern of pseudo-female and male roles in which the mother made all the running, and the father, except in very important matters, gave way to her. This background hardly helps the child to develop a healthy personality. Sexual differences appear as mutually exclusive opposites and as conventionalized role-playing, not as genuine and basic qualities of personality. Masculine and feminine are thought of as muscle and softness, toughness and gentleness, strength and weakness, aggressiveness and timidity, forced activity and passivity, whichever sex displays them. The understanding of male and female elements in the personality as being mutually necessary and complementary in development, cannot be got at. In these pathological forms, the pseudo-male attitudes substitute for both healthy doing and healthy being, while the pseudo-female attitudes of passivity or weakness essentially express non-being, not being a proper person. If the healthy 'female element' is disassociated the healthy 'male' element is lost as well.

Thus, the bachelor patient I have just mentioned said: 'As a little boy I was a sissy, I didn't play rough games like boys, I cried easily if hurt. I feel now that my physique is weak and girlish, but I felt I was becoming masculine when I got a motor-bike. Now I have a car but I still fantasy myself as a ton-up youth taking a shadowy girl on the pillion. She never has any real personality but is only there to admire me. When I feel anxious I still put on my leather jacket and tight belt round my waist and look at myself in the glass and feel tough and masculine.' Adler's 'masculine protest' was an early indentification of this pseudo-male, pathological sex role which can appear in both men and women. It often develops into sadism and destructiveness, and carries the complementary idea of the woman as the weaker sex; an idea which, except in the crude muscular sense, has no counterpart in reality, but has great importance in psychopathology. When male is equated with sadism, then female is equated with masochism. Disturbed women harbour these ideas as much as disturbed men. Thus a female patient, a spinster in her early fifties, when anxious, depressed, or when she felt she was being 'made into nothing' at work by coercion or undervaluation, would fly into violent rages to master her fears, and scream out: 'I'm not a woman, I'm a man, a man. They cut off my penis and left me with a filthy hole.' It emerged that this 'hole' symbolized her pathological version of the female element, a sense not only of her weakness but of her sense of 'non-being', of there being nothing there, an emptiness at the heart of her. As a little girl she had once been left at home with an older male cousin who had undressed her and stood over her exposing his penis and bragging of his strength. This terrified her and made her feel 'just a weak helpless little thing'. But the extent of her fear in that situation had pre-existing causes. Her parents presented her with the inverted pattern of pseudo-sex roles, a mild father who never effectively protected her from a mother who did not want children, hated her and beat her, and took charge of the family money and business. In such patients one sees clearly the conflict between opposed pseudo-male and pseudo-female attitudes, always involving them in hatred of the supposedly female characteristics (located in the weak parent irrespective of sex). *The pseudo-female side in these cases is not dissociated but rejected and if possible repressed, both in men and women, in favour of a pseudo-male role.* The true female potentiality remains dissociated. Here are the pathological versions of 'being and doing', 'female and male', in the forms of 'passivity' (weakness, submissiveness, helplessness, nonentity) and 'forced activity' (toughness, strenuousness, aggressiveness, destructiveness, compulsive over-activity). What is lacking is always a strong, secure primary sense of 'being' from which healthy activity could flow unforced, in terms of objective interests without secondary anxious subjective motives. Healthy 'being' and 'doing' are complementary.

Healthy 'Being' and 'Doing' as True Female and Male Characteristics

If pathological 'being and doing' appear in sexual guise, it seems probable that their healthy forms have a genuine sexual connotation. In what sense is 'being' characteristically 'female' and 'doing' characteristically 'male'? And in what sense does 'female' specially characterize the female sex, and 'male' the male sex, since the pure female and male elements do not mean woman and man, for both elements must naturally be developed together in both sexes? Yet we must expect women, in their constitutional make-up, to be 'weighted' on the side of the 'pure female element', and men to be similarly 'weighted' on the side of the 'pure male element', without the opposite sex element being absent. Pathological 'weighting' occurs in the masculine protest in a woman and effeminacy in a man. How shall we describe the 'weighting' in healthy persons? It must come from the original circumstances which led to the differentiation of the sexes and shaped for them different functions in the procreation and rearing of children. From the outset the terms 'being' and 'doing' seem appropriate to describe these functions, the mother having the more intrinsically important part to play. The female receives what the male gives in the sexual act, and when she becomes pregnant her part at first is not so much to 'do' as to 'be' for the child. There is nothing she can 'do' but if she ceases to 'be' the child will cease to 'be'. Her being and the baby's being are linked inseparably as a physical fact, and *this 'oneness' is carried over into the beginnings of the infant's psychic life. Only gradually can he stand separation on the basis of undisturbed oneness*, in some sense preserved psychically after physical separation, as the ground of the possibility of 'relationship'.

Meanwhile the father's part is to sustain the 'being' of both mother and infant by his 'doing' as hunter, foodseeker, and protector, without whom they would most likely die. At first, his part has not the same deep intrinsic importance *for the start of the child's personality* as the mother's, though it increases in importance as time goes on. The mother must later develop her capacities for 'doing' for and with the child as he develops separate individuality apart from her, and at the same time as the child develops a personal relationship with the father, he too must become able to have a maternal capacity simply to 'be' as a basis for the child's secure development. 'Male' and 'female' are thus not primarily sexual terms in the narrow genital sense. Genital functioning reflects the total personality functioning of the mother and father. A man and woman expressing together their mutual love in sexual relationship will both alternate in reacting on the basis of both female and male elements. A man and woman making love passionately together are both reacting with their maleness, actively 'doing'. A man and woman lying quietly and restfully in each other's arms, simply aware of mutual well-being and security are both reacting from their female element, simply experiencing their secure existence each in themselves but in the medium of their being securely together; so much so that they can afford, without danger to their separate individualities, to forget their separateness, and experience identity and oneness, as they may also do at the height of mutual sexual orgasm. This relives on the adult level the primary identification each of them had as infants with mother if all went well. Furthermore, one may be male, actively 'doing' while the other is female, quietly and receptively 'being', each in turn.

This oscillation of both partners between male and female element reactions, not only characterizes their narrowly sexual relations, but their whole relationship in marriage. Each will, in so far as they are integrated and whole mature persons, be able to relate to each other and to their children on the basis of both 'female being' and 'male doing'. Nevertheless, *the capacity for 'being' is fundamentally the female and maternal element, because the relationship of the mother to the child is fundamental in a way the father's is not.* Winnicott illustrates this by reference to the two different kinds of object-relating, (*a*) object-relating in terms of drives for satisfactions, implying separateness, activity, doing, and (b) object-relating in terms of identification, simply as an experience of subject-object identity as the basis of the capacity to 'be' as an emotional experience. The first is a male relating, the second a female relating. Winnicott writes: 'The male element *does* while the female element (in males and females) *is*.' So totally dependent is the infant at first that the very possibility of the start of his ego-development rests entirely on the mother's capacity to 'be' an adequate source of security. This makes the equation not arbitrary. He writes:

> However complex the sense of self and the establishment of an identity eventually becomes as a baby grows, no sense of self emerges except on the basis of this relating in the sense of BEING.

The 'sense of being' is the gift of stable mothers to both males and females, and is the basis of strong ego-growth and therefore of mental health, in the beginning.

One male patient said: 'I always think of a real mother as not a bustling, busy, organizing woman who "runs" the household, but as a quiet, serene, warm, deep character whose very presence makes the family feel secure.' Such a woman is quite capable of 'doing' but is likely to get things done with little fuss and without seeming over-busy. The same is true of a stable male. In both sexes we must say that the typically male element of 'doing' must rest on the typically female element of 'being', and the sense of 'being' is to be regarded as female because it depends for both sexes on adequate mothering from the start. The mother must first enable her baby to have a sense of the reliability of his own secure existence, by being the kind of person with whom the baby can share in her secure 'being'. Only then can the baby go on to develop a full capacity to express his own reality by spontaneous unforced self-expressive activity, because he has a self to express, a strong ego to be active with. A spinster in her fifties who was hated by her mother and whose life had been one long angry struggle to drive herself on, said, 'I can't cope with life. I've got nothing to cope with life with.' She was not referring to abilities, which she did not lack, but to her not having any inner feeling of being a whole real person. The struggle to substitute 'doing' for 'being' is always nearer to breakdown point than the individual cares to know. This made one patient say: 'I'm only a thin veneer of the intellectual professional man over a chaos of deep-down emptiness, terror and ferocity.'

Male and Female Relating and Knowing: Thinking and Feeling

The 'male way of object-relating' presents no difficulty in definition. It is the active way of 'doing', and in much of recreation, sexual activity, work co-operation, intellectual pursuits, and scientific investigation, both males and females are relating with their male element capacities, doing something with someone. The 'female element' plays a sustaining part varying with the nature of the activity. The 'female way of object-relating' presents some difficulty. Winnicott is, apparently, in two minds about it. He writes:

I wish to compare and contrast the unalloyed male and female elements in the context of object-relating. . . . The element I am calling 'male' does traffic in terms of active relating or passive being related to, each backed by instinct (i.e. specific impulses). . . . By contrast, the pure female element relates to the breast (or to the mother) in the sense that the object is the subject. . . . Here in this relatedness of pure female element to breast is a practical application of the idea of the subjective object, and the experience of this paves the way for the objective subject—that is the idea of a self, and the feeling of real that springs from having an identity. . . . No sense of self emerges except on the basis of this relating in the sense of BEING . . . The term primary identification has perhaps been used for just this. . . . As the ego begins to organize, this that I am calling the object-relating of the pure female element establishes what is perhaps the simplest of all experiences, the experience of 'being'.

Nevertheless, he later writes:

This pure female element has nothing to do with object-relating. Object-relating belongs to the boy aspect of the personality uncontaminated by the female element.

There is an ambiguity in his use of the term 'relating', so that he both affirms and denies that 'female element identifying' is a way of relating.

This ambiguity carries over into the problems of 'communicating' and 'knowing'. He distinguishes between a male element breast and a female element breast. The male element breast is characterized by 'doing', when actively feeding the baby. By contrast the female element breast is not *doing something for*, but *being something for* the baby, simply being there as a safe, reliable, warm, comforting contact; giving not food but relationship, love, interest, attention, everything that enables the infant to feel securely 'in being', protecting him against premature disturbance before he is able to deal with it. At first the infant knows no difference between himself and the breast, but feels that he 'is' because the breast 'is'. Here is the origin of all 'knowing by identification'. Thus there are two ways of 'knowing'. The *male way of knowing* in its highest development is objective analytical scientific investigation. The *female way of knowing* in the completest sense is the mother's intuitive knowledge of her baby. Thus Winnicott writes:

'Primary maternal pre-occupation' . . . is the thing that gives the mother her special ability to do the right thing. She knows what the baby could be feeling like. No one else knows. Doctors and nurses may know a lot about psychology, and of course they know all about body health and disease. But they do not know what a baby feels like from minute to minute because they are outside this area of experience. (*The Family and Individual Development*, p. 15.)

They are scientists, not mothers. Thus we may say that *'feeling' is the female element, a state of being, of being in touch, of knowing by identification:* while *'thinking' is a male element, intellectual activity.* Both men and women are capable of both thinking and feeling. Both can concentrate too exclusively on intellectual activities and remain undeveloped in their female and maternal capacities, to the impoverishment of their personalities and of their capacity to 'know' in a deeper sense. Marjorie Brierley, as previously quoted, writes:

One thing I feel pretty sure about is that we feel before we think, even in images, and that feeling is therefore our means of discrimination with respect to what happens to us well before we become capable of strictly cognitive discrimination.

This ambiguity of meaning of 'relating' and 'knowing' with respect to the female element, seems to supply the key to the problem (discussed in Chapter VIII) posed by Winnicott in his paper on 'Communicating and Not Communicating', namely, 'Is the individual ultimately and at bottom an isolate?' He states:

Although healthy persons communicate and enjoy communicating, the other fact is equally true, that *each individual is an isolate, permanently non-communicating, permanently unknown, in fact unfound*. . . . At the centre of each person is an incommunicado element. . . . The violation of the self's core, the alteration of the self's central elements by communication seeping through the defences: for me this would be the sin against the self. . . . The question is: how to be isolated without having to be insulated?

He summarizes this as:

The non-communicating central self, for ever immune from the reality principle, and for ever silent. Here communication is

> non-verbal . . . absolutely personal. It belongs to being alive. . . . It is out of this that communication naturally arises.

Here, however, is the same ambiguity in the meaning of 'communicating'. He does not really mean that the central self is non-communicating but that it does not communicate in the male way:

> Here communication is non-verbal . . . absolutely personal . . . it is out of this that communication (i.e. verbal communication based on the male function of 'thinking') arises.

The difference is not between communicating and not-communicating, but *between communicating verbally and non-verbally, on the basis of thinking and feeling, the male and female ways of relating, knowing, and communicating*. If the central self were really non-communicating, it would be an isolate, and this would destroy the very thing Winnicott contends for: namely that

> No sense of self emerges except on the basis of this *relating* in the sense of BEING,

the 'knowing' and 'communicating' involved in the basic mother–infant relationship of primary indentification. Since the central self can communicate non-verbally, personally, in this way, it cannot be an isolate. The term 'isolate' also is used ambiguously.

'The central core of the personality' must be the same as 'the uncontaminated female element that leads us to BEING'. 'Doing' is a secondary development. The 'core of the self' does not communicate verbally in the male way or enter into active object-relations, but it does communicate personally and pre-verbally, and enters into object-relations in the female way. There are two ways of relating, knowing and communicating; *the male element way* of relating by active doing, knowing by thinking, and communicating by verbal symbols of ideas. It centres on the intellectual processes. *The female element way* is that of relating by identifying and sharing in a sense of being, knowing by feeling, and communicating by emotional empathy. This is the mother's way with the baby and it enables the baby to establish his ego-identity. Only when this way of relating breaks down does the baby grow up to be really an 'isolate' at heart, unable to communicate and in terror both of being found and of remaining unfound. All this is recognized in the familiar line, 'Thoughts that do often lie too deep for tears', or for any expression in words, an experience common in earliest motherhood, profound friendship, and true marital love. The criticism may be made that this implies extrasensory perception, but that only draws a red herring across the trail. Sensory experience plays its part in both emotional and intellectual processes. In the former it merges in feeling; in the latter it is the basis of images, ideas, and thoughts.

We may summarize the whole line of thought thus: 'doing' flowing naturally from a secure sense of 'being' is a state of balanced and integrated mature development of our bisexual make-up. 'Doing' should not have to be carried on to create and sustain a sense of 'being', but should express and satisfy the needs and interests of an ego that can take its secure and reliable on-going being for granted, because the mother took care of that physically, and, even more important, mentally. The infant can grow up with no feeling of having to work hard to keep himself mentally functioning and alive. When activity has to be devoted to that, the resulting strain, tension, and exhaustion blocks full free development.

The problem of the female element of being and the male element of doing, as different factors in our nature which should be complementary but may be forced into conflict, can appear clinically in a particular form. The female element may be defined as *the need to be emotionally susceptible*, *the capacity for sensitiveness to what others are feeling*. This is most necessary to the mother if she is to understand her baby and sense his needs. By contrast, the male element, seen as *the need to be able to take practical action in an often difficult and dangerous world*, and if necessary to harden the heart to do what is unavoidable, had to fall to the lot of the father who could not afford to be too sensitive. That is how it worked out in a rough-and-ready way, though both capacities needed to be available to both men and women. None fights fiercer than the animal mother in defence of her young, and the male must do a share of mothering. However, considered as elements in our total make-up, the female element is the emotionally sensitive self that can be more easily hurt, and can then be felt as a weakness to be resisted, resented, and hidden behind a tough exterior. Patients who have not been able to develop the tough superficial defence but have remained too vulnerable and sensitive, may generate an intense unconscious hate of their female element, project it, and experience frightening destructive impulses towards little girls and women. Thus two patients, one a married man, the other an unmarried woman, both in middle-life, had become self-sacrificing slaves to other people's interests. The man had a breakdown which began with a need to go to the lavatory in the night; but this involved passing his small daughter's bedroom door, and he was unable to move because of a terror that he would go in and strangle her. He then became a prey to fears that he would do some injury to his very sympathetic wife. The female patient, early in her breakdown, went to stay with some very helpful friends who had a particularly friendly small daughter. The patient became terrified of being left alone with her because of an impulse to strangle her, and also felt sudden urges to attack the mother. Thus the capacity for sensitive and sympathetic feeling so especially necessary in the mother with her baby, is felt to be the female element in human nature, and if projected may be either desired as the one thing needful or hated as a weakness to be destroyed in some female person, as often as not a girl child.

Representation of Male and Female Elements by Michelangelo

The female element as 'being' and the male element as 'doing' is strikingly illustrated by Michelangelo in four Madonnas, produced between 1503–6, in one of his most creative periods. There is an obvious continuity of unconscious intuitive thinking in the four works. The first, the Doni Madonnà, is a painting of Mary, Joseph, and Jesus as an intensely active group. It seems that at that point Michelangelo was driven back to what lay behind and led up to that capacity for vital activity. He then produced a marble statue, the Brughes Madonna, and two marble reliefs, the Pitti Tondo and the Taddei Tondo in which he worked out his answer. We may treat the painting as the fourth, not the first, of the series. The Brughes statue gives simply the Madonna and Child in a state of complete quietude and repose. The Madonna is sitting quite still with an expression of calm and peace on her face that perfectly expresses 'life without activity' or 'being without doing'. The Child stands motionless at her knee in the same state of complete restful composure. The mother is simply 'being' for the child who shares in her state and can simply 'be' for the mother. They are not looking at each other but are simply 'at one' and together, in a way that expresses the most complete and absolute security, the experience of identification and 'sharing in being' of mother and child. Here is the true starting-point for the growth of the human being to a capacity for confident and vital activity, and therefore 'activity' develops slowly through the other three works. In the Pitti Tondo movement has occurred. Again the child stands at the mother's knee while the mother sits calmly with an expression of deep and restful peace. But instead of simple 'togetherness', the beginning of active object-relationship has occurred. The child has turned towards his mother and is resting one elbow on her lap. The Brughes and Pitti Madonnas portray the laying of the foundations of security and therefore of subsequent activity on the part of the child, in his relation to the calm and stable 'being' of the mother. This is the female element in human existence, and therefore no male figure other than the child is present in either of these two works.

In the third, or Taddei, Madonna a striking development has taken place. The child Jesus has sprung into action and a third figure, a male, the boy St John is included. He holds out a fish to Jesus, who moved by curiosity has started forward to see what it is, and then has suddenly become anxious and shrinks back while loath to leave it. He is still looking back at it while he runs to his mother for safety. The mother sits there calm and undisturbed holding out a protective arm to her son but with a reassuring expression towards St John. Anxiety is clearly allayed in this experiment of 'doing' on the basis of stable 'mother–child being', and we turn back to the first work, the Doni painting, which must be seen as the end result of Michelangelo's experiencing of the mother–child relationship. We now have a scene of full and unrestrained healthy activity on the part of the child, as actively supported not only by the mother but also by the father, the male figure who is now appropriately present in a picture in which the male element of 'doing' is the theme. Jesus, a strong and muscular little boy, is vigorously climbing on his mother's shoulder, while Mary, clearly a woman of strong physique, though retaining her basic gentle mothering quality, is holding him up there, and Joseph standing behind them is lending a helping hand to support the child's vigorous outflow of energy in action; yet Joseph's expression contains something of mothering solicitude for the child while he enters in spirit into the child's activity.

Ego-Identity in Privacy and in Relationship

While Winnicott's view that 'each individual is an isolate . . . permanently unknown, in fact unfound' seems to me to be unreconcilable with his fundamentally important view that 'no sense of self emerges except on the basis of relating in the sense of BEING' in the identificatory relationship of mother and infant, nevertheless he calls our attention to one of the two ultimate problems, the need of the individual to preserve his individuality from violation. Relationship and dependence must not compromise separateness and independence, but must sustain and nourish them.

The mother first supplies the baby with his basis for 'being' while he is still in the womb, and must be able to prolong that secure experience of 'being-at-one-with-her' after birth, so that as the baby begins to experience his physical and psychological separateness from the mother on a conscious level, he is protected, by the unconscious persistence of the feeling of 'being-at-one-with', from the shock of what might otherwise be experienced as a feeling of being 'cut off', lost, dying. *A secure sense of being, shared with a stable mother both before and after birth, must remain as a permanent foundation in the unconscious, on the basis of which a separate ego-identity can develop stably and elaborate into a highly individual personality.* The infant could not stand without grave disturbance the upheaval of first physical and then psychic birth into separateness, ultimately at a conscious level, if he had lost the rock bottom experience of 'being in touch' and 'in being' and 'at one with' in his deepest unconscious feeling. The mightiest oak can only go on being an oak because it has deep hidden roots in mother earth. *The conscious ego is the ego of separation, of 'doing', of acting and being acted on, and in that sense is the location of the male element in personality. It must derive its strength from the deepest unconscious core of the self that has never lost the feeling of 'being-at-one-with' the maternal source of its life.* This ultimate source of inner strength may become 'dissociated' and inaccessible if the mother fails the infant badly and allows his sense of primary security in identification with herself to be shattered by her rejection or neglect. Two patients who answer exactly to that description, say they feel 'lost', in a 'wilderness' and 'in despair of being found'. Even then at the very deepest level of the unconscious there must remain some buried memory of this original 'oneness', and the patient goes in search of it when he breaks down into a profoundly regressed illness based on a fantasy of a return to the womb.

If the primary security of the mother–child relationship does become thus unreliable too early, ego-development fails to get a proper start or falters and breaks down. There supervenes a condition in which psychic impulses operate in disconnected or dissociated ways, because the ego they should express is still only a latent possibility; there is no effective ego to which they can belong. The patient can never then become a real person unless by 'therapeutic regression' he can find his way back to the starting-point of primary identification, now in the transference relation to the analyst. But the process of ego-development is, in itself, the normal process by which an undisturbed psyche grows its coherence and differentiation, in unity and wholeness. The feeling 'I am' leads to the question 'What am I?', i.e. the experience of 'being' leads to growth of self-consciousness, self-knowledge, and self-realization.

There is, however, always some tension in human beings between the need to defend their separate individuality and the need to keep in relationships. We have seen this in the schizoid person's 'in and out' way of living. My own experience of patients suggests that the fear of isolation, of the ego being emptied by feeling completely cut off from all object-relationships is deeper and more overpowering than the fear of the ego being violated or smothered in object-relationships. Total separation, absolute complete separate individuality, seems impossible to human beings for it renders existence meaningless. If an ego forms and then loses the sense of relationship to any depth, it begins to disintegrate. We begin as literally a part of another person, of 'nature', and only if that basic sense of unity and the security it gives persists as a permanent unconscious foundation, can we sustain separateness and individuality without anxiety. The psychic factor that underlies everything else, the experience of identification, of oneness, of the sense of belonging, of not being an 'isolate', is the psychological replacement for the security of the original literal organic oneness with the mother and 'nature'. The need of the human being to retain a fundamental sense of organic unity which is at the same time a latent sense of relationship, and which will develop through a good mother–infant experience into a specific capacity for ego-object relationship, ultimately with the universe itself, the final reality, must have been the core of religious experience all down the ages, however varied and transient its expressions in 'historic religions' may have been; i.e. Buber's 'yearning for the cosmic connexion' as something entirely different from projecting a father-image on to the universe.

However, we have to recognize that individuality and separate ego-identity, however strongly achieved, are always precariously held against threats from the external world. A practical exploitation of this fact is seen in third-degree interrogation, and still more in the brain-washing techniques and the physical and psychological high pressure methods used by totalitarian political systems to break down the resistance of those who dare to be real individuals, by breaking down their entire personality. When people have a 'nervous breakdown' and feel they are 'going to bits' under the pressure of life, this is only a commoner version of the same thing. We cannot stand what Winnicott calls 'the violation of the self's core by communication seeping through our defences'. We must feel able to shut out the external world and maintain our right to an inviolable privacy within ourselves at need if we are to remain healthy persons. We cannot tolerate being psychologically 'flooded' by alien invading experiences, or again, as Winnicott puts it, suffering in reality 'the frightening fantasy of being infinitely exploited'. I cannot see that this implies that 'the self's core is an isolate and incommunicado'. It seems to me that if ever the ego feels itself to be approaching that condition it begins to disintegrate for the opposite reasons, not because it feels invaded and violated but emptied, left to flounder in a vacuum, without the basic 'ego-relatedness' that must develop out of the primary oneness of identification. Thus a patient who had the unpleasant experience of being unexpectedly physically assaulted by a man who lost his temper in an argument, defended himself adequately, but afterwards said: 'I've gone back to my old feeling that the world is a horrible place one can't succeed in, I feel utterly worn down. I feel the fundamental part of me is a little bit of me that is really utterly alone and cut off and will drag me down into that level.'

Two things must remain inviolate if a human personality is to remain strong: (i) An inner core of the sense of separate individuality, of 'me-ness', of ego-identity, strong enough both to relate to and accept communication from, or at need to withdraw from the outer world without anxiety over possible ego-loss; (ii) a still deeper ultimate core of the feeling of 'at-oneness' which is the soil out of which the sense of separateness can grow. To feel separate and individual while cut off from any foundation of 'at-oneness' is terrifying and destroys the ego. This, however, involves also the opposite danger of the basic need for 'at-oneness' threatening to paralyse and extinguish the separateness, as when an insecure person defends his independence with fanatical determination because he is so afraid of losing it if he allows himself to depend in any real way, say on a therapist. *It is hard for individuals in our culture to realize that true independence is rooted in and only grows out of primary dependence.*

Winnicott expresses his sense of the complexity of the question whether the central self is an isolate, when he says, 'This line of argument involves me in great difficulties.' But I feel these disappear if we do not infer that, because relating, knowing, and communicating as we generally understand them are 'male element' activities, therefore the 'female element' (the basic 'feeling' psyche prior to the growth of 'thinking and acting') does not relate, know or communicate. The point of Winnicott's work on the mother–infant relationship is that the 'female element' has its own definite ways of relating, knowing, and communicating which are fundamental. He writes:

> The sense of being is something that antedates the idea of being-at-one-with because there has not yet been anything else except identity.

But it is only because of the factual existence of a state of being-at-one-with, that the sense of being and the emergence of a sense of self can come about at all. We are having to try to make distinctions within an experience rich with possibilities and never for a moment static. *Even as identity and being are experienced, they must be in process of developing the experience of being-at-one-with and of incipient relationship, which is the factual basis of their possibility. If this is the absolute start of experience, the core of the self can hardly be an isolate.*

The deepest thing in human nature is 'togetherness'. From that starting-point the psyche passes through the separation of birth into 'aloneness' which would be insupportable unless beneath it, as its foundation, there still persisted that oneness of the child with the mother, and through her with 'mother-nature', in the sense in which Buber quotes:

> the mythical saying of the Jews 'In the mother's body man knows the universe, in birth he forgets it'.

But he never forgets it at bottom. It remains as the secret foundation of the stillness, security, and peace of the Brughes Madonna, a foundation which must be preserved and developed in post-natal growth through identification to object-relationship. Buber writes:

> Time is granted to the child to exchange a spiritual connexion, that is *relation*, for the natural connexion with the world.

But in the deepest unconscious it is never lost, and human beings struggle to return to it when their 'ego' is most desperately menaced. Only when this foundation of security is retained is it safe for the reality outside to impinge on the ego of consciousness; and two human beings can be together in silence and yet know that they are 'in touch' and 'relating' and 'communicating' in deep feeling without words or actions, at that deep level.

This most elementary psychic level is the 'female' element of pure feeling, starting off as the experience of 'being' which in fact is an experience of 'being-in-touch-with' and could not exist except in an actual relationship of 'being-in-touch-with'. It is the starting-point and permanent foundation of ego-identity and ego-strength, a quietness at the centre, a core of personality which must be preserved inviolable, beyond the reach of external world pressures. I think this is what Winnicott means by

> the violation of the 'self's core' . . . by communication seeping through the defences . . . the sin against the self.

It is all a question of 'what kind of communication'. There needs to be an ability to defend against 'male element' impingement at a conscious level without losing 'female element' relationship in depth. Grave questions are raised by psychiatric attempts to bypass the conscious ego and contact the unconscious direct.

A patient once mentioned how impressed he had been with a description of Danny Kaye as a whirlwind of activity, wit, and humour on the stage, though 'the source of his rapport with his audience was a stillness at the core'. This 'self's core', embedded in indissoluble 'being-in-relationship' and communication of the special kind necessary and possible at that level, not verbally but in feeling, was his source of rapport with others. Only if that is dissociated, cut off and made unavailable as the foundation for ego-growth (it cannot be destroyed) by too bad mothering, is the self forced into the position of an isolate, and becomes unable to develop the sense of 'basic ego-relatedness'. This is the ultimate meaning of 'ego-weakness' and loss of ego-identity. In this disastrous predicament, the basic 'being-in-relationship' is there in the unconscious depths for the schizoid suicide to take flight back to. For health, the female and male elements need to be released from dissociation and integrated. This is possible because it is the essence of the female element that it can relate, know, and communicate in a more fundamental way of feeling, than the more external relating, knowing, and communicating of the male element. This is the foundation of ego-identity, individuality, and object-relationship. Put simply, the silent relating, knowing, and communicating of love is a profounder thing in human experience than science.

Science never knows 'the person'; it only has information about the 'person'. Finally, 'being and doing', feeling and acting, are not intrinsically female and male except by biological accident, but have acquired that broad significance as the two elementary constituents of personality. They transcend sexual differences and are simply what belongs to being a whole person. As the separate functions of the two sexes emerged, each had to specialize in one of these constituents without losing the capacity for the other. *There cannot be a whole complete human being without an integration of feeling with thinking and acting, provided by 'doing', arising spontaneously out of the fundamental experience of 'being'.*

Part IV

SOME IMPLICATIONS FOR PSYCHOTHERAPY

X

DIFFERENT LEVELS OF PSYCHOTHERAPY

IN the previous chapters an attempt has been made to pursue the analysis of the disturbed personality to the deepest possible levels and to arrive at a truly radical understanding of mental ill-health. This endeavour must go on, and no doubt much more remains yet to be understood. Perhaps the search can never be pushed to an absolute final conclusion. When, however, we turn our attention to the problems of psychotherapy, it is well to remind ourselves that theoretical ultimates must here give way to practical possibilities. The analysis of the schizoid problem must have profound and far-reaching implications for psychotherapy, but only relatively few therapeutic analyses can be carried to that depth. In psychotherapeutic practice we are limited to what the patient wants, and to what his circumstances in a variety of respects make possible. Psychotherapy is a function of at least three variables: the personality and experience of the therapist, the incentives and the nature of the problems of the patient, and the facilitating or frustrating nature of the environment both materially and personally. This is especially clearly emphasized in Freud's cautionary comment, that things cannot be raised from the unconscious purely by analysis, and we often have to wait for the impact of life itself to trigger off what is repressed. Thus psychotherapy in practice is not a uniform thing and certainly does not go to the same depths with all patients. If we were to consider solely the deepest problems revealed by analysis of the basic schizoid level in the personality, we might be tempted to conclude that radical psychotherapy was beyond our powers. It can certainly only be carried out when therapist and patient can go on together for a very long time.

Fortunately there are different levels of psychotherapy, and we do not have in practice to be perfectionist, but to aim at the possible. No doubt all therapists working with psychoanalytical methods, have had a number of cases where only symptom relief was called for, and could be achieved fairly quickly. This may, in one sense, be no more than psychoanalytical first aid, but can be very valuable. A simple example is afforded by a man who thought that he had lost his sexual potency because he could not respond with any sexual feeling to a woman of whom he had grown truly fond. In fact, his first marriage had broken down to his dismay and left him very depressed until at last he felt that he must take himself in hand and start mixing with people again. He did this and presently developed an entirely good friendship which he felt could develop towards marriage, only to find himself freezing up emotionally. He was not aware that his underlying feeling was 'Once bitten twice shy; don't ever risk it again; don't be drawn.' When this became clear to him, he was able to face and get over that fear, and his sexual responsiveness returned. A dozen sessions sufficed for this, and though they also revealed the existence of personality problems that could well have been analysed, there was no justification for embarking on such a venture. Malan's account (1963) of the experiments of Balint's group in short-term planned psychoanalysis, gives strong reasons for holding that we must be practical rather than perfectionist. In any case, the early idea of 'a fully analysed person' has long since been abandoned as a myth.

It is with these reservations in favour of what is practical, that we can feel free to explore the possibilities of psychoanalytic therapy 'in depth', simply because it can contribute so much of value that might be used in shorter analyses. Even with more radical treatments there are still different levels to which analysis can proceed. No rigid scheme of 'stages' could be true of the bewildering variety of unique individuals calling for treatment. I shall indicate three stages which I have observed, which in some patients have developed in orderly fashion, though in other patients there has been what might be called a disorderly oscillation to and fro between these stages before a stable result could be come by. But the 'disorder' is only in appearance, for the actual progress of any analysis has its own inner logic. However, I have observed in some patients a fairly consistent pattern of three stages of treatment, which could be called the stages of (i) oedipal conflict, (ii) schizoid compromise, and (iii) regression and regrowth. All these three stages are complex and no two patients ever work through them in the same way or in any fixed order. They may go back and forth between them, but they are broadly recognizable.

Before we explore these stages or phases in more detail, this seems to be the place to mention two matters of general importance. In my book *Personality Structure and Human Interaction* (1961) I described Fairbairn's theory of endopsychic structure as 'a *complete* object-relations theory of the personality'. This, I now feel, may be somewhat misleading. It may be taken, as it was by one critic, that by 'complete' I meant 'final', as if Fairbairn's theory was 'the last word' on a difficult problem, which would be absurd. I would now, therefore, rather describe his views as 'a *consistent* object-relations theory of the personality'. What I intend by either 'complete' or 'consistent' is to stress the fact that in Fairbairn's theory 'personal object-relations' is the basic concept of the theory in its entirety and of every part of it, which would not be true of Freud's concept of the 'id' which is impersonal. For Fairbairn, an originally whole though undeveloped pristine infantile psyche undergoes processes of internal structural differentiation under the impact of the infant's mixed experience of part satisfaction and part frustration in the earliest object-relationships. This results in good ego-growth as a result of good-object experience, and processes of ego-splitting as a result of bad-object experience. Such a theory plainly calls for concentration of research, on the facts of ego-development in the earliest stages of infancy and Fairbairn's work on schizoid problems pointed in the same direction. His work was not only a stimulus to, but also itself a part of a general trend of psychoanalysis in that direction, taking us ever deeper into the most fundamental problems, as we saw in Winnicott's work. As Fairbairn once said to me, 'The more we analyse the ego, the longer analyses get.'

This brings me to the second matter. With the ever-increasing concentration on the ego, its nature, origins, early development, significance as the core of the human being's 'selfhood as a person', and on the patient's struggle to achieve and preserve a viable ego with which to face the outer world, psychodynamic science emerges as specifically a 'Personality Theory'. It is well to consider the implications for psychotherapy of this position. It does not mean that we are committed in every case to call in question and analyse the entire structure of the patient's personality as a whole. Not every patient needs or should be committed to a radical analysis, if he can achieve sufficient stability without it. In a private communication J. D. Sutherland has written:

There is a difficulty that may well get brought into consideration of your thesis although strictly it does not apply. What I had in mind was that in describing your basic process and its far-reaching importance, both in depth and width, within the personality, you may be accused of not doing justice to all the other kinds of specific manifestations that underlie the traditional nosological categories.

You will at once feel that this would be an unjustifiable criticism, as you do, for example, in connexion with the Oedipus complex, make the point that what has been studied classically is the end product of a process stemming from certain major conflicts in the early stages of development. I think the substance of what I am saying is just to suggest that it is worth repeating in various ways and at various points, even to what would seem a quite unnecessary degree to yourself, the point that *your basic conflict is an underlying factor which can be found in almost all the conditions where, of course, it is complicated by the effects of more specific developments particularly related to subsequent experience.*

That is a wise precaution with which I unreservedly agree. In fact I regard the schizoid problem as a basic condition that is an *underlying factor* in varying degrees not only in all manifestations of mental illness but also in what we accept as mental health, a relative concept. It does not by any means always have to be analysed, and in fact very often 'good enough' stability is achieved, as it were, over the top of it, both with and without analysis. On the other hand, we shall not thoroughly understand any condition of personality without taking into account the fact that this underlying problem is there, in some degree. My clinical experience is, nevertheless, that even when the patient brings problems of schizoid withdrawnness at the very beginning, the oedipal level of analysis always gets brought in and cannot be by-passed by a premature attempt to resolve schizoid problems as it were in isolation. *If schizoid problems represent a flight from life, oedipal problems represent a struggle to live, and the two types of reaction interact constantly all through life itself, and all through psychotherapeutic treatment.* If schizoid problems of ego-weakness and retreat are presented at first, their analysis is quite likely to lead, not to a headlong plunge into deep regression but into a mobilization of defences against regression, bringing the patient back to the pressing problems of his personal relationships both at home and at work and in his more private life. Only later, when his oedipal patterns with their guilt and self-punishment have been worked over, may it be possible for him to return to facing the full force of his schizoid flight from reality. Too early emergence of the schizoid problem is not necessarily the best condition for its resolution. The personality undergoes an important strengthening in working through the oedipal conflicts. When it is not possible for treatment to stop there, this is still probably the best preparation for dealing with still earlier matters. Thus Winnicott cites a woman who had an earlier oedipal analysis but came to him because she knew that there was something deeper still to be dealt with (1958b, p. 279). A patient once wrote to me to say that she had had eight years' analysis and had benefited greatly, in that constructive social relationships and a happy marriage had become possible: but she said it had not eliminated what she called her 'earliest separation anxiety'. Sometimes it is possible to analyse mild though important schizoid reactions usefully in the midst of dealing with oedipal ambivalent love–hate and guilt problems and they may represent no more than a flagging, at that stage, of the patient's 'will to recovery'. Patients can hate, not only people, bad objects, but their illness, feeling profound irritation and anger at the frustration of living under its limitations. The patient has known and enjoyed enough at various times to know how good life can be, and yet feels himself to be struggling on, forever trying to reach a carrot dangled in front of him. He recurrently feels the weariness and futility of struggling on year after year always hoping for a final breakthrough to mental health. Freud said that at best we can only help the patient to exchange his neurotic suffering for ordinary human unhappiness. That, I believe, is too pessimistic a view, and the patient has glimpses of feeling the possibility of experiencing himself and life in a much more real and stable way. Yet there are no quick short-cuts to his goal, and 'hope deferred maketh the heart sick'. Times of hopelessness, staleness, of longing to give it all up and have done with it all will intervene, expressed in a sense of futility and a withdrawn mood. This may well contain a reliving of similar moods in childhood, without implying problems of the most ultimate kind. We may proceed then to examine three stages or levels of psychotherapy, taking them in what is perhaps their most natural order, oedipal conflict, schizoid compromise, and regression, without implying that this is in any way a fixed scheme.[1]

1. *Oedipal Conflict.* Whatever diagnostic label may be stuck on a patient, hysteric, obsessional, anxiety state, depression, etc., the first few years of analysis are likely to deal with the problems of the child struggling to adapt and maintain himself in an unhelpful family widening out into the social environment. This is broadly the 'classic oedipal analysis' of defences and conflicts concerning ambivalent object-relations of love and

[1] The rest of this chapter is a revision of section two of 'Psychodynamic Theory and the Problem of Psychotherapy', *Brit. J. med. Psychol.*, **36** (1963), pp. 167–73.

hate, primarily with parents and siblings, and then transferred into wider areas of living. As symptoms fade, the underlying conflicts over sex, aggression, and guilt will emerge, and classic depression in varying strength will have to be dealt with. Such analyses can lead to marked improvements which are very welcome, yet sometimes leave the feeling of something else unspecified still to be dealt with. The analysis produced valuable but not sufficiently complete results, since in this case it dealt with defences rather than ultimate causes. Nevertheless, it can prove quite possible for a patient to find he can stabilize at that point, especially if his infancy was good and his disturbance arose in later childhood.

Thus twelve years ago a man came to me very depressed after the death of his father. He said, 'I can afford time and money for 100 sessions.' I advised him to spread them over two years since growth is a matter of time. In addition to his depression, he was in a rut in his work, and his childless marriage was hardly happy. At the end of his hundred sessions he was definitely improved. He had got out of his rut at work, taken a better job, and was doing well. He and his wife had faced their problem, and adopted a child. I heard from him recently that he was carrying on well. I had told him that his whole problem could not be cleared up in a hundred sessions and he accepted that. He said he still had occasional moods but he felt he understood and could manage them, and his work and home life were satisfactory. The adoption had proved a success. That is a worthwhile result if not a complete one. In practice, the greater part, certainly of short-term therapy, is on this level. In the early days of psychoanalysis a year seemed generally to be adequate for treatment. But while we should always be happy to be able to let matters rest at that stage, this may not be possible.

2. *The Schizoid Compromise.* We may find that the patient, instead of utilizing real improvements, is only marking time in analysis, and retaining improvements by effecting a more rational control, i.e. a modified and more reasonable obsessional or schizoid character. Even then, if maintained, this may well represent, for all practical purposes, a 'cure'. But it may, however, turn out to be far more some degree of schizoid compromise, a half-in-and-half-out relationship to life in which the patient is not really satisfied. The patient does not do without personal relations, yet cannot do wholly with them, or cannot stand their being too close and involving. He takes up a half-

way position in which he hopes to get by and remain relatively undisturbed. If the patient *can* survive in that way, it is not good to probe deeper, for it may mean asking him to face more than he can stand to go to the depths of his insecurity. Nevertheless, these relative stabilizations cannot be guaranteed to last, and most patients, when they leave treatment, want the security of knowing that they can contact the analyst again if in real need. The patient may leave and later encounter real life stresses which are too severe and break him down again. Or he may stick at analysis without really making use of it, seeking to make analysis itself his compromise solution, gaining enough support from sessions but not changing much. This may break down; the patient feels frustrated, leaves in a resentful mood, and finds that his resentment of the now absent analyst is a quite useful if hardly constructive motivation helping to keep his ego functioning. Lastly, the patient may stick at analysis and allow his compromises to be analysed till slowly he gets beneath them. Whether he had returned to analysis with a second breakdown or carried on doggedly till the deepest levels were reached, the result is much the same.

The way in which the schizoid compromise solution is attempted and is liable to break down is best illustrated by two actual cases. A male patient in his fifties who had decided to end a long analysis and move to another city to start life afresh said, 'The height of my ambition now is to get through life without trouble. It's not that bad an aim, a bit negative; it has a certain vegetable feel about it, a kind of blankness. Under such circumstances you don't feel anything much at all. That's a preferable state to feeling awful. Big changes have gone on in me really. It's a tremendous relief not to feel so frightened, nor so excited in a bad way. Yet it feels also like losing something.' The last remark showed that he was aware that this was not a final, positive result, but a compromise solution aiming at maintaining improvements. It lacked the vital sense of reality in living. Yet only he *could* know if he could have gone deeper and in the end fared better. In fact, over a number of years to date, he has reported post-analytic improvement.

How a well-established compromise solution can break down is seen in the case of a woman in her late forties. She had recovered complete physical health after a long analysis, and at a late age took a University course to qualify for a profession, established her independence of parents, got a flat and a car of her own, and made all the progress it was possible to make along those lines. The fact that this welcome improvement and independence also included a schizoid compromise, protecting her from any real involvement in personal relations, became clear when she suddenly panicked at the prospect of marriage. She said: 'I think I'll be best keeping my freedom and independence, my job and money, flat and car, and not feeling too deeply about anything. I don't want to feel love or hate. If I feel, I become a baby. If I skate over the surface and don't feel much, I can be more grown up, and in a way I enjoy life better then, especially driving my car. Really I'm a child and don't want to do anything; I only want to go home to mother and father. I picture our family living on a desert island and never going out of it. I can't really face life. I never wanted to do a job; only stay at home and do housework with mother. But I know they can't live for ever and I've got to think out a different way of life. Perhaps really I'll drift into marriage, though with my eyes open, and make something of it.' The challenge of marriage, however, made it increasingly difficult for her to maintain her improvement on the basis of schizoid compromise, and she was pushed into the more radical experiencing of her basic fears of any real involvement in personal relationship, and she did succeed in marriage in the end.

3. *Regression and Regrowth.* At this stage problems are entirely different, specifically schizoid rather than depressed. One begins to gain contact with the terrified infant in retreat from life and hiding in his inner citadel: the problem to which, in its various aspects, Chapters I to IX were devoted. Fairbairn wrote:

> Such an individual provides the most striking evidence of a conflict between an extreme reluctance to abandon infantile dependence and a desperate longing to renounce it; and it is at once fascinating and pathetic to watch the patient, like a timid mouse, alternately creeping out of the shelter of his hole to peep at the world of outer objects and then beating a hasty retreat. (1952a, p. 39.)

Two cases illustrate this decisively. (i) A married woman of fifty, during a prolonged hysteric phase, dreamed of a hungry, greedy, clamouring baby hidden under her apron, the symbolic representation of an active orally sadistic infant who had to be kept under control or none would like her. When she had worked through that phase she became markedly schizoid, quiet, shut-in, silent, finding it hard to maintain any interest in life, beginning each session by saying 'You've gone miles away from me.' She then produced a fantasy of a dead or else a sleeping baby buried alive in her womb, and felt that she had a lump inside her tummy as if pregnant. (ii) The second patient was a male who had an earlier period of analysis of exceptionally sado-masochistic oral material and intense conflicts over both sexual and aggressive impulses which he controlled with great difficulty. He reached a stage where his original guilt depression faded and he could carry on as a successful if obsessionally hard working professional man. Then an unusually severe run of family troubles broke him down again. When he returned to treatment he was plainly struggling against a powerful regressive drive, feeling exhausted, and having fantasies of an infant wrapped away in a warm and comfortable womb.

It was this material that first suggested to me, as set forth in the earlier chapters, that what Fairbairn calls the *libidinal ego*, corresponding to the libidinal aspect of the Freudian 'id', the dependent needy infant, itself undergoes a further and final split. It is already split off and isolated in the personality by repression, by the Freudian ego and superego, or what Fairbairn calls the central ego and antilibidinal ego. This amounts to an internal persecution to which the infantile ego produces a double reaction of 'anger and fight' and also 'fear and flight'. This leads to the deepest ego-split of all, into an active oral ego and a helpless regressed ego as a final hidden danger. Psychoanalysis has taken full account of the 'ego vicissitudes' of anger and the aggressive or fighting impulses in face of threat. It has not taken the same full account of the 'ego vicissitudes' of fear and flight from life, and never fully fitted regression into the conceptual framework. In practice, regression is usually treated, psychiatrically, as a nuisance to be checked. This is far too superficial a view. Regressive trends are in fact derived from a structurally specific part of the total self which is deeply withdrawn, the schizoid ego *par excellence*, the hidden self in the schizoid citadel. It has undergone a two-stage withdrawal, first from a persecutory outer world of external bad objects; and secondly, from a persecutory inner world of internal bad objects, and especially the antilibinal ego (cf. Chapter VII). In working back to this depth, we are led at last to the unevoked potential of the patient's true self.

Psychotherapy may produce valuable results *en route* which in many cases, and for practical purposes, may prove sufficient; but it cannot be radical unless it reaches and releases this lost heart of the total self, which is not only repressed but in too great fear to re-emerge. So far as I can see, though we have come to this by different routes and our terminology is different, this is what Winnicott is saying when he describes a patient as having had a successful oedipal analysis, and later coming to him for a treatment which he calls strikingly 'therapeutic regression aiming at the rebirth of the true self', necessitated by the fact that the 'classical analysis had somehow left the core of her illness unchanged' (1958b, p. 249). This justifies us in saying that what psychoanalysis has so far discovered is just how difficult radical psychotherapy is.

We are left with two final problems for psychotherapeutic research.

(1) First, that of *resistance to treatment*. This is due not only to unconscious guilt over unconscious destructive fantasies and impulses, sexual or aggressive, but also to guilt over weakness, the fear of humiliation over disclosing weakness, and deepest of all over the sheer fear of collapse into a self which is too weak and fear-ridden to face living. The infantile dependence which Fairbairn regarded as the basic cause of neurosis, is something which the patient has been taught culturally to despise in the process of growing up, and emotionally fears as undermining his efforts to carry his adult responsibilities. He is always to some extent resisting any real dependence on his therapist, believing that it will throw him back on the weakest part of his personality, rather than put him in a position of emotional security setting him free for regrowth. What Balint (1952) calls 'primary passive love' is the necessary starting-point for his 'new beginning', when the basic ego has been too badly damaged in early childhood. But the patient has spent his life often in fighting against just this, and feels intense contempt and self-hate over it. It is just because the hysteric appears not to fight against it but to accept it too easily, that he incurs so much impatient criticism. This is more elementary than the moral superego: not fear of bad impulses but fear of weakness, though it can also involve guilt over 'sponging' on others. One patient says, 'I lose all my friends. They can't stand my demands on them.' I think the ultimate meaning of Fairbairn's antilibidinal ego is that it enshrines the frightened child's fear of his own weakness, his desperate struggle to overcome it by self-forcing methods, and by the denial of all needs, especially passive ones, a struggle based on identification with rejective persons in real life. This is a 'libidinal cathexis of the bad object' (Fairbairn, 1952a, pp. 72ff), which sets up resistance to a good therapeutic relationship with the analyst, by means of which a controlled constructive regression could be undergone to whatever extent necessary to make regrowth possible.

'Resistance' was explored in Chapter VII but its complexities call for much more work to be done on it.

(2) If at last the patient can undergo and accept a therapeutically controlled regression, the second and worse problem emerges. He will experience terrifying states of despair, feeling utterly shut in and hopeless about any rebirth. For a long time he oscillates between regression and resistance. The analysis of oedipal conflicts seems relatively straightforward by comparison with the complex infantile schizoid fears and persecutory anxieties which originally prevented the growth of a strong basic ego, and now bar the way to the rebirth of the lost heart of the self. One patient reported that while she was sitting in a bus she suddenly had a queer purely mental experience. 'I felt that I was nobody, neither body, soul nor spirit. I felt that I, the real "I", was nothing at all.' Here is the patient's discovery of the basic need to find a real self.

The problem is constituted, not only by the existence of persecutory fears, but also by the persistence of the undeveloped weak infantile ego state; a vicious circle in which the fears block ego development and the weak ego remains over susceptible to fears. Psychotherapy has somehow to provide a new security in which a new growth can begin. Just how afraid the patient is, is shown in a letter from the female patient in her late forties referred to on page 281f.

I am consumed with fear. I have always been and still am terrified of everything and everybody. Terrified of doing things, too afraid to live at all. All my life I have been running away and trying to hide. That is what I am doing here in this job and this flat. I want to hide and be undisturbed by the world and other people. I want to sleep and let the world go by. Yet there is another side of me that longs to *live*, and wants to be able to do things and live an interesting life free from *fear*. But it is such a struggle always fighting *fears*. The prospect of marrying has brought this to the fore. I want love desperately yet I am afraid to accept it or even to believe in it. I have been trying to force myself to go the pace alone but I need help desperately.

It would seem that the very real gains and developments in her 'ego of everyday living' which resulted from orthodox analysis at the outset of her treatment, enabled her to face the uncovering of a regressed infant in herself. But until that was regrown, no therapy could be complete. Is it safe or possible to go so deep with everyone?

At this point three practical problems arise: (i) The question may be asked whether increased knowledge of the regressed infantile ego in the schizoid citadel will enable us to uncover it more quickly and so shorten the ever-lengthening process of psychoanalytical treatment? In any absolute sense I cannot think that this is practicable. Premature interpretation of the existence of the most withdrawn part of the complex ego will yield no better result than premature interpretation of any other problem. The patient will either not understand or else grasp the meaning only in an intellectual way. If the patient is nearer to the emergence in an emotional way of this basic withdrawnness, interpretation of it before he can stand it will only intensify his defences. There is no short cut. The patient's strongest defences are permanently mobilized to keep his regressed ego and his passive needs hidden, for when they begin to emerge he feels he is really 'breaking down'. All the oedipal and compromise positions involved in his defensive system must be patiently worked through and in that process the patient comes to feel strong enough and well enough understood and supported to face the ultimate test of bringing the fear-ridden infant into the treatment relationship.

(ii) If it is agreed that the schizoid problem is the ultimate one, to insist on this with too narrow and rigid logic could betray us into the trap of thinking that nothing else matters. If we were to try to drive at once straight to this tap-root of all problems, we would only risk fitting the patient into a theory, and block him by trying to take up problems not in the natural order of their unfolding, and we would learn nothing new. This would lead to a premature attempt to reduce all problems to one problem in psychotherapy, much as Rank (1929) thought he could go straight to his 'birth trauma' and clear everything up quickly. That would be a delusion. The patient will dictate how fast the analysis can move by what and how much he can cope with as it goes along. One can only deal with what the patient presents and let the next phase grow out of that. One can only keep a sharp lookout for whatever signs of 'withdrawnness' the patient actually does present, and take care not to hold up the analysis by treating conflicts over sex and aggression as ultimates when the patient is ready to go behind them. We cannot afford to concentrate attention exclusively on any one thing, whether it be the oedipal problem, the depressive problem, or schizoid withdrawal and regression. We can only recognize that psychoanalytical investigation has discovered these problems in that order, as it has worked deeper. We must use all concepts which are relevant to whatever the patient presents, and keep an open mind for anything 'new' he discloses. Psychodynamic theory will not come to a final closure in our time. When patients begin by presenting schizoid and regressed reactions, they are more than averagely ill, and even then its complexity is enormous, and we know all too little about primary ego development as yet. So we must not allow theory to become dogma but use it as a signpost.

(iii) A third question likely to be raised is that the regressed schizoid patient *wants* to be treated as a baby, with the implication that he should not be indulged in this. This gravely over-simplifies the case. Even when gross hysterical dramatization of illness is obvious, there is an infant in the patient, an undermined basic ego, who *needs* to be accepted for what he is, by being helped through whatever degree of 'therapeutic regression' proves necessary. But there is an antilibidinal ego in the patient who hates this. If the patient senses that the therapist is on the defensive against his deepest needs, this may force them to the front and drive him to become demanding and manipulative towards the analyst (parent) who basically rejects him. If, however, he slowly realizes the analyst will accept and help the baby in him, it has the effect of bringing his antilibidinal defences into the open, and we witness the intensity of the patient's resistance to treatment as a struggle *not* to depend on the analyst for help. The analysis of this situation leads to far more real progress towards a more secure, relaxed, non-anxious, and spontaneously loving personality. The demanding patient, like the demanding child, clamours for a love he feels is being refused. The resistant patient fears to accept a love that he suspects will be smothering. In either case the patient is likely to be sensing accurately the analyst's basic attitude behind his overt behaviour. Probably the patient with the deepest schizoid problems of all is the patient most dependent for a successful result on the degree of real maturity in the therapist, in the long run. We need to know more about the processes of rebirth and regrowth of the profoundly withdrawn infantile ego hidden in the depths of the unconscious, and about what kind of relationship to the analyst the patient requires to make that possible. One patient said simply: 'If I could feel loved, I'm sure I'd grow. Can I be sure you genuinely care for the baby in me?'—a statement which makes it clear that what the patient is fundamentally seeking is a relationship of a parental order which is sufficiently reliable and understanding to nullify the results of early environmental failure.

XI

THE SCHIZOID COMPROMISE AND PSYCHOTHERAPEUTIC STALEMATE

THE schizoid quest for compromise in human relationships was described in Chapter II, pages 58–66, in some of its most general manifestations in everyday living. In Chapter X the schizoid compromise was considered from the very different point of view of its emergence as a stage, or a recurring phase, in psychotherapy. This raises so many questions of detail that it must be considered at this point as a problem in itself.[1]

The Schizoid Compromise

Ostensibly, every patient wants to be cured of neurosis quickly, so that he can get on with living. Whatever 'resistances' the patient thereafter puts up, wittingly or unwittingly, to treatment, there is no doubt that his 'Reality-Ego' does want to be finished with the illness as such, and as soon as possible. The length of time involved in psychotherapy is a sore trial to him. He feels that his progress is too slow and too small, and that life will have gone by before he is capable of living it properly. It may be that better understanding of the problems involved will shorten treatment, though in the nature of the case a healing process which is a regrowing *process* just as much when it concerns the mental self as when it concerns the body, cannot be artificially hurried, however much we may wish it. All that we can do is to discover the obstacles to regrowth, provide a relationship in which the patient can come to feel secure, and leave 'nature' to prosecute her healing work at her own pace. The time factor in psychotherapy can never be simply in the therapist's power to more than a small extent, and it is much easier for all concerned to hinder and lengthen treatment than to shorten it.

What is usually not realized at the outset, nor for a long time, by the patient is that he himself will play the largest part in hindering, that he will do so mostly unknowingly, and that

[1] The following is a revised version of a paper under the above title in the *Brit. J. med. Psychol.*, **35** (1962), pp. 273–87.

this is inevitable because it is bound up with the very nature of this kind of illness. I did have one patient who, at the outset, said, 'I'm very afraid I'll ruin this treatment in the end.' Most patients do not have so much insight. This bears vitally on the criticism often made that psychoanalysis is in fact an interminable process. The psychoanalytical researcher can only go on pondering the actual clinical data he meets. There is certainly no quick and easy way of making a mature and stable adult personality out of the legacy of an undermined childhood. It is always a question of how deep a patient can go, wishes to go, or has the chance to go into his problems. Moreover, the patient, however ill, is still a 'person in his own right'. He is ill because in some way he was not treated as one in his childhood. He feels an urgent necessity to *defend* his own independence and freedom of self-determination as a person; and he feels this all the more, the less of a person deep down he feels himself to be. In a sense he wants to be rid of the illness without changing his familiar self-identity, even when he has some insight into the fact that this kind of illness robs him of genuine freedom. Still he cannot allow anything to be put across on him, even if it is supposed to be for his good. Because he feels menaced in the very essence of his selfhood, he is bound to be on the defensive against the very person whose help he seeks. All these difficulties have their roots in the schizoid problem, for the one thing above all others that is so hard as to seem at times almost impossible for the aloof schizoid personality is to affect a genuine relationship with any other human being, including the psychotherapist. In proportion as a patient is schizoid, he is afraid of people just as much as he needs them. This is a dilemma in which he cannot avoid seeking compromise solutions until such time as his fears diminish and allow his needs to be met. All through his treatment he will be tossed about between his fears of isolation and his fears of emotional proximity.

A patient in his forties, married and with a family, who suffered very severe anxieties over every kind of family separation, summed up his position thus: 'I'm the prey of deep, terrifying, fundamental fears if I'm not in control of all our relationships with regard to separation. If my wife is away and late returning or I don't know when she will be back I panic. I feel I'm in control of the situation if I can be certain she'll be back at the stated time, or if I can go away and come back and know she'll be there. I don't mind her being away if I can get at her, and then I don't want to. I even feel relief at being alone, so long as I can have them all back the moment I need them. But I hate and fear and loathe this dependent weak part of me, and it makes me hate those I depend on.' Thus, this kind of insecurity makes it important to have an absolute guarantee of never being deserted and left really alone; yet it also carries with it a dread of weak over-dependence on the needed person, the fear of being betrayed into a subordinate, submissive clinging to one's protector in which one's own individual personality will be stifled. In *Vanessa* Hugh Walpole makes the heroine say:

> We affect one another. To live with another is to have to fight for your own integrity morning and night. I suppose if you love someone enough you lose your own integrity and find another much finer. But if you don't . . .?

To the schizoid person this risk seems too terrifying. This patient had to have his wife always there, but so that he could both leave her and return to her at will. This kind of relationship, the 'in and out programme' described in Chapter II, is not only typical of schizoid persons but practically inevitable for them. It is the only way they can maintain a viable compromise between their equally intense *needs* and *fears* of personal relationships. Naturally, this patient had exactly the same problem with me and this is the major 'sticking point' in psychotherapy. He could feel severe anxiety at the thought of not having me to come to, and yet when he came he found it extremely difficult to bring out frankly his 'weak and dependent self', the legacy of his insecure childhood. To be altogether 'out' or altogether 'in' would mean to be plunged into emotional storms. His compromise was often to come and discuss things on an intellectual level, being present physically and intellectually but, as it were, absent emotionally. I once had a patient who would say: 'There's a part of me I never bring in here.'

Schizoid patients suffer from what Laing (1960) has called 'ontological insecurity', using the terminology of existentialist philosophy. This philosophy regards human existence as fundamentally rooted in anxiety and insecurity, and, if one may judge from the clear signs of a schizoid mentality of aloofness and detachment in the writings of Heidegger and Sartre, this philosophy is an intellectual conceptualization of the fundamentally schizoid plight of practically all human beings, even if in varying degree. I have referred to schizoid patients, but what patients are not schizoid at bottom to some extent? As Fairbairn pointed out, schizoid problems are far commoner in clinical practice than classical depression, and when patients say they are depressed they usually mean not guilt-burdened but apathetic, devitalized and feeling that life is futile. 'Ontological insecurity' means insecurity as to one's essential being and existence as a person, insecurity about one's ego-identity, the feeling of basic inadequacy in coping with life, and inability to maintain oneself as in any sense an equal in relationships with other people. It involves therefore urgent needs for support but at the same time a great fear of too close relationships which are felt as a threat to one's own status as an individual. The schizoid person, to whatever degree he is schizoid, hovers between *two opposite fears, the fear of isolation in independence with loss of his ego in a vacuum of experience, and the fear of bondage to, of imprisonment or absorption in the personality of whomsoever he rushes to for protection.* A patient once said to me: 'I know that all my active feelings about you are only defences against the feeling of wanting to be safe inside you.' Fairbairn once said to me in conversation: 'The person one breaks away to, turns into the person one has to break away from again.' That is the schizoid dilemma, equal inability either to do with or without the needed protector, the parent-figure whom the insecure child inside must have, but whom the struggling adult conscious self cannot tolerate or admit. This presents the greatest possible obstacle to psychotherapy.

This is strikingly illustrated in the case of a female patient who seemed, on the face of it, to be a gentle-natured person who made no secret of her nervousness, timidity and fear of being alone and need for constant support. Nevertheless, in a quiet and rather secret inward way, she revealed a most unyielding need to keep herself going without help, and found it exceptionally hard to put any real trust in and reliance on me. She wanted to but 'it did not happen'. She complained repeatedly that she felt I was a support during session time but she had to live her life when I was not there, so that I was not really of much use to her. She knew that she was free to ring me up when she was in a panic, but for the most part she would rush to a drug instead. It took her a very long time to admit that the trouble was not really that I was not physically present with her at work and in her home life, but that the moment she got out of the consulting room she mentally dismissed me: 'Now I'll have to get on without help and do it myself.' Then she fell into panics of isolation, would be driven in desperation to carry on long conversations with me in her head, and yet when she arrived for the next session would have nothing to say. Often the session began with her not even being able to sit down. She would stand immobile and speechless, aloof and uncommunicative. As usually happens with such patients, as the end of the session began to draw near she would have so much to say that she found it hard to get it all in. But even then it was a monologue that kept me at a distance. This constant oscillation between 'near and far', dependence and independence, trust and distrust, *acceptance of and resistance to treatment, the need of a security-giving relationship and fear of all relationships as a threat to one's separate existence as a proper person* presents itself for analysis under a thousand forms all the way through the process of psychotherapy. *When the patient can establish a persistent compromise halfway between the two extremes, the result is 'blocked analysis' and therapeutic stalemate.*

This is illustrated by two dreams of the above patient:

I was having a meal with a friend alone, and suddenly my sister and her whole family came in and just sat down and began to eat. There wasn't enough food to go round and no one noticed that I was having to go without.

It did not occur to her that she herself had made up the dream that way and that was how she wanted it. It was far too much of an unreserved commitment to be alone with one friend in a cosy *tête-à-tête*. This had to be broken up, yet not so as to shut her out altogether. She was still there but not very deeply involved in what was happening. That was her basic attitude to sessions. She also dreamed of coming to see me and finding me busy with other patients. That dream recurred several times, and she would express jealousy of my other patients and say that I ought to have only her. These complaints faded away only when I pointed out that this apparent jealousy masked her fear of any real relationship, and in fact the existence of my other patients reassured her. They were like the other members of her family that she brought into the first dream to dilute the personal relationship situation, and leave her free to maintain her 'half-in-and-half-out' position. She wanted some person all to herself, yet was secretly glad of the protection of rival claimants to that person's attention so that she should not be swallowed up in the relationship.

Forms of Schizoid Compromise as a Defence Against Psychotherapy

Before we seek to uncover all the cleverly hidden forms of schizoid compromise, a brief statement of the theoretical position already outlined, will lead into the subject. Incidentally, *theoretical stalemate*, the congealing of theory into a rigid orthodoxy which does not admit of fresh approaches, must itself be a defence, of the nature of a schizoid compromise, against new truth that would bring us closer to real life. We have traced the shift in the centre of gravity of psychodynamic theory from impulse-control to the fundamental problems of ego-growth and distortion involving structural ego-splitting. It is significant that Freud's last unfinished book *An Outline of Psycho-Analysis* (1940), stops short in the uncompleted Part 3 with the subjects of 'ego-splitting' and 'the internal world'. James Strachey tells us in his preface that Freud broke off at this point and did not return to the subject, turning instead to another piece of writing, itself unfinished. Could it be that Freud knew that he had raised the vital problem for future theoretical developments, but that the clinical data did not yet exist for its satisfactory solution? Now it is possible to see that whatever clinical problem is dealt with, if analysis has to go far enough, one finds oneself going behind the more accessible conflicts over sexual and aggressive drives, to the deeper conflicts over primary fears, and the secret flight from life of the weak and undeveloped infantile ego, hidden deep in the unconscious. We are here considering some of the peculiar difficulties that stand in the way of psychotherapeutic treatment when it comes up against the schizoid factor in the personality. In other words, what light does the schizoid process throw on 'resistance'.

Freud made it clear that *every* patient *resists* treatment, no matter how much he may also want it, and that the resistance can be so serious as to lead to 'blocked analysis'. We have seen that this cannot be wholly accounted for by unconscious guilt over sex and aggression. Guilt is felt also over weakness and fear, and tends to take more and more the form, not of moral guilt, but of contempt and hatred of that part of his personality which the patient feels will 'let him down'. A striking example of this as the cause of resistance, is the following comment of a male patient: 'I play a "cat and mouse" game with myself. "Why can't you stop being a mouse?" Then I turn the tables and say: "Why can't you leave me alone?" It's all very well coming here but at bottom I don't want to get better, or only part of me does.' I suggested that his 'cat and mouse' game with himself was a rival policy to psychotherapy, a struggle to solve the problem his own way. He was being a cat to himself to prove that he wasn't nothing but a mouse. He replied: 'It's like putting your head in a gas oven to get your name in the papers.

Do the stupid thing in a big way. I've had years of analysis and I'll go on for ever. I'm not going to be one of those people who can be cured in six months. One must have some distinction.' Fairbairn's 'internal closed system which shuts the analyst out' is the struggle to master and defeat chronic infantile dependent needs by internal violence, and force the outer world self to carry on in a state of maximum independence of other people. Here the schizoid conflict between needs and fears of human relationships turns into the patient's seeking a treatment which he then cannot fully accept. He will go on being ill and suffering the miseries of neurosis, unaware of the fact that he cannot admit the implication of weakness by the full acceptance of the therapist's help. Yet he is in truth weak because so gravely damaged in infancy and childhood, and he craves all the time for a good parent figure with whom he can get a new start. Thus *he can neither fully accept nor fully reject the therapist, and many of the difficulties of treatment lie in his intense need to set up and maintain some form of compromise relationship.*

(i) *Blocked Analysis Itself as a Compromise*

The essence of the schizoid compromise is to find a way of retaining a relationship in such a form that it shall not involve any full emotional response. It is easy to do this with psychoanalytical treatment. The patient keeps on coming but does not make any real progress. He exhibits recurring moods of restlessness, complains of feeling 'stuck', says 'We're getting nowhere with this' and toys with the idea of dropping treatment. But he does not stop. He keeps coming without opening up any real emotional issues for analysis. Some patients give the impression of being prepared to go on indefinitely like that, deriving some quite valuable support from sessions but not undergoing any real development of personality. I have come to regard too prolonged a therapeutic stalemate of this kind as a very important indication of the severity of the deepest-level anxieties the patient will have to face if he ventures further. He dare not give up, or serious anxiety will break out, and he dare not 'let go' and take the plunge into genuine analysis, or just as serious anxiety will be released.

This situation was manifested by the female patient whose dream of coming up against a huge wall was quoted on page 121. It simply barred the way forward and implied that there was something quite 'cut off' within herself which she could not face. I suggested that this was also her way of saying that her progress in treatment was completely at a standstill. She was at a dead end. The fact that she had made this plain to herself saved her from a blind wearying blocked analysis. But that did not of itself enable her to move forward. It meant that if she found herself unable to move forward, she was going to have to give up treatment, and that in fact is what happened. Instead of continuing analysis on a dead monotonous level of unbroken stalemate, for a time she kept breaking off and returning again. Concerning the dream she had said: 'I've got to go on, if you can stand it' and I had replied: 'I can stand it if you can.' But every time any important development looked like occurring, she would begin to argue, criticize, work up a quarrel, and break off. Then after becoming depressed, she would write a few months later asking to return. This was repeated several times, till at last she revealed the plain fact that she could not stand that committal of herself to another person that a real therapeutic relationship would have implied, for on resuming analysis for the last time, she brought to the first session the following dream:

I got on a tramcar and walked straight through to the driver's platform, turned the driver off and drove the car myself.

I put it to her that the tram was the treatment and I was the driver, and she felt the situation to be one in which she was in my power, as she had once been in her father's; and this she could not tolerate. Only if she could take complete charge of the analysis and run it herself, could she go on with it: but in that case it would not be treatment, it would be merely turning the tables on father in my person, and nothing would really be changed. She did not come next time and ended her analysis at that point. Yet this was still, after all, a blocked analysis which she kept alive, for she did not really give me up. Much later she sent me a copy of one of my own books, filled in all the margins with highly critical comments. She was still carrying on her critical and angry attacks on me and on psychoanalysis in her mind instead of in sessions. She was still 'keeping herself going' by holding on to a now internalized struggle for power with the analyst *in loco parentis*, which never produced any constructive results but only kept her half in and half out of relationships.

A blocked analysis is always liable to break down sooner or later in some such way as this. So long as it does not break down there is a chance of analysing the forms of compromise the patient sets up and promoting some progress. Yet there is no certainty about this. The male patient also quoted on page 121 as having the fantasy of coming up against a circular wall inside which the heart of his personality and its problems were locked away, persisted steadily in a long analysis. It became clear, at any rate in an intellectual way, that what lay behind the circular wall was the self of his early childhood which he felt was a 'miserable little worm', terrified of a psychotic father and starved of true love by a dictatorial mother. The only emotional indications of its presence deep inside were occasional feelings that it would do him good to have a good cry, and sudden attacks of exhaustion when he would go home and go to bed and sleep it off. In general he was a tightly organized, obsessional hard worker, liked and respected by his employees to whom he was fair and just. He could not involve himself in any closer kind of human relationships, though he had always wanted to be married. After the 'circular wall' fantasy he would say, 'I can't let anything disturbing out this session. I've got an important business meeting tomorrow', and constantly commented, 'There's something I'm doing that holds up the analysis. I wish I knew what it was.' This was analysed from many points of view, all relevant, but he never succeeded in giving up this stalling reaction. Then one day he did not turn up and I learned that he had been found dead from a coronary thrombosis. That gives the measure of the severity of the internal tensions he locked up inside himself. If he could have risked a complete regressive illness (as he would have had to if it had been, say, pneumonia) at an early enough period, he could no doubt have escaped the thrombosis and solved his psychic problems. But it is not easy to get a regressive illness accepted and understood: also he had a business to run. His steady and determined persistence in what came to be a blocked analysis, was a schizoid compromise which probably he had no option but to maintain; and to support him in it was the only way of giving him such help as he could accept.

Such a case makes it clear that *resistance* is not just perverseness, or negative transference merely, or moral fault, but a defence of the patient's very existence as a person within the limits of what is possible to him. Such resistance and blocked analysis, in so far as it is successful, must seem practically preferable to opening up devastating conflicts in order to reach a 'final' solution.

I am confirmed in this view by the severity of the struggle to get the deep hidden schizoid ego reborn, in a number of patients who have been able to go beyond a purely defensive compromise solution. From one point of view the schizoid compromise is a struggle to maintain stability, even though from another it is a resistance against further psychotherapy, the kind of treatment that involves opening up disturbing inner problems to get a chance to solve them. In this sense, this kind of stability is an evasion of a more thorough-going solution, but it is not for us to say lightly whether a patient should or even can lay himself open to the radical 'cure'. That depends partly on whether he gets the kind of understanding he needs from his human environment, and the supportive relationship he needs with his therapist, but ultimately on the degree of severity of his deepest problems. My impression is that if the patient can face it he will, and if he cannot, no amount of analysis will make him do so.

(ii) *Compromise Techniques in the Patient's 'Management' of Analysis*

These are much simpler matters and fairly easy to recognize, and need not detain us at length. They often take the form of trying to turn analysis into an intellectual discussion. One patient began by saying that he looked on the analysis as a 'valuable course in psychology'. Others will bring for discussion their intellectual problems about religion, or morality, or human relations in society, or their doubts about psychoanalysis. I do not think that this kind of material can be just rejected outright as a defensive manœuvre. It can well be that the patient feels that his intellect is the one part of his personality that he can function with, and if he is just ruthlessly stopped from using it in sessions he may well feel merely 'castrated', or reduced to a nonentity, depersonalized. This is all the more likely to be the case if his early attempts to form his own views were ridiculed at home. The grown-up self needs support and understanding in analysis as well as the child, for the grown-up self has to stand the strain of carrying the child with him. For that reason, when treating patients who work in medical, psychological, or social fields, I have always accepted the discussion of some of their own 'cases' in the session, for in fact these always lead back to their own problems. It is on a par with the parent-patient wishing at times to discuss the problems of his children, for they are his own problems as well. One could be too purist in this matter. The patient is quite likely genuinely needing help, and does feel that the analyst is a person capable of giving it to him. It is all the more important when he afterwards says: 'I was never able to discuss anything frankly with my parents.'

It is best to go through with this and use it to help the patient to see where his difficulties in dealing with others are bound up with his own problems. Then it can lead back into analysis proper. Only when too persistent use is made of this kind of discussion must it be challenged as a schizoid compromise, an attempt to keep going in relationship with the therapist while keeping the inner self withdrawn.

One male patient proceeded with his defence against analysis by flooding every session with long recitals of endless dreams, simply recounting one after another without a stop. That this was a quite serious compulsion was evident from the fact that for a long time my assertion that these dreams were a waste of time since he never made any use of them, made no impression on him. By cramming sessions with dreams he was seeking to prevent my saying anything that might stir up anxiety. When at last he did consent to have a look at a dream before hurrying on to the next, he would set about the intellectual analysis of its meaning (which he was able to do since he was well versed, professionally, in symbolism), or else keep on asking me questions as to what I thought this or that meant. I judged it inadvisable to let him come up against too blank a wall of non-response on my part, and carefully selected the points on which I did comment, to help him to become aware of his deeper anxieties. Gradually he became able to drop this compromise method of coming for analysis without having it, and then he began to 'feel' how much his very schizoid personality was out of real touch with his environment. The theme of loneliness took the place of somewhat excited dreaming.

This is a convenient place at which to stress that *dreaming is, as Fairbairn pointed out, a schizoid manifestation; it is itself the schizoid compromise par excellence and, as such, dreaming often functions as a rival policy to psychotherapy*. This is why it is, as Freud said, the royal road to the unconscious, but it is a road that the patient will not always allow the analyst to tread. There are patients who will occasionally say: 'I'm not going to tell you my dream. You'll only spoil it', or who begin to tell a dream and suddenly forget it completely in the very act. One patient dreamed furiously every night, yet could never remember a thing in the morning. He then decided to take pencil and paper to bed and write down his dreams during the night, while he had them clearly in mind. To his surprise he just stopped dreaming and after a few nights he no longer troubled to take up his paper and pencil. At once he began dreaming furiously again. It will come as no surprise that this patient finally dreamed of going down into his cellar to free a young man who was in the grip of an octopus. He opened the door, and then shut and locked it again and came upstairs, and promptly decided to end his analysis. If a patient is aware of dreaming at the time and then forgets it, he is at least in contact with his inner fantasy life, which is better than having it totally cut off. One patient, an entirely intellectual financial expert, had only about half a dozen dreams in some three years of analysis, and made only superficial if useful adjustments of personality.

Dreaming is the maintenance of an internal world, withdrawn from the outer world, in which the outer world including the analyst may not be allowed to share. It is a schizoid phenomenon based on the fact that the over-anxious or insufficiently formed ego cannot maintain itself in existence without object-relationship. The loss of all objects simply leads to depersonalization. Therefore, when the infant makes a mental withdrawal from a too traumatic external world, he runs the grave risk of losing his own ego, the deeper he takes flight into himself. I have had a number of patients who clearly remembered as tiny children having 'queer' states of mind in which they did not know who they were and felt everything to be unreal. Lord Tennyson as a boy must have withdrawn into himself from a very gloomy and bitterly depressed father, and was once found alone staring into space and mechanically repeating his name, 'Alfred, Alfred'. He grew up to be intensely shy and to suffer from marked 'absences of mind'. In proportion as the infant ego is not basically 'ego-related', in real-life experience and therefore in fundamental feeling (in the sense discussed in Chapter VIII) the child must counteract this by setting up an internal world of imaginary object-relationships in the mind, a world of dream and fantasy. Thus, young Anthony Trollope, ostracized by everyone at Harrow and Winchester schools on account of his poverty, developed a persistent and elaborate fantasy world which he carried on from day to day and even from year to year, until at last he disciplined it into a gift for novel-writing. This fantasy is the expression of a complex feeling-state, and in so far as it occurs at a far earlier age, it develops into an unconscious structural aspect of the total self, persisting and re-emerging as dreams.

The two indubitably real parts of the personality which must ultimately grow together, are the utilitarian self of everyday conscious living and the fear-ridden infantile ego in a state of schizoid withdrawnness and arrested development deep in the unconscious. The intermediate dream world is to a considerable extent a defensive artefact, a struggle to maintain an ego in face of dangers from outer reality and inner withdrawnness. As a wish-fulfilment it is primarily an expression of the wish to remain in being, by having a world to live in when the real outer world is largely lost to the inner core of the self. Wish-fulfilment would here be better described as ego-maintenance. That is why dreaming is regarded as a phenomenon of the night-time. We certainly dream by day, but do not generally notice it because our attention has to be concentrated on the outer world. In the night that is lost, and our dream world is all we have. In proportion as tendencies to feel depersonalized are strong (or basic ego-relatedness is weak), night and sleep are felt as a dangerous risk of ego-loss. Patients will say 'I fear I will never wake up again', or as one patient said: 'I have to keep waking up at intervals to see how I'm getting on. It's so difficult going to sleep because it feels like going some place where there isn't anybody and you're really by yourself.' Then dreaming keeps the ego in being. If too much interest is allowed to become 'fixated' on dreams in analysis, it positively helps the patient to maintain his schizoid defences, and it may well be that much dream analysis that looks fairly convincing and useful is, from the patient's point of view, much more intellectual than emotional.

I have been very impressed with the way patients will begin to live out in a consciously emotional way, states of mind that they expressed quite clearly in one or two notable dreams probably one or two years previously. When that happens, the patient is giving up dreaming as a defensive inner world, a rival policy to psychotherapy and a struggle to solve his problems by himself, and bringing his real self into the analysis. There are various levels of dreaming. On the top level the patient is ready to communicate his inner life via the dream to the analyst. On the bottom level the dreams belong to Fairbairn's 'static internal closed system', the private world which is the patient's answer to the badness of his real world, and into which he does not trust anyone else to intrude: perhaps a parallel to Winnicott's 'core of the self as an isolate'. Thus, when we have learned all that may contribute in a dream to the patient's insight into himself, the dreaming-activity itself needs interpretation as, to varying extents, a form of his *resistance* to the whole outer world including the analyst. Otherwise dream material can be handled in such a way as to give the patient an excellent chance of maintaining his schizoid compromise of being only half in touch with the analyst.

I should, perhaps, stress that I am speaking of dreaming as we come upon it in patients. It cannot be said that all dreaming is schizoid and pathological of necessity, even though probably most dreaming in fact is. We may illustrate the problem by comparison with abstract thinking. When we are doing something that presents no difficulty, our thinking is tied to our immediate activity step by step, and is directly orientated to outer reality. The schizoid intellectual, on the other hand, has retreated from direct dealings with the outer world, must interpose theories and impersonal ideas between himself and reality, makes thinking an end in itself, and is 'sicklied o'er with the pale cast of thought'. Thinking has become an interior life carried on in withdrawnness from real object-relations. Most dreaming, and certainly the dreaming of patients, is of that nature. There is, however, another kind of abstract thinking in which the thinker, having come up against an unsolved problem which halts his activity, 'withdraws' and 'stops to think'. The construction of a scientific theory, or the planning of a battle by a general who is trying to see beforehand what his opponents' moves are likely to be, illustrates this. This is a kind of abstract thinking which is not aimed at 'withdrawal from reality' but at 'mental preparation for further action'. It does not belong to a self-contained 'static internal closed system', but is directed towards action in the real world all the time. There is no reason why a healthy-minded person should not at times do some of his deep inward 'preparation for future living' in dreams. Maybe Jung's view that some dreams have an outlook on the future is relevant here. But such dreams will not be a disturbing compulsion like the dreams of pathological anxiety.

One patient said: 'I begin to see what you meant when you said that dreaming is an alternative policy to psychotherapy. I'm not interested in anything real, because if you're interested in anything you come slap up against people. I can only live my dream and fantasy life. If I were interested in people I could be interested in lots of things. But I'm afraid of people. In my dream world I'm really all by myself and that's what I want to be, to get back to my dream world, a protected world. If I get too deep into it I may not be able to get back from it, but what will I do if I stop dreaming. My real interests are so few. I've nothing to think or talk about.' I reminded him that he was too afraid of people to have any interests. He replied, 'I'm cross with you now.' I said I thought that was because I am a real, not an imaginary person, and called him out of his dream world into the real one. He said: 'I'm angry because I feel anything you say is interference in my private world. Dreaming is against psychotherapy and it's against life.'

Sometimes a patient's general behaviour expresses this compromise. One patient found great difficulty in deciding where to sit. She felt the couch was somehow unnatural and isolating, yet the patient's armchair seemed to be 'too adult' a position. Anywhere too near to me was, she felt, frightening. Finally she compromised by sitting on the floor fairly close to me but with her back to me, obviously at one and the same time seeking and yet rejecting any relationship with me. Another patient made use of a small stool which she could move closer to or further away from me, according to which way her anxieties developed. One male patient lay on the couch and wanted me to place my armchair close to it where he could see me, which I did. But after a while he got anxious and needed me to take my chair away to the other side of the room. This 'to-ing and fro-ing' often has to be repeated and analysed many times before its significance really gets home to the patient. Some patients will keep their overcoats on, buttoned up tight, expressing their self-enclosure and withdrawnness from the therapist even though they are with him, and it is a good sign when of their own accord they begin to take it off in the natural way and leave it outside the room.

(iii) *Schizoid Compromise in Real Life Which is not Brought into Analysis*

Hold-ups in analysis are sometimes discovered to be related to a successful schizoid 'half-in-and-half-out' relationship which the patient is maintaining in real life, but is keeping hidden from the analyst. He fears, of course, that if it is analysed he will have to give it up or else enter more fully into it, and either way he would lose the protection of the relative stability it gives him. Sometimes one finds that a patient's entire practical life is conducted in terms of 'brinkmanship' (cf. p. 64). He does not properly 'belong' to anything but is a dilettante smatterer, toying with life rather than living it. It is amazing how far systematic non-committal can be carried in relationships with friends, organizations, jobs, houses, or what not, so that the patient is for ever on the move, like a butterfly alighting for a time and then flitting on. One patient mentioned casually, not thinking that it had any significance, that he never went to the same place twice for a holiday. That this has meaning is clear when it is compared with the opposite fact of the person who goes always to the same safe and familiar place, and would not dream of going anywhere else. The way ordinary life is conducted gives plenty of material for studying the conflicts that go on between needs and fears of close relationship. One patient at once dislikes the clothes she buys as soon as she has got them home, however much she felt 'I just must have that dress' so long as it is in the shop. Many patients will not think of mentioning such things as these, because they cannot risk seeing their inner meaning. They slip out by accident as 'casual asides'. One such observation may lead to the opening up of whole areas of successful compromise in which the patient is entrenched.

A not-uncommon compromise that is kept out of analysis and operates as a successful defence against real progress is the secret sexual affair. One patient's regular sexual relationship with a married woman provided for the emotional support of his dependent infantile self in a way that saved him from the dangerous close involvement of marriage, but also saved him from really bringing his fear-ridden infantile inner self into the treatment relationship. The position enabled him to maintain in real life a duplicate version of the schizoid split between the infant and the adult in himself. The infant was, so to speak, 'kept quiet' by a sexual affair which was completely cut off from all the rest of his life, and left his adult hard-working self free to go its own way. Two parts of himself were kept out of relationship with each other. Prostitution and homosexuality are clear cases of schizoid compromise in their evasion of the full commitment to the real relationship of marriage. That is one reason why they are so hard to cure. Under these conditions clearly no progress is going to be made in analysis. An analogous situation is sometimes met with in the treatment of a medical man. He is always trying to do without the analyst by depending on his own self-prescribed drugs, yet he still comes to sessions. So long as any of these compromises in real life are kept out of analysis, the result is a serious blocking of progress.

(iv) *Classical Analysis Utilized as a Defensive Position to Mark Time in*

By classical analysis is meant the theoretical position that the cause of neurosis is the Oedipus complex, the conflicts over the patient's incestuous desires for the parent of the opposite sex, and fear, guilt, and hate for the parent of the same sex. This is the theoretical position which results from the analysis of depression, and was Freud's first great pioneering contribution. It was not orientated to the schizoid problem which had not yet been explored. The measure of success which can be obtained by analysis on this basis is amply illustrated by the case of the patient who had the 'circular wall' fantasy. He came for treatment for an orthodox depression, a gloomy, angry, guilt-burdened, resentful but paralysed state of mind. He presented oedipal material in plenty, dreams of being in bed with mother, of fighting and castrating father and being castrated by him, of being dragged before courts of justice and condemned for criminal activities. His conscious fantasy, both sexual and as it concerned car-driving, was sadomasochistic in full detail. Anal material in both dreams and symptoms was plentiful. The analysis of all this did without doubt moderate his depression so that life became practically more comfortable for him, and his work was less interfered with by his moods. At his very first session he had said: 'I feel as if I've got a bag of dung inside me which I want to get rid of and can't.' Over a number of years he held to this idea and could not give it up. It stood for the notion that his trouble was something in his personality or make-up which was bad, unclean, which his mother (who had been a martinet in cleanliness training) would frown on and about which he felt guilty. He clung to this idea long after his depressed moods had faded. It is not, therefore, to be wondered at that he remained a very highly organized obsessional character. His was one of the cases that led me to feel that the results of classical analysis were not fundamental, and led not so much to radical change but to an improvement of the patient's character-pattern in the form of either *a milder and more livable obsessional character* in which very efficient self-control and self-management were maintained or else *a milder and somewhat easier schizoid character* in which analysis halted at the typical schizoid compromise of being only half-related, a position managed in a sufficiently socialized form to make daily life more possible without risking any dangerously strong feeling being aroused.

This means that if we were to encourage patients to regard sexual and aggressive problems as ultimate factors in their own right rather than as symptomatic of a deeper undermining of the ego, we would help them to halt at the stage of improved impulse-control without recognizing these problems as defences against the most primitive fears. Of course the primitive fears will break through, but it depends on the interpretations put upon them, as to what will happen to them. If fears are regarded only as secondary phenomena, anxiety reactions to bad impulses, then obsessional and schizoid defences will be strengthened and the primary fears will be buried. In some cases where that proves possible, this may in fact be the best course. Where it is not possible, to persist in applying only the classical analytical concepts would lead to stalemate and frustration.

In considering the Oedipus complex, we must note that an oedipal fantasy is neither on the one hand an adult marriage with real life commitment, nor is it on the other frank regressed infantile dependence. Oedipal fantasies are the end-product of infantile fantasy life and represent a child's struggle to overcome infantile dependence by disguising it in semi-adult form. Yet the hidden infantile dependence is but thinly disguised, as may be judged by Fairbairn's (1954) comment that hysteric genitality is so extremely oral. We have to distinguish between a healthy stimulating oedipal phase in normal development where parent–child relationships are good, and a pathological oedipal fantasy life which forms the basis of neurotic symptoms. This oedipal fantasy life arises when the anxious child withdraws from his outer world, and seeks to compensate for inability to make progress in real life, by setting up a substitute for it inside. We have already seen that the whole of this inner world life is basically a defence against the dangers of too drastic withdrawal. The pathological Oedipus complex always masks poor relationships with parents in reality, and should be analysed in such a way as to lead on to the discovery of the hopeless, shut-in, detached infantile ego which has given up real object-relations as unobtainable and sought safety in regression into the deep unconscious. In the case of one patient who had actually been seduced by her father, the physical relationship was certainly a schizoid compromise on his part between his inability to give her a genuinely personal relationship and his prevailing tendency at other times to ignore her altogether. This oedipal relationship had been the patient's one anxiety-burdened hope as a child of meaning something to her father, and therefore of feeling herself to be something of a person. In analysis she naturally produced a fully developed oedipal transference, and clung to this stubbornly as a defence against a true therapeutic relationship; for this would have meant bringing her disillusioned, apathetic childhood self to a real person for real help in regrowing, the most difficult of all psychotherapeutic experiences to encounter. Sexual relations both in reality and fantasy are a common substitute for real personal relations. One bachelor patient, who was a quite remote person with little feeling about anything, described his occasional sexual affairs as due to the need to discharge 'an intermittent biological urge which has nothing to do with me'.

In classical transference analysis on the basis of instinct-psychology, it is easy to confuse together the healthy oedipal phase and the pathological oedipal fantasy which is a schizoid compromise between real life and flight from reality. The patient may then believe that his pathological oedipal transference feelings are genuine natural instinctive reactions, though transferred from his parents of long ago. In this situation the patient would be helped to concentrate attention on the unrealistic as if it were real, and will be helped not to experience in an undisguised way what his actual basic and quite realistic feelings for his analyst are. What he is really feeling at bottom, without being able to let it emerge plainly, is that he is a frightened, weak, and helpless small child needing to depend on his analyst for support and protection, while at the same time he is afraid he will be ridiculed and rejected if he shows this openly. If he were allowed to believe that his Oedipus complex were the ultimate root of his neurosis, his attention would be diverted from the real ultimate problem and a schizoid compromise unwittingly maintained.

Classical oedipal analysis is, however, a much less specific entity in practice today, than it may appear to be in theory. The work of Melanie Klein has forced analysis ever deeper into the pre-oedipal, pre-genital levels, to the earliest paranoid and schizoid problems. Here we are not dealing with the child struggling with problems of socialization in a multi-personal family group; but with the primary two-person mother–infant relationship in which the ego begins to grow and the earliest ego-splitting and the creation of internal objects occurs. The position remained confused for a long time because, as Balint pointed out, theory lags behind practice. Writing in 1949, some six years after Fairbairn's proposed revisions, Balint still found theory tied to 'the physiological or biological bias' rather than 'the object-relation bias', and based on the data of depressions and obsessional neurosis rather than on hysteric-paranoid-schizoid phenomena (Balint, 1952). What I have said about the possibility of using analysis on the basis of the classical psychobiological oedipal theory as an unwitting support for resistance, simply re-emphasizes the need for theory to catch up with practice. There is much less need to emphasize this now

(1966) in view of all the work that has been done on the earliest mother–child relationship and its power to determine ego-formation.

The Necessity of the Schizoid Compromise as an Intermediate Phase to the Emergence of the Regressed Ego

Though I have sought to show how this need to set up a middle position, in which the patient is neither completely isolated nor yet fully committed to object-relationships, is the cause in general of psychotherapeutic stalemate and blocked analysis, it must also be added that this situation should not be too ruthlessly exposed. It is, in fact, often a necessary stage through which the patient has to pass on his way to facing at long last, first his frightening sense of fundamental isolation, and then his fears of the real good relationships which alone can heal his hurt and liberate his devitalized infantile ego for healthy and vigorous growth. The emergence of the ultimate withdrawn infantile self is the hardest of all ordeals for the patient. In the earlier chapters I have given reasons for the view that, in proportion to the severity of the patient's illness, a definite part of his total self is specifically withdrawn into the unconscious in a state of extreme infantile regression. This 'regressed ego' is the headquarters of all the most serious fears, and it feels a powerful need for complete protected passive dependence in which recuperation can take place and rebirth of an active ego be achieved. Nevertheless, *patients experience the most intense fear as this regressed ego draws near to consciousness. It brings with it a sense of utter and hopeless aloneness and yet also a fear of the good-object relationship as smothering*. The patient fears that his need for some measure of regressed dependence on the therapist will involve him in the loss of self-determination, of independence, and even of individuality itself. He cannot easily feel it as the starting-point of new growth in security. In truth, the need to regress cannot be taken lightly. In the most ill, it often involves hospitalization. In others, sufficient regression can be experienced in sessions while the active self is kept going outside. Regression can be understood and controlled, and insight can convert even normal 'resting' at home into a purposive regression. One business executive would quite suddenly feel exhausted, and as soon as possible put up the engaged sign, lock his office door and put his feet up for fifteen minutes. Mentally he was repeating the regression and passive relaxation he had learned to achieve in sessions, and with very great benefit, so that in time the need faded out. In some other cases, it seems that specific regression is not needed, and 'withdrawing tendencies' can be reversed in the normal process of transference-analysis.

The schizoid problem and its compromise solutions show, however, where the ultimate difficulties of psychotherapy lie, and just how difficult it is and why. The patient *cannot* easily and quickly abandon his inadequate solutions or defences for what he feels to be the uncertain promise of a real solution, bought at the price of encountering such severe anxieties. He can only do so by easy stages, and meanwhile he must use whatever schizoid compromises between accepting and rejecting treatment that he can. In truth, he endures other anxieties by holding on to his own attempts to carry on in his own way, which are as severe as the fears of over-dependence, and far more destructive. But since the real 'cure' *seems* to involve sinking his own personality in passive dependence on that of another person, at least at first, we must admit that the patient is confronted with a formidable prospect. Often, if he could not effect some compromise relationship to tide him over till he can face progress again, he would have to break off treatment. I once had a patient who had spent several years *using* psychiatrists as 'someone to argue with', giving them no chance to help her because, as they happened to be males of roughly her own age, she felt that the degree of dependence involved would be too humiliating. It would take a major cultural revolution to create an atmosphere in which patients might find it easier to accept psychotherapy; a cultural atmosphere in which not only Ian Suttie's 'taboo on tenderness' had disappeared, but also its deeper implication, the 'taboo on weakness'. Then, perhaps, illness of the mind could be treated with the same acceptance of the need for 'healing in a state of passive recuperation' as is already accorded to illness of the body. But then there might be fewer mentally ill people.

Yet the final difficulty is in the patient's own mental makeup. Two patients of mine needed to go through a regressive illness which involved hospitalization. One with a gentler nature who made no difficulty about accepting help, 'gave in' to the situation thoroughly and made an excellent recovery in a few months. He came out to return to work straight away, and with diminishing frequency of analysis, maintained his improvement. The other, an obsessional hard-driving and at times aggressive worker who could not at that stage be tolerant to himself, could not surrender his struggle to drive himself on.

Having got over the acute crisis, he came out of hospital still with a lot of tension and conflict. His own comment was: 'I couldn't make the best use of hospital. I couldn't give in. I felt I had to be adult and keep myself active.' He had seemed to be more keen on helping the other patients than on getting better himself. But three months later he was back in again and this time for a far longer and deeply regressed illness. Yet we can understand why he put up such resistance, for though he got over this illness in time and returned to work in a better state than before, still he was left with a clearly hysteric dependence on others which he feared, and had to face. Where it is not possible for the patient to have a long analysis, the choice may be between a bad breakdown willy nilly, or the achievement of a useful schizoid compromise. If the patient feels a very intense need to safeguard his independence and freedom for self-determination, which he feels to be compromised by accepting help, we must recognize that the solution of this problem will take a long time. If for any reasons the patient cannot go through with such a long analysis, he may need to be helped to accept the fact that he cannot force himself beyond a certain point in making human relationships, and must find out what compromises between being too involved and too isolated work best for him. Yet given enough time and reasonably supportive circumstances, this problem can be solved for many people by psychoanalytical therapy.

We need to concentrate our best efforts in research to this end, for the feeling of angry frustration, of being caught in a trap which is their own mental make-up, of being entangled in a web of difficulties within themselves and only becoming more and more entangled the more they struggle to get free, is a terrible problem for all types of patient. The naturally energetic and capable persons who cannot succeed, or be contented, in becoming cold, emotionally neutralized individuals, and yet cannot effect stable and happy human relationships and get on with living, can reach a point of volcanic eruption. They cannot stand the utter frustration of their inability to escape from their own need for compromise, half-in-and-half-out, solutions. If such a person can find no understanding and reliable therapist, the result can be tragedy both for himself and others. It is well for him if he has the safeguard of a genuine therapeutic relationship at such a time, which offers him a chance to grow some deep-level security on the basis of which he can find his way out of his trap.

XII

OBJECT-RELATIONS THEORY AND PSYCHOTHERAPY

GENERAL CONSIDERATIONS

Fairbairn's Unfinished Work

IF the development and maintenance of the ego has come more and more to be seen as the fundamental psychodynamic process, and an ego can only develop in the medium of personal object-relationship, it follows that psychotherapy at any level, but particularly at the deepest level, can only occur as a result of a personal therapeutic relationship. Symptom relief can be produced by non-personal techniques with varying success, though I recently heard a behaviour therapist say that it was now recognized that results tended to be better when the technique was always administered by the *same* psychologist. Thus the therapeutic value of the personal relationship cannot be excluded, it seems, from any type of therapy of 'persons'. Nevertheless, the more we are concerned about the 'person' and the less about the 'symptom', the more the personal therapeutic relationship comes to dominate the entire situation. This insight is not the exclusive possession of any one school of psychodynamic thought. Though certainly the work of Fairbairn and Winnicott is at the centre of this situation, the names of an ever-growing number of therapists spring to mind whose writings point this way.

It is, I think, necessary, at the outset, to put aside a possible misconception. I have from time to time received enquiries both from Britain and America as to where one could get a 'Fairbairn analysis'. One letter from the U.S.A. stated:

> There are a considerable number of us who are very interested in the work of Fairbairn. . . . It might be advisable to show how the theories of Fairbairn cause modifications in the classical technique, and in the type of interpretations, dosage, etc. . . . The Kleinians quite clearly spell out how they carry out analysis in the classical tradition, but change only the way they make an interpretation by utilizing the concept of fantasy. . . . The nature and range of their

fantasies are oftentimes quite clearly spelled out and are available. No such protocol exists for the Fairbairnian technique. This is badly needed. Those of us who practise what we feel is a form of Fairbairnian analysis primarily do have our own ideas about this, one of which is the maximal use of the interpretation of basic trust and mistrust in the external object's ability to help the patient integrate his disparate fragments.

I feel it should be said at once that there is no such thing as 'the Fairbairnian technique' or a 'Fairbairnian analysis', but I must make clear what I mean by this. Over the fifteen or so years of my acquaintance with Fairbairn, I never gained any impression that he thought of himself as founding a distinct school of psychoanalysis, or that he had any wish to do so. His attitude was always that of simply contributing to the common stock of psychoanalytical knowledge, such insights as seemed to him new and important. He certainly had a great faith in the power of significant ideas to look after themselves and spread themselves abroad, and this is exactly what is happening to his ideas. He would have been quite happy with the situation expressed by my correspondent as: 'Those of us who do practise what we feel is a Fairbairnian form of analysis primarily do have our own ideas about this.' 'Schools' tend to dogma. 'Freely circulating ideas' tend to fresh thinking. I think, however, that he would have deleted 'a Fairbairnian form of analysis', and substituted 'an object-relations form of analysis'. Not that he would have been prepared to give any exact description or definition of what this meant. He rather regarded it as the major practical problem awaiting investigation. One aspect of it would certainly be that the therapist must be the kind of person with whom 'the patient can integrate his disparate fragments'.

Nevertheless, he would not have expressed his thought like that. He held strongly that the use of impersonal conceptualization, as if that alone could constitute 'scientific thinking', led to a subtle falsification of understanding in psychodynamics. He abhorred such terms as id, mental mechanisms, and would not have spoken of 'the analyst–patient relationship' as 'the external object's ability to help the patient integrate his disparate fragments'. The nearest he came to expressing this thought in his own way was when he wrote:

> . . . The patient cannot surrender his internal bad objects until the analyst has become a sufficiently good object to him.

He would certainly have said that this will not happen unless the therapist is the kind of person who actually can help. To use Winnicott's distinction between 'doing' and 'being', technique is a matter of what the analyst is 'doing', how he is operating his protocol for interpretations and so on, but the therapeutic factor lies in what the therapist 'is', what he is 'being' unself-consciously in relation to the patient. Fairbairn wrote that he would not like to be without the guidance of scientific concepts in this field, but I do not think he would ever have attempted to create a protocol for treatment. He once said to me in discussing this matter that he thought the most important thing was to be human, natural, and real. 'Insight' cannot be learned from a text-book, any more than musical composition can be learned from a text-book. What can be learned from text-books is much that is essential and useful for the 'expression' in a concrete way of the 'insightful interpretation' or the 'symphonic composition' which in themselves are spontaneous creative responses of a whole personality gifted in these directions. The reason, basically, for a training analysis, is not primarily to 'learn a technique', but to make sufficient progress towards becoming a whole or integrated person, capable of effecting a real relationship through genuine care for and understanding of the patient enmeshed in his subjective difficulties. Only that could justify us in thinking that we have the right to offer to another human being a chance to find his own unity or true selfhood in and through his dealings with us.

Fairbairn's thinking was as personal as that, which accounts for the fact that he was very cautious about therapy while he was so very radical about theory. His work raises the whole question of what is the nature of the psychotherapeutic relationship. What I have said above may perhaps disappoint some who have found in Fairbairn's work insights of basic importance for the re-orientation of psychodynamic theory. It would not, however, be correct to say that Fairbairn originated this re-orientation. If anyone did that it was Freud himself, when he put ego-analysis in the centre of the field of enquiry. Perhaps nobody really originates a major development of this kind. It is part of the historical and social process, of the movement of life and thought all around us. It is in the air, and many people contribute to its growth, while here and there someone seizes on some aspect of it and gives it clearer definition, to set going in turn ever-widening circles of fresh thinking. In this Fairbairn played an outstanding part, conceptualizing with great intellectual clarity, the way psychodynamic thinking was moving ever deeper, beyond impulses and symptoms, oedipal, and depressive problems, to the earliest vicissitudes of the infantile ego, and the intense need of the schizoid ego for an object with whom security could be found. In particular, he followed up the work of Melanie Klein, showing how her object-splitting involved corresponding ego-splitting. His clear conceptualizations would not have been possible without the prior work of Freud and Melanie Klein, and the fast developing psychoanalytical therapy of children. Perhaps only now, *more than a quarter of a century after he began to publish his findings*, is the intellectual force of his work beginning to have its proper impact on those whose minds are open to seminal ideas.

Nevertheless, he was not able to bring his own work to completion, by working out its full application to psychoanalytic therapy. One can see now that the first signs of failing bodily health were beginning to manifest even before his last published paper, 'On the Nature and Aims of Psychoanalytical Treatment' (1958). He had approached this extension from the theoretical to the practical only slowly. He said to me at that time: 'The implications of object-relations theory for psychotherapy are so far-reaching that we must proceed with great caution.' My guess is that probably many analytical therapists have been more experimental in practice than Fairbairn was. I have never discussed his methods with anyone who had an analysis with him, but my own experience of Fairbairn the analyst was that he was remarkably orthodox. Analysis began and proceeded on the oedipal and transference problems level, and I was surprised that he seemed to make so little use of his own distinctive theoretical orientation in practical analysis. Fairbairn the analyst helped me to understand Freud so far as theory went; it was his writings that opened new horizons. I believe that some critics inferred from the fact that he was known to be a very kindly man who in some cases gave patients some badly needed extra-analytical help, and that his theoretical views implied the recognition and acceptance of a great measure of dependence of the patient on the analyst, that he could not deal with or did not sufficiently understand or recognize hate, aggression, and negative transference. That was not my experience of him. Some of my own personal gains from analysis related directly to his recognition of negative transference.

Although in one paper he expressed the view that the idea of 'free association' belonged too much to the old nineteenth-century Utilitarian philosophy and ought to be replaced by the more dynamic concept of 'maximum freedom of expression short of action' during a session, nevertheless he could permit and handle some 'acting out'. He told me of one female patient who suddenly turned on him and pushed him down, and he added, 'She got on a lot better after that.' He also described to me a patient who 'acted out' a lot of tension and resentment over cleanliness training by using a small stool to stand for the pot. His own experience as a family man no doubt enabled him to understand this acting, with constructive results. He once gave me his opinion that the nearer adult analysis came to child analysis, the better the result. My own experience leaves me in no doubt about that, and also that this is the main source of resistance to analysis, that the adult in the patient finds it so disturbing and humiliating to go back to having to experience himself on the level of a child with another adult. Fairbairn's remark encouraged me to go through with a patient over a long period of 'acting out' and reliving her childhood in sessions, from bottle feeding to games on the floor (tearing up paper and flinging it around, drawing, plasticene modelling in which the whole family were stamped on and destroyed) to the ultimate embarking on friendships with men with me as a father to whom she could talk freely without moralistic criticism. Treatment ended when she became capable of a serious courtship and marriage.

On the other hand he expressed the view to me that the more we analyse the ego, the longer analyses become. Perhaps this perception, along with a certain conservatism in his make-up (for most things other than psychoanalytical theory), combined with his isolation in Edinburgh, in the medico–religious–intellectual climate antipathetic to psychoanalysis, to make his practice lag behind his theory in therapy. He certainly did not evolve any specific 'Fairbairnian technique'. He practised orthodox psychoanalysis while recognizing that object-relations theory was bound to involve further developments of therapeutic method. In conformity with this, he definitely changed his personal attitude to patients over the years. He told me that in his early days he began with the usual view that extra-sessional contacts with the patient should be ruled out, and that when a female patient entered hospital for a surgical operation and requested him to visit her, he told her that this would be bad for the analysis, and refused. But he afterwards became convinced that this was a mistake which made it hard for the patient to realize him as a real human being.

He also once refused to treat an agoraphobic patient who

wanted all sessions to be conducted in his own home, and probably would have made that same decision again in the same circumstances; nevertheless, he accepted a very regressed patient from abroad who had fled from an extremely formal analyst, and when after a time she became unable to attend at his rooms, he conducted sessions with her at her hotel. Over a period of two years she recovered sufficiently to go back to her own country and has worked consistently ever since. It is clear that he was beginning to concentrate specifically on the problem of the therapeutic relationship, when his health and strength began to fail. When I first knew him, he was intending to write a major book on hysteria and it was found that he had gathered a great deal of material for this and was not able to complete the task. His last projected paper, which also he never got written, he outlined to me towards the end in conversation. It was on 'Psychoanalysis as Science' and was concerned with the impersonality of the purely objective 'natural science' methods as contrasted with the deeply personal nature of the psychotherapeutic relationship. I made two attempts to get him to discuss this so that I might put something on record but his health did not make this possible.

The implications for therapy of the extension of theory into the lowest depths of ego-growth, are today being explored on a wide front. Fairbairn's 'object-relations theory', which links ego-growth in all its vicissitudes with the human environment of personal relationships, has been carried back to its ultimate beginnings by Winnicott's work on the mother–infant relationship. Here the 'maturational processes' given by the psychobiological inheritance are seen to be completely dependent for their development on the 'facilitating environment' of personal object-relations, with the mother as the first and all-important object. With regard to the implications of this for psychotherapy, I shall for the moment only mention Winnicott's distinction between *classical analysis* for psychoneuroses on the oedipal level, and *management* or 'holding the situation for the patient' in a mothering sense with as much analysis as is useful for schizoid, regressed, and potentially psychotic patients. This problem of the management of regression had arisen for Fairbairn with one patient in an acute way at the end, and had to be abandoned when Parkinson's disease and cerebral thrombosis overtook him. We shall return in the next chapter to this problem as presented in Winnicott's terms, but must first take a more general look at the nature of psychotherapy in its inevitable setting in real life.

Deeper Levels of Therapy and Changes of Technique

We can only answer the question about the nature of the psychotherapeutic relationship in a comprehensive way, if we keep in mind and find the answer to a further question: can oedipal problems be seen as simply oedipal, once we are aware of the existence of the deeper level schizoid ego-problems? Winnicott regards these as requiring something more than straightforward classical analysis, something which he calls 'management' which is closely related to the mother–infant relationship. Must not the psychotherapeutic relationship then *at every level even though with differences of degree*, include not only transference relationships calling for classical analysis, but also and along with that, in keeping with the severity of the illness, an *ad hoc* reality-relationship of a supportive, growth-promoting and finally personally liberating kind. The fact that this question was always latent in the psychoanalytic enquiry is clear from Freud's original limitation of (classical) analysis to the transference neuroses. Here is a recognition of the fact that this only related to one area of human problems, and that sooner or later deeper levels would have to be investigated and their therapy considered. Analysts have been driven willy-nilly into treatments going far beyond the limits Freud prescribed for classical analysis. The concept of the classical analysis belongs to the pioneer period of partial and incomplete knowledge, but since all moves beyond that have been basically psychoanalytical in principle, there seems no reason to limit the term psychoanalysis to oedipal treatments.

Actually it becomes increasingly difficult to conceive of a stereotyped psychoanalytic procedure, and we have to be content with main guiding lines. The highly individual nature of every separate analysis calls for understanding, since no two patients are ever exactly alike. Every human being is a unique individual person. Psychotherapeutic success depends ultimately not on theory, and not on a stereotyped technique, but on the individual therapist's ability to understand intuitively and accurately this particular patient, and to sense what is truly this patient's problem. Theory is a great help but it does not confer intuitive gifts of understanding or a therapeutic personality. It provides a more or less useful guide for them. In this, psychodynamic science differs from natural science, where theory determines and controls exact procedures. Psychotherapy is a living personal relationship. A therapeutic personality in the therapist is, however, the central desideratum around which a complex of other factors group themselves. This becomes more evident the more ill the patient is. Hence the necessity for careful selection of patients for deep therapy, and for our earlier discussion of different levels of psychotherapy.

External and Internal Conditions for Psychotherapy

The conditions for successful psychoanalytical therapy can be roughly divided into external (or environmental) and internal (or psychodynamic). Environmental conditions are not so important if one is dealing with a fairly straightforward case of oedipal psychoneurosis. Oedipal patients can 'stand' their real-life environment better than, say, regressing ego-weakness patients can. But while there are cases that can be helped to an adequate stabilization on that level without probing deeper, *it is not so possible today as it used to be to leave matters alone at the stage of the resolution of purely oedipal conflicts.* It used to be said that an 'intact ego' is a precondition for psychoanalysis. But in the light of the most recent psychoanalytical advances, it is precisely this that is so hard to find. We are much more likely today than were the earlier analytical therapists, to find ourselves coming upon indubitable signs of basic ego-weakness obtruding into the middle of oedipal analysis. I have found this to be true even within the thirty years of my own work as a psychotherapist. The overall conclusion from the material here studied would seem to be the fact that *the deepest researches of contemporary psychoanalysis show that 'radical' psychotherapy must aim, not simply at the resolution of specific conflicts, but at the fundamental regrowing of the basic ego, the whole personal self* (with the proviso that such 'radical' psychotherapy is certainly not possible or even wanted in every case, though it is the true goal in the light of which all else must be judged).

Not that the resolution of specific conflicts has lost its importance and reality. This is the pathway to the undermining of all symptoms and defences, and we can be grateful when it is possible to leave it at that. But this so often leads remorselessly on to the ultimate problem, the need for a rebirth and regrowing of a 'whole person'. This can easily be dismissed as an impossibly idealistic aim, though if patient, therapist, and circumstances are adequate to the need, there is a genuine possibility which in some cases is actually accomplished. However, in practice, we so often get no chance to aim at that ultimate goal because the coincidence of all the necessary factors is rare. This is easiest to illustrate if we look first at the environmental circumstances, and the extreme case of the deeply disturbed patient who may need an actual breakdown into severe illness before he can turn the corner and get well. His circumstances may be such that he cannot risk it, or that if it happens he may be financially or professionally ruined, or that his environment may not be adequate to sustain him in his convalescence. I have quoted the case of one patient whose father was psychotic, and whose exceptionally rigid defences probably contained something psychotic in the depths of his own unconscious; he was a bachelor living alone, and managing a small but highly specialized business, and there was no one to look after it or him if he cracked. He became a genuine case of blocked analysis. There was no chance of finding out whether or not he could have faced the deepest repressed elements in his mental make-up. Another, female, patient in similar circumstances, with a similar psychotic factor in her problems, felt that if it ever came to a real breakdown and having to enter a mental hospital, she would become thereafter suspect in her profession and would have no economic future.

If a patient needs a long regressed illness which cannot be coped with at home, he may find himself taken out of analysis and into hospital, and made the subject of concentrated efforts to suppress his illness forcibly by drugs or ECT and hospital discipline, while his deep problems simply cannot be glimpsed or understood by psychiatrists and nursing staff whose aim must of necessity be to get him well quickly. On the other hand there is the patient who, after a long analysis which by its very success at last opens up the deepest levels, finds himself in such an appalling state of mental suffering that he simply cannot stand it and at some point can only want to have it buried by ECT or else suicide. Thus one middle-aged married woman whose mother had simply ignored her in infancy apart from routine physical attention, grew up very seriously schizoid. She had in fact no mother who felt any genuine personal attachment to her, and therefore no mother to whom she could feel any personal attachment; in effect, no personal relationship in which she could make a start in experiencing herself as a person. She was not the only member of the family who suffered, but being the eldest she suffered most. Late on in treatment she visited her parents' home on one occasion, and found her father alone in one room, her mother and several other members of the family in another, all sitting in deadly silence after some quarrel. After a time, she could not stand it and went, and on the way home suddenly remembered 'But I've often known it like this in the past'. About the same time, a younger sister remarked to her one day, 'The trouble is that there isn't enough affection in our family.' I will summarize this case, as it shows, particularly clearly, the interaction of external and internal factors in therapy.

After a long analysis she began to experience the outbreak of feelings of quite appalling isolation on waking up in the night. This made her suicidal without the protection of pills. One day her general practitioner suddenly declared to her husband that he had no time to give to cases like this and said, 'Take your whole family off my list to another doctor.' This traumatic rejection so terrified her that in an emergency session that afternoon I was unable to get any real contact with her. She was in the grip of the fear that another doctor would not understand and would refuse to give her the sleeping pills she needed, a fear that proved to be not without a basis in reality. This made her feel that I too was useless in this kind of emergency and that her husband would be unable to cope with the situation; the strain would give him a second coronary thrombosis. That night she took all her remaining pills and was only just saved by intensive hospital treatment. When she regained consciousness, her first words were 'Does G (myself) know? Does he understand.' Her husband told her 'Yes'. When later she was able to return to analysis she made rapid progress, realized what great efforts had been made to save her, felt that after all she must be 'wanted' by her family, and finally said to me, 'What really convinced me was when I saw that your attitude to me had not altered a bit. I thought you would be angry with me and refuse to treat me any more.'

For the space of nine months she developed quietly and steadily into a trustful communicative and friendly person. Her husband and daughters said that the home had become a more normally happy one for the first time. Then suddenly, just before the Easter holiday break loomed up, a dramatic change occurred. It was clear that in spite of her welcome improvement her need of large doses of night sedation meant that her deep dread of utter isolation still remained to be dealt with. She failed to arrive for the last two sessions before the holiday, and her husband rang to say she had a migraine attack. Both I myself and the patient and family were going away for two weeks and I could do no more than have two phone talks with her before the 'separation', with no definite result. During the holiday the patient's sister had to go into a mental hospital and had ECT for depression, and then the patient broke down. When I saw her again I was shocked at the change in her, physically fat and swollen with marked signs of oedema, and mentally very withdrawn. She too had to be hospitalized. She put it down to the shock of her sister's illness, but on her return home she resumed sessions and the rapport of the previous nine months was definitely absent. I took her back to the two migraine attacks before the holiday, and gradually it dawned on her that she had begun to feel ill before her sister's illness and had made that an excuse to divert her anxiety from herself. At last a critical insight came. She remembered that before the holiday she had been feeling so much better for so long that she suddenly got the idea that I would soon be saying to her that she did not need me any more and her treatment could come to an end. This had caused her to panic and she had migraine attacks to stop herself coming to sessions to have the dread verdict passed on her.

As the ultimate outcome showed, her problem was more complex than this. Really she feared going on with the analysis because it would mean having to face her ultimate terrifying sense of isolation; yet she was equally afraid to stop, and was in a cleft stick. The migraine attacks masked the acute tension between the fear of stopping and the fear of going on, and combined with the holiday made her feel that she had lost me already. As her resumed analysis proceeded, I found that she had begun to re-experience the appalling isolation states that she had felt before her previous suicide attempt. Her husband became alarmed and told me that she was definitely drifting back into the state of mind she had been in before. There was no doubt that this sense of utter isolation had its origin in maternal neglect in the first year, but she had been to a considerable extent defended against that by the fact that a grandfather who was very fond of her and she of him, lived with the family and cared for and protected her. He died when she was about four years old, and she was thrown back again on her basic isolation. What emerged at this stage was that she was identifying losing me through ending treatment, with the death of her grandfather which had evidently precipitated a severe crisis at the age of four which no one recognized, and which left her a seriously withdrawn child. The analysis of this threw her back on her original experience of maternal deprivation; and her feeling of utter isolation now emerged in full force, plunging her into despair. She could do nothing but sit at home sobbing, and feeling suicidal, till she suddenly made up her mind. In the next session she said, 'I can't stand this mental suffering any longer. I can't attend to analysis. I must have it buried or I shall commit suicide. I want ECT.' She was in no state to be told that this might not do for her what she wanted, and as she insisted, I made arrangements for it. Here was a sad dénouement. Successful analysis had unearthed something that the patient just could not face.

The ETC gave her relief from the intolerable mental suffering but impaired her memory so that she could not remember why she had it, and why she was not now seeing me. When a few days after its termination she seemed much calmer, the psychiatrist said he hoped this would last, that it could be unwise to stir up the mud again, and he hoped she would not need to see me for further analysis. She thought she was being forbidden to see me again and that same night her suicidal despair rushed back in full force. She had to return to analysis, and we found that in fact ECT had put some brake on uncontrollable emotion in a crisis, that she could now stand going back earlier than her grandfather's death, and was clearly reliving the basic trauma of the primary maternal neglect. The ensuing analysis of the isolated infant who could not develop a true self in an empty world was a fascinating experience, of which I shall give some account in the next chapter. I may mention here that while she was in hospital the first time, after her suicide attempt, she was exceptionally well cared for and sympathetically understood by the consultant, but on one occasion his junior took it upon himself to give her a severe lecture to the effect that other people had had a difficult childhood besides her, and it was time she pulled herself together and got over this suicide nonsense. He came near to undoing for a time the good that was being done.

Environmental factors over which we have no control can in this way greatly complicate the handling of the inner problems, which may themselves be greater than the patient can face. One may well feel that, in spite of advances in understanding, it may often be a practical impossibility to secure the conditions in which radical psychotherapy can be carried to a successful issue. For the deeper we go, the more vulnerable the patient becomes to the impact of external reality, as vulnerable in fact as he was in infancy. Nevertheless, there are actual successes even in very long-term cases. Given a fair chance, some can win through and some cannot, but we must go on to explore this problem as thoroughly as possible.

Freud's Caution[1]

It is well known that as Freud grew older he grew more cautious in his estimate of the therapeutic value of psychoanalysis, though he retained an undiminished regard for it as an instrument of scientific research on the psychic life of human beings. It may well be that Freud's scientific interest was greater than his human interest, for he expressed very low views of human nature in general. I have little doubt that his psychobiology and instinct theory made him regard as inherent in human nature what were in fact psychopathological developments. This is not a good basis in theory for psychotherapy. It must be apparent now that in practice psychoanalysis only has value as an instrument of scientific research into the most painful areas of unconscious feeling and impulse, if the patient has reason to believe that the method has therapeutic value and will help him to become the 'person' he feels he has failed to be. No one is going to lay bare their intolerable hidden distress to satisfy someone's scientific curiosity. They will only do so if they become steadily convinced that we will stand by them and in the end relieve their misery, and even then, cooperation is opposed by tremendous inner resistances. If faith in the therapeutic value of psychoanalysis proved unwarranted, it would have no more value as a scientific method than have the laboratory methods of 'objective' psychology. The person investigated just does not allow any of these methods to touch the painful areas of his inner life. All that is obtained is some objective knowledge of the patient by the investigator, with no transforming healing process involved. Scientific understanding of the *dynamic subjective* development and functioning of human personality will only be gained by combining investigation and therapy. This is what psychoanalysis claims to do, not by mere observation of *behaviour* from the outside, but by sharing the painful subjective *experience* on the inside, which lies behind the patient's behaviour. This is our only hope of entering this closely guarded, tenaciously defended area of the patient's suffering privacy.

This makes Freud's cautious estimate of the possibility of psychotherapy all the more challenging. Therapeutic optimism

[1] At this point material is incorporated in revised form from an article, 'The Therapeutic Factor in Psychotherapy', *Brit. J. med. Psychol.*, **26**, 2 (1953) up to the point where Winnicott's view of psychotherapy is examined, on p. 357. Ch. XIII.

and pessimism have alternated in the history of the psychoanalytic movement, which simply shows that analysts have never been blind to the difficulties. On the one hand there are blocked analyses, negative therapeutic reactions, the gaining of intellectual insight without accompanying emotional change, and the fact that distortion and embitterment of human personality can go so far and be so deep-seated, that the individual seems to be virtually inaccessible to healing influences: and there is the ever-present fact of unconscious resistance to treatment. On the other hand there is the simple fact that a number of patients do actually show important changes in personality in ways that manifestly would not have occurred but for their psychoanalytical treatment; not only losing symptoms but becoming happier and more effective people. It is difficult to present publicly the evidence for this, firstly because the nature of the work is so highly confidential, and secondly because there are so few analysts and therapists that the pressure of sheer urgent clinical work leaves all too little time for detailed research on results. Furthermore, since the patient goes on living, treatment cannot produce *final* results but rather puts him in a position to manage the rest of his life with greater insight and to go on growing. Thus it is not uncommon for patients to write even a long time after they have ended treatment, to report post-analytic improvement. A male patient wrote over six years after he had ceased analysis to say that he definitely had not stood still but felt that insight and improvement had gone on steadily. He had just dreamed of being with the Queen (the symbolic mother) and 'to my surprise she took quite a friendly interest in me. I feel that this marks a favourable turning-point in that what was previously an inhuman and frightening object becomes more human and warmer.' His mother had been cold and introverted. He added, 'I am still staggered by the amount of fear and insecurity we all carry, making for blindness, false targets, wrong judgment's inactivity, etc. It is like travelling in a heavy fog but just occasionally getting a glimpse of a sunlit landscape in an unspoiled world.' Prior to psychotherapy his inner world was almost entirely dominated by internal bad objects and a paranoid atmosphere. The motivational element of simple compassion for suffering human beings which plays an important part in leading one to become a psychotherapist who treats patients by 'understanding' them rather than by 'working on' them, makes it impossible simply to write off the patient who does not oblige by getting better quickly as if it were the patient's fault. One has to be prepared to go right through with the patient, whatever his difficulties, and it would be impossible to go on doing this year after year, if one did not see genuine evidence that this work has, not only great limitations but also real effectiveness. The problem of the nature of psychotherapy calls for continuous investigation.

Scientific Validation of Psychotherapeutic Results

It may be worth while at this point to glance briefly at the difficulties of validating therapeutic results. Those who like Eysenck attempt statistical assessment of results designed to highlight the failures of psychotherapy, should be required in every case to present them only alongside the parallel statistical study of the failures of psychiatry and behaviour therapy. A hospital psychiatrist recently told me that thirty per cent of their admissions are readmissions, and I have been given higher figures than that. The psychiatrists are now in many cases trying out behaviour therapy techniques but no one has to my knowledge published statistics of failures. I personally know of such failures. The only firm conclusion that can be drawn is the correct one that mental health problems are far more subtle and complex than our present understanding and treatment methods can cope with. Partisan attempts to decry any one method of treatment should disqualify the critic as prejudiced and unscientific. Thus, Eysenck, to take only one example, seeks to prove statistically that two out of every three neurotics are cured or improve within two years without psychotherapy. However, in 1950, the present writer broadcast some short talks on 'Nerves' which brought in over 1,500 letters from radio listeners. The outstanding fact in this correspondence was the very large number of letters from elderly people who reported that they had suffered their first breakdown in their late teens or early twenties, and that since then they had experienced repeated relapses at intervals of three to five years up to their fifties or sixties (their age at the time of writing). Some of these patients had been hospitalized more than once and treated by a variety of methods; many had recovered spontaneously, but all broke down repeatedly at intervals. All these cases would be included in Eysenck's category of 'cured or improved within two years', which turns out to be simply meaningless.

It is not surprising that remissions of overt neurosis occur, since such illnesses are emotional crises and emotion invariably ebbs and flows in intensity. Anxieties of even deep origin are greatly affected, stimulated or damped down by every change of circumstances. Emotional crises are reactions to changing situations both within the mind and in the outer world, and the natural and automatic defence of repression is not a fixed and constant factor. The struggle to suppress disturbed feeling is always going on, and repression is being constantly weakened or reinforced by the ever-changing life situation. Disappearance of symptoms is not 'cure'. Faced with such an enormous problem as mass mental ill-health in the community we can be grateful for any *symptom-relieving treatment* that can be proved to be helpful, whether behaviour therapy, drugs, ECT or any other kind; but *psychotherapy accepts the responsibility of working for something more fundamental; long-term stabilizing changes in the total personality*. Whatever disappointments are encountered, this is still the real aim of psychotherapy, even when the psychotherapeutic method itself can be used for valuable short-term improvements. Psychoanalytic therapy can only fairly be judged in the light of what it ultimately aims at.

It may be useful to look a little closer at this question of scientific validation of psychotherapeutic results, partly because it will clarify the nature of psychotherapy, but especially because many psychodynamically orientated social and case workers and teachers, trained in the broadly psychoanalytic approach, find themselves under fire from psychologists and other colleagues who have had a purely objectively scientific education and are often lamentably ignorant of realities beyond the scope of 'science' in the narrow sense. The social workers have usually come to their subject from the background of an arts education, and are not seldom at a loss to know how to meet the 'scientist's' criticisms that their work is purely subjective guess work and cannot be scientifically validated, or even scientifically based. This raises the gravest and profoundest intellectual problem of our time. For centuries we had a civilization based on 'faith' in which the whole of reality was 'personalized'. In the last few centuries this has been increasingly replaced by a civilization based on 'objective scientific knowledge of material reality', and everything tends to become depersonalized. But now at last, and very much through the work of Freud, in whom the intellectual battle raged fiercely, science has run up against the fact of human personality itself. Here it is faced with a new dimension of reality and knowledge, and is very loth to admit the facts. Scientific orthodoxy struggles to deal with the 'person' by the old 'objective methods of investigation' suitable to dealing with material reality. The 'scientific' study of the 'person' has split into two quite different approaches, so-called 'objective' psychology, and 'psychodynamics' which studies the 'subjective experience of the human being as a person', and to which the 'objective' school wish to deny scientific status. I used the term 'so-called objective' psychology, because our subjective experience of ourselves as persons is just as much an objective reality, a stubbornly existing fact, as any material fact or process. Nevertheless, it cannot be studied simply from the outside. It is a kind of fact or reality that we can only 'know' on the inside. Psychodynamic studies are the very spearhead of intellectual progress today and will lead to yet another major reorientation of our culture and civilization. Those who foolishly try to deny scientific reality to psychodynamic studies are, by implication, saying that the progress of human thought has come to a final end in their type of scientific theory and philosophy: a proposition which only has to be stated to be seen to be absurd. This question is of such great importance today that I have dealt with it at greater length in Chapter XIII, on 'The Concept of Psychodynamic Science'.

I will only add here that a great deal of psychiatry and behaviour therapy today is an unrecognized attempt to make science take over our responsibilities for human living. At a time when philosophers of science are themselves expanding the concept of science, psychotherapy must disentangle itself from a false subordination to the orthodox scientific outlook of the last few centuries. The business of science is not to be a substitute for our human living as 'persons', but to give us the tools with which to carry out our purposes. Science cannot take over, or provide any substitute for, the essential human activity of making personal relationships in which we can experience the reality of both ourselves and other people, and thus find meaning and value in living. Psychotherapy is a part of this essentially 'human living' and its aims cannot be achieved by any impersonal material technique. Psychotherapy must use psychodynamic knowledge, which has its own objectivity and is the only truly 'psychological science', as a tool in the service of human personality and its rights to be given personal relationships of a kind which will permit and 'facilitate' (*vide* Winnicott) growth to maturity of personality. We are sometimes told, not only by scientists but also by some theologians, that 'man' has in this present scientific stage of history at last 'come of age'. This is surely blind and arrogant nonsense. All that has happened is that 'natural science' has made available to us knowledge, much of which is being used in widely destructive ways, because of our chronic psychological immaturity. Only in our lifetime has the work of Freud and his successors begun to disturb our complacency and compel us to face this fact.

In the light of this we can return to the consideration of statistical studies of psychotherapeutic results, and see that they are really completely devoid of meaning, for three reasons.

(1) They have no way of taking into account the motives patients have for recovery or non-recovery. Tests that can only be applied to objective data, just do not deal with subjective data. Many patients feel guilty about taking treatment because of the opposition of disapproving relations, or because they feel involved in talking about parents and friends behind their backs, and feel they ought not to do that even to get well. This guilt is all the more serious and obstructive when it is unconscious, as Freud pointed out in 'The Ego and the Id'. It is part of psychotherapy to deal with such problems but success is not likely to be invariable. Some types of patient who are aggressive and wish always to be master of other people, or to be independent at all costs, find extreme difficulty in accepting psychotherapy at all. They are always secretly wanting to frustrate and defeat their therapist even at the price of remaining ill. Accepting help feels like 'giving in', and when they have been compelled to 'give in' systematically to a domineering parent, this is the last thing they feel prepared to do with anyone else. Other patients are genuinely terrified of the emotional upheaval they must face in radical psychoanalysis; they are perhaps constitutionally deficient in capacity to stand tension and anxiety. Sometimes a patient's human environment is so frustrating that it offers no better alternative than illness, and there is no real incentive to get well. One sensitive refined female patient whose husband was plainly a brutal, uncomprehending man, felt unable for important reasons to leave him, and illness was in fact her only protection if she stayed with him. It did at least keep a doctor in touch to afford some brake on his behaviour. Yet again, some patients enter on psychotherapy not because they themselves really want it but because some other person, doctor or relation, recommends it, and they come not really knowing what is involved. As they find out, they may or may not respond. An underlying resistance may not be surrendered.

(2) Statistical studies have no way of taking account of a fundamental factor which has concerned us all through this study of schizoid personalities. The schizoid patient who is so

fear-ridden that his basic strategy in life is to keep outside all real personal relationships in spite of his need of them, and not to allow any feeling to be evoked in him if he can help it, may be unable to form any sufficiently real relationship with the psychotherapist to allow psychotherapy to proceed. There is a real dilemma here; until psychotherapy has helped him to become less afraid of relationship, he cannot make much use of the treatment, yet while he cannot effect this relationship spontaneously because of his anxieties, the treatment cannot get under way. The problem is not insoluble or psychotherapy would never get going at all, but it constitutes probably the major difficulty in treatment. One can only keep quietly on, sympathetically directing attention to the fears of relationship, keeping them conscious so that the patient can repeatedly test them against the reality of his experience of the therapist. Every therapist is familiar with the patient who is just beginning to develop some rapport and then suddenly shoots off into detachment. This has to be analysed over and over again. Since not all patients experience this difficulty in the same degree, simple statistical comparisons are impossible.

(3) This brings us to the most serious omission in any statistical analysis of psychotherapeutic results. It fails to take account of the relationship between the patient and the therapist. If therapy were a purely objective scientific procedure or 'method' this would not matter. The patient's reaction to the doctor in purely organic disease is not so primarily important, though this ceases to be true as we enter the realm of psychosomatic disease. The therapeutic powers of the old family doctor rested to an incalculable extent on his personality and the relationship between the doctor and patient. In the sphere of psychological healing this becomes the all-important factor which no statistical analysis of results can either record or evaluate. Analysts as individuals do better with some types of patient than with others. It is not solely a matter of training and technique. Patient and therapist need to be 'matched' to secure the best results. Groddeck would refuse to treat a patient if he did not take to him. 'Choice of analyst' is highly important from the patient's point of view. Not anybody can be assigned to any therapist with equal chances of success, on the assumption that 'the psychotherapeutic process' will go on automatically. This may be an inconvenient complication in organizing clinics, but is nevertheless a fact. Such highly relevant factors are too subtle to be weighed in merely statistical scales. Eysenck's sweeping conclusion that 'the data fail to confirm

the hypothesis that psychotherapy alleviates or cures neurotic illness', is only a hasty unscientific generalization or prejudice based on inadequate methods of investigation. It may well be that some early distortions of personality become irreversible, that no psychotherapist could be found to expose himself to a frankly murderous psychopath. But we do not need to prove that psychotherapy must be one hundred per cent effective, or even partially effective, in *every* case, to show that it is a real valuable possibility.

A far stricter definition of psychotherapy is needed. Some refer to it as 'the talking cure' as if any kind of talking by any kind of psychiatrist or psychologist however untrained in psychotherapy, can be considered to be the practice of psychotherapy. I am inclined to say that psychotherapy is the only method of treatment doctors are permitted to practice without specific training. Others again speak of it as 'counselling' which could mean anything from experienced understanding to pep talk and authoritarian advice. Psychotherapy is a term that now becomes meaningless unless it stands for trained psychodynamic treatment of the personality in depth. Everything else is 'psychological first aid', however valuable and necessary that often is in practice. It is the dynamic personal factors which are the crux of the matter in psychotherapy, as becomes ever more clear when we probe to deeper levels of human disturbance, and these factors are altogether too subtle to be taken account of by statistical studies of the results of varying samples of psychotherapy. Such investigations do not envisage the necessity of studying the personalities and the developing relationship of both patient and therapist *in every case* before it would be possible to assess the nature of the results or the reasons for success or failure. Eysenck speaks of 'cure' or improvement 'without benefit of psychotherapy' but he makes no attempt to give meaning to that phrase by studying the life-situation and the personal relationships in the midst of which the patient did or did not recover. There is no such thing as improvement 'without benefit of psychotherapy' for life itself has its psychotherapeutic factors of which professional psychotherapy is a scientifically specialized development. The meshes of the statistical scientific fish-net (*vide* Eddington) are too large to catch these facts of interpersonal relationships, but we cannot therefore conclude that they are not facts.

In a letter to the Editor of the *Quarterly Bulletin of the British Psychological Society* (April 1952) Eysenck compared 'papers devoted to scientific (experimental and statistical) studies in abnormal psychology' with 'papers dealing with ideographic, psychoanalytic and other "dynamic" topics'. The first he called 'factual' and the second 'speculative', and he has consistently maintained that point of view in subsequent publications. The fallacy of refusing the status of 'fact' to what one's own favourite method is incapable of taking account of, should be obvious. But this dangerous narrow-mindedness of the exclusively 'scientifically' moulded mind is so widespread still, that I have reserved a fuller study of it for Chapter XIII, Psychotherapy is a practical procedure involving the art of sustaining an actual kind of personal relationship. It can be studied scientifically but not by methods which fail to take into account the all-important personal factors of motivation, understanding, and emotional relating. At this point the very concept of science must be broadened beyond the scope of the purely objective study of the 'facts' of the material universe. In psychotherapy two therapists can be treating two broadly similar types of patient, using the same kind of technique and interpretations, and yet what really goes on in the two treatments may be utterly different, leading in the one case to a blockage and in the other to a therapeutic success. We shall be led astray if we attribute therapeutic results solely to our technique of investigation, and/or to our theory. *The technique helps us to investigate the problems which the therapeutic relationship, when it is therapeutic, enables the patient to reveal. It is the relationship with the therapist that creates the situation in which the problems can be solved.* This 'object-relationship theory of therapy', which has always been implied in the various aspects of the 'transference' problem, was first laid down by Freud himself, when he wrote of his decision to drop hypnosis and the abreactive, cathartic technique as follows:

> It was true that the disappearance of the symptoms went hand-in-hand with the catharsis, but total success turned out to be entirely dependent upon the patient's relation to the physician. . . . If that relation was disturbed, all the symptoms reappeared, just as though they had never been cleared up. (1922, p. 237.)

XIII

OBJECT-RELATIONS THEORY AND PSYCHOTHERAPY

THE PSYCHOTHERAPEUTIC RELATIONSHIP

THE previous chapter emphasized that the extent to which the psychoanalytic technique can be 'worked' depends on the relationship between the therapist and patient, and that, in the words of Freud, 'total success turns out to be entirely dependent on the patient's relation to the physician'. We must then examine closely the dynamic personal factors which are the crux of the matter in psychotherapy.

The Personal Relationship of Patient and Therapist: Transference

It is best to approach the deeper discussion of the patient-therapist relationship from the starting-point of Freud's recognition of transference phenomena, for though transference does not cover the whole problem, it is an enormously important part of it. It is one of those problems that have been so thoroughly explored that there is perhaps not much new to be said about it, but we must seek to present it in such a way that it can be integrated with newer views of the therapeutic relationship. I have felt that some writers dealt with transference as if all relationships of every kind were nothing but transference, and that nothing new in the way of relationship could occur. If that were true there could be no progress in psychotherapy. *Fairbairn's 'object-relations' view of psychotherapy was certainly that it is a process in which transference relationships, both positive and negative, are worked through until they lead on and give way to a good realistic relationship of whatever kind is possible and appropriate between therapist and patient.* Some patients can arrive at a quite good result and end treatment and go away to attribute the result to something other than the therapist's help. They cannot owe him anything. This shows that the results may be good enough for practical purposes, but have not fully resolved the patient's difficulties in human relationships. While no treatment can reach perfection in results, a really good result should leave the patient able to feel happy in a genuine sense of gratitude and friendly feeling for the therapist, along with a quite realistic appreciation of him as a human being. I can perhaps explain what I mean best by referring to my own case. My analysis with Fairbairn eventuated in a normal friendship between us, expressed by correspondence, usually on psychoanalytical matters, and occasional visits whenever any business took me to Edinburgh. We had a lot in common in psychological and philosophical concerns. I know he respected my understanding of his work, and I respected his integrity, ability, and deeply humane qualities of character. From time to time he expressed views on other matters with which I disagreed, and had his health permitted more vigorous discussion in his later years, I have no doubt we would have discovered, and I think respected, some quite extensive differences of outlook, without our friendship suffering. This seems to me a 'realistic relationship of whatever kind is possible and appropriate between therapist and patient'.

Naturally, not all treatments end in that degree of friendship. Good results can be obtained with patients with whom one would not have much in common outside the therapeutic situation, provided the basic 'human therapeutic relationship' is genuine. In other cases it is simply a matter of lack of opportunity. Nevertheless true feelings of friendship will exist. Recently a patient who had ended her treatment two years earlier, rang to say: 'I thought you would be interested to know that my eldest son has been chosen to play in a Young England Rugby Trial match.' I was very interested, knowing what difficulties this family had encountered and surmounted, and we had a very interesting chat. A successful psychotherapeutic treatment should end by contributing something permanent and intrinsically good in human relationship to the patient's life, even in cases where patient and therapist never see each other again. No doubt all therapists rejoice in the occasional letter from a past patient indicating that they are going on well, and have not forgotten how they have been helped. We are, however, anticipating, and must go back to the beginning and look first at transference.

The factor of personal relationship between analyst and patient was quickly recognized by Freud and incorporated into the body of psychoanalytical teaching under this term of 'transference'. He saw how large a part the patient's emotional reactions to the analyst played in treatment, and one of his major discoveries, valid for all time, was that these included repetitions of what the patient had felt and was still unconsciously feeling towards parents and other important people in his childhood. Some patients largely repress what they are feeling towards their therapist for a long time, and want to maintain a consciously good relationship with him, on the moral level of winning and keeping his approval. Others begin with openly hostile and resistant attitudes bound up with resentments about having to seek help for this kind of illness. Therapists in general find that it is much better when the hostility comes out frankly at the start. In reality patients always feel both ways, and whichever reaction is conscious, the other is unconscious. This repression of part of their feelings is, needless to say, like all repression, itself unconscious and automatic. This is simply a repetition of the early situation as seen in the conformist, and the problem, child.

Sometimes the patient is unaware of feeling anything at all about the analyst, and becomes very resistant to any interpretation of his behaviour designed to help him to become conscious of this emotional reaction. The withdrawn patient hates feeling 'lured' into a personal relationship. One patient said, 'I'd rather hate you than love you', and another, 'Hate is much safer than love.' But if possible they prefer to feel nothing and so long as they can maintain that stance, nothing much happens. Freud saw that the patient 'transfers' on to the therapist repressed and forbidden infantile reactions to parents of both love and hate. He held that the present-day neurosis must be replaced by a transference neurosis, in which all this is felt for the therapist, if a 'cure' is to be achieved. As usual, Freud had taken the first step in the unravelling of a problem of extremely complex proportions. Not everything can be seen at the start. Freud seized on the importance of this personal relationship factor in treatment, but he looked at it more from the point of view of the patient's reactions to the analyst as a substitute parent, than from the point of view of what impact the analyst made on the patient *in reality*, as the kind of person he actually was. These two factors are subtly intermixed and analytical treatment has to unravel them, so that ultimately the patient can come to feel objectively without the distortions introduced by transference reactions.

After a time it came to be realized that analysts have countertransferences to their patients, which should likewise be analysed. They will be in proportion to the incompleteness of the analyst's own analysis. That must at least have gone far enough to enable him to recognize and work on his own countertransferences. When I once said to Fairbairn 'Countertransference must be harmful to a patient', he replied, 'You may do more harm to a patient if you are too afraid of countertransference.' The reason, clearly, is that if a therapist eliminates all personal feeling for a patient (which actually he can only do by repression or by being something of a schizoid intellectual) in the interests of pure scientific objectivity, the patient will be all too justified in feeling that he is dealing with someone who has no genuine interest in *him as a person*. Patients easily feel that anyway. They will say: 'You can't really be concerned about me. I'm only one of a crowd of patients to you. I'm only a name in a list of cases to you. I need something more personal, more human than analysis. I need to feel you care for me, that you are my friend.' There is naturally a great deal of transference in this. It conceals unsatisfied legitimate longings for parental affection, and these may be disguised in sexual fantasies of intimate relationships with the therapist. There is nothing here that is not always occurring whenever human beings make each other's acquaintance in everyday living, but the analyst has to separate out what comes from the past and what can genuinely and realistically belong to the present-day meeting of two real human beings, when one is concerned to help the other to find his human reality. This latter only becomes clear as the transference is got rid of (though there is no perfection in human life, and this process can never be absolutely complete).

Repressed sexual fantasies towards therapist and parents can become conscious if the patient feels safe enough with the therapist. Sometimes these can be quite simply pregenital and infantile, and may then be even more embarrassing to the patient, as in the following two cases. A married woman in her thirties with three children, feeling unequal to her responsibilities, suddenly felt she wanted to run over to me, climb on my lap and curl up and go to sleep, as she used to do with her father. The other, a headmaster in the forties, felt a strong wish to lay his head on my shoulder and have my arms round him, and recalled being held in his father's arms and laying his head on his father's shoulder. The experience was so real to him that he could smell the tobacco of his father's pipe. But are these to be analysed as just 'early erotic wishes to be outgrown'? Were they not precious memories of a time when the parent–child relationship had been good, a regression under present-day strain to an early security which had been lost? Their revival in the transference was a sign that the parents, from that time onwards, had failed to help the child to go on to a more maturing relationship. The headmaster's father had in fact become a cold aloof man as his son grew up, and they lost contact. He needed me to be someone with whom he could go back to that point of arrested development to free himself for further growth. This could not be done by a literal recreation of the original father–child physical relationship, but it could be done by an accepting and sympathetic mental understanding of his whole position.

The Analyst as Projection Screen and as Real Object

The early view of the analyst as simply a 'projection screen' for the patient's fantasies has today already been left behind in its stark simple form, but must still be taken into account. The patient has *personal* needs towards the therapist which are not exhausted by the transfer of infantile eroticism, since he needs his therapist to help him as a real person. When transference analysis succeeds, the patient's realistic emotional needs towards the analyst emerge, and they are none the less realistic for emerging at first in immature forms, belonging to that level of his unconscious childhood life which the analysis has reached and opened up. Psychotherapy depends ultimately on their satisfaction. The patient's infantile ego can only grow in a genuine object-relationship. If the therapist persists in being, in reality, a merely objective scientific intelligence with no personal feeling for the patient, he will repeat on the patient the original emotional trauma suffered at the hands of parents, which laid the foundations of the illness. Those who are one of a sibling group will say, 'I'm only one of a lot of patients to you,' while others, and not only those who had no siblings, will say, 'You ought not to have any other patients but me.' When such reactions have been analysed in terms of the patient's inner world, I often add a purely realistic comment, 'If you think you can only feel sure of being loved in the absence of rivals, then you will never feel secure. When you think you have got someone all to yourself, you will really be living in dread of a rival turning up, and if that happens you will feel convinced that the person you are needing will desert you for the other party. You can only feel secure by discovering that you can be valued and cared about as a person in your own right while others are present.' These patients are seeking a parent–child relationship because what they had in that respect was not adequate to laying the foundations of a strong personality.

They may want it, unconsciously or consciously, in erotic forms, both infantile and oedipal, but if they got that and nothing else, it would keep them in an emotionally immature state. No doubt that is what happens in some marriages where the partners emotionally stagnate.

Yet, if the patient were in reality only 'one of a crowd of patients' to the therapist, how could he be helped to develop a sense of his own reality and worth as a person in his own right. What the patient *needs* as a basis for recovery can be described in three stages. First, he needs a parent-figure as a protector against gross anxiety. He may recognize or resist this, but either consciously or unconsciously he feels like a drowning man without a lifebelt. The psychotherapist is at first a rescuer to him, from the hopeless losing battle with problems he does not understand. If a good rapport is established, he is likely to say: 'I feel you are the first person who has ever understood me, or taken the trouble to try to.' As one patient put it: 'An analyst is better than prayers.' But such frank dependence is equivalent to one aspect of the parent–child relationship. It is the child's need for a purely supportive, protective, reassuring love as a basis for existence. The second stage involves the analysis of all the ways in which this is interfered with by the legacy of old inadequate relationships with the actual parents and in the family group. This is the transference proper.

Whatever we mean by 'cure' or 'maturing' or becoming able to end treatment, depends on getting beyond that to the third stage. Not that these stages are distinct, separate, and marked off from each other. They are subtly intermixed all through analysis. They are more aspects, often co-existent aspects, than stages, except that the third aspect should become more and more predominant towards the end of treatment. Here, the patient begins, at first dimly, to feel that what he really needs is the basically non-erotic love of a stable parent in and through which the child grows up to possess an individuality of his own, a maturing strength of selfhood through which he becomes separate without feeling 'cut off', and the original relationship to parents develops into adult friendship. The three aspects or stages may be summarized as rapport, transference, regrowing or maturing. It is usually over the last issue that the most critical question arises, as the patient begins to work clear of transference problems. Has this patient now got enough of a basic ego to be able to go forward to maturity, or are we uncovering an inner emptiness, corresponding to the fact that the original mothering was not good enough to get an adequate ego-development started? This is the most difficult therapeutic problem, and in this case the psychotherapist must be the kind of person who can relate to the patient in a way that enables him to find his own reality and experience a true 'ego-birth and growth' in a way he could not do with his parents. This is something far deeper than questions about the satisfactions or conflicts concerning instinctive needs. They are subordinate aspects of a total self, mature or immature. Here we are concerned with the *possession* of a meaningful self as distinct from a mere psychic existence which has lost its primary unity. In pursuit of this, the psychotherapist must be able to support the patient with unfailing care and understanding while leaving him free to become his own unique self in an 'on the level' relationship. This he cannot do for the patient unless he has genuine feeling for him, and is not afraid of a truly personal relationship which the patient needs to find with him.

Nevertheless, however adequate the therapist is, it still takes the patient a very long time to accept him as a liberating person, and longer still to experience him as someone with whom the patient can find a true self of his own. There is no evading transference analysis, as all his fears, distrusts, and resentments felt towards parents rise up again, and all his dependent needs countered by fears of involvements with all their restrictive and rejective attitudes are projected on to the analyst. Here the classical psychoanalytic technique is indispensable. The therapist's psychoanalytic insight must guide his intuitive understanding based on experience, to enable him to help the patient to bring his problems to consciousness and face them, both on the oedipal and the schizoid levels. For as frankly oedipal transference phenomena are analysed, the result may well be, not that the patient is straightway released to grow up to a mature adult love, but is rather deprived of a main defence against the ultimate problem, the profound sense of inner emptiness which shows that no very real ego got a start at all. Now the therapist must be the kind of person with whom the patient can find some sense of reality in his own experience of him, and who can at times see something in the patient that he cannot see for himself, because he has never before adequately experienced it. The therapist must now sense, not the patient's repressed conflicts but his unevoked potentialities for personal relationship and creative activity, and enable him to begin to feel 'real'.

All this cannot go on unless the therapist is a 'real' person himself, giving the patient the possibility of a 'real' relationship in the treatment situation, over and above the transference relations. These can come out more openly on the basis of a steadily deepening realistic confidence of the patient in the therapist without which the patient will let out very little, however correct the technique. He must have *some firm standing ground in present-day reality* if he is to revive, recognize, and work through problems originating in the past, all the more so if these come from the very earliest infancy level. Even then there is no automatic guarantee that the patient can or will use the analyst's help to grow out of his unreality. After all, he is still an individual who can harbour and pursue purposes of his own other than those which led him to treatment. The therapist can do no more than make the possibility of a therapeutic relationship available, and perhaps by being real himself give the patient some reason for feeling that this is the worthwhile goal. He has no power, nor should he have, to force the patient to get well against his will. All through treatment, the patient is constantly discovering that he has what feel to him more important purposes to serve than getting over his illness or solving his personality problems. He may still feel determined to revenge himself on his family, or by transference on the therapist. In that case he will use the analysis to get worse, and will accuse the therapist of destroying everything he had to cling to: beliefs, duties, ideals, hopes, illusions or what-not. Thus he can finally say to the analyst: 'Look at the mess you have made of my life, look what you have done to me.' He may be unprepared to accept the transference elements in this because he wants, not the memory of a dead parent, but a live present person to hit back at. A negative therapeutic reaction enables him to expose the bad parent or even the whole bad family, and the bad analyst all in one.

Hate has its satisfactions in destructiveness even at the ultimate price of self-destruction, for those who feel they cannot ever become constructive. At least it sometimes enables a patient to feel better after he has given up his therapist, though this may not prove to be very firmly based. The path from schizoid and depressive states to reality and maturity of selfhood is like an area sown with land mines. There is hidden explosive material at every step. Traversing this path can never be easy either for therapist or patient. The final result a patient achieves may well be the result he secretly sets out to achieve, in the sense of having unconsciously aimed at all along, and it may be exceedingly difficult to save him from himself by successfully analysing this. If his aim is constructive, he will respond to his therapist in the end, but he must have a 'real' person to respond to. No one will be saved from profound personality disturbance by talking to an impersonal projection screen. In fact, the difficulties the patient encounters within himself are so formidable that he is not likely to be able to overcome them, unless through all the ups and downs of treatment he comes to realize that the therapist is so to be trusted and relied on that it becomes possible and safe to be quite open with him.

Internal Difficulties Operating Against Psychoanalytic Therapy

In Chapter XII, section (3), we glanced briefly at the fact that the deeper psychoanalytic therapy goes the more dependent the patient becomes on an external supporting environment for the time being, so that external factors can easily frustrate our endeavour. We must now look more deeply at the internal obstacles, constituting 'resistance'.

(1) The hysteric defence of substituting a body problem for a personality problem is usually easier for the therapist to detect than for the patient to relinquish. The patient mentioned on pages 318–21, the middle-aged deeply regressed woman, succumbed to a serious infection during a particularly important period of treatment and had to stay in bed and have massive doses of antibiotics. At that time she grew quite calm in her state of mind, only to find that her extremely disturbed condition began to return as she got over her physical illness. There is still in some medical quarters the tendency to treat the hysteric as merely 'attention seeking' and as a wilful nuisance. Certainly hysterics can be extremely irritating, but they are 'attention seeking' in the sense that a drowning man is 'attention seeking'. When it comes to conversion symptoms, physical pain can cover and defend against far worse mental pain which is going to emerge if the physical pain is lost. Unless the patient feels the therapist can really help ultimately with the mental pain, he cannot give up easily the physical pain which is far easier to bear, and more accepted by other people. Professor Bonamy Dobree, in a broadcast talk on Kipling, spoke of the poet's interest in mental breakdown and his knowledge of inner mental hells which have 'to be experienced to be appreciated'. He referred to the charge that Kipling was 'callous about physical pain' but replied that he knew 'it was as nothing

compared with spiritual agony. This he [Kipling] states unequivocally in the *Hymn to Physical Pain.*'

'Dread Mother of Forgetfulness
 Who, when Thy reign begins,
Wipest away the Soul's distress,
 And memory of her sins. . . .

Wherefore we praise Thee in the deep
 And on our beds we pray
For Thy return, that Thou may'st keep
 The pains of Hell at bay.'

This is the situation the psychotherapist often faces in the patient, and the phrase 'memory of her sins' reminds us of the part Freud saw that guilt, often of a deep unconscious kind, played in this self-punishing hysteric defence against something much harder to bear. This situation often arises towards the end of treatment, as in the same case of the deeply regressed woman, especially when the patient has produced a marked improvement which in fact hides a deep and as yet untapped problem. Through fear of approaching this hidden danger, the patient may first produce a 'flight into health' and then find himself in the dilemma of ending treatment with an unsolved problem on his hands which might well be triggered off by the separation anxiety of losing his therapist, or else going on and facing the analysis of what he is afraid of. In this situation he may well try to do neither, but fall back on a relapse into hysteric conversion symptoms to sidetrack the treatment from the main issue. Since the ultimate issue is always the patient's need for a personal relationship which will enable him to grow a real self, the last and deepest problems are always some version of one or other of the two final fears, the fear of having no relationship at all and losing one's ego in a vacuum; and the fear of entering into a relationship and feeling that one's weak ego will be overwhelmed. In this dilemma, hysteric conversion symptoms have the special value of diverting attention for the time being away from the problems of human relationship, on to some bodily symptom.

An elderly woman known to me developed eczema all over her body following the death of her husband. For more than a year medical treatments secured no more than improvements, followed always by relapse. She was then cured by a kindly elderly woman herbalist who personally massaged a wonderful ointment into her for an hour twice a week. She was 'cured' so effectively that the eczema never returned. This was due, no doubt, not to the wonderful ointment, but to the 'mothering', albeit of an infantile order of soothing attention to her body by someone in whom she rapidly acquired great faith and trust, in her loneliness and distress. Nevertheless, an analyst would be thankful to produce so permanent a result so quickly. Her bereavement had laid bare a deep-seated infantile insecurity in her which had been hidden by her dependence on her husband. As she certainly had no faith that medical treatment would provide an answer to that problem, she could not give up her eczema by which she cried out through her body for 'mothering attention'. The patient cannot give up the illness unless something better can be put in its place. What kind of 'something better' can the psychotherapist give? Certainly not a cold, impersonal scientific technique of investigation, or as in the case of behaviour therapy, of 'symptom elimination'. Certainly for the elderly woman one would prescribe the motherly herbalist rather than psychoanalysis; whereas for anyone young enough to want radical changes in personality, the psychotherapist must provide a kind of personal relationship that enables the basic psyche to grow out of ego-weakness into ego-strength.

(2) A further and extremely stubborn obstacle to psychotherapy, though in fact it is the same obstacle viewed in a deeper way, is what Fairbairn called 'the libidinal cathexis of the bad object' (1952a, p. 72). In 'Analysis Terminable and Interminable', Freud (1937, p. 332) describes psychotherapy as supporting the patient's ego against the quantitative strength of his innate instincts. He says:

> The quantitative factor of instinctual strength in the past opposed the efforts of the patient's ego to defend itself, and now that analysis has been called in to help, that same factor sets a limit to the efficiency of this new attempt. If the instincts are excessively strong the ego fails in its task. . . . The power of analysis is not infinite . . . it is limited. . . . We shall achieve our therapeutic purpose only when we can give a greater measure of analytical help to the patient's ego.

We have moved far today from this simple instinct theory and the biological and therapeutic pessimism it would force on us. We would today be evading our responsibilities as therapists if we told a patient that we could not help him because his instincts are too strong. The actual impulses and emotions with which we deal in patients are not in themselves fixed innate biological factors. They are reactions of an ego, though a weakened ego, to persons and situations encountered in the process of living, and in psychotherapy to the situation created by the therapist. They are appropriate to the way the ego perceives the object, and express the ego's relation to the object. In analysis, this is a mixture of transference factors and of what the analyst is in reality. Change the object, either in reality or in the patient's perception, and the impulses and emotions change. Supposing the analyst to be adequate as a real person to the therapeutic situation, then what he must analyse is his patient's ties to his internal bad objects in his inner world. It is the patient's internal bad object world, not his instincts, that are the cause of trouble. The turbulent impulses and emotions of the neurotic are not fixed inborn instincts, they are personal reactions of a weak infantile ego at the mercy of and yet unable to give up the frightening and frustrating figures in the deep unconscious. They would die down if these internal persecutors were got rid of.

But that is just the problem. The infantile ego cannot just give them up, for in that internal world it feels like being left with nobody at all. Psychoanalysis is not reinforcement of instinct-control. As Fairbairn says aptly, it is more like exorcism, the casting out of devils from the inner unconscious world, devils who can often be seen clearly enough in the patient's dreams. Yet it is not strictly speaking like exorcism, but is a subtler process. Where lies the difficulty? One might think that patients would be only too glad to let go their devils, but nothing is further from the truth. Thus a spinster in her late fifties was still dreaming of her father thrashing her and said, 'If that were happening, at least I wouldn't be an aging woman living alone.' A man of thirty, who in real life could not bring himself to leave a home in which he was violently unhappy, dreamed

> . . . of being on a muck-heap frantically raking to find something valuable. A cyclist went by and called to him to come away and join him, but he stayed on his muck-heap.

'Mucky' was one of his epithets for his mother. He couldn't give up his muck-heap that he was still trying to get something valuable out of. Yet another patient said, 'My husband and father are devils but I never give up my devils.' Patients cling tenaciously to their *external* bad objects because they represent *internal* bad objects whom they feel incapable of leaving. To part with internalized bad parent figures sets up two kinds of fear-reaction; it plays on repressed death-wishes against the bad parent in childhood, arouses the unconscious feeling of having now destroyed this bad parent in the inner world, leading to guilt and self-punishment; it also creates the unconscious feeling of being now for the first time in life left utterly alone, bringing with it the fear of ego-loss, of depersonalization, of dying, unless and until they are replaced by someone better. Bad parents are better than none. Both a depressed and a schizoid reaction can follow the loss of internal bad objects as the following case shows with great clarity.

A spinster in her middle fifties, who had had an unusually bad mother, was physically very vigorous but emotionally very vulnerable and given to violent outbursts of rage. She was constantly dreaming of the hate-relationship between her and her mother, and would project her into any woman who invited such projection, often with catastrophic results in her daily work. After a very long analysis, she passed slowly into a phase in which she began to lose her physical energy, and then halfway through one session she suddenly fell silent for a long time, and then said quietly: 'It's safe now. She's gone. This is the turning point. I'm going to get better now.' She left feeling definitely better, but turned up for the next session quite markedly depressed. She was surprised when I said that I had expected this. She had at last let go and got rid of the bad mother inside and now felt all alone because she had lost her. She felt cut off from her friends. I suggested that I myself, and the very good friend she lived with, and an excellent friend she had made about a year previously, were not yet installed adequately in her deeper feelings, in her unconscious where she had been tied to mother for so long. As we talked about this her depression lifted, and for two or three weeks she emerged into an entirely new personality. She lost her hate and temper outbursts, and her loud raucous voice, and her 'queer' intolerances of ordinary things, and became as her friend said 'a normal, more healthy-minded, and also a gentler and more lovable person, much easier to live with'; though she also felt physically weak, like a small child facing the big world. Then she seemed to come to a standstill, and was unwell, miserable, and discouraged. Though she did not lose the gains made, she seemed unable to make any further progress. Then one night her friend was out later than she had expected, and she began to fear that she was dead. In telling me about this, she realized that she had begun to have ideas that those she loved would die, and she developed an unreasonable dislike for her friend's aged mother, about whom she said, rather oddly, 'I shall have to go on fearing her till I die.' I put it to her that she was showing clear signs of feeling guilty as if she had murdered her mother in fantasy to get rid of her, that no doubt death-wishes against her mother from childhood had been activated, and that now she was feeling that she must be punished by being unable to get any benefit from her new freedom; she must remain ill and weak, her own loved friends must be taken from her, and that in her unrealistic reaction to her friend's mother she had in fact put herself back in her own bad mother's power, this time decreeing that she herself must be the one to die first. Only with the bringing out of this depressive guilt, as well as the first schizoid reaction, was she set free to enjoy a steady recovery of physical health as well as mental stability.

The major source of resistance to psychotherapy is the extreme tenacity of our libidinal attachments to parents whatever they are like. This state of affairs is perpetuated by repression in the unconscious inner world, where they remain as subtly all-pervasive bad figures generating a restrictive, oppressive, persecutory, inhibiting family environment in which the child cannot find his real self, yet from which he has no means of escape. There are only three things he can do, fight desperately, suffer passively, or fly, i.e. withdraw into himself, break off all object-relationships, and experience the 'unthinkable anxiety' of utter isolation in which he will lose his ego. Then, when he gets over negative transference, i.e. the fear of meeting his bad parents again in his therapist, his fear of losing them remains so great that he will regard the analyst as someone who is going to rob him of his parents, even though it is also true that he looks to the analyst to rescue him from them. He will then face an awful period in which, if he loses his internal bad objects while not yet feeling sure enough that his therapist will adequately replace them, he will feel that he is falling between two stools, or as one patient vividly expressed it, 'plunging into a mental abyss of black emptiness'. It takes the patient a very long time really to feel that the therapist can be and is a better parent with respect to giving him a relationship in which he can become his own true self. Long after he is consciously and intellectually persuaded that this is so, the child deep within cannot feel it. In this uncertainty, even accepting the therapist's help may still feel like a fundamental disloyalty to parents and arouse guilt, or else he will go back to negative transference and feel he encounters his smothering internal bad objects all over again in his therapist.

Thus one patient who had made great progress began to come up against the smothering of his spontaneity in the early family set-up. He dreamed that he was watching a mother and small son, and the mother was saying, 'Everything you know belongs to me, I gave it to you.' He was so furious that he pushed the mother over, and the dream ended suddenly. Here was the smothering mother and in his next session it was clear that he felt he had come up against her in me. He had dreamed:

> I was driving an old car I had years ago and came to a place where I wanted to get up to some bridge over to where I was going. I could go up in a lift, but there was a side road up a steep hill that I could get up by and I decided to go up that way.

I commented, 'It looks as if you decided not to accept help but to get up by your own way, to do it yourself.' He said 'I'm claustrophobic in lifts. There is a very closed-in one where I work and often I can't go in it.' I told him that I thought he was feeling claustrophobic in relation to me, that he was feeling I was like the mother in the previous dream, putting her knowledge into the son and then possessing him, and this was how he had felt about his own mother who had brought him up on a very marked social conformity pattern. He said 'Yes, she was always on at me to behave nicely, to be generous, or you never knew what people would be thinking about you. I often feel when people are talking to me that they are pushing things into me. When you were saying something just now I was trying not to listen, and then had to repeat your words over again to myself before I could bring myself to attend to their meaning.'

But even when this kind of problem is got over, the fear of having no roots in a family past can dictate the defence and justification of parents against all outsiders. As one patient said, 'I sometimes feel this business is against my parents, that they haven't brought me up properly which I deny (though in fact she had recently been saying exactly that), and secondly that it's pulling me away from them, which I don't want.' She had for the moment forgotten that it was in defiance of her parents' opposition that she had sought treatment of her own accord to achieve greater independence of them. Fairbairn wrote:

> The resistance can only really be overcome when the transference situation has developed to a point at which the analyst has become such a good object to the patient that the latter is prepared to risk the release of bad objects from the unconscious. (1943, p. 332.)

And again:

> It is only through the appeal of a good object that the libido can be induced to surrender its bad objects. . . . It may well be that a conviction of the analyst's 'love' (in the sense of Agape not Eros) on the

part of the patient is no unimportant factor in promoting a successful therapeutic result. At any rate, such a result would appear to be compromised unless the analyst proves himself an unfailingly good object (in reality) to his patients. (*Ibid.*, p. 336.)

J. C. Flugel wrote in 1945:

Though the negative phase of the transference is unavoidable and also essential for a 'deep analysis', it is the positive phase which is the ultimate stepping-stone to therapeutic success, for it is only by means of the projection of the more positive aspects of the super-ego on to the analyst that the patient can face the task of becoming aware of his own repressed impulses and inner conflicts. He needs the help, understanding and security afforded by the analyst before he can venture to relax the control exercised by his own super-ego. This is well brought out by Fairbairn in 'The Repression and Return of Bad Objects'. (Flugel, 1945.)

This, however, falls short of Fairbairn's position while it supports it. The patient's superego may not contain the 'more positive aspects' Flugel refers to, and the patient may need to find them for the first time in the analyst. It is curiously artificial to say that the patient can only be helped by the analyst if he projects some part of himself on to the analyst. Object-relations theory calls for the analyst to be a good-object in reality, in himself, just as the mother has to be a good-object in reality to the baby. Flugel's simpler statement is more realistic, that the patient 'needs the help, understanding and security afforded by the analyst' who will have to provide that particular kind of parental love that the patient's parents failed to provide at first, i.e. in Fairbairn's words, to care for him 'for his own sake and as a person in his own right'. The therapist must be more than just a projection of good elements in the patient's own superego. He must, in his own reality as a person, bring something *new* that the patient has not experienced before.

(3) The view of psychotherapy here maintained is that the patient cannot be weaned from, and become independent of, internalized bad parental objects, and so cannot become healthy and mature, unless he can consolidate a good relationship to his therapist as a real good-object; since otherwise he would feel left without any object-relationships, the ultimate terror that the withdrawn schizoid person is always dreading. Here emerges the third fundamental obstacle to psychotherapy in practice, namely the severe difficulties patients have about entering into any relationships at all with real human beings

in their outer world, even though such relationships are what they most deeply need. Thus they both seek and resist a real good-object relationship with the therapist. In the depressive position their trouble is the ambivalence of their reactions. They cannot love him without finding that hate and aggression surge up as well. But the deeper and more difficult problem is their reaction in the schizoid position. Here their need of love-objects is so starved and intensified, and their basic attitude to people is so greedy, hungry, and devouring, so that they feel destructive, that they are afraid to need and want and love anyone. This is further complicated by the fact that all this arose because they had reasons to fear their unsatisfactory human environment at the outset, and also, as Melanie Klein has shown, by 'projective identification', they feel that their objects have exactly the same destructive attitudes to them. Hence, for a complex of reasons, they retreat into a cold, aloof, unfeeling detachment. Real relationships are felt as too dangerous to be risked, however much this feeling is masked by a superficially co-operative attitude. Genuine rapport is gained only to be lost again, and they become 'cut off' through fears of being destroyed or absorbed, if they risk too genuine and spontaneous a response of trust.

This difficulty is shown by a female patient who alternated between response and withdrawal. In the earlier stages of her analysis she was fully conscious of feeling guilty of disloyalty to the family and especially mother if she let the therapist help her to any independence of them. Long after she had ceased to feel conscious of this, traces of it would reappear in her dreams whenever negative phases alternated with positive ones in her sessions. After a period of much more definite responsive trust in me during which she had begun to feel that her treatment really was supportive while she was at work and between sessions, she suddenly cut herself off again. She commented, 'I lost you almost as soon as I left last time, and have felt to be struggling alone all the week.' She then reported a dream:

I was with my family and I just wandered out, left them and went off alone, and I got lost. I knew they were angry with me for leaving them, but I could not find my way back to them.

Here is the real schizoid predicament. Even when she had relinquished her original unsatisfactory objects in their mentally internalized form (in real life she still had responsibilities to an aged mother, and a sister), she still could not commit herself steadily to a growth-promoting relationship with the therapist, and wandered in an empty no-man's-land in her dream world.

The more radical difficulty of not being able to accept a therapeutic relationship at all, in spite of a conscious need of it, is shown by a male patient who was exceptionally rigid in his detachment. As he came into one session he observed: 'I feel an uprising of tension but the thought occurs, "I'm old but you're older still." One becomes less physically attractive as one grows older, and less likely to be loved. As I grow older there are fewer people by whom I can be loved in a paternal way. One's props get less. I feel angry but if I were aggressive you'd resent it, it would become a personal matter between us. It's only because between analyst and patient there's no personal relationship between us that I can let things out at all.' I explained that he wanted but was afraid to see me as a real human being who could have a genuine concern for him. He would only see me as an impersonal professional object called 'an analyst' lest the therapeutic relationship should become emotionally alive and real, when he would have to face all his deeply disturbing difficulties about personal relationships. This was an effective defence which halted real progress in treatment, so that he made only superficial improvement. I reminded him that he once said that he could only talk at all if he lay on the couch where he could not see me, and could talk to the wall. In that situation, nothing of any emotional significance would be likely to emerge and he would be safe from anxiety attacks. He replied, 'I find any personal relationship with anyone impossible. I don't really know what it means. I want a personal relationship but am too proud to ask for it, too independent.'

The Therapist as a Real Good Object

If the patient cannot part with his bad psychic objects in his inner world because of guilt and the risk of ego-loss, in what sense must the therapist become a real good object whose 'love' helps him out of this dilemma towards finding his own true self? Gitelson, in a paper on 'The Emotional Position of the Analyst in the Psycho-Analytical Situation' (1952) wrote that:

> Recent developments in the psychotherapeutic functions of psychoanalysis . . . have pointed to the importance of the analyst as a real object.

His paper, however, was confined to dealing largely with countertransference, the fact that 'the analyst may bring into the analytical situation interfering emotional factors'. To off-set these he held that the qualified analyst brings to the patient

> . . . intellectually sublimated curiosity. . . . Object-attitudes including empathic compassion which is distinguishable from sympathetic identification, and helpfulness which is distinguishable from omnipotence or masochism . . . Finally, an emotionally 'open' and flexible [personality] in a spontaneous state of continuing self-analysis. (1952, pp. 3–4.)

This, however, does not carry us far enough. Gitelson rightly says that

> The analyst as a mere screen does not exist in life. He cannot deny his personality nor its operation in the analytical situation as a significant factor. (p. 7.)

'Helpfulness distinguishable from omnipotence and masochism' is definitely required but 'sympathy distinguishable from sympathetic identification' raises far subtler questions, and here Gitelson appears to retreat from the full implications of the analyst as a real person in the therapeutic relationship. Home, in 'The Concept of Mind' (1966, pp. 43–4), writes:

> In discovering that the symptom had meaning, and basing his treatment on this hypothesis, Freud took the psychoanalytic study of neurosis out of the world of science into the world of the humanities, because a meaning is not the product of causes but the creation of a subject.

By science he means the impersonal study of dead facts, explaining them in terms of causes, and by the humanities he means the personal study of living subjects in terms of meanings and reasons. He holds, and I believe rightly, that the only way we can know 'living subjects' is by identification.

> This gives us an *understanding* of the object (i.e. the live object or living subject) and particularly of how it is feeling and therefore of how it will behave.

Provided perception is accurate and 'refined by the withdrawal of projections', 'cognition through identification gives us accurate information and information which can be obtained in no other way'. It is 'this mode of cognition which is used by the analyst in analysis'. In that case, by denying that the analyst's 'empathic compassion' is the same thing as 'sympathetic identification', Gitelson denies the only means by which an analyst can 'know' his patient at all in a truly personal sense. Gitelson's argument should logically have concluded with the affirmation of the psychotherapeutic relationship as a fully personal relationship, but he drew back from that when he wrote:

> This is far from saying, however, that his [the analyst's] personality is the chief instrument of the therapy which we call psychoanalysis. ... It is of primary importance for the analyst to conduct himself so that the analytical process proceeds on the basis of what the patient brings to it. (1952, p. 7.)

It is, of course, easy to see that what he seeks safeguards against is the danger of the therapist becoming bogged down in a neurotic emotional involvement with the patient. This can only be avoided by the maturity of the therapist, not by maintaining a theory of the therapeutic relationship which denies its fully personal nature. The personalities of parents are the chief instruments in bringing up the child. What the patient brings to analysis is, at bottom, behind all his defences, a need for a relationship with someone who *in loco parentis* will enable him to grow, a need which must be met by what the therapist brings to the analysis.

Gitelson almost but not quite reaches to this point when he concludes that the

> ... sustaining psychotherapeutic factor in the conduct of an analysis, the real ego-support that the patient needs, resides in the actuality of the analyst's own reality-testing attitudes. (p. 8.)

And

> One can reveal as much of oneself as is needed to foster and support the patient's discovery of the reality of the actual inter-personal situation. (p. 7.)

But he still does not give a definite statement of the nature of the specific element in 'the reality of the actual inter-personal situation' which meets the patient's need. One does not usually have to 'reveal much of oneself' for example, as a private individual; the analyst's personal interests, activities, friendships, family life, history, are not as such essential to the patient. *What does concern the patient, and it is the only thing about the therapist that does really concern him, however much other things may crop up accidentally or incidentally, is whether the therapist as a real human being has a genuine capacity to value, care about, understand, see, and treat the patient as a person in his own right.* Obviously any given therapist will find that he has more natural affinity with some patients than with others, but if he can truly and humanly care and understand, then he can be therapeutic. This *disinterested personal 'love' (agape not eros) is the true parental love*, which does not regard the child as a nuisance, or as a piece of clay to be moulded, or as there to fit in merely with the parents' convenience or to fulfil their ambitions for themselves, or what not. It is *the capacity to respect and to be concerned about the other person's reality in himself and apart from oneself, and to find true satisfaction in helping the other person to find and be his own properly fulfilled nature*. It is a matter of being a sufficiently *real* person to the patient to give him a chance of becoming a *real* person himself, and not an assemblage of defences, or a role, or a conforming mask, or a mass of unresolved tension. If the patient cannot meet with personal reality in the therapist, he cannot give up his struggle to keep going a spurious reality by means of internal bad-object relations and external forced effort.

The urgency and reality of the need felt by one patient in this matter was vividly expressed in a dream:

I'm looking for Christ on the seashore. He rose up as if out of the sea and I admired his tall magnificent figure. Then I went with Him to a cave and became conscious of ghosts there and fled in stark terror. But He stayed and I mustered up courage and went back in with Him. Then the cave was a house and as He and I went upstairs, He said, 'You proved to have greater courage than I had,' and I felt I detected some weakness in Him.

The patient associated the admired tall figure of Christ with his athletic father and then said: 'I also associate Him somehow with you. I've got the idea that somehow you may inveigle me into courage to face ghosts and then let me down. Mother was a menacing figure. Father was weak, mute before her onslaughts. He once said it wasn't a good thing to have one parent constantly dominating the other in front of a child, but he never showed any anger at all.'

Here is the patient oscillating between the old fear that father lets him down if he tries to stand up to his violent-tempered mother, and the new wavering hope that the therapist will not let him down in facing the 'ghost' of the angry mother within. In a later dream he encountered the ghost of mother coming out of a room, while a figure representing myself stood by him. He was gradually internalizing me as a reliable parent-figure in his inner world around whom he could reorganize his security as a person. It was such phenomena that suggested to

Fairbairn the parallel between the analyst and the exorcist casting out the ghosts or devils who haunt the patient in his inner world; though the analyst does not in fact 'cast out' these internal bad objects, but gives the patient a sound personal relationship in which his ego can grow secure enough not to need them any longer.

The psychotherapist naturally does not seek to play the role of a Christ or Saviour, or indeed to play any role, least of all the 'role' of a professional therapist. But without him, the patient cannot either cope alone with his disturbed state of mind or give up his internal bad objects and be left with no one. His only hope lies in his internal bad objects being replaced by the internalization of a good therapist, i.e. the therapist who gives him a relationship which at one and the same time supports him and leaves him free to develop his own nature. By then, the therapist will have become a non-possessive good parent-substitute with whom the patient will have outgrown the dependencies and fears of childhood, and achieved the kind of mature satisfactory relationship which is not lost or damaged by his ending treatment to live his own proper life, akin to the grown-up child leaving home.

The centrality of the personal relationship factor in psychotherapy has been steadily gaining recognition now for some time. Speaking of psychotherapy at the Sixth International Congress of Psychotherapy, Laing (1965) said, 'We live on the hope that authentic meeting between human beings can occur.' Only when the therapist finds the person behind the patient's defences, and perhaps the patient finds the person behind the therapist's defences, does true psychotherapy happen. This relationship factor has sometimes been crudely expressed as 'loving the patient better' but we need to be careful what is meant by that. Certainly if we simply hate patients, are on the defensive against them, and want to make them get better quickly to get rid of them, we shall do no real good, and may even encourage them to maintain a hate-relation as a defence against a real solution. On the other hand, uninformed sympathy for the patient, however genuine, would only draw him into interminable dependence which gets nowhere. Moreover, since it is a main part of the patient's problem that he is afraid of a relationship to anyone, it may still be a problem to the therapist that he could be afraid of a relation with the patient. All that Gitelson said about 'continuing self-analysis' is highly relevant. This personal relationship factor is what makes psychotherapy the most difficult of all therapeutic procedures, and makes many favour more impersonal objective 'scientific' methods. It is possible to carry out diagnostic labelling and prescription for the control and suppression of symptoms on the basis of a knowledge of medicine. Psychotherapy can only be carried out on the basis of a knowledge of oneself and of the patient as a person.

Psychotherapy can only be carried on by those who are prepared to be exposed to all the subtle reactions that go on between two human beings who meet on an emotional rather than on an intellectual plane; and who are prepared to accept awareness of these reactions as essential to treatment. The emotional plane is that of the patient's suffering, his loneliness, his insecurity as an ego and his anxiety about life. The psychotherapist is not a *deus ex machina*, an authority diagnosing and prescribing from some position outside the patient's personal world. The psychotherapist must be primarily a human being who has faced and sufficiently understood himself to be worthy to be admitted into the patient's private pain and sorrow. He will understand the patient's inner life, not because he has a theory (though if it is a good one, it helps) but because he can feel with and for the patient; and he knows, not just theoretically but in his own experience, what the patient is passing through. Sharing in the same humanity with the patient, he is able to identify with him in order to know him. Only that enables the patient no longer to feel alone. Neither love nor insight alone cures. Fairbairn pointed out that deep insight only develops inside a good therapeutic relationship. That is because the patient cannot stand it if he feels alone. What is therapeutic, when it is achieved, is 'the moment of real meeting' of two persons as a new transforming experience for one of them, which is, as Laing said (1965), 'Not what happened before [i.e. transference] but what has never happened before [i.e. a new experience of relationship]'. Thus a patient who had had a paranoid-schizophrenic breakdown, suddenly said to me, after two-and-a-half years of analysis: 'I feel safe with you now. I haven't done hitherto.'

But this meeting of two people is far from easy. Transference analysis is the slow and painful experience of clearing the ground of left-overs from past experience, both in transference and countertransference, so that therapist and patient can at last meet 'mentally face to face' and know that they know each other as two human beings. This is without doubt the most important kind of relationship of which human beings are capable and it is not to be confused with erotic 'falling in love'. People can and do fall passionately in love sexually and later discover that there is no genuine relationship between them as persons. In that case, the sexual passion generally fades out into disillusionment. Neither does this deep and truly personal relationship necessarily involve sexual love. It can exist between people of the same or of different sexes; sexual relationship cannot be truly satisfactory without it, but it can and does exist where a sexual relationship is not appropriate or desired and does not exist. It is the fundamental purely 'human personal' relationship. It cannot exist fully between parent and child because the child is as yet immature and not capable of 'equal' relationship. But I would say that its ideal realization is to be found where the child grown adult and the parent remaining young enough in spirit, achieve a deep mutual affectionate understanding of each other. This I regard also as ideally the goal of psychotherapy, which is basically a relationship of the parent–child type at the start. We shall see in the next section how profound an interpretation of this Winnicott gives.

Most psychotherapeutic sessions are experiences of transient flashes of reality amidst a lot of unreality. Real psychotherapy does much for the maturing of the therapist as well as the patient. The patient's need dominates the situation, but the therapist cannot meet it and remain a stagnant human being. He cannot pretend or play roles. If he does, the patient cannot find him and nothing happens. Psychotherapy is a progress out of fantasy into reality, a process of transcending the transference. The extent to which Freud regarded sex as the basic factor in object relations has, I am convinced, introduced misunderstandings and unnecessary complications into psychotherapy, and also exerts a dangerously misleading influence in current popular culture. Unless the term 'sex' is used with such a wide connotation that it loses all specific meaning, it cannot be said to be the essence of meaningful personal relationship. It must be seen as biologically innate need that can only find real fulfilment as part of a truly personal relationship.

I must add that I feel suspicious of 'active stratagem' technique. It looks too like experimenting on the patient, who is then treated as an object not a person. The surest guide is simply to keep asking oneself: 'What is this patient's genuine need at this moment, whether he realizes it or not? In what way can I help him to understand it and how can I meet it to help him forward?' Once patients know that they can reveal their need and be sure of a response of understanding and acceptance, of a kind they failed to find in childhood, then through many ups and downs the genuine meeting of two human beings as persons begins to occur. That is the only thing that is ever really therapeutic, enabling the patient to feel real in himself.

It seems that in the last hundred years, the schizoid element in human experience has become more obtrusive and recognizable, perhaps because this is a century of cultural transition in which human beings tend to become spiritually displaced persons. The rise of the psychological novel from the work of Henry James is a symptom of this. Recently a radio reviewer of a book on 'Loneliness' said: 'Loneliness has always been with us but it is only recently that we have become aware of it.' Our age has become more generally aware of the isolation of the individual within himself, and the tenuous nature of his relationships with other isolated individuals. Existential thinking is another symptom of this, with its stress on life as rooted in anxiety, and on the personal encounter as the important fact in human life. Without that we are only sub-human, and apart from it our anxiety cannot be dealt with. What existentialism is in thought, psychotherapy seeks to cope with in practice; they are parallel manifestations of our need to overcome our alienation from ourselves, from one another, and from our whole outer world, so that humans no longer hide away inside themselves, insecure and only half alive in an internal fantasy world that binds them to the past, but become able to emerge into real personal relationships and live a whole life.

It follows from this that a psychotherapist is not a therapeutic good object merely by virtue of being a good technician or analyst. The technique of psychoanalysis *as such* does not cure. It is not endowed with any mystic healing power. It is simply a method of psychodynamic science for investigating the unconscious, an instrument of research. It plays an essential part in psychotherapy but is not itself the therapeutic factor. It is a way of helping unconscious mental experience to become conscious, by providing a patient with an opportunity to talk to someone with complete freedom to say anything and everything without encountering disapproval or retaliation; so that he can bring the unconscious operations of his personality to conscious awareness, and discover himself to himself in self-expression, aided by the therapist's experience and insight. But what is to be done with what becomes conscious? Abreaction, 'talking out', 'acting out' gives some temporary relief to pent up feeling, and temporary security is experienced in an *ad hoc* good relationship, but this does not of itself lead to permanent changes. Thus the analytical technique itself is more an instrument of research and of temporary relief than of radical therapy.

The analyst's interpretations will be given to the patient as suggestions for him to respond to, not as dogmatic or authoritative pronouncements for him to accept blindly. It is the sustaining of this analytical process in the continuing relationship of therapist and patient on an emotional, personal level, that enables the patient to deal with what is made conscious. It is only the kind of self-knowledge that is arrived at as living insight, which is felt, experienced, in the medium of a good personal relationship, that has therapeutic value. Insight, integration, individuation, and personal relationship are but distinguishable aspects of one and the same thing, which is called 'mental health' from the psychiatric point of view and 'peace' or 'salvation' from the religious point of view. Whatever terminology different interests use, the therapeutic change can only come about in, and as a direct result of, a good relationship. This is true in real life. The best chance of progressively modifying the bad objects internalized in infancy and repressed, lies in the child experiencing increasingly good relationship to parents in the post-infancy period, before the whole mental make-up consolidates. That is the cue for psychotherapy

As a radical process, it has a better chance in childhood than in adulthood, but either way the maturing of personality takes place by natural growth and development on the basis of the right kind of parental love. In infancy, parental love has an erotic element and is expressed in physical handling in bodily contact and care. This physical relationship is profoundly necessary to the child, especially in the earliest preverbal period. As the child grows up, this erotic factor will have done its work of giving an elementary sense of security, and is reduced to minor proportions, so that ultimately the child can transfer its erotic response and become capable of marriage. Parental love changes into a non-erotic, non-possessive, non-dominating affection which supports the child in his development of separate and independent personality. He is backed up and encouraged to think, feel, and act for himself, to explore, experiment, take risks, use and develop his own powers and is helped to 'be himself'. This kind of parental love, appropriate to latency and adolescence, leads finally to the replacing of the early erotic attachments which are dependent in the child and supporting in the parent, by mature relationships of adult mutual respect, equality and affection in friendship. Then the grown-up child is free without anxiety or guilt to enter an erotic relationship with an extra-familial partner, and to form other important personal relationships in which there is a genuine meeting of kindred spirits without the erotic element, and further to exercise an active and spontaneous personality free from inhibiting fears. This kind of parental love, which the Greeks called *agape* as distinct from *eros*, is the kind of love the psychotherapist must give his patient because he did not get it from his parents in an adequate way.

Winnicott's View of the Basic Psychotherapeutic Relationship

In Chapter IX I sought to relate the work of Winnicott to the developing phases of psychoanalytic theory. His work on the mother–infant relationship from the very beginning, as the indispensable medium in which the psyche of the infant begins to realize its latent possibilities of ego-growth and the achievement of true selfhood, is an advance beyond the work of both Melanie Klein and Fairbairn. It is an advance beyond Klein in that it is fully object-relational. It rescues us from the implicit solipsism and subjectivism of the Kleinian view of the infant's inner world of fantasy as held to be built up primarily by the interplay of entirely innate, subjective forces, the inherited life and death instincts. I have devoted Chapter XV to the closer consideration of the Kleinian metapsychology. It is sufficient here to say that the objective world in her system is quite secondary. It functions as a projection screen on to which the infant's fantasy can be extruded thence to be introjected again so that the object world can never be experienced in its own right. In Winnicott's work, on the other hand, the all-important primary object, the breast and the breast mother, is a real object directly influencing the infant, and entirely responsible for the infant's security. Only the mother who is capable of 'primary maternal preoccupation' and 'identification' with her baby, is capable of giving it a sound start in ego-development. The mother is not just a projection screen but a real person, so real that the baby's ego will be weak or strong in proportion as the mother's ego-support of the baby is weak or strong. This view plants human personality squarely in the soil of personal 'object-relationships' as the starting-point of all human living, prior to the development of Klein's internal fantasy-world.

Winnicott's work also goes beyond that of Fairbairn, in that Fairbairn's analysis had to take the existence of the ego for granted, in order to trace out the splits it suffers in its early experience of good and bad object-relations. But Winnicott takes us deeper than that to the most elementary experiences in which the first dim and uncertain beginnings of ego-growth occur as a result of the infant's existing in the peculiarly intimate primary mother–infant relationship. If we take all this into account, it is clear that Winnicott's work must have a very large implication for psychotherapy, where the last and deepest problem to be dealt with is always the profound basic ego-weakness of the patient. Winnicott, indeed, has seen this and left us in no doubt about his views on the matter. It is only when theoretical analysis and therapeutic practice are carried back to the very beginning that the implications of the personal nature of the therapeutic relationship emerge in their simplest form and become fully clear. Short-term treatment of the milder neuroses can be carried out successfully with no more than a very straightforward cooperative relationship developing. The earlier the causes of trouble in the patient, the more fundamental his ego-weakness, and the more we move beyond psychoneurosis into the deeper schizoid, borderline and psychotic problems, the more profoundly important does the quality of the therapeutic personal relationship become, until ultimately it faces the question of the possibility of a *replacement* for the failure of original mothering.

It is at this deep level that Winnicott's most important contribution is made. He distinguished between 'psychoanalysis' for 'oedipal cases', and 'management' for 'pre-oedipal cases' where initial good enough mothering cannot be taken for granted. When Winnicott first made this distinction I could not feel happy about its being made in such a clear-cut form, at least in the one respect that analysis cannot be excluded from the treatment of pre-oedipal cases. Even with respect to the earliest experiences, the patient needs interpretation of the experience, if he is to gain insight and integrate the experience in the context of the therapist–patient relationship. But Winnacott does not make the distinction rigidly. In his paper on 'The Aims of Psychoanalytical Treatment' (1962), he says:

As we come to gain confidence in the standard technique through our use of it in suitable cases, we like to feel that we can tackle the borderline case without deviating, and I see no reason why the attempt should not be made.

But he makes an important qualification which high-lights the personal relationship aspect of treatment. He speaks of analysts who

> . . . deal with more primitive mental mechanisms; by interpreting part-object retaliations, projections and introjections, hypochondriacal and paranoid anxieties, attacks on linkages, thinking disturbances, etc., etc., they extend the field of operation and the range of the cases they can tackle. This is research analysis, and the danger is only that *the patient's needs in terms of infantile dependence may be lost in the course of the analyst's performance.* (*Op. cit.*, p. 169; my italics.)

With this mention of the 'patient's needs in terms of infantile dependence' *the ultimate psychotherapeutic problem* is raised, that of *how to start off the growth of an ego which has not yet properly begun to be.* Winnicott bases his view of psychotherapy at this depth, on his view of the nature of the infant–mother relation. I shall summarize this briefly before quoting his own words. The mother is being there for the baby in such a way that he can feel in touch with, share in, partake in her psychic state of secure being, even before he can distinguish between her and himself. Here, at the very beginning, the foundations of ego-security are laid in a situation experienced by the mother as her state of 'primary maternal pre-occupation' with the baby, and by the baby as 'primary identification' with the mother. The baby must be able to feed actively at the 'male' breast (cf. Chapter IX) that is doing something for him or else he must protest at deprivation; but he can sleep without anxiety at the 'female' breast that is simply 'being there' for him, and there is the beginning of the secure sense of 'in-being-ness', of ego-identity, that as he grows the baby can take for granted and does not have to worry over and work hard to maintain. Only the mother can provide this experience at first, while the task of the father lies in 'doing' all that is necessary to protect and support the mother–infant pair in their very special and formative relationship. In psychotherapy at the deepest level, this situation has to be recovered, with the analyst meeting the patient's need for both mother and father. Thus one female patient in her late fifties, herself a grandmother, but who had been severely schizoid all her life, said, after a very long analysis, 'I don't want analysis now. I just want to be here and to be quiet, and know that you are there and let it sink in.' Shortly after that she brought a dream:

> I opened a steel drawer and inside was a very tiny naked baby staring with wide open eyes as if looking at nothing.

Suddenly she saw a filing cabinet in the corner of my room and said, 'The steel drawer was like that.' Thus her unconscious fantasy and experience was of coming to birth out of me, and of bringing her tiny infant self to me, simply to get a start in feeling secure and real. 'Analysing' is a male function, an intellectual activity of interpretation, but based on the female function of intuitive knowing experienced, as Home reminds us, through identification. Ultimately 'being there for the patient' in a stable and not a neurotic state, is the female, maternal, and properly therapeutic function, which enables the patient to feel real and find his own proper self.

Winnicott writes:

> There is something about the mother of a baby, something which makes her particularly suited to the protection of her infant in this stage of vulnerability, and which makes her able to contribute positively to the baby's positive needs. The mother is able to fulfil this role if she feels secure . . . (Her) capacity does not rest on knowledge but comes from a feeling attitude which she acquires as pregnancy advances, and which she gradually loses as the infant grows up out of her. (1965a, p. 3.)

> We notice in the expectant mother an increasing identification with the infant. . . . The predominant feature may be a willingness as well as an ability on the part of the mother to drain interest from her own self on to the baby. I have referred to this aspect of a mother's attitude as 'primary maternal preoccupation'. In my view this is the thing that gives the mother her special ability to do the right thing. She knows what the baby could be feeling like. No one else knows. Doctors and nurses may know a lot about psychology, and of course they know all about body health and disease. But they do not know what a baby feels like from minute to minute because they are outside this area of experience. (1965a, p. 15.)

In this passage Winnicott draws a clear and absolute distinction between intuitive knowing or knowing by identification, by emotional or personal rapport, and intellectual or scientific knowing. The qualified doctor or nurse approaches the baby as a scientist, from outside observation, and with intellectual knowledge, a kind of knowing that was described in Chapter IX as 'male element knowing'. This is valuable when it is a matter of dealing with the baby's bodily health, but it is useless for 'knowing from minute to minute what the baby could be feeling like'. This 'mother's knowing' comes through an emotional 'feeling at one with' the baby, and as Home maintains this 'knowledge by identification' cannot be come by in any other way. Home regards it as the way in which the psycho-analytical therapist 'knows' his patient, and it was described in Chapter IX as the typically 'female element knowing'. Many years ago in an obituary notice on David Eder, Edward Glover stated that the true psychoanalytical therapist had to have a strong maternal element in his make-up, which Eder had.

Accordingly Winnicott does not hesitate to take this mother–infant relationship as the model for and basis of psychotherapy. Just as the good mother is free to use whatever valuable intellectual knowledge she may possess about the baby's bodily and mental processes, as an adjunct to her more intimate personal knowing of the baby, so the psycho-analytical therapist is free to use whatever intellectual knowledge his study of psycho-dynamic science has given him, but it must be as an adjunct to, not as a substitute for, his personal knowing of the patient which is emotionally perceptive, working by identification and intuition. Winnicott writes:

In our *therapeutic* work over and over again we become involved with a patient; we pass through a phase in which we are vulnerable (as the mother is) because of our involvement; we are identified with the child who is temporarily dependent on us to an alarming degree; we watch the shedding of the child's false self or false selves; we see the beginning of a true self, a true self with an ego that is strong because like the mother with her infant we have been able to give ego support. If all goes well we may find that a child has emerged, a child whose ego can organize its own defences. . . . A 'new' being is born, because of what we do, a real human being capable of having an independent life. My thesis is that what we do in therapy is to attempt to imitate the natural process that characterizes the behaviour of any mother of her own infant. If I am right, it is the mother–infant couple that can teach us the basic principles on which we may base our therapeutic work.

This view of the basis of psychotherapy has bearings not only on the treatment of the most ill, regressed cases where the ego may be so weak as to be barely there at all. It has bearings on the treatment of lesser degrees of illness, for if psychotherapy is a belated replacement for original inadequate parenthood, the way the parent–child relationship changes steadily as the child grows will illuminate the entire therapeutic process. The therapist has no choice but to be deeply involved with the patient who is at last compelled to give up the futile struggle to keep going on the adult level and relapses willy nilly into the depths of infantile terror, isolation, and the evaporation of his ego into a feeling of nothingness. He must keep as constant and close contact with him as is humanly possible, especially if the patient's human environment is not as supportive as one might wish. He must see the patient through into the ultimate acceptance of a therapeutic regression from which he must be mentally nursed to a rebirth and regrowth of a real self. The therapist is utterly indispensable to him at that stage.

This is well illustrated by the case of the deeply regressed woman mentioned in this and the previous chapter. Some concluding remarks on that case may now be made. As mentioned on page 321, after many vicissitudes, she began to relive the basic trauma of her primary maternal deprivation and her sense of utter isolation at heart. Her husband had a very adequate grasp of all that was implied in this and we were able to work together to meet her need for a belated maternal security. But there were times when it was inevitable that she was left alone in the house, and I was kept informed of these. They were dangerous occasions for her, and I did all I could to contact her on the telephone at these times. Her state of mind was invariably like that of a person alone and lost on an empty plain without landmarks. On various occasions she said such things as: 'Till the phone went and I realized it was you, I've been sitting here paralysed, unable to move, with a queer feeling as if there's nobody else in the whole world except me.' Again, 'I can't stop sobbing and I feel I can't hear a single sound anywhere except the sound of my own crying.' Yet again, 'I'm so glad you've rung. I knew you would but I felt so afraid something would stop you, and this terrible loneliness would never be broken. I've had hard work not to panic. Yet when I heard the phone go I felt terrified that it would be someone I didn't know.' Her husband said to me, 'I've given up being a husband just now and I'm simply being a mother.' Gradually the neglected and isolated infant in her deep unconscious must have been reached and contacted, reassured, and given a new start with a feeling of security, for she began slowly to drop her resistance to regressing, accepted her husband's help without resistance, felt more and more overcome with exhaustion and the need to sleep, and found that she could go to bed and drop fast asleep at any time without any sleeping pills, waking after three or four hours to feel much better. At this stage the ordeal of a journey from her home town to Leeds became too much for her. There was one morning in the week when her husband could be free to bring her, and I arranged to see her then. She took no medication at all on those mornings, and would arrive feeling pretty ill, but always by the end of the session felt much better and found that a 'person' was better than a 'pill', a highly important discovery for her, for she had been under heavy medication for years. At her other usual session times, I would ring her and after a short talk she would then go to bed feeling that I was mentally with her, and go to sleep (like the baby in the pram who can't see mother but has no doubt that she is there).

Gradually this must have set going an inner sense of a new security, and this was expressed in a dream. She consciously dreaded mental hospital as a place where she would not be understood. Now she dreamed that she was back in the hospital where the superintendent had been so very understanding. But this time it was a real home; doctors, nurses, and patients (i.e. father, mother, and siblings) were all friendly, and there was a graded scheme of stages through which everyone was getting better, and she herself moved from the first (entry) stage on to the next one. For years her dreams had been frankly persecutory or anxiety-saturated. Now here was the sign of the development of a foundation of inner security on which a new life could slowly be grown. At such times the therapist's involvement with the patient is maximal.

Winnicott, however, says of the mother's 'primary maternal preoccupation' with her baby that it is an

> . . . extraordinary condition which is almost like an illness, though it is very much a sign of health. . . . It is part of the normal process that the mother recovers her self-interest, and does so at the rate at which the infant can allow her to do so. . . . The normal mother's recovery from her preoccupation with her infant provides a kind of weaning . . . we can find parallels to all these things if we look at our therapeutic work. (1965, pp. 15–16.)

Thus, the degree of involvement of the psychotherapist with the patient, as with the mother and her child, will change. At first it must be adequate to the patient's need for a stable parent, according to the nature and degree of the illness for which he seeks treatment. If that is successful, it will slowly adapt to the patient's growing need for greater independence and will turn into support for and respect for his development of an individuality of his own. Throughout, psychotherapy is a personal relationship on the basis of which the therapist can make use of his intellectual knowledge gained from psychodynamic research. Our patients are always to some extent isolates hiding behind defences, in a persisting state of anxiety and insecurity. Their 'cure' can only come about in a therapeutic relationship in which the core of their potential self can be found and communicated with in such a way that it shall not feel threatened, but protected and supported for self-discovery and self-realization. On this basis of a new-found self-possession and ego-strength, he can lose his schizoid fear of human contact and involvement, and find relationships enriching and fulfilling.

Part V

OBJECT-RELATIONS THEORY AND EGO-THEORY

XIV

THE CONCEPT OF PSYCHODYNAMIC SCIENCE

I mentioned in Chapter XII that social workers, who nowadays are usually trained in psychodynamic concepts, often find themselves criticized by psychologist colleagues who claim that their work is scientific and objective, while the social workers operate with subjective guess-work. It seems important therefore to give full consideration to this problem of the scientific nature and standing of psychoanalytic, or as I prefer to call it in this context, psychodynamic investigation, and its relationship to traditional 'natural' science. I dealt with this problem at length from a somewhat different point of view in Chapter VII of *Personality Structure and Human Interaction*, under the title of 'Process Theory and Personal Theory'. Some of the argument of that chapter must be here repeated in this different context, the starting-point of which I shall take from the paper by Home, 'The Concept of Mind' (1966). Home takes up the challenge of the scientist by asserting boldly that psychoanalysis is not science, but an example of the equally necessary but quite different 'humanistic' thinking.[1] He defined 'mind' as the 'meaning of behaviour'. We do not speak of the 'behaviour' of *dead (inanimate) objects* but only of their activity, because it has no 'meaning'. 'Meaning' only exists for *live objects* and constitutes their subjective experience of their own activities and those of other live objects, in terms of their aims and purposes. He regarded science (i.e. 'natural' science) as the study of the activities of dead objects. The objective methods of such science are incapable of dealing with the 'meanings' of the subjective experience of live objects, but this is what psychoanalysis sets out to study. Home is absolutely right in saying that the traditional methods of objective 'natural' science are incapable of dealing directly with subjective experience and its meanings. His conclusion that psychoanalytic thinking is therefore not 'scientific' but 'humanistic' thinking is, however, open to further discussion, but this must start from acceptance of the plain fact that psychoanalytic thinking is based on our subjective knowledge

[1] The rest of this chapter is a revision of a paper of the same title in the *Int. J. Psycho-Anal.*, **48** (1967), pp. 32–43.

of ourselves, and our capacity to identify with (and therefore to know inwardly) other people.

The problem that emerges is that of *the status and nature of specifically psychodynamic studies*. Home worked out thoroughly one of the two possible answers, namely that *psycho*dynamics is not a scientific but a humanist study. The other possible answer is to question and enlarge the traditional meaning of science. Like the philosopher Home, he pursues an important line of argument to its logical bitter end and so high-lights all the problems involved. This present discussion of the concept of psychodynamic science falls into three parts: (i) a discussion of the terms 'physical' and 'mental' science, or the 'natural' sciences and psychology; (ii) the question 'Have we really got a "mental" science?'; and (iii) is 'Object-Relations Theory' a true psychodynamic science?

'Physical' and 'Mental' Science

We must guard against befogging the theoretical issue by confusing it with a false antithesis between a scientific and a human approach. A surgeon can be capable of sympathy with his patient however objectively and impersonally scientific is his medical theory and practice. He does not have to know his patient subjectively as a person in order to perform an accurate surgical operation, though such knowledge may well enable him to help the patient to get over the aftermath. It is true that a person who has a flair for personal relationships is likely to feel drawn to psychotherapy, while others are more at home in laboratory research. This does not bear on our problem, unless someone who cannot do or is antagonistic to psychotherapy, prefers a definition of science that rules out a personal relationships approach. Thus Eysenck says that psychologists explain but do not understand human beings. Psychiatrists not infrequently comment that the majority of their colleagues are cynical about psychotherapy as unscientific.

What concerns us is *the theoretical definition of science*. If psychodynamic studies are scientific, then there are two kinds or levels of science. There are fundamental differences between the methods and type of conceptualization employed in the physical sciences and in the *psycho*dynamic studies which are the theoretical basis of psychotherapy. I shall speak of 'physical' or 'material' science, not 'natural' science, for psychic phenomena are as 'natural' as physical ones. The term is a relic of a time when scientists thought that psychic phenomena did not deserve to be given the status of reality, as in Huxley's view of mind as an epiphenomenon, related to the body like a whistle to a train, playing no part in its running. The train would 'go' just as well without the whistle. Only physical phenomena were thought worthy of, or regarded as open to, scientific study. Many regard that stage as now over. In a more subtle sense I do not believe it is over. Home put the question 'Is psychodynamics a science after all?' If it is, we have not yet really decided in what sense.

The classic view of science still holds in many minds. The extraordinary material and technological success of physical science compared with the very modest achievements of mental science support that. There is an emotional addiction to a view of science which is, in fact, being intellectually superseded. This seems to be strong in psychiatry, and to be subtly present in much psychoanalytical writing, because in this field we operate closest to our own psychological weaknesses; more so than in the physical sciences, which therefore provide us with an escape. Even Freud, when anxious, longed to get back to the physiological laboratory, where he felt on safer ground. Astronomy, physics, and chemistry provide the primary model, with mathematics, for what is entitled to be called science. They were the earliest sciences to arise, because they dealt with the kind of phenomena which were easiest to treat scientifically, and they did not encounter so much subjective emotional resistance in the investigator, as when we study human nature. Physiology, neurology, and biochemistry were built up on the same scientific model. They dealt with 'material' phenomena, and the pseudo-philosophy of scientific materialism classed mental phenomena with religion and fiction, as not only outside science but not really important, mere imagination.

I shall, however, refer here to 'material' and 'mental' science. This does not imply any definition of 'matter' as opposed to 'mind' as entities. I mean simply that material science studies those aspects of reality which we investigate by sensory perception and experimental methods based on it. One can study behaviour this way and create the behavioural sciences, but it is not psychology. It is not about the psyche, but only about the outward expression of some aspects of it as behaviour, a most incomplete guide to the full nature of a 'person' and the whole range of his subjective experience. To quote Dicks:

> While behaviour is subject to scientific observation of an objective kind, experience is not—it needs to be shared and understood.

Physical scientists do not usually regard psychic phenomena as having the same trustworthiness for investigation as material facts. In whatever way we acquire our knowledge of our thoughts, feelings, and volitions, we do not get to know them by seeing, hearing, touching, tasting or smelling them, but by *a wholly subjective inner process which we call recognition or realization of our immediate experience*. They are what Gellner calls 'warm mental entities, introspectible mental experiences'. Of course, sensory perception also is a subjective experience, but it has an objective reference which is entirely absent from our experiencing of ourselves. Sensations are the basis of our knowledge of the external world. Our thoughts, feelings, and volitions (and our fantasy images, dreams) give us knowledge of ourselves, of our internal reality as subjects of experience.

We know that our thoughts and feelings do not have any necessary objective counterpart in the outer world, but they have a reality of their own, *psychic reality*. This direct immediate knowledge of psychic reality is quite different from our sensory experience of the outer world. *Our knowledge of our thoughts and feelings is our experience of ourselves as 'subjects'*. We can mentally know ourselves in this manner without any intermediary method or technique of investigation. There is nothing else *at all* that we can know in this direct manner. We may, and often do for our own motives, deceive ourselves and distort our immediate experience of ourselves. In that case we directly experience the distortion. It is still true that when we realize that we are thinking this thought or feeling this emotion at this moment, that knowledge has an absoluteness about it which cannot be questioned. Free association rests on this. We never consciously know all that we experience, but whatever else a free-associating patient may or may not know about himself, he knows with a certainty that he *is* thinking and feeling whatever associations occur to him as he talks, and that that is knowledge about himself and is dependable. Psychoanalysis bases itself on this fact, that even if only slowly, *psychic reality reveals itself to us directly, that the analytic method in the therapeutic relationship frees more of it to do so, and that it has to be taken seriously as a fact*. It is only of our *own* experience that this is true, and our capacity to know and understand other people's experience is based on our knowledge of our own. Our understanding of others is, at the intellectual level, an inference based on our knowledge of ourselves, it will not be more thorough than our knowledge of ourselves, and must be tested and justified by further experience. That is why a personal analysis is indispensable for a psychoanalyst. But *we can know others 'on the inside' by identification, as Home stressed, because we know ourselves directly 'on the inside'; and this is a phenomenon entirely absent from the physical sciences*. In this sense 'material' objects have no subjective or 'inside' aspects, and can be wholly satisfactorily studied objectively.

We may illustrate this difference by comparing the explosion of a firework and an explosion of anger. We do not know how the firework is feeling by its explosion, because in fact it does not feel and its explosion has no meaning. It is a purely physical fact fully comprehended by objective study of cause and effect. When a person explodes in anger, he creates a tense situation which we sense even before the explosion. It is true we perceive by our senses his tight face, harsh voice, clipped speech, angry words and gestures, just as we see the sparks and hear the bang of the firework. But we know the state of mind behind what we see and hear of the person, because we have felt like that and in response to him we can feel like that now. We know his psychic reality by identification based on our own experience. Possibly because of this difference, many scientifically trained people seem reluctant to recognize psychic reality as a fact. Mayer-Gross, Slater, and Roth say that

> instability in the attitude of psychiatrists is made all the easier by the subjectivity and *lack of precision of psychological data* [their italics]. Mental events can only be described in words that are themselves often open to varied interpretation. Many terms in psychiatry are taken from everyday language, and are not clearly defined. . . . Much psychiatric literature of today owes its existence to the possibility of playing with words and concepts; and the scientific worker in psychiatry must constantly bear in mind the risks of vagueness and verbosity.

But they are really complaining of something deeper than carelessness in the precise use of terms. They speak of 'the instability of attitude' of students of psychiatric phenomena. 'Attitude' to what? They mean instability of attitude to what is and is not science. They write: 'This book is based on the conviction of the authors that the foundations of psychiatry have to be laid *on the ground of the natural sciences*. [Their italics.] An attempt is made to apply the methods and resources of a scientific approach to the problems of clinical psychiatry.' They simply equate Science and 'natural' science, and reject any description of psychic reality that does not conform to natural science terminology, as 'not clearly defined', 'vague and verbose', and 'playing with words'. But it is not for a scientist to try to dictate to facts, but to try to understand what is there; and psychic reality is indisputably there, and moreover its study cannot be carried on 'on the ground of the natural sciences'. We need a 'mental' or 'psychodynamic' science, distinguished from 'physical' science. This conclusion is supported by Taylor in *The Explanation of Behaviour* (1964). He writes:

> To assume from the superiority of Galileo's principles in the sciences of inanimate nature, that they *must* provide the model for the sciences of animate behaviour, is to make a speculative leap, not to enunciate a necessary conclusion. (p. 25.)

He concludes that 'behaviourist psychology' shows the invalidity of one form of mechanistic explanation of behaviour, which can only be explained teleologically by reference to purpose; that Behaviourism is 'non-psychological psychology'.

Have we got a 'Mental' Science?

It has been reserved for psychoanalysis to show respect for, and create a definite concept of, 'psychic reality', denoting as stubborn a fact as can be found anywhere, in the sense that a fact is what is effective. Yet it is not a fact that can be studied by the same kind of methods used in physical science. We gain nothing by avoiding the use of the term 'mental' even though we do not work with a dualistic philosophy or regard 'mind' as a separate 'thing'. *'Matter' and 'Mind' are the age-old and honoured terms by means of which mankind has expressed its direct recognition of the fact that there are two quite different aspects of our existence.* This is a fact that it seems many people have not yet come to terms with on the level of scientific thinking. They still hanker after the false simplification of 'scientific materialism'. When 'natural science' arose, scientists with the usual human desire to get everything under their control and in their power, simply denied 'mind' and dogmatically asserted that it was nothing but 'brain'. One is reminded of the surgeons who dissected Beethoven's brain after his death to find his musical genius. The simple-'mindedness' of this assumption and the way it flies in the face of actual experience is not at all obvious to those trained exclusively in 'natural science'. If we refuse to turn a blind eye to this ineradicable dualism in our experience of existence, then there are only two possible solutions: (i) to limit science to the study of material phenomena and agree with Home that mental phenomena call for a different kind of thinking; (ii) to expand the meaning of science to include the study of 'mental' phenomena in its own and not in physical terms. Can we really do that? It is not satisfactorily done by the development of the Social and Behavioural sciences. They either look to psychoanalysis to supply a psychodynamic science for them to work with, or fall back on neurological conditioning, dealing only with behaviour, and studying it objectively.

Nor do I think that biology provides the type of thinking required to do justice to psychic phenomena. I agree with Home that biology comes under the heading of physical science, though I feel there is an ambiguity in his thought here. He distinguished between studying live and dead objects. The word 'object' thus covers both personal and impersonal objects, a difference which matters to psychodynamics. The objects we are interested in are capable of being, and in fact are, *subjects of experience.* The objects of natural science are either not capable of being subjects, or when they are it does not matter to science, which ignores that aspect of their reality. When live objects are studied as subjects we have psychodynamic science. When live subjects are studied as objects only, as is done by biology, neurology, behaviouristic psychology and sociology, then we have the classic model of 'natural' science. There is an element of objectivity in every kind of study and relationship, but I would prefer to sum the matter up thus: *psychodynamics studies its objects basically as 'subjects', while traditional science studies whatever it does study as 'objects only'. It is this exclusively objective approach of classical science that fails to do justice to 'persons' as 'subjects of experience'. Psychodynamic studies pose a genuinely new problem for science, which cannot be handled by the classic scientific methods of investigation and conceptualization.* Either science in the traditional sense will have its absolute limits revealed, or else it will undergo radical revision as to the meaning of science. It is not that classic terms like observation and experiment, inductive and deductive reasoning are questioned. There are both observation and experiment, and we may reason both inductively and deductively, in personal relationships. It is rather a question of a new kind of 'object' to be studied, i.e. subjective experience, and a new primary source of information, not sensory perception of the outer world, but immediate experience, direct knowing, of an inner personal world. *In psychodynamics*, the data are obtained by subjective observation of ourselves and identification with others. It is not the nature of scientific thinking that is at stake. That remains 'objective assessment'. It is the nature of the data themselves and of the method of obtaining them, that is different. A revision of the meaning of science is, however, already under way with the philosophers of science, for it is evident that there is not the old-fashioned solidity and simplicity about matter, space, and time that used to be assumed.

There may, however, be more to be said for Home's view that science can only deal with dead objects, or with live objects as if they were dead. There is an arresting passage in Bion's *Learning From Experience*, Chapter 6. He calls sense-impressions β-elements, which a hypothetical α-function works up into α-elements, thoughts that can be used. He says of some patients that 'evading the experience of contact with live objects by destroying α-function' makes them unable to have a relationship with anything except as *an automaton*, i.e. a dead object. He then observes:

> The scientist whose investigations include the stuff of life finds himself in a situation that has a parallel in such patients. The breakdown in the patient's equipment for thinking leads to dominance by a mental life in which his universe is populated by inanimate objects. The inability of even the most advanced human beings to make use of their thoughts, because the capacity to think is rudimentary in all of us, means that the field for investigation, all investigation being ultimately scientific, is limited, by human inadequacy, to those phenomena that have the characteristics of the inanimate. We assume that the psychotic limitation is due to illness; but that that of the scientist is not. . . . It appears that our rudimentary equipment for 'thinking' thoughts is adequate when the problems are associated with the inanimate, but not when the object for investigation is the phenomenon of life itself. Confronted with the complexities of the human mind the analyst must be circumspect in following even accepted scientific method; its weakness may be closer to the weakness of psychotic thinking than superficial scrutiny would admit.

Bion sees that traditional science would depersonalize man, or as Wordsworth said 'We murder to dissect'. The psychotic and the scientific limitations appear to meet in the schizoid intellectual (and there are many among scientists) who can only think about inanimate objects, not about living subjects, for he is too basically anxious to risk identification and the sharing of experience. For him, as for power politicians, persons are things. Home can claim Bion as a powerful ally. Science is limited to the investigation of inanimate objects, which seems to imply that some other kind of thinking must deal with live subjects.

Nevertheless, I would prefer to accept Bion's shrewd observavation about the nature of most of what is scientific or 'natural' science thinking, and go on to explore whether the concept of science cannot still be expanded to take in the study of 'live subjects'. Bion provides a reason for science remaining for so long bound up with the ideology of scientific materialism, which Macmurray described as neither scientific nor philosophical, but only a popular prejudice based on the prestige of science. But it may have deeper causes; partly emotional, in that people feel safer on what they *think* is the more solid ground of material facts, but more, according to Bion, because of the sheer limitations of our capacity to think beyond the range of inanimate facts. The 'reach' of our capacity to 'experience', is far greater than the 'grasp' of our intellectual capacity to explain. This involves an intellectual humility we do not always show as 'thinkers'. It is of a piece with this that many physical scientists regard the human sciences such as anthropology, sociology, and psychology, as either an inferior sort of science, or even not properly science at all. A reviewer of Teilhard de Chardin depreciated his claim to be regarded as a scientist because his anthropological pursuits did not have this exactness required by the sciences with their mathematical tools. For this very reason psychology, in its fight for scientific status, has always had to encounter attempts to reduce it to something less than psychology, such as neurology, biology, or physiology. We know what a terrific struggle Freud had to move in an opposite direction.

We cannot, however, reduce psychodynamics to psychobiology. This does not involve ignoring biology for its proper contributions, as for example in problems of heredity, but it avoids the confusion of thought arising from two different levels of abstraction. For example, terms like 'meaning' and 'experience' belong specifically to the psychological level. As I understand it, biology does not deal with a living creature as a 'subject' whose experience and actions have meaning for himself and others, but as an objective phenomenon to be studied from the outside by experimental methods, rather than appreciated from the inside by identification, sympathy, empathy, or what have you. Biology for most scientists surely means biochemical, just as psychology for material scientists means psycho-physical. I fancy that in those compound terms the important components are 'chemical' and 'physical'. 'Bio' and 'psycho' are added as consolation prizes. In spite of the powerful support of Bion's argument that the scientific intellect is too limited to deal with anything but the inanimate, I would rather not distinguish, as Home does, between the 'live' and the 'dead' as the fields of study respectively of psychodynamics and physical science, for this seems to me to indicate only the difference between biology and physics. We are more concerned with the difference between the merely animate and the personal, i.e. between the personal and the subpersonal and impersonal: for there are forms of existence which are alive but of no interest to us in psychodynamics because they are not personal (such as fleas, bugs, mosquitoes, and plants). *We are concerned with the study of the 'person', with that level of abstraction at which we speak of the human being as not a 'thing' or an 'organism' but a 'unique individual'*. We only talk significantly about persons when we talk about their experiencing their environment and themselves in a way that has meaning. The difference between these two levels of thinking is clear from the fact that a person has no meaning for his merely material environment, but that environment has meaning for him. I mean nothing to the mountains of Glencoe but they mean a great deal to me. *It is the 'person', the unique and individual 'subject' of meaningful experience*, that the methods of traditional science so fail to deal with. *Psychodynamics is the science of the personal subject, not of mere objects. Psychodynamics is the touchstone of whether psychology in its own right has really been accepted as a science.*

Psychotherapists, whether psychiatric like Stack Sullivan, or psychoanalytic like Szasz and Colby, have produced stout protests against the reduction of psychodynamics to something less than itself. Szasz (1956) wrote:

> Mathematics can function as a tool in physics and astronomy without the identity of those sciences suffering thereby. Psychology cannot so use mathematics without thereby altering its own identity. It appears that in psychology the very process of expressing experiences in highly abstract symbols—even if they pertain to phenomena which are ordinarily thought of as psychological—alters one's conception of the nature of the problem.

Sullivan and Colby are, however, somewhat equivocal. Sullivan writes:

> Biological and neurological terms are utterly inadequate for studying everything in life . . . I hope that you will not try to build up in your thinking correlations (i.e. 'of "somatic" organization with psychiatrically important phenomena') that are either purely imaginary or relatively unproven, which may give you the idea that you are in a solid reliable field in contrast to one which is curiously intangible.

If a person really thinks that his thoughts about nerves and synapses and the rest have a higher order of merit than his thoughts about signs and symbols, all I can say is, Heaven help him.

So far, so good, but then Sullivan rules out the study of the person's 'unique individuality'. He says it is a great thing in our wives and children but we are not concerned with it in science. But it is the very point in question when we ask what is the nature and status of psychodynamic studies. 'Unique individuality' is just what we are concerned with, for in Sullivan's 'interpersonal relationships', what we are and how we react is most closely bound up with what the other person is, and vice versa. Sullivan is saying that something knowable is outside science. After proclaiming the limitations of physical science, he fails to establish a psychodynamic science on its own proper level, which may warn us of the difficulties.

Colby also illustrates the failure of a thinker, who certainly understands the limitations of physical science, to establish psychodynamic science satisfactorily. He speaks of levels of integration in reality and of abstraction in thought, and writes:

At each level of integration characteristic and new properties emerge which are not entirely explainable in terms of levels below them. For these new properties, special methods of study and a special language are required. . . . At the psychic level of integration, between the neuronal and the social, we assume certain properties to be the consequence of what our language calls psychic functions. . . . The higher we go in theoretical abstraction, and the further away we get from material tangible substances, the more difficult it seems for some to grasp what it is that is being discussed. Many simply cannot understand what it means to theorize on a psychic level. We must now abandon them as ill-starred and continue on in a psychological language.

What then is Colby's psychological language? We find we are after all no further forward. He says:

We consider psychic functions to be performed by a hypothetical psychic apparatus. It is an imaginary postulated organization, a construct which aids our understanding of certain observable properties. . . . But there is no point-to-point correspondence between the psychic apparatus and the brain.

He avoids the reduction of psychology to physiology but has not arrived at a true psychology. An 'apparatus for studying observable properties' is a physical science concept, quite unsuitable for representing personality. At best it could only conceptualize the study of behaviour, not of the experience of a personal self which has unique individuality. 'Meaning' which is so vital to the reality of psychic experience and everything that psychoanalysis studies, is not an 'observable property'. We can see or hear certain agreed ways we have of conveying our meanings to one another, but the meaning in itself is not observable; it can only be subjectively realized, appreciated. So true is this that, when we have written or said something and believe that we have made it crystal clear, we can be disconcerted to find that someone thinks we have written or said something entirely different from what we meant. Colby proceeds to elaborate a diagram of endopsychic structure which might well pass as a diagram of a computer or electronic brain, processing in-put and delivering out-put. Thus even those who see that psychodynamics call for a new and broader conception of science, do not yet see clearly what a truly 'psychodynamic' science will be like.

The contribution of E. H. Hutten (Professor of Physics, London) is important at this point. He writes:

> [In psychodynamics] we describe all happenings in terms of psychical reality, and so can dispense with that framework of physical space-time which does not apply to mental phenomena.

He accepts multiplicity of causes and over-determination as essential to psychological theory and in no way militating against its scientific status. It is heartening to find a professor of physics who does not use the term 'cause' with its old scientific meaning in the realm of psychology. He says:

> Classical physics is taken as the standard when it is said that a scientific theory must explain a given phenomenon in one way only; but that is not really true even there, and certainly not in modern physics. Underneath this ideal is, I think, the metaphysical belief in the mechanical determinism of past centuries, according to which everything in the world is connected by the iron chain of necessity.

Hutten confirms my feeling that a view of science which is gradually becoming outdated intellectually, is still held for unconscious emotional reasons. Just as Freud said that the religious believer projected the father-image on to the universe for security reasons, so many a scientific believer projects on to the universe the 'Iron-chain-of-necessity image', scientific materialism, also for security reasons. They feel on safer ground then. There is nothing like dealing at first hand with *psychic* reality, for encountering disturbance.

Psychoanalysis itself grew up so much under the sway of the classic scientific outlook, that Freud could not really escape that projection himself. Thus many attempts to make psychoanalysis scientific have in fact been unrecognized attempts after all to press it back into the mould of the material science type of theory. This becomes increasingly unsatisfactory as the modern philosophy of science makes it plain that physical science no longer sanctions the old solid reliable deterministic universe, a closed system in which we know to a certainty exactly what is what. Thus Popper in *The Logic of Scientific Discovery* (1959) writes:

> The empirical basis of objective science has nothing absolute about it. Science does not rest upon rock bottom. The bold structure of its theories rises as it were above a swamp. It is like a building erected upon piles. The piles are driven down from above into a swamp, but not down to any natural or given base; and when we cease to drive our piles into the deeper layers, it is not because we have reached firm ground. We simply stop when we are satisfied that they are firm enough to carry the structure, at least for the time being.

By the swamp I take it Popper means the area of ultimate ignorance beyond our limited knowledge or (*vide* Bion) beyond our capacity to 'know'. Bertrand Russell's prophecy many years ago that one day science would have discovered everything and provided a giant card index in which we could look up the answers to every possible question, seems now unconvincing: an example of the lack of humility due to failure to see our intellectual limitations. It is clear that physical scientists and philosophers have been every bit as dogmatic within their closed systems as theologians, and are having to learn humility in face of ultimate reality. Since the movement of science has been from the physical to the psychical, it is comforting, when we are puzzled by psychic reality, to remember that physical reality is part of the same swamp, and we are only trying to drive the piles a bit deeper. How are we doing this?

Hutten has thoroughly excluded physical models for psychic reality, but I do not feel that he has yet arrived at a full *psychodynamic* science. He writes:

> The usual cause-and-effect language breaks down when we want to treat processes in which we cannot immediately recognize some constant element. The language works only if the process is no more

than the displacement of a permanent thing in space-time under the influence of a constant force. This is largely true for physics, but even there exist examples where this no longer holds. . . . A psychoanalytic explanation is about a conflict or a process. . . . The same set of data (may) lead to exactly opposite results . . . which shows that the processes underlying human behaviour are dynamical in the sense that they represent a conflict or tension between two opposite poles.

What this demonstrates is that psychoanalysis has a right to its own terminology and cannot be strictly modelled on physical science. Hutten looks in the right direction when he says that in psychodynamics we speak not about

. . . causal laws but about the *aetiology* of an illness. Instead of description and prediction we have *diagnosis* and *prognosis*. . . . Unlike mass points human beings have a history and we cannot hope to predict their future from their present alone.

But neither can we hope to predict their future at all, even from their present plus their history. What Hutten is glimpsing is *the human personal subject of experience as the source of psychodynamic phenomena.* Unless we think of Hutten's 'processes' and 'tensions' and 'opposite poles' as manifestations of the life of a personal subject, we shall find we have slipped back into some kind of physical science terminology, and are not on the proper level of psychodynamics. At a time when all traditional and classic concepts are in the melting pot, including those of science, we should not hesitate to speak of a genuinely *psycho*dynamic theory not tied to the physical conception of science, yet not giving up the claim to be scientific. *Psychodynamics is called on to conceptualize what science has never hitherto regarded as coming within its purview, namely the human being as a unique centre of highly individual experience and responsibility.*

Is 'Object-Relations Theory' a True Psychodynamic Science?

In what terms can we construct psychodynamic science? I have much sympathy with Home's view that some metapsychological statements *literally* do not mean anything, as for example when Hanna Segal tells us 'the infant projects the death instinct into the breast'. This extraordinary statement is due both to careless use of words (if the infant has such a thing as a death instinct, it certainly cannot project it anywhere else), and a confused mixing of psychodynamic and biological concepts. 'Projection' is a psychodynamic concept, 'instinct' is a biological concept. An instinct cannot be projected. Moreover, though Freud said 'Instincts are our mythology', and on its first introduction spoke of the 'death instinct' as a speculation, he, and certainly Klein and Segal thereafter, treated it simply as an undisputed fact. Credible theory cannot be created in this way.

This difficulty of the confused mixing of psychodynamic and biological concepts is perhaps clarified indirectly by a statement of Foulkes (1965) on group therapy, at the Sixth Psychotherapy Congress. He said:

> Psychoanalysis is a biological theory which has only very reluctantly been pushed into being a social theory by the pressure of psychotherapy. Group therapy is not psychoanalysis.

The first sentence is, I am sure, entirely right. Psychotherapy is a social, personal relationship problem. This is obvious in group therapy but not really less so in individual analysis. Thus, psychoanalysis, which came into being as a result of a search for a method of, and a theoretical basis for, psychotherapy, did not after all, *in its original form*, provide one. Psychoanalysis *began* as a biological theory, i.e. as a stage in Freud's emancipation from neurology, and has been very reluctant to be pushed into being more than that, lest it be charged with becoming unscientific. But it has been so pushed by the pressures of psychotherapy, which needs a social and personal relations theory. Is not that the explanation of the great difference between the pre-1920 biological stage of Freud's work, and the post-1920 more fully psychodynamic stage, growing out of the theory of the superego, a concept which owed nothing at all to biology but is a pure psychodynamic concept? What Foulkes called 'the pressure of psychotherapy' is the pressure of the facts about human beings as persons, demanding a theory which goes beyond both physiology and biology, to the highest level of abtraction, where we study the unique individual, not only in immaturity and illness but also in maturity and health. In his first period Freud struggled to transcend physiology and arrived at psychobiology. In his second period he began the struggle to transcend psychobiology and move on to a consistent *psycho*dynamic theory of personal object-relations. With his concept of the super-ego, we begin to see, not an organism dominated by instincts, but an ego which has instincts among its various properties, shaped as a whole in the matrix of human interaction. But the drag of biology and of the metapsychology built on it proved strong, and the result is seen in the work of Melanie Klein. She moved steadily towards a fully-developed object-relations theory, while at the same time clinging all the more tightly to an instinct theory metapsychology, giving us the unfortunate death instinct, constitutional envy and so on. Nevertheless, the direction that development was taking, was bound to demand a re-evaluation of the term 'ego', as more than just a control-apparatus. In the work of Fairbairn, and now in that of Winnicott, it becomes what it really is etymologically, a term denoting the 'I', the core of the personal self, the essence of the 'whole human being'.

The difficulties in psychoanalytic theory arise from its having remained too tied to classic 'natural science' concepts, particularly in biological form. This could not have been avoided. Psychoanalysis arose in the natural science era. It was only Freud's work that forced recognition of psychic reality in a new way. Everything cannot be done at once. New insight grows gradually out of a period of confusion in which old and new overlap. But Foulkes was surely right when he said that the pressures of psychotherapy have forced theory to move on. Nowhere is this more conspicuous than in the work of Winnicott. *The goal is a consistently psychodynamic theory of the unique individual in his personal relations. This is what the emergence of 'Object-Relations Theory' is about.*

The argument so far can be brought to a head by a closer look at the work of Bion. He criticizes psychoanalytic theories for being a 'compound of observed material and abstraction from it'. He seeks a theory of the 'practice of psychoanalysis' which uses only 'pure scientific abstraction'. What is meant by 'pure scientific abstraction'? Abstract terms must be appropriate and relevant to the level of reality at which the abstraction is made. Is he making a psychodynamic theory of the person? His abstractness might seem a target for Szasz's criticism, that in expressing psychological experiences in highly abstract symbols we alter our conception of the nature of the problem. Nevertheless *Bion's concepts imply a dynamic experiencing person whose processes he symbolizes.* Whatever judgment ultimately emerges about his particular conceptual scheme, its basis in this respect is sound. He uses the symbols α and β to avoid prejudging issues by premature description. Thus he speaks of our capacity for thought-making as α-function so as to avoid the risk of defining it concretely in advance of adequate knowledge. This is entirely legitimate. He postulates β-elements as primary sensory experiences of, and α-function as a basic dynamic activity of, an individual psyche. α-function in fact operates on two different sets of data, sense impressions of the outer object world, and emotions as immediate experiences of our inner subjective being. These data are the β-elements which α-function works up into thoughts usable for thinking. Wisdom points out that the theory requires two levels of both consciousness and comprehension, a primitive consciousness and comprehension of β-elements or the raw materials of experience, and then a more developed level of consciousness and comprehension on which α-function does its work and produces 'thoughts'. If α-function fails we cannot think for we have no thoughts to think with. Here again we must distinguish two levels of thinking, thinking as a process that develops 'thoughts' and thinking as a process that uses 'thoughts'. There seem then to be *three levels of psychic activity*, *immediate experience* (sense data and emotions), *thought production*, and *reflection on experience* (science). These can only be theoretically distinguished in our actual experience, except where pathological states artificially isolate them. β-elements are the starting-point of all our experience, α-function is our 'digestion' of it (Bion's term), and science is our reflection on it.

The immediate experience of sense impressions must be the raw material of physical science, from which our α-function builds up such understanding as we are capable of, of the external world. But that cannot be the model for *mental science*, *for the raw material of that is not sense impressions of the outer world, but emotions, i.e. our experience of ourselves as subjects in relation to objects*. Our α-function may well operate less adequately on emotions than on sense impressions, so that we find thought-building easier about objects than about subjects. Here may lie the innate limits of our capacity for thinking that Bion refers to. One result is that it is difficult to talk about mental phenomena in any other than metaphorical language. Our language is based primarily on sensory experience. We apply the terminology of sense-perception to psychic phenomena when we speak of the unconscious as 'deep down', or of the schizoid person as 'shut in', or of the ego as 'split'. But patients themselves describe their experience that way and what other language would express it as accurately, for the purposes of 'primary description'. This is no doubt what Home meant when he said, in a private communication, that he regarded the language of psychology as ordinary language. This is the criticism of Mayer-Gross and others that 'terms in psychiatry are taken from everyday language' and that psychic phenomena 'lack precision'. But *they do not lack precision if we look for the right kind of precision, precise expression of emotional, not sensory experience.* 'Shut in' does not express a spatial relation but a state of mind, a substitution of self-communing for object-relationship, a withdrawal into the self through fear of the outer world. The possibility of thought-building is easier for physical science, but cannot be an impossibility for mental science, for after all we are dealing with facts, the facts of psychic experience and reality.

Using Bion's ideas, *physical science* is the result of his hypothetical α-function turning our immediate experience of sense-impressions of objects into thoughts of objects, which are then developed through the levels of dream-thoughts, concepts, scientific systems, and finally algebraic calculus. But this *physical science is simply an account of the easier half of our experience to think about and conceptualize. Mental science is about the more difficult half of our experience to conceptualize, not the objective world but ourselves as the subjects of experience. It must be thought of as α-function turning the β-elements of our emotional experience of 'ourselves in relation to others', into thoughts that can be developed into psychodynamic science.* This is the difference between the science of objects known from the outside, and of subjects known from the inside. We have made more headway with the first than the second. My own feeling is that 'Object-Relations' theory is the nearest we have got yet to a true psychodynamic science. It is not all the way there but it is on the way. It appears to me that Home's 'Humanistic thinking' is the description of our immediate experience of ourselves in ordinary everyday language. If that were substituted for 'Psychodynamic science' I think it would be open to Gellner's (1959) criticism of 'ideographic science', as:

> . . . a study which claims to know individual things 'in their full individuality' and without the intermediary of general terms or concepts.

We must have general concepts, but derived from the study of experience, not of behaviour. There must be a further stage of reflection, or thinking about experience, which is psychodynamic science, working with general abstract ideas of personal, not impersonal reality.

Freud's work has developed into the exploration of the subjective personal life of man, the understanding of our inner experience, as distinct from the objective description of behaviour. Instincts are no longer all-important and the central place in the theory is now taken by the ego, the core of the personal self, in living relations with other persons or selves. Freud's supreme achievement was to rise superior to his scientific origins and challenge science to go beyond treating human beings as laboratory specimens to be investigated and manipulated, and see them as persons whose lives mean something to themselves and others; persons who can only really be known and helped by someone who does not just objectively diagnose their illness and prescribe treatment, but who knows and in a way shares their experience of suffering, goes along with them in seeking to understand it, and offers them a relationship in which they can rediscover their lost capacity to trust and love. The analytic session and the psychotherapeutic relationship is the laboratory in which psychodynamic science is formulated, and all the time it is a problem of understanding what is going on here and now between two persons, how their past experience contaminates their present meeting, how that can be eliminated and replaced by realistic mature relationship; i.e. how two 'egos' can meet in a fully shared experience. This is what the object-relations theory, emerging from the work of Melanie Klein and Fairbairn, is in process of exploring and formulating, what Martin Buber called the 'I–Thou' relation in contrast to the scientific 'I–It' relation.

Before we look specifically at object-relations theory, it must be noted that so far use has been made of Bion's views only as they concern 'thought-building', the development of the intellectual function with its ultimate consequence, the creation of science. This corresponds to Winnicott's use of the term 'mind' as distinct from 'psyche'. Mind is not there from the beginning as psyche is. Later in the first year, brain maturation makes intellectual activity possible, and Winnicott then speaks of 'mind' or the infant's 'thinking' capacity as gradually becoming able to take over the care of the child from the mother. The primary psyche he regards as not simply a reflection of somatic experience, for it may be but loosely related to the body in the first months of life. Soma and psyche are distinguishable aspects of the whole 'person'. Winnicott writes:

> The psyche of a normal infant may lose touch with the body, and there may be phases in which it is not easy for the infant to come suddenly back into the body, for instance, when waking from deep sleep. (*The Family and Individual Development*, p. 6.)

The psyche must learn to integrate somatic experience, and this it can do only if environmental adaptation to the infant's needs is adequate. The fact that the infant psyche can lose touch with the body and regain it frequently in the earliest months, emphasizes what psychoanalysis calls 'psychic reality' as distinct from 'material (somatic) reality'. The psyche (Fairbairn's 'pristine ego'), which Winnicott says is 'from the beginning . . . already a human being, a unit' (*op. cit.*, p. 5) experiences the soma, and develops an inner relation to it, comes to 'own it' or feel at one with it, and this is part of the integration of personality as experience develops.

In 'object-relational' terms, the infant psyche is from the start potentially an ego as yet undifferentiated as to internal structure, and it needs a good enough human environment to make possible the actualization of the ego through a developing process in object-relations. Here we may return to Bion's 'emotions' as 'β-elements'. He includes in his list of basic 'functions of the personality' the emotions of loving and hating. I do not understand why 'fearing' is omitted. He includes in his basic functions 'reaction between the paranoid-schizoid and depressive positions' and fear is the basis of the paranoid-schizoid position in the same way as hate is the basis of depression. The omission of fear seems to be due to the persistence of the traditional psychoanalytical view that the fundamental conflict is that between love and hate. Freud held that hate is the primary human reaction to the environment and that fear is the secondary result of hate. The study of the schizoid position as antedating depression makes it clear that the very opposite is the truth. Human beings hate because they are afraid. If the weak and dependent infant finds his environment unsupporting and even hostile while he is as yet quite unable to defend and support himself, fear dictates withdrawal and the breaking off of relationships. It is fear that makes it impossible to love, and the conflict between love and fear is the fundamental problem. In an intractable environment, the infant is left with only one choice, that between 'flight' and 'fight' between schizoid withdrawal and the development of hate, of fighting back at those who make it impossible to love, as the only means of maintaining object-relations. It takes a strong and stable person to love; hate is a defence of weakness and fear.

The simplest elements of our psychic experience in its emotional aspect are: (i) a natural capacity to trust, depend on and *love* (at first unconsciously) the good object, and grow with it feeling secure; (ii) *fear* of the bad object, precipitating schizoid withdrawal and the breakdown of object-relationships, which can only be maintained at the price of paranoid persecutory anxiety; (iii) hate of the bad object in an attempt to retrieve the situation, force it to become helpful and restore object-relations (this refers to pathological hate; there is a healthy hate which a mature person will feel as a response to, say, intentional evil such as deliberate cruelty); (iv) *guilt*, in so far as, unlike fear, hate implies love and involves hurting love-objects, thus evoking the urge to reparation; and/or (v) *self-punishment*, self-suppression, the sadistic 'superego' or 'antilibidinal ego', with resulting loss of physical and emotional spontaneity, and the growth of rigidities of character and inhibition of functions. (vi) Out of this inherently unstable and highly complex inner situation, having fear and the lost capacity to love at the bottom of it, personality illness arises. This is not the result of failure of mere gratification of instincts, but of the tension and conflict of the desperate struggle to achieve and maintain a viable ego, a self adequate to living in the outer world. These are the emotional experiences which α-function must 'digest' (Bion) and turn into 'thoughts' if we are to be able to understand them and build up a psychodynamic science. *They are all object-relational experiences. We have to deal with the ego-growth in object-relations.*

At the Sixth Congress of Psychotherapy Laing made a criticism of object-relations theory which it seems pertinent at this point to examine. He said:

> The object-relations theory attempts to achieve, as Guntrip has argued, a synthesis between the intra- and the interpersonal. Its concepts of internal and external objects, of closed and open systems, go a considerable way. Yet it is still 'objects' not 'persons' that are written of. (1965.)

In the first draft of his paper he put this more strongly: 'The objects, in object-relations theory, are internal objects, not other persons.' This latter criticism would appear to me to be true in the long run of Kleinian theory, where internal objects are formed first of all, not by external experience, but by the internal operation of a biological factor, the innate conflict of the life and death instincts, which is then projected on to external objects. The internal life of the ego *could* be worked out as a solipsistic affair and the external world need be no more than a blank projection screen. So far as Fairbairn's object-relations theory is concerned internal objects belong properly to the realm of the psychopathological, since they are internalized in the first instance because they are bad objects. This, it seems, is supported by Bion's view that good experience is digested and worked up by α-function into thoughts. Bad experience remains undigested, a foreign body in the mind, which the psychic subject then seeks to project. *In health, ideally, our objects are not internal objects but real persons, even though in fact none of us can be as healthy as that.* But our internal objects are reflections of our experience of real persons from earliest infancy. Psychotherapy aims at cure by real relationship between two human beings as persons. In it, the psychopathological relationship of the ego to its internal objects as revealed in the transference, steadily changes into the healthy reality of objectively real personal, or ego to ego, relations, first achieved by the patient with the therapist, and then becoming capable of extension to the rest of life. The 'ego' for Fairbairn was not an 'apparatus' nor merely a structural part of a psychic system. It is the personal self, so that when the primary ego is split in experience of other real persons, each aspect of it retains 'ego' quality as a functioning aspect of the basic self.

Should we speak of 'Object-Relations Theory' or of 'Personal-' or 'Ego-' or 'Subject-Relations Theory'? In one way the term 'object-relations' begins to date. It reminds one of Freud's 'sexual object' which was there to gratify an instinct, not to provide a two-way relationship. On the other hand, there is no intrinsic objection to the use of the term 'object' as an abstract term in psychodynamic science, provided it is not held to imply an exclusively impersonal object. Even then, a science of human experience must include Buber's 'I–It' relation, the ego-object relation where the object is impersonal, since this is a valid part of the experience of the ego, both in the sense of the scientific investigation of material objects, and in the sense of, say, the appreciation of beauty in nature. Nevertheless, what really concerns psychodynamic science is the ego-object experience where the object is another ego. Only then do we have the full reality of personal experience and personal relations. *Psychodynamics is the study of that type of experience in which there is reciprocity between subject and object*, and of the experience of ego-emptying and ego-loss when relationship and reciprocity fail.

I made my own view clear in Chapter 17 of *Personality Structure and Human Interaction*. I described immature relations as essentially *unequal*, of the 'one-up-and-the-other-down' type. This may be natural dependence in the case of child and parent, but is pathological as between adults, as in the sado-masochistic relation. There each *uses* the other rather than *relates personally* to the other. Such relations tend to the 'I–It' pattern. Mature relations are two-ways relations between emotional equals, characterized by mutuality, spontaneity, cooperation, appreciation and the preservation of individuality in partnership. There can be no 'turning the tables' for the relation is the same both ways. Each goes on being and becoming because of what the other is being and becoming, in their personal interaction and mutual knowledge. Object-relations theory has not yet adequately conceptualized this. It does now have a truly psychodynamic theory of the development of the individual ego in personal relations; but not of the complex fact of the personal relationship itself between two egos. From Freud's ego and superego, through Melanie Klein's internal objects, projection and introjection, to Fairbairn's splitting of both ego and objects in relationship, and finally Winnicott's tracing of the absolute origin of the ego in the maternal relationship, we have a highly important view of what happens to the individual psyche under the impact of personal relations in real life. But the theory has not yet properly conceptualized Buber's 'I–Thou' relation, two persons being both ego and object to each other at the same time, and in such a way that their reality as persons becomes, as it develops in the relationship, what neither of them would have become apart from the relationship. This is what happens in good marriages and friendships. Winnicott describes its beginnings in the evolving pattern of a good mother–infant relation. This raises the fundamental question: how far can we know and be known by one another? It is what psychotherapy seeks to make possible for the patient who cannot achieve it in normal living. It raises the question Winnicott (1967) says psychoanalysis has not yet faced: 'What is life about, apart from illness?'

XV

HEINZ HARTMANN AND THE OBJECT-RELATIONS THEORISTS

THE rapid survey of 'basic theoretical orientations' here attempted, from the standpoint adopted in the last chapter, must be confined, through considerations of space, to the ego psychology of Heinz Hartmann, so influential in the United States, and the broadly 'object-relational' type of theory that has grown in Britain from the 'internal objects' theory of Melanie Klein. It is not useful to speak of Hartmann and Klein as American and British 'schools'. That is purely historical accident, not logical necessity. In truth, both the Hartmann type of structural theory, and the Klein, Fairbairn, Winnicott type of object-relational and 'whole person' theory, were bound to be developed sooner or later, and they have to be 'thought together' as parts of the overall search for an ever more complete and satisfying theory.

In general, Hartmann developed the already existing potentialities of the classical theory where it was visibly incomplete, in ego-analysis. The British 'internal objects and object-relational' thinkers developed those 'personal relations' implications of the classical theory (as seen so clearly in the Oedipus or family complex, and the superego concept) which were bound to lead sooner or later to a theory that transcended the 'natural science' orientation, and established a fully developed and consistent 'psychodynamic science'. Hartmann and his followers may be found commenting that this or that leads back ultimately to physiology, or that his ego theory may ultimately prove capable of correlation with brain physiology. Without disputing that, one may say as a rough analogy that it is like describing the human life of a family with all its social, artistic, and personal interests as leading back finally to the bricks and mortar of the house and concrete of the foundations. Of course there is a connexion, but this 'reductive' type of 'natural science' explanation avails us little in the study of the 'personal'. It is more important for us to think the other way round, and say that the concrete, the bricks, and the mortar of the house (physics and physiology) provide a basis for the flowering of a fully personal and valuable human living of 'whole persons', and that this is the really important aspect of reality. The scientific study of the 'foundations' is necessary but ancillary to the study of 'personal reality', which is the special province of psychodynamic research. The 'persons' who can create a science of atoms and organisms, are more significant than the material basis of their existence.

In the last chapter I sought to show that psychodynamic science is a new scientific development, going beyond the conceptualization of impersonal objects and subpersonal organisms, needing a new type of conceptualization. In dealing with 'persons', the familiar type of 'natural science' concepts, which are abstract concepts of the 'impersonal', is inappropriate. Thinking in terms of entities, structures, processes, apparatuses, mechanisms, ceases to be relevant and illuminating in psychodynamics. Such a term as 'structure' may be used metaphorically only with great safeguards. What we need is to abstract and conceptualize in terms of the 'personal'. 'Object-relational concepts' and 'ego-concepts' in the sense of 'self' or 'whole person' concepts are, I believe, an effort to do just that. Thus, in voicing criticisms of Hartmann's work, I do not underestimate his great achievement in massive detail, in developing the greatly neglected ego-psychology of the classic theory. I rather question the basic modes of conceptualization and orientation in both, as inadequate to the study of man as a person whose be-all and end-all of existence is his relational life with other persons. For this, only object-relations terminology is adequate.

There never was a time when psychoanalytic theory remained static for long, but there are landmarks that stand out, such as Freud's work on dreams, and the Oedipus complex at the turn of the century, and on ego-analysis and structural theory from 1920. But Freud could not be creative for ever, and even before his death in 1938, important new explorations came from other minds in the 1930's. Melanie Klein, migrating from Europe to Britain, published *The Psychoanalysis of Children* in 1932, and Hartmann gave his essay on *Ego Psychology and the Problem of Adaptation* in 1937 to the Vienna Psycho-Analytic Society, before migrating to the United States. Time relations are significant here, for the two movements of thought in Britain and America overlapped though they did not start together. The ferment of ideas started by Melanie Klein in Britain began with her lectures in 1925, twelve years before Hartmann's essay. Probably preoccupation with the development of object-relations theory in Britain accounts for the fact that more notice was not taken earlier of Hartmann. On the other hand, preoccupation with Hartmann has meant that only of recent years have American analysts begun to take more serious notice of what was going on in Britain. Object-relations theory has developed a different type of ego-psychology from that of Hartmann. Ultimately the two streams had to meet.

Klein's ideas were developed vigorously in the 1930's and 1940's, and Fairbairn, striking out an original line under inspiration of her work, completed his main contribution between 1938 and 1946. Her paper on 'Manic-Depressive States', which so deeply influenced him was given in 1935, two years before Hartmann read his essay, which unfortunately was not made available to the wider English-speaking audience till 1958. Of the papers collected in *Essays in Ego Psychology* (1964), the most direct development of the ideas of the early essay came in four important papers written between 1948 and 1952, on instinctual drives and ego-psychology. This situation was reflected in my earlier book, *Personality Structure and Human Interaction*, which, although not published till 1961, was written between 1945 and 1958. Chapters 1–9 were written between 1945 and 1950, at which time I had to confine myself to the consideration of the paper by Hartmann, Kris, and Loewenstein on 'Comments on the Formation of Psychic Structure' (1946) in Chapter 6 on 'Later Freudian Structural Theory and Analysis of the Ego'. In Chapters 10–18, written between 1950 and 1958, when Hartmann's work was gathering momentum in a series of essays, I was concentrating on the work of Klein, Fairbairn, and Winnicott, and tracing out the general development of the broadly object-relations theory in Britain. In this present volume I hope I have made it clear that *I regard Winnicott's clinically-saturated theoretical work, especially of the last ten years*[1] *as developing the object-relations type of ego theory to its starting-point in living experience, so that fruitful comparison with the work of Hartmann is now possible.*

This is perhaps the place to mention one criticism that has been made of Hartmann's writing, that it is too abstract. By contrast I have just described, intentionally, Winnicott's writings as 'clinically saturated'. In their valuable biographical sketch of Hartmann (Chapter 1 of a book of essays in Hartmann's honour entitled *Psychoanalysis—a General Psychology* edited by Loewenstein *et al.*, 1966) Ruth and Kurt Eissler paint a portrait of a most attractive personality: stable, serene, unpolemical,

[1] Written 1967.

of direct and objective intellectual integrity, as well as great intellectual capacity, a liberal humanist who understood with sympathy those who disagreed with him; a man of astonishingly wide culture and far-ranging interests, perhaps one of the last representatives of the great nineteenth-century encyclopaedic liberal humanists, with tremendous powers of intellectual synthesis. The Eisslers are then compelled to say:

> The criticism has been made since 1939 that Heinz Hartmann's work has been mainly of an abstract character, tending to shy away from clinical exemplification. This is true and it is quite surprising. (p. 9.)

This is certainly my own personal reaction to reading Hartmann's work, and but for the Eisslers' valuable pen-portrait, I would have imagined him to be a very different kind of man. One would think that he was more human as a therapist than as a theorist. Could it be that a rigorous scientific training and the vast erudition of the liberal humanist imposed on him such an intellectual discipline as a synthesizer, that the live creative intuitive person was stifled *in his writing* by the intellectual clarifier and developer of what he had inherited from Freud? Melanie Klein wrote as she thought with clinical intuition, not as an intellectual, and part of the difficulty of reading her is that one can feel her struggling with her live developing thought as she writes. Fairbairn, a man of very wide culture and intellectual discipline, a product of both Scottish and German Universities, was more of an intellectual thinker, and made the mistake of publishing his 'Revised Theory' before he had published his clinical evidence for it. Nevertheless, his writing is definitely closer to clinical material than is Hartmann's.

In contrast with both of them, Winnicott is a man of great clinical intuition, and his writing is 'clinically saturated'. I have had the experience, on first reading some of his writings, of the opening of a hitherto closed door. I had that experience more on reading Fairbairn than in listening to him in sessions, where his interpretations were usually short and intellectually clear, though not theoretical. It was in his writing, as he told me himself, that Fairbairn struggled and laboured to clarify emerging insights which 'light up' for the reader. I do not get this experience of 'enlightenment', of the opening of a door into a dark region of human experience, in reading Hartmann. He reads more like a text-book of philosophy or scientific theory, what the Eisslers call 'the magnificent abstract edifice that Heinz Hartmann built'.

In this particular subject, my own predilection is for clinically-saturated writing, as more creative. Hartmann himself wrote: 'Progress in the development of analysis is mostly based on clinical discoveries' (*Essays on Ego Psychology*, p. 142). His own theorizing, however, is remote from direct clinical experience and highly intellectually abstract. In psychodynamics, an abstract concept, however exactly defined, has a somewhat indeterminate factual reference if it is not precisely anchored to and illustrated by the relevant clinical material. Thus in fact, whatever Hartmann was in conversation and in therapy to those fortunate enough to know him, the only Hartmann most of us can know is the abstract theoretical writer. This, I think, has an important bearing on the fact that *Hartmann's theory presents us with an ego that is a 'system', one part or substructure of a complex structural organization, while Winnicott presents us with an ego that is a 'self', an infantile psyche that is an incipient ego-self, and in process of getting, or being prevented from getting, a start as a real ego-self in the relation to the mother.*

This discussion has been necessitated further because of its bearing on Hartmann's efforts to extend psychoanalysis so as to make it a 'General Psychology'. Certainly psychoanalysis must ultimately have much to contribute to a General Psychology, but that is hardly its major task, which is to provide a basis of understanding for psychotherapy. A general psychology will include much that is of no immediate importance for psychotherapy, much that may be more relevant to education and sociology. They are primarily concerned with the processes of development and maturation that go on in sufficiently or 'relatively' normal persons whose mental health can be assumed. In so far as mental health cannot be assumed, educationalists and sociologists must turn to learn from psychoanalysis. It is important for psychoanalysis to understand what is meant by 'mental health', if it is to have a true criterion of what is 'mental illhealth'. But psychoanalysis does not have to use in therapy, a knowledge of normal developmental processes. That concerns what has gone right, while psychoanalysis is basically concerned with what has gone wrong and needs to be set right. When we can help a disturbed personality to outgrow the blocking effects of its internal conflicts, we can trust the normal developmental processes to take over. Thus, I was recently asked to see a University student of good intelligence who had completely failed in his exams. He was suffering from an anxiety state bound up with serious family troubles over a long period, but some six months of analysis freed him from his intellectual blockage and he took his next exams with complete success. I did not have to concern myself with his resumed use of his intellectual capacity or with its modes of functioning. That took care of itself. The case would have been different had he been a schizophrenic with fundamentally disordered thought processes, but the analyst's task would not have been even then any different 'in principle'. It would have been to discover what had got in the way of normal development. Hartmann wrote:

> Today we actually know much more (about the ego) than we are able to use technically in a rational way. (*Essays on Ego Psychology*, p. 143.)

Is not that perhaps due to the fact that some of it is knowledge that was obtained in the process of extending psychoanalysis in the direction of a general psychology, and so is not really relevant to the major psychoanalytical concern, which is psychotherapy?

With regard to the general question of 'abstractness', all scientific concepts are abstract, but in psychodynamics they must be specifically abstractions from concrete clinical experience. In the long run, this always comes down to the human being's experience of struggling to achieve an ego, not as a system of apparatuses for control, adaptation and so on, but an ego as a 'real self'. What at long last our patients arrive at is that they feel lonely, empty, and unreal at heart because they had no relationships in infancy that could give them an abiding sense of 'belonging', and of personal reality. *Appetitive drives and ego techniques belong to the instrumental aspects of personality; the ego as a real self belongs to its essence.*

What the Eisslers call the 'abstract structure' is to some extent true of much psychoanalytic theory prior to the emergence of the problem of the ego as a true self originating in the mother–infant relation, an advance that the psychoanalysis of adults owes primarily to the development of the psychoanalysis of children. Hartmann speaks of Freud's earlier ambiguous use of 'ego'

> to designate not only what we now call the ego as 'system' but at the same time also the self, and one's own person in contradiction to other persons. (*Op. cit.*, p. 279.)

He holds that it was fortunate that Freud's interest in the ego was retarded by his work on the unconscious and drives (*op. cit.*, p. 281). He mentions that it was in Freud's middle period that he thus used the term ego in more than one sense, but in his third period as in his first, the organization of the ego was again emphasized. *For Hartmann the ego is defined as a system of functions* (*op. cit.*, pp. 286–9). *He came down definitely in favour of the ego as 'system', not 'self'*. He writes:

The term 'ego' is often used in a highly ambiguous way, even among analysts. To define it negatively, in three aspects, as against other ego concepts: 'ego' in analysis is not synonymous with 'personality' or with 'individual'; it does not coincide with the 'subject' as opposed to the 'object' of experience; and it is by no means only the 'awareness' or the 'feeling' of one's own self. In analysis the ego is a concept of a quite different order. It is a substructure of personality and is defined by its functions. Which functions do we attribute to the ego? A catalogue of ego functions would be rather long, longer than a catalogue of functions of either the id or the superego. No analyst has ever endeavoured a complete listing of ego functions. (*Op. cit.*, p. 114.)

Hartmann states further:

That Freud's investigation of the id preceded his approach to structural psychology is one of the most momentous events in the history of psychology. (*Op. cit.*, p. 113.)

That is true but I feel bound to add that it was also one of the most disastrous, even though it was inevitable, from 1880 onwards in the scientific and intellectual climate of that time. For it meant that *Freud did not begin with an over-riding sense of the wholeness of the 'person' or else took it for granted and did not make it fundamental for theory; and it has therefore taken well over half a century for psychoanalysis to begin to grasp the fundamental importance of ego-psychology as the psychology of the whole person in object-relations*. The assessment of Hartmann's work must therefore be concerned, not so much with the details, the mass of valuable analyses of the functions of the 'system ego', though we cannot ignore these, but rather with the fundamentals, the questions of the id-ego dichotomy and of the ego as system or self.

Hartmann set out (i) to remedy the neglect of ego-theory in the first phase of Freud's thinking, when all the emphasis was on the so-called 'id'. (The extent of that neglect, perhaps we should even say repudiation, shows in Anna Freud's statement in 1936, that prior to 1920 when Freud himself took up the problem of the ego, 'the odium of psychoanalytical unorthodoxy . . . attached to the study of the ego), (ii) to remedy the major problem created by this excessive emphasis on instincts, which left analysts with no real means of understanding human beings as 'human' beings, as 'persons', as achieving what Spitz (1957) called 'the dignity of the human being', and Rapaport (1953) called 'the achievement of man's estate'. One cannot overemphasize the importance of these two aims, but the judgment of Gill and Brenman (1959) that

> . . . the central advance in the theory of psychoanalytic psychology in the past two decades has been the concept of relative autonomy (i.e. of the ego). (Hartmann, Rapaport.)

overlooks the quite different type of ego theory that emerged in the object-relations orientation, based not on the assumption of the fundamental hostility of ego to id, but on the growth of the psyche as a 'whole person'. I believe this involves a more radical development beyond Freud than does the theory of Hartmann. The emergence of the concept of 'ego-autonomy' *is* the emergence of the one key idea needed to turn psychoanalysis from a psychobiology into a psychodynamic theory of 'persons' but only if by 'ego' we mean more than a partial system, an organ of adaptation. 'Ego' must mean the 'realized potentiality' of the whole psyche for developing as a whole self, a person. In fact Hartmann's concept of 'ego-autonomy' would be more important if his concept of the ego was more adequate.

Already in 1937 Hartmann showed convincingly that there was more in the ego than defence mechanisms against id-drives, but when he wrote:

> The psychology of the id is the preserve of psychoanalysis, and ego psychology is its general meeting ground with non-analytical psychology. (1939, p. 6.)

this is misleading. It is more significant to differentiate non-analytical psychology as a non-dynamic science of behaviour, from psychoanalysis as a psychodynamic science of experience. Hartmann's view arose out of his orthodox view of psychology as a 'natural science' and of psychoanalysis as one of the biological sciences. Gitelson (1965) was impressed with Hartmann's statement in 1937 that:

> It is only when we consider the social phenomena of adaptation in their biological aspect that we can really start 'getting psychology rightfully placed in the hierarchy of science, namely as one of the biological sciences'.

This view was natural in the early days of psychoanalysis and was bound to continue for a long time, but it does not do justice to the revolutionary nature of Freud's gradually developed concept of 'dynamic psychic reality'. This implies that psychoanalysis has moved beyond the scope of biological science and that the concept 'id' must be transcended, and with it the 'id-ego' dichotomy. Hartmann, in carrying Freud's theory to its fullest point of systematization, especially in ego-theory, added much to the picture of man as going beyond conflict with primitive instinctive drives to achieve truly human dignity in social and intellectual capacity, but he did not question the id concept. He retained it, yet was driven to transcend it in his theory of an autonomous ego. The id is no longer the sole source of energy, with an ego which is nothing but structure, the theory which Fairbairn regarded as Helmholtzian and out of date scientifically. *The ego has its own innate sources of energy for Hartmann, and we must regard this as a great stride forward in realistic conceptualization, if only its full implications had been worked out;* but Freud never abandoned, and Hartmann never questioned searchingly the adequacy of the clinical actuality of the original id-instinct theory. His concept of a primary undifferentiated phase prior to the id-ego, could have led to the questioning of the traditional 'instincts versus social controls' model of human nature, redefined as the id-ego dichotomy which he saw was absent in animals. But this did not happen and the id concept remained responsible for the long neglect of ego-theory, and continued to control Hartmann's research. This model was not only a continuation of centuries-old assumptions, but was easy to fit into the 'natural science' ideology in which Freud was trained. When physiological research failed to answer psychological questions, Freud naturally turned next to biological concepts with the feeling that he was not abandoning the scientific approach, but was basing everything on scientifically respectable data in studying the vicissitudes of instincts. He could not have foreseen that his work was destined to open up an entirely new level of scientific enquiry, as much beyond biology as that was beyond physics, namely 'psychodynamics' or 'the science of the *person*'. *Freud began and Hartmann completed the attempt to graft a theory of the 'person', in the form of a structural psychology with a 'system-ego', on to the stem of biology.* Neither recognized that while body, organism, and person are all one whole in the human being, we cannot mix and confuse our different categories of thinking about these quite different aspects or levels of abstraction in the scientific study of man without subtly dragging down the higher into the lower. This happened in the beginnings of psychoanalysis when id theory practically excluded ego theory in all but superficial respects. The result was an ever-elaborating description of forces, processes, mechanisms, apparatuses, and so on, but nowhere did the meaningful 'whole person' dominate conceptualization, nor can he so long as he is sundered into an id and an ego.

The behavioural sciences have much to learn from Hartmann's detailed analysis of ego-processes. Rangell writes of Hartmann as going beyond the study of conflict and defence and says:

Hartmann looks now from the wider view of general psychological theory. From this point of view, techniques of achievement and adjustment to reality emerge in a more explicit way than they do from the angle of pathology. (1965.)

However, *Hartmann's 'system-ego' with autonomous power (as against the id) to adapt and adjust to outer reality, does not give us a 'person' with capacities for spontaneous self-expression and creative originality, not simply adapting to external reality but producing from internal reality*. I would summarize at this point by saying that the restriction of the term 'ego' to the meanings of 'internal defensive ego' and 'external-reality adaptive ego' is too narrow. The id-ego dichotomy and hostility is transcended once we see that the so-called id itself has 'ego-quality' as must every aspect or part of the psychic individual. *The isolation and description of apparatuses and techniques of the outer-reality ego is secondary to the over-riding problem, studied in Chapters VIII and IX in connexion with the work of Winnicott, the problem of how a whole 'ego' in the sense of an 'I', an experience of stable selfhood, as a real person in ego-relationships gets a secure start at all, in the earliest mother–infant relations.*

The evidence gathered in this book all goes to show that the one fundamental thing that matters to human beings is to possess a stable experience of themselves as whole and significant persons. It is ego-growth out of primary psychic unity, and ego-maintenance in internal security, not instinct gratification or control, or even ego-adaptation to outer reality (one aspect of which is Winnicott's 'false self on a conformity basis'), that is the ultimate motivating force, and conscious and unconscious aim. Questions of instinct-gratification can only arise within that overall context.

The impact of Hartmann's work has caused much radical thinking among American analysts. A useful measure of this can be gained from a perusal of four papers in the *International Journal of Psycho-Analysis*, 1965–6. Rangell (1965, pp. 5–29) is a wholehearted exponent of 'a man considered by most to be the leading living theoretician in our field'. Holt (1965, pp. 151–67) first quotes Chein as saying that 'psychology must decide between two images of man . . . the active responsible agent . . . and the (scientific) view of man as an impotent reactor' to internal conditions and external forces. Holt then regards Hartmann's 'ego-autonomy', as representing man as a responsible agent 'who actively intervenes as a "third force" in the operation of causal pressures' from the id and the environment. However, he goes on to point out that this 'autonomy' is only a negative concept of 'freedom *from*' environmental pressures and id drives, and states that 'autonomy in the sense most appealing to us, the positively defined "freedom *to*" can only be won by the person himself'. In a footnote he states:

Rapaport was well aware of this. He acknowledged that he was neglecting 'freedom to' but deferred for the future . . . the crucial task of the study of the autonomous ego's motivations.

Holt then clearly renounces his initial suggestion that Hartmann treats man as

. . . an active responsible agent. . . . I believe [he writes] that autonomy is the utopian ideal of ego psychology, a slogan emblazoned on the banner of the ego psychologists in their struggle against the excesses of traditional id-orientated psychoanalytical thinking. Indeed, I believe that the main reason we have a concept of autonomy is the unbalanced development of psychoanalytic theory. . . . If we try to imagine what psychoanalytic theory would look like if re-written on a clean slate, I think we may find that the concept of autonomy will not occupy an important place. One would instead be mainly concerned to describe the relative roles of drive, external stimuli and press, and various inner structures in determining behaviour, and the complex interactions between them.

This remarkable statement seems to me to involve an acceptance of all Hartmann's work in detail together with a repudiation of his ego-autonomy view, and with it a repudiation of the view of man as an 'active responsible agent' in favour of the supposedly scientific view of man as simply a reactor to internal and external forces and factors. This simply shows how urgently we need a radical 'whole ego' theory of the kind that object-relations theory has led to. Holt rejects just that concept of Hartmann that held out most hope of progress. He is still an 'apparatus theorizer'. He ends his paper with the words:

The complex interactions between external inputs, endogenous inputs, and the structure of the psychic apparatus itself, explanatory concepts which I believe will eventually make the descriptive evaluative concept of autonomy take a relatively minor role in psychoanalytic theory . . . Although I agree that it is misleading to conceive of two separate autonomies (from the id and from environment) I believe that the theory will grow in the direction of further specification rather than simply by the unification of the autonomies. This growth awaits, however, clarification of the central concepts of drive and structure, which in turn presupposes a fundamental reconsideration of the entire psychoanalytic model.

My own judgment is that in fact this amounts to a cancellation of all the implications of Freud's psychodynamics, and a regression to the severely physicalistic 'natural science' mode of thought that Freud was always struggling to outgrow. Holt specifically rules out the one concept needful for a true psychology of the 'person', namely a unified autonomy of an ego that is the core of selfhood in a whole person. Apfelbaum, in a far more detailed critique of the structural ego theory, quotes Sutherland as saying:

One of the main features of ego psychology seems to be a need to formulate theories in terms that are thought to be more appropriate to science, or more accurately, to other scientists.

This must apply even more drastically to Holt. In 'Ego Psychology, Psychic Energy, and the Hazards of Quantitative Explanation in Psycho-Analytic Theory' (1965) Apfelbaum writes:

The determining concern of contemporary ego theory is to establish its physicalistic-organic model, in the belief that this will bring an eventual joining with physiology and general psychology.

He regards Holt as seeking to reinstate Freud's early 'Project' and comments:

This interest on the part of theoretical ego psychologists in recovering Freud's early quantitative principles is also illustrated by Kris

who takes us back to the constancy principle and the fluid energy model. That all this takes us ever further away from our true interest, the clinical concern with real human persons, is evident to Apfelbaum, when he says:

Simplified representations of impulse and control are an identifying feature of the quantitative approach. This would be more noticeable were Hartmann and Rapaport more often to use clinical examples. Instead they use physicalistic and organic visual metaphors and analogies in which fixed quantitative conceptions are taken for granted.

In all such trends psychoanalysis is forsaking its own proper role, which is to understand the functioning of the human being, not as an organism, but as a 'person': i.e. not to reduce psychology to physiology, but to develop a truly psychodynamic science of persons.

Rangell writes: 'It was Hartmann who, more than anyone else, systematized the existing fragments of ego psychology into a composite whole' (1965). The psychology of Hartmann is about this relating of bits and pieces of psychic life to each other, id-drives and ego-apparatuses. The emphasis is not primarily on the central fact of a 'whole person' whose growing processes these are. Such a theory becomes bogged down in the complex difficulties which Apfelbaum surveys in 'On Ego Psychology: A Critique of the Structural Approach to Psycho-Analytic Theory' (1966). The ultimate difficulty is that the id-ego analysis involves a permanent division in the psyche. Only a 'whole ego' theory in which pathological conflicts are seen as ego-splitting, can give real meaning to integration (as, for example, Winnicott's 'true and false selves', an arrested infantile ego, and a conformist semi-adult ego). Hartmann writes: 'the forces of the mind are pitted against one another' and

> the ego must treat certain instinctual drives as dangers . . . The inherent antagonism of the ego towards the instinctual drives (is) described by Anna Freud. (1939, p. 28.)

This is completely depersonalized conceptualization. In fact, *what has to be conceptualized is* something quite different, *the co-existence of different developmental levels of experience within the same psychic whole, setting up internal strains and tensions which split the unity of the basic psychic self.* Psychotherapy seeks to restore wholeness and growing maturity to the ego, making possible a meaningful relatedness to external reality.

Hartmann, however, regards the concept of 'somatic apparatuses to execute action' as legitimately transferable to psychic reality as 'ego apparatuses to execute action'. But this is not legitimate. Apparatuses cannot be personalized, but the ego becomes depersonalized, mechanized, and there is no true self. He writes:

> The apparatuses, both congenital and acquired, need a driving force in order to function: the psychology of action is inconceivable without the psychology of the instinctual drives. (1939, p. 101.)

We are back to the id as blind dangerous energy or drive, and ego as pure structure, apparatuses, which, even with partial autonomy, must still draw on id-energy to control id-drives. To make this possible, speculative concepts are invented such as desexualized, deaggressivized, neutralized energy. Apfelbaum sums up:

This is the heart of contemporary ego theory; drives remain infantile; only the ego develops. The original potency of drive may be weakened, endlessly diverted and refined, but at the ultimate levels of maturity it simply reaches neutrality. . . . The ego, as intellect and judgment, must free itself from emotion as represented by the id.

Aptly he cites Erikson:

Mechanization and independence of emotion characterize the impoverished ego rather than the healthy one.

This was in fact seen by Rapaport when he recognized that the autonomous ego was all too like the obsessional ego. To save this autonomous ego with only neutral energy from being quite depersonalized, he has to allow 'regression in the service of the ego' in order to make gratifying sexual functioning and creative activity possible again. At this point the id-ego dualism has become impossible to work consistently and is self-defeating.

The only escape from this artificiality of theory is to abandon the theory of a permanent antagonistic id-ego dualism, and *develop a consistently psychodynamic theory of the development of a 'whole person ego' from the original 'psyche with ego-potential', a process which can only get really started in a good enough mother–infant relationship*. The over-riding concern for the 'whole person' which is crucial for object-relations theory appears also in the work of Erikson. Apfelbaum points to his 'almost exclusive concern with the synthetic function . . . perhaps the cardinal ego function' and his description of the child's 'unsatiable desire for independence, mastery and investigation'. Here is a whole personal self, not just an ensemble of apparatuses. 'Synthetic function' is an abstract theoretical term for the basic wholeness and unity of the personal self, a dynamic structure in all its aspects, actively living. Thus Apfelbaum notes that even when Erikson speaks of 'drive-fragments' 'these fragments are themselves synthesis-seeking', a view I have expressed as 'every part of the whole but split ego, retains ego-quality'. Again,

Erikson finds no inevitable opposition between ego and instinct, and consequently makes no appeal to the idea of ego autonomy, in Hartmann's sense. Erikson writes:

> Man's 'inborn instincts' are drive fragments to be assembled, given meaning, and organized during a prolonged childhood. (1950.)

It seems to me even *more accurate to describe instincts as the properties of a dynamic psyche which is a potential ego or whole self*. Fairbairn expressed this view by saying that instincts are not entities that invade the ego from outside 'giving it a kick in the pants', and he preferred the adjectival form 'instinctive', to avoid the danger of reifying these aspects of psychic functioning. Erikson's point of view is very close to Fairbairn's concept of 'dynamic structure' in which there is no separation or opposition of energy and structure as id and ego, though Erikson does not discard the non-personal, non-psychological term 'id' as Fairbairn does. Fairbairn pointed out that such separation is a relic of nineteenth-century science in Helmholtzian physics, in which Freud was educated. Present-day physics finds no place for a concept of energy without structure, or structure without energy. Such ideas belong to the old notion of the billiard ball universe, in which inert atomic structures were pushed around in space by an independent energy.

The concept of an 'inner world' is perhaps the best point at which to make a transition from Hartmann to the 'object-relations theory' thinkers. Hartmann writes:

> In the course of evolution, described here as a process of progressive 'internalization', there arises a central regulating factor, usually called the 'inner world', which is interpolated between the receptors and the effectors . . . one of the ego's regulating factors. . . . The biological usefulness of the inner world in adaptation, in differentiation, and in synthesis, is obvious in the biological significance of thought processes. Perception, meaning, imagery, thinking, and action are the relevant factors in this connexion. The inner world and its function makes possible an adaptation process, which consists of two steps, withdrawal from the external world, and return to it with improved mastery in the world of thought and the world of perception . . . elements of the adaptation process which consists of withdrawal for the purpose of mastery. (1939, pp. 57–9.)

Hartmann's 'inner world' as one of the regulating factors in the ego as an organ of adaptation to the outer world, is simply our conscious capacity to stop and think and use our consciously available intellectual resources to guide our action. This is indeed 'general psychology' and far removed from clinical psychopathology and psychoanalysis as a basis for psychotherapy. It is far removed from the 'inner world' as conceived by Melanie Klein, Fairbairn, Winnicott, and object-relations thinkers generally. Their 'inner world' is a psychodynamic legacy, compound of all the unsolved problems of disturbed ego development in infancy and childhood; it is a purely psychic world that the individual lives in, largely if not wholly unconsciously, where his lack of internal unity as a self is manifested in dreams, fantasies, and symptoms, as experiences of highly emotionally charged relationships of parts or aspects of himself with internalized bad and good objects. In this 'inner world', which is both withdrawn and repressed though it breaks into consciousness as pathological disturbance, a needy deprived infantile ego clamours for good objects, and an angry sadistic infantile ego hates its bad objects, and the whole is shot through with the fears of internal bad objects destroying internal good objects in fantasy, leading to depression and despair. This whole pathologically dynamic 'inner world' is the active unconscious, and it masks the more secret phenomenon of the regressed, withdrawn, or even as yet barely evoked true or natural self, a potential self awaiting a chance to be reborn into an environment in which it is possible to live and grow. The work of Melanie Klein on fantasy, following and developing Freud's work on dreams, gave us a full view of the 'contents' of this inner world. The work of Fairbairn on the correlations of ego-splitting and object-splitting gave us insight into the disruption of the infant's psychic 'wholeness' in a too bad early environment, and the work of Winnicott takes us to the experiential beginning, the start of ego-growth in the infant–mother relationship. In all this work, the emphasis is all the time on 'object-relations' as the *sine qua non* of the development of a healthy, mature, whole, personal self. Hartmann's 'inner world' is a process of reflective judgment forestalling hasty action in outer reality, a view which does not take us anywhere near the tremendous dynamic problems of personality that psychoanalytic psychotherapy has to grapple with. The 'inner world' of 'object-relations' writers is the dynamic heart of the psychic experience of 'persons', with varying content in illness and health. The 'id' of Hartmann and of classical psychoanalysis, is simply the dynamic or energy aspect of this infantile inner world, abstracted, depersonalized, and conceptualized, with the structural infantile-ego aspect omitted.

The problem is not that of conceiving of a rational intellectual ego-structure controlling blind biopsychic forces, but of understanding how the psychosomatic whole human being, the biologically based infantile psyche, realizes its potentiality for becoming a 'person', utilizing all its energies and capacities as they mature, in the good environment of maternal support; growing towards the 'ideal' goal of a 'whole' mature adult person, capable of fullness of living in personal relationships, with no pathological splitting between emotion and intellect, or between infantile and adult. We are not concerned with blind forces and mechanical control apparatuses, a natural way of thinking in the atmosphere of nineteenth-century science. *We are concerned with a living whole human being and how he can become a viable ego, a real self, a personal 'I', with all his inborn energies flowing together as an inwardly free and spontaneous capacity to enjoy, love and create.* This can only be expressed theoretically in terms of the vicissitudes of the primary unitary psyche as 'dynamic structure', and its natural development as a whole personal ego in good enough object relationships, beginning with the mother–infant pair. To clarify this, I shall survey briefly the work of Melanie Klein, Fairbairn, and Winnicott, with only passing reference to Fairbairn as I have dealt at full length with his contribution in a previous book. A further review of Melanie Klein's work and of Winnicott's latest work is essential.

The 'Object-Relations' Theorists

The work of Melanie Klein appears to me to be the decisive contribution which marks the transition from classical to present-day psychodynamic research. Just as for psychological studies in general, we have to think in terms of 'before and after Freud', so I think the historians of psychoanalysis will come to think in terms of 'before and after Melanie Klein'. One can disagree with Freud on fundamental matters and yet recognize with gratitude the greatness of his new departure in the study of human nature. Similarly, one can disagree with Melanie Klein on matters of crucial importance and yet recognize with gratitude that without her work psychoanalysis today would not have achieved many of its fundamental insights. In the body of this book I have laid most stress on the work of Fairbairn and Winnicott because they are closer to the elucidation of schizoid problems as I see them, and because of their implications for wider thinking. Yet the work of both of them pre-supposes that of Klein. At a dinner given to Fairbairn on his seventieth birthday, he stated publicly that it was hearing Mrs Klein give her paper on 'The Psychogenesis of Manic-Depressive States' in 1935, that provided the great stimulus to his thinking, and led to his own creative writing from 1938 to 1951. Prior to that he had produced nothing of marked originality. Strachey, Winnicott's analyst, specifically urged him to study what Melanie Klein, then newly arrived in Britain, was saying. Neither Fairbairn nor Winnicott accepted anything like the whole of her metapsychology. They were both independent and original thinkers and had to explore their own ways. But their debt to Klein's work was immense.

As I have not made much specific reference to Klein's views in this book, I feel it is due to the importance of her work that acknowledgment should here be made of my own agreements and disagreements, with emphasis on the fact that I regard the agreements as indispensable, because of the fundamental nature of her basic contribution. It is a measure of her greatness that her critics are as much influenced by her work as her disciples. I made a detailed study of the essentials of her theory in Chapters 10–12 and 16 of *Personality Structure and Human Interaction* (1961). I shall therefore base this review on Segal's *Introduction to the Work of Melanie Klein* (1964) as affording an opportunity of assessing what Kleinian metapsychology is today. The book is so clearly written that it is a pleasure to read, and performs a valuable service, for most readers find Klein's own style not easy going, due in part to the fact that she was wrestling with a subject-matter which was growing all the time under her touch.

Melanie Klein's fundamental and major contribution was to develop a new conception of endopsychic structure. Before Klein, the human psyche was regarded as an apparatus for experiencing and controlling biological instincts originating outside the ego. The ego was a superficial development 'on the surface of the id', hostile to it and with only very imperfect capacity to control what Rapaport called the 'battle of the Titans', the 'seething cauldron' of id drives. *After Klein, it became possible to see the human psyche as an internal world of a fully personal nature, a world of internalized ego-object relationships, which partly realistically and partly in highly distorted ways reproduced the ego's relationships to personal objects in the real outer world.* This conception of endopsychic structure as an inner world of personal object-relations, revealed to consciousness in dreams, symbolically expressed in symptoms, and represented in fantasy, is 'the great divide' in the development of psychoanalysis. It is in Klein's work that object-relations first begin to replace instincts as the focal point of theory. This is making possible a subtle but enormously important change of 'atmosphere' in psychoanalytic thinking; from the *mechanistic* to the *personal*, from the study of mental phenomena, the clash of psychic forces, to the study of the human being's struggle for self-realization as a person in personal relationship. Melanie Klein as the originator of this concept was not able to realize that in fact it replaced the earlier concept of psychic life as simply an area of superego and ego control of antisocial instincts. The fact that she introduced the new view without giving up the old has been confusing, but all the implications of a revolutionary new departure cannot be forseen at the start. Freud himself, like all thinkers who break new ground, was caught up in the same problem. Others have to discover what far-reaching modifications of earlier ideas will be made necessary by a new insight. In fact, Klein's views on inner psychic reality, on internal objects, and internal object-relations, created the necessary conceptual framework in which Freud's later emphasis on ego-psychology could be fully developed, and this is what has happened.

Recognition of the importance of fantasy has its origin, psychoanalytically, in Freud's work on dreams and his theory of the superego. It was, however, Melanie Klein, dealing directly with the fantasy life at its source in early childhood, who showed that it constitutes the secret heart of our mental self, and reveals the structure and working of the whole personality, and therefore of neurosis. She showed how specifically human beings live an inner world secret life, organized round the twin fantasies of the internal good and bad objects; how this fantasy life forms a second world competing with the first, external world; and how interplay between the two by projection and introjection gives the clues needed to understand the problems of psychopathology. By means of this material Klein described the paranoid-schizoid and depressive phases of development, giving rise to paranoid-schizoid and depressive 'positions' or developmental levels in the psyche, which do not pass away but endure as

> specific configurations of object-relations, anxieties, and defences which persist throughout life. (Segal, p. xiii.)

It should be noted that Klein originally spoke of 'paranoid' and 'depressive' positions, but Fairbairn's work on schizoid problems led to her adopting the term 'paranoid-schizoid' for the earlier position, though with some differences of meaning. With Klein, schizoid means 'splitting' while with Fairbairn it predominantly means 'withdrawal', a point to which we must return. All this amounts to a tremendous stride forward in psychoanalysis, whereby it gets far closer to inner psychic reality than was possible in terms of the instinct and oedipal theories which paved the way. Klein's contribution is permanent, fundamental, and secure. Klein's concept of the inner unconscious fantasy world goes beyond the earlier simpler concept of a repressed unconscious. It is not merely an impersonal unconscious into which impulses that are not ego-syntonic are thrust away. It is an unconscious mental world to live in, the maintenance of a hidden life that is additional to that lived in the outer material world, and is the heart of our personality.

Segal devotes her first chapter to the exposition of the concept of 'fantasy' because it is the basic concept, Freud's recognition of 'psychic reality'. She says:

> Some psychologists used to object to Freud's description of the mind on the grounds that it was anthropomorphic—a strange objection, . . . since psychoanalysis is concerned with describing man. . . . Freud, in his description of the super-ego, is not implying that there is a little man actually contained in our unconscious, but that this is one of the unconscious phantasies which we have about the contents of our body and psyche. Freud never refers specifically to the super-ego as a phantasy, nevertheless he makes it clear that this part of the personality is due to an introjection—in phantasy—of a parental figure. (p. 1.)

'Fantasy-forming is a function of the ego' and Segal makes it clear that in Kleinian theory

> . . . the ego assumes a higher degree of ego-organization than is usually postulated by Freud. It assumes that the ego from birth is capable of forming . . . primitive object-relationships in phantasy and reality. From the moment of birth the infant has to deal with the impact of reality. . . . Phantasy is not merely an escape from reality, but a constant and unavoidable accompaniment of real experiences, constantly interacting with them. (pp. 2–3.)

> The structure of the personality is largely determined by the more permanent of the phantasies which the ego has about itself and the objects that it contains. (p. 9.)

It is this conception of human beings living in two worlds at the same time, inner and outer, with mutual interference, that makes Klein's work of such momentous importance, and there is wide agreement as to the salient features of this inner world life of good and bad object-relations. Though the term 'object-relations theory' came to be applied in a special sense to the work of Fairbairn, that is too limited a use of the term. *'Object-relations theory' was primarily the creation of Melanie Klein's work on internal and external object-relationships and their interplay in fantasy. The full implications of this were, however, obscured by her retention of Freud's original instinct theory. Fairbairn's work lay in the specific disentanglement of 'object-relations theory' from 'instinct theory'*. Unless this is done the full scope of the radical nature of Klein's contribution is obscured.

It is at this point therefore that fundamental differences of view arise as to how this unconscious fantasy life comes into being. When Segal writes: 'Phantasy is a mental expression of instincts through the medium of the ego' (p. 2.), there is no facing of the problems so much discussed in American ego-psychology of recent years, those that arise from the idea of the id as an 'ever-seething cauldron' of forces or drives which have no structure, and an ego pitted against them but having no energy of its own. These problems were closely discussed, as we have seen, in the 1950's in relation to Hartmann's ego-psychology, but were fully realized by Fairbairn from between 1940 and 1946, and were the cause of his moving beyond the instinct theory of Freud and Klein, to a consistent object-relations theory. To show how this came about we may consider the four parts into which Klein's theory may be divided.

(1) *Description of the Inner Fantasy World*, and of internal object-relations. The basic clinical data here are pretty well agreed. Klein in part confirmed and in part greatly elaborated what Freud had inferred as to the fantasy life of infancy. The criticism that she 'read back' later developments into earlier stages seems now to have lost its force. Her work has compelled analysts to put more stress, in therapy, on the analysis of *the present endopsychic situation* as revealed in fantasy, than on genetic and developmental analysis which is valuable mainly as illuminating the patient's existing personality structure.

(2) *The Ego Defence Processes*. (The term 'mechanisms' is out of place in a personal psychology.) Projection, introjection, splitting, idealization, denial, identification, are concepts common to all analysts, but Klein made special use of combinations of projection and introjection with identification, as a natural result of her concept of 'the inner world'. Though she continued to use 'instinct' language, it is really 'internal bad objects', not 'instincts', that are defended against; a point made extremely clear in Fairbairn's paper on 'The Repression and the Return of Bad Objects' (1943).

(3) *The Scheme of Ego Development.* This is much closer to the requirements of a psychology of personality than the earlier concept of oral, anal, and genital phases based on instinct maturation. Klein's scheme represents the psychodynamics of personal object-relations, and is a genuine concept of the growth of the individual as a 'person'. The concept of a paranoid-schizoid phase antedating a depressive phase, i.e. experiences of internal objects in terms of first fear and withdrawal, and second hate and guilt, leading to the development of a paranoid-schizoid 'position' underlying depressive phenomena, clearly carries Freud's analysis to a deeper level. It raised decisively the problem of the earliest beginnings of ego growth as the fundamental problem, that has been so radically investigated by Winnicott in particular. We should remember that psychoanalytical theories are based on psychopathological evidence, and that very clear-cut paranoid-schizoid and depressive phases and subsequent 'positions' are not necessarily markedly noticeable in the adequately mothered baby. They represent the essence of mental ill-health, but they are also hazards in the process of growing up that the environment is never so good as to protect us from completely. For that reason no doubt Winnicott prefers the more normal term 'stage of concern' for the psychopathological 'depressive position'.

(4) *Basic Explanatory Concepts; Metapsychology.* Here we face the great difficulty in Klein's views. She did not evolve a total systematic theory. That is not surprising for it was her own clinical work that created the need for theoretical revision. She herself began with Freud's instinct theory, as all analysts had to do, and never realized how its narrow bounds were burst by her own discoveries. This was largely due to the fact that she centred everything on Freud's 'death-instinct', so that she did not use her own discoveries about internal object-relations to achieve a more satisfactory structural theory, which could take account of ego-splitting as the id-ego-superego scheme could not. Probably it was impossible for her to run so far ahead of her own work. Thus her theory remained a mixture of biology and psychology, with (like Freud) no true ego-theory as a foundation for her study of the psychodynamics of ego-object relations. Her internal object-relations discoveries demanded a consistently psychodynamic ego theory, a theory of man as a personal self.

Klein's metapsychology rests on a theory of *ego-development by hereditary predestination* but her work on fantasy calls for *ego development by environmental object-relations*. Segal makes it clear that Kleinians have moved in this direction on two basic points: (*a*) There is a real ego at birth (pp. 2–3). (*b*) 'Instincts are by definition object-seeking.' Whether admitted or not this is a clear acceptance of Fairbairn's revision of theory. He pointed out that as early as 1929 Freud wrote in *Civilization and Its Discontents*, 'Love seeks for objects', and in distinguishing between ego-instincts and object-instincts he wrote: 'For the energy of the latter instincts and exclusively for them I introduced the term libido.' Fairbairn commented in 1944: 'Nevertheless the ever-increasing concentration of psychoanalytical research upon object-relationships has left unmodified the original theory that libido is primarily pleasure-seeking' (p. 83). This 'ever-increasing concentration on object-relations' was due to Klein's work, and led to Fairbairn's 'revised Psychopathology' (1941) based on the specific rejection of the view that 'the course of mental processes is automatically regulated by the pleasure-principle' (Freud, 1920). He stated that '*the ultimate goal of libido is the object* [Fairbairn's italics]'. Only this view could be the starting-point for a true object-relations theory and ego-psychology, a psychodynamic theory of man as a 'person'.

Such a true object-relations theory is implicit in Klein's work but is prevented from becoming explicit by the retention of instinct theory. This is made abundantly clear in the following quotation from Segal.

> In Melanie Klein's view, unconscious phantasy is the mental expression of instincts and, therefore, like these, exists from the beginning of life. Instincts by definition are object-seeking. The experience of an instinct in the mental apparatus is connected with the phantasy of an object appropriate to the instinct. Thus, to every instinctive drive there is a corresponding actual phantasy. To the desire to eat, there is a corresponding phantasy of something which would be edible and satisfying to this desire—the breast. (p. 2.)

This is a plain statement to the effect that like the biological instinct, the fantasy of its corresponding object 'exists from the beginning of life'; i.e. that the fantasy of the object exists prior to any experience of an object, that the infant has an innate fantasy of the breast before he has actual experience of a real breast. This is clearly an unprovable assumption. It fully warrants Laing's criticism, if this were in truth an object-relations theory, that the objects in such theory are internal objects not real objects. In Kleinian theory instincts are by definition not real-object seeking, but fantasy-object seeking.

Experience of real objects has to be fitted into this predetermined pattern. Segal further overlooks the fact that it cannot be true of the death instinct that it is object seeking, for by definition it does not seek a proper relationship but the destruction of the object. Clinical experience has been pushing Kleinians towards a full object-relations theory from which instinct-theory in general, and the 'death instinct' concept in particular holds them back. If there be a death instinct, there cannot be a properly whole ego at birth, nor can object seeking be the basic nature of our instinctive endowment. Segal raises questions about the death instinct which she does not face. This remains the crucial issue.

Kleinians explain the build up of the inner fantasy world as a result of a theory of our psychobiological make-up which includes a death instinct. They do not see it as created out of unsatisfactory experiences in object-relations in real life, a view which would make much more clinically verifiable sense. The death instinct is in no sense a scientific hypothesis derived solely from clinical data. It is a theoretical construct imposed on the data, which has now become a dogma. We must draw a clear distinction between Klein's highly important clinically descriptive account of personality and neurosis, and certain theoretical ideas she used to explain it. The very clarity of Segal's exposition magnifies the problem. Kleinian 'metapsychology' is an inverted pyramid resting on an unsubstantial apex, the concept of a 'death instinct', the most speculative and subjectively determined of all Freud's ideas. It was rejected, as Jones showed, by practically all analysts except Kleinians. One would have thought, therefore, that Segal would have recognized an obligation to justify this concept, but she introduces it with the simple assumption that it represents an undisputed self-evident fact:

> [The ego] has from the beginning a tendency towards integration. At times, under the impact of the death instinct and intolerable anxiety, this tendency is swept away. . . . Faced with the anxiety produced by the death instinct . . . the ego splits itself and projects that part of itself which contains the death instinct outwards into the breast. Thus the breast is felt to be bad and threatening to the ego. . . . The original fear of the death instinct is changed into fear of a persecutor. (p. 12.)

This is pure unproven dogma. The only kind of proof implied is the circular argument: the death instinct produces such-and-such a phenomenon, therefore this phenomenon proves the death instinct. Yet this notion controls the entire build-up of the Kleinian scheme, the necessities of the theory being imposed on the clinical material. The ego splits itself because of its fear of its own death instinct, without and prior to any relationship with objects; the badness of the object is determined, not by experience of the object, but by projection of the death instinct, and the badness of the self is felt, not in relation to objects, but because it is in part constituted by a death instinct. Everything begins with the ego's fear of its own death instinct. The result is a dogma of 'original evil' strictly parallel to the theologian's dogma of 'original sin'. Human nature contains an enormously powerful innate destructive force which is anti-social and anti-libidinal. What a fascination this idea has had for men over the centuries, from Zoroaster, Plato, and St Paul down to Freud and Klein. If this is true, then the ego is 'split' from the start, not by bad object-relations experience in real life, but by its biological inheritance, 'the inborn polarity of instincts—the immediate conflict between the life instinct and the death instinct' (p. 12). Since this split is there before the infant has any experience of objects, all his experience of objects becomes automatically and inevitably split, not because of what the objects are but because of what the infant's nature is. He is, in fact, incapable of experiencing objects simply on the basis of his experience of their treatment of him. The influence of the environment is only secondary and confirmatory. The whole Kleinian psychopathology, so clinically penetrating, *could* be built up, metapsychologically speaking, with an external world that was no more than a blank projection screen.

Segal seeks to avoid this implication. She writes:

> If unconscious phantasy is constantly influencing and altering the perception or interpretation of reality, the converse also holds true: reality impinges on unconscious phantasy. (p. 4.)

But that is hardly the point. One would think no one would dispute either of these statements. The question is, which comes first? For Kleinians, unconscious fantasy rests on an inborn factor, not on experience of outer reality. It is given with, and as part of, instinctive endowment. Having actually stated that, Segal seeks to soften its implications: 'Environment has, in fact, exceedingly important effects in infancy and childhood . . .' (p. 4). Surely everyone takes this as obvious, but it has to be stressed by Segal because Kleinian theory *does* make the environment an entirely secondary factor. She writes:

The importance of the environmental factor can only be correctly evaluated in relation to what it means in terms of the infant's own instincts and phantasies. . . . It is when the infant has been under the sway of angry phantasies, attacking the breast, that an actual bad experience becomes all the more important, since it *confirms* [my italics] not only his feeling that the external world is bad, but also the sense of his own badness and the omnipotence of his malevolent phantasies. (p. 4.)

Note 'confirms', not 'originates'. One would think that such confirmation was superfluous, so malevolent is the infant by nature anyway. Segal adds:

Good experiences, on the other hand, tend to lessen the anger, modify the persecutory experiences and mobilize the baby's love and gratitude and his belief in a good object. (pp. 4–5.)

Such good experiences, however, could only make a superficial reduction of 'anger', etc.; they have no chance of producing any basic modification in the inborn 'death instinct' and its consequences. In any case on this theory, both good and bad object fantasy life is held to exist independently of experience of outer reality which only 'confirms' what is felt already anyway. Clinical data support rather the view that good and bad object fantasy life arises out of the infant's difficulties in coping with his real outer world. The whole weight of Winnicott's work concerning the 'facilitating environment' is against this theory, and particularly the way he shows the total nature of the baby's dependence on the mother for the very start of ego development at all. All this is clinically verifiable certainly in later life. One can watch a patient driven back into fantasy when he cannot cope with reality, as well as observe his fantasy distorting reality. It is most natural to expect that this is how pathological fantasy (as distinct from healthy imaginative exploration of life) begins. Kleinians only assert the opposite view: they do not prove it.

Segal writes: 'It is not true that without a bad environment, no aggressive and persecutory fantasies and anxieties would exist' (p. 4). This oversimplifies the problem. We have no experience of an infant, *from his point of view*, without a bad environment. No environment can ever be perfect, but, what is even more to the point, the infant is so weak and helpless that what is not from our point of view bad, can seem so to him because he is so vulnerable. Here is all the possibility of bad-object experience, fear and anger, arising with even the best of mothers. Nevertheless, there exist accounts of some very friendly and quite non-aggressive primitive societies. There is no clinical warranty for assigning the whole origin of infantile fantasy to an unproven concept of an innate factor like a 'death instinct'. (It may be noted that the evidence of experimental animal psychology shows that 'destructiveness' is a 'learned', not an 'innate' response.)

When we turn to *psychotherapy*, the logical implication of Kleinian theory is that we are up against fixed and final limits to what can be achieved. It would be possible to analyse the permutations and combinations of life and death instincts with ego defences, and the alternations between the paranoid-schizoid and depressive positions. Thus some differences could be, and can be, made to the elaborate piling up of defences on defences that we always find in disturbed persons. But one cannot analyse a 'death instinct'. If it existed it would be an ultimate and ineradicable datum like the life instinct. It would preclude basic analysis of the problems of aggression, and any real integrative healing of the split ego. Thus, if envy is the direct manifestation of the death instinct which cannot be eliminated, then neither can envy be overcome. On this theory we envy other's good not because we *feel* we are bad or have actual bad disturbed emotions, but because *we are bad by nature, having a permanent destructive urge in us. That is the theory.* Incidentally it implies that there is not really any more good in anyone else to be envied than in ourselves, for they too have this same ineradicable destructive death instinct in them. I have mentioned the strange fascination that this idea of 'original evil' has had over the centuries. It involves that psychotherapy could only be a matter of superficial adjustments and improvements. Marie Bonaparte drew the correct inference when she wrote:

> So far as the aggressions are concerned, there seems little prospect of man's ever achieving equal happiness and goodness.

I believe, as I have stated earlier, that this traditional dogma is man's oldest self-deception. We prefer to believe that we have 'mighty instincts' (Freud) even if they are bad or antisocial because we can then believe that we are basically strong. It is frightening for human beings to believe that they are made for social relationship and love while yet they are small and weak in face of overwhelming reality.

Churchill was close to facts when he said, 'We are all worms but I think I am a glow-worm.' Most of us, if we are realistic, would wish yet hesitate to add even that qualification. The individual human being may have tremendous intelligence and in combination with others can achieve wondrous things, yet if he is emotionally alone he is helpless in face of reality. All human beings know this at heart, and the theory of the destructive 'aggressive instinct' is an attempt to overcompensate. In fact, aggression is a problem for analysis and cannot be ultimately shelved by being treated as an innate drive *per se*. It is nearer the truth to say, with one of my patients: 'When I can get angry, I can feel plenty of energy. Otherwise I feel timid and weak.' I cannot but wonder at Kleinians resting their whole theory on such a shaky concept as that of a death instinct and innate destructiveness, especially when this inherited concept so dangerously obscures Melanie Klein's really original findings.

Finally, the question of the meaning of the term 'schizoid' arises. For Klein, 'schizoid' refers primarily to '*ego-splitting*' as a result of the death instinct. Granted the death instinct, that is logical. The ego that goes to pieces under the impact of its death instinct, will be unable to effect true contact with external reality, and will appear 'withdrawn'. If, however, disturbance is caused by external bad-object relations (Fairbairn) or by the not-good-enough-mother failing to support the vulnerable infant ego (Winnicott), then schizoid would primarily mean '*withdrawal* from outer reality under stress of fear'. Ego-splitting will be secondary and the result of the need both to withdraw and at the same time keep in touch. In this case, psychotherapy, instead of being ultimately impossible, becomes a realistic attempt to reconcile the withdrawn frightened infantile ego in the inner world to external reality. For Kleinians, it could only be, so far as the theory goes, the dubious business of seeking to minimize the effects of the death instinct. No doubt, because clinical practice is often better than theory and more human, better results than this are produced. If so, they do not support the theory. For progress towards integration can only come by outgrowing the unreal abstractions of separate good and bad objects, allowing them to merge back into what they originally were, good and bad aspects of one and the same real person. Then in real life it becomes possible to treat real people as neither ideal lovers nor sinister persecutors, but as human beings with limitations and imperfections, with whom it is quite possible to form genuine good relationships. On Kleinian theory, our fantasy life could never support this realistic development, for the internal good and bad objects have their origin in fixed instincts which are permanently opposed.

Fortunately, as in the case of Freud, Melanie Klein's genius for intuitive understanding of personal reality, for knowing the unconscious experiences of others through an available inner knowledge of, or closeness to, her own unconscious, could not be imprisoned by the logical implications of rigid theoretical ideas. She took over Freud's death instinct, but it did not stop her from seeing clearly the intense fantasy life going on in the inner world of very small children: and her account of it laid the foundations for a reorientation of theory away from merely the psychobiology and physiology of instinctive satisfactions and frustrations, as if that were the whole of living, and towards the primacy of good and bad object-relations as the meaningful experiences in which the ego either grows strong and mature, or is stifled at birth, or fragmented and lost.

This I believe to be the most momentous development in psychoanalysis, which in different ways stimulated both Fairbairn and Winnicott. Fairbairn traced out the basic pattern of ego-splittings which followed on the object-splitting Klein described, and he centred attention on the schizoid condition as the ultimate problem underlying depression and psychoneurosis. Winnicott, as I have sought to show in Chapters VIII, IX, and XIII, pushed research beyond the pattern of ego-splitting to the point of exploring the beginnings of ego-development in the infant–mother relationship, not an apparatus or a system-ego, but a person-ego. I shall close this rapid theoretical review by indicating the far-reaching importance of his latest conclusions, as stated in 'The Location of Cultural Experience' (1967).

Winnicott here indicates a gap in Freud's theory: 'Freud did not have a place in his topography of the mind for things cultural.' Without committing himself to any particular definition of 'culture', it is clear that he means the product of the continuing and accumulating efforts of mankind through thousands of years, to find ways of expressing the essence of man's experience of 'what life is about' in terms of 'personal being' and 'personal relations'. He writes:

> Our psychotic patients force us to give attention to this sort of basic problem. We now see that it is not instinctual satisfaction that makes a baby begin to be, to feel that life is real, to find life worth living. . . . It is the self that must precede the self's use of instinct. The rider must ride the horse and not be run away with. (p. 370.)

With this statement it becomes clear that the growth of the theory of ego-development as a function of personal object-relations, has now brought about a total revolution in psychoanalytical thinking. Winnicott must be aware of this for he writes: 'It is part of my thesis that the psychoanalytic literature does not, in fact, include what I am putting forward.' The question 'What is life about?' would be an astonishing one, if asked in the context of the classical psychoanalytical theory. The only answer that could be given would be that life is about the quantitative reduction of instinctive tensions, in obedience to the 'constancy principle'. Such an answer has only to be stated to make its inadequacy, even absurdity, plain, for it conveys no intelligible meaning in terms of the mutual valuation and affection of persons in relationship. Nor does it give any clue to the significance of man's creation of culture through the centuries, but this is precisely what Winnicott does give us.

To explain this, he takes us back to his familiar concept of the 'transitional object', a bit of blanket, a cuddly toy or what-not, that the infant will not be parted from. He says:

> When we witness an infant's employment of a transitional object, the first not-me possession, we are witnessing both the child's first use of a symbol, and also the first experience of play.

The enormous importance of this observation is realized the moment we remember that 'culture' is entirely made up of the products of centuries of man's efforts to achieve 'symbolic expression' of the fullness of his 'personal living'. Culture is symbolism, the symbolic expression of what is personally meaningful, in contrast to science, which is the impersonal, neutral, non-emotional description of matters of material fact, which have utilitarian but not personal value. (Words, mathematical signs, etc. are commonly spoken of as symbols, and so they are, but in a quite different sense from the symbols that represent personal reality. The difference is that between a mathematical equation and a poem or painting that moves us profoundly to a deeper experiencing of human living.)

It follows that 'culture', all the arts and religions of mankind, are 'playing'. This is not to trivialize culture, but to reveal the enormous significance of 'playing' at the beginning of life. In fact, it is in his 'playing' that a child is really 'living', not in the carrying out of routine biological functions such as eating, excreting, sleeping, etc., which keep the body healthy and alive. They belong to the area of science. 'Playing' belongs to the area of the developing personal life. In it the child is experimenting with himself and his friends in personal relationships to find out 'what life is about, what makes it worth living'. That is why children play at being mothers and fathers, teachers and scholars, doctors and nurses and patients, cowboys and Indians. They are exploring the range of experiences of personal relationships, so that *there is a direct link between children's playing and the social and religious rituals of adults. They explore the imponderable reality of human living as personal relationship, a field of reality in which science cannot operate; for when it tries to do so, it only depersonalizes it, as in behavioural psychology.*

The starting-point of all this is where the infant first begins to differentiate out from the mother, and discover himself and her and the relationship between them. I give this in Winnicott's own words.

> The transitional object is a symbol of the union of the baby and the mother (or part of the mother). This symbol can be located. It is at the place in time and space where and when the mother is in transition from being (in the baby's mind) merged in with the infant, and being experienced as an object to be perceived rather than conceived of. The use of an object symbolizes the union of two now separate things, baby and mother, *at the point of the initiation of their state of separateness*. . . . There must be the beginning of the setting up in the infant's mind or personal psychic reality of an image of the object (mother). But the mental representation in the inner world is kept significant, or the imago in the inner world is kept alive, by the reinforcement given through the availability of the external separated-off and actual mother, along with her techniques of child care. . . . *This is the place that I have set out to examine*, the separation that is not a separation but a form of union. (p. 369.)

This positive statement Winnicott reinforces by a negative one, which I will summarize. The 'feeling of the mother's existence' lasts at first only so long, say x minutes. If mother is absent $x + y$ minutes, the imago fades but on her return she can, by 'spoiling', mend the baby's distress. But if she is absent $x + y + z$ minutes, the baby is *traumatized*, and mother's return cannot mend matters.

> Trauma implies that the baby has experienced a break in life's continuity, so that primitive defences now become organized to defend against a repetition of 'unthinkable anxiety' or of the acute confusional state that belongs to disintegration of the emerging ego structure. . . . Madness . . . means a *break-up* of whatever may exist at the time of *a personal continuity of existence*. After 'recovery' from $x + y + z$ deprivation a baby has to start again, permanently de-

prived of its own root, which would be *continuity with the personal beginning*. (p. 369.)

Here is the ultimate explanation of the schizoid phenomenon; 'the personal beginning', the core of the true ego, is split off and lost, partly repressed by primitive defences, partly withdrawn in deep fear, and yet containing so much personal potential that remains unevoked, and undeveloped. It is a matter of degree, but the worst degrees clearly involve schizophrenic madness. I put Winnicott's $x + y + z$ formula to one patient who is a mathematician, to see how he would react. After silently pondering, he said, 'I don't think my case was as bad as $x + y + z$ but it was worse than $x + y$. It was certainly $x + 2y$.'

The implications of this for theory are far-reaching. The stage at which the baby begins to emerge from primary identification with the mother, and begins to have the experience of separateness, is *the danger-point in development* if the mother does not give the baby adequate ego-support. And *the danger is not that his instincts are unsatisfied, but that his basic ego-experience is lost*. Thereafter, as all our schizoid patients sooner or later complain, he feels an 'emptiness', a 'nonentity' at the heart of him. Here are the facts that make possible a final settling of the problem of 'instincts and self', of 'id and ego'. Winnicott states the position plainly.

The phenomena I am describing have no climax. This distinguishes them from phenomena that have instinctual backing, where the orgiastic element plays an essential part, and where satisfactions are closely linked with climax. Here comes in Hartmann's concept of neutralization. But these phenomena that have reality in the area whose existence I am postulating, belong to *the experience of relating to objects*.

Winnicott observes:

I can see that I am in the territory of Fairbairn's (1941) concept of object-seeking (as opposed to satisfaction-seeking). (p. 371.)

In the paper Winnicott refers to, Fairbairn stated that his study of schizoid phenomena had resulted in:

the emergence of a point of view which, if it be well-founded, ... must necessarily have far-reaching implications both for psychiatry in general and for psychoanalysis in particular ... a considerable revision of prevailing ideas ... and a corresponding change in current clinical conceptions of the various psychoses and psychoneuroses.

It is at this point that I find myself differing somewhat from Winnicott, i.e. as to the implications, of what he presents so clearly, for existing theory. He states:

Psychoanalysts who have rightly emphasized the significance of instinctual experience and of reactions to frustration have failed to state with comparable clearness or conviction the tremendous intensity of these non-climactic experiences that are called playing (p. 370) [i.e. 'the experience of relating to objects'].

He illustrates this by referring to 'the "electricity" that seems to generate in meaningful or intimate contact . . . when two people are in love'. But in distinguishing this from 'instinctual, orgiastic, climactic satisfactions' he says: 'Here comes in Hartmann's concept of neutralization.' But Hartmann's 'neutralized energy' was a speculative assumption that the energy of the sexual and aggressive instincts could be desexualized and deaggressivized and placed at the disposal of the ego for non-instinctive ends. We have seen that this idea came to be regarded as such a threat to the reality of ego-experience, that Rapaport suggested a 'regression in the service of the ego' back to the energy of unneutralized instincts. I cannot think that Hartmann's 'neutralized' energy would generate any 'electricity' in a personal relationship. Moreover, if the baby's non-orgiastic experience of relationship is an example of Hartmann's 'neutralized energy', then it would mean that the experience of relationship is a secondary thing, derived from energy withdrawn from instinctive satisfactions. Winnicott's position, as I understand it, necessitates the exact opposite of such a view. *The experience of relationship is primary in that it alone brings into being an ego, a self that feels real, and only then is there a 'rider' who can ride the 'horse' of instinct.* Otherwise, instinct is merely a disconnected element in a psychic chaos, a part-function which Winnicott says becomes a '*seduction* unless based on a well-established capacity in the individual person for total experience'. Instincts can only operate satisfactorily when they belong to a stable ego, and therefore cannot be the source of the ego's energy for object-relating. It seems more conceivable that *the energy of the ego for object-relating is the primary energy; as Fairbairn put it, 'libido is object seeking'. In this sense libido is the fundamental 'life-energy' and sexual and aggressive energy are specialized aspects of it*, aggression being the reaction of the 'whole person-ego' to frustration. I do not think that Winnicott's present position can be reconciled with the old instinct theory by resort to Hartmann.

It seems to me that Winnicott's 'object-relating' theory can and should stand on its own feet in its theoretical assumptions. He rejects the death instinct, and regards the experience of object-relating as essentially different from that of sexual orgiastic satisfaction. We know that in fact sexual orgiastic satisfaction can take place in the absence of, and as a substitute for, true personal relating. *What then is the energy that makes 'object-relating' possible. It is not hate, nor fear, nor sex. It can only be the primary need to receive and give love.* Winnicott writes of object-relating as occurring

between any one baby and the human (and therefore fallible) . . . mother-figure, who is essentially adaptive because of love. (p. 391.)

Again he writes of the initial joining and separating of

. . . the baby and the mother when the mother's love, displayed as human reliability, does in fact give the baby a sense of trust, or of confidence in the environmental factor. (p. 372.)

Here at last we are released from some of the nightmare interpretations of human nature enforced by the classical instinct theory, and can hold that a healthy and natural human being is loving, and hate and fear (when not realistically aroused by environmental danger) are psychopathological. *Mother love, and the infant's innate capacity to respond to it with trust, to return love for love, is the basic reality*, not a death instinct; while sex will function in the service of whatever emotional state dominates the total self, be it love or hate or fear.

Winnicott sees clearly that his theory of the primacy of object-relating is a serious challenge to the traditional psychoanalytical point of view. He writes:

Starting as we do from psychoneurotic illness and with ego defences related to anxiety that arises from the instinctual life, we tend to think of health in terms of the state of ego defences—we say it is more healthy when these defences are not rigid, etc. But when we have reached this point we have not yet started to describe what life is like apart from illness or absence of illness. That is to say, we have yet to tackle the question of *what life is about.*

But he then goes on to say:

This theory does not affect what we have come to believe in respect of the aetiology of psychoneurosis, or the treatment of patients who are psychoneurotic; nor does it clash with Freud's structural theory of the mind in terms of ego, id, superego. What I say does affect our view of the question: what is life about? You may cure your patient and not know what it is that makes him or her go on living. (p. 370.)

We can agree that the aetiology and treatment of psychoneurosis remains as it was in the classical theory, provided one is faced with a relatively straightforward example of psychoneurosis, of oedipal conflicts for example. But 'object-relations theory' does affect our views of the aetiology and treatment of psychoneurosis in a far more fundamental way. It shows that the classically analysable psychoneuroses are relatively superficial phenomena, and when they are not, then the analysis of them takes us deeper and deeper into the depths of schizoid problems. We then find ourselves concerned less and less with the treatment of sexual and aggressive symptoms and their attendant anxieties and guilts, and more and more with fundamental ego-weakness, the nature of which Winnicott has made so clear.

Nor, finally, can I agree that Winnicott's theory of object-relating and ego-formation makes no difference to Freud's id, ego, superego theory. It seems to me that *the demonstration of the primacy of object-relating in terms of the mother's capacity to love and the baby's innate capacity to respond to love, and thus in turn become capable of loving, is the factual starting-point for rethinking structural theory*. We cannot pretend that there is any quick and easy way of eliminating aggression and destructive behaviour from human society. But if, indeed, the capacity to love is the basic element in human nature, then the problem is not *intrinsically* intractable. It may, in fact, be *practically* nearly intractable in many cases (and perhaps wholly intractable in the case of some psychopaths) because once fear and insecurity have been aroused, human beings get caught in vicious circles of deteriorating relationships, as individuals, classes, nations, and races. Where fear rules, attack seems the best defence, and so creates the very dangers that are feared. In psychoanalytic therapy we constantly come across this situation in husband–wife relations, where both parties long to remedy an intolerable situation, yet both fear to allow the vicious circle to be broken from their side because of a deep dread that it means surrender, defeat, and loss of personality. Neither can believe that the need to love and be loved is the basic nature of both of them, so completely does this seem to be swamped by fear and aggression, once aroused.

Nevertheless, these vicious circles can be broken and do get broken, and the will-to-peace is discovered behind all the turmoil of conflict. This happens on a social scale whenever negotiation ends conflict. It happens in a far deeper and more radical way when people discover that they can, through a long therapeutic analysis, outgrow their hates and fears, and find a 'true self' in a positive capacity for making and maintaining good personal relations.

The id, ego, superego theory, with its implication of an intractable dualism of id and ego, blind drives and social controls, is an analysis of the hopeless vicious circle situation in which, admittedly, masses of human beings are all too bogged down. This terminology fosters pessimism, for the term 'id' retains an aura of constant suggestion that our problems arise out of innate anti-social instinctive forces, the only answer to which is ego and superego control. Winnicott himself stated that

> Starting as we do from psychoneurotic illness and with ego defences related to anxiety that arises from the instinctual life, we tend to think of health in terms of the state of ego defences—we say it is more healthy when these defences are not rigid. But when we have reached this point we have not yet started to describe what life is like apart from illness. . . . We have yet to tackle the question of *what life is about*. (p. 370.)

'Less rigid defences' is too negative a definition of mental health to have more than superficial validity, and is quite unimaginative. Mental health should mean the vitality of the spontaneous and creative living of a 'whole person' in good human relations. This becomes practically meaningful on the basis of Winnicott's demonstration of the primacy of loving-relating of the mother and infant at the very start of life. Structural theory should have as its starting-point our latent natural health, not the forms of illness so soon imposed by an unfacilitating environment. 'Id, ego, superego' was at best a first attempt to conceptualize the split-ego condition, the early loss of psychic unity, which is the common human lot even though it differs in degree from one individual to another. Nevertheless, 'id' is a bad, non-psychological term for the frustrated, hungry, maternally deprived child. If we imagine a perfectly mature person, he would have no endopsychic structure in the sense of permanently opposed drives and controls. He would be a whole unified person whose internal psychic differentiation and organization would simply represent his diversified interests and abilities, within an overall good ego-development, in good object-relationships.

We cannot, however, hope for such perfection, but we can

hope to see, and in psychoanalytic therapy we do see, individuals who, through long tribulation and recurring disappointments, win their way at last to peace of mind, an outgrowing of the legacy of infantile fears and hates, and a feeling of self-fulfilment in an increasing capacity to make and enjoy genuine friendships. Structural theory must start, not with an 'id', but with a primary unitary infantile psyche, capable of becoming a mature loving person in a loving 'facilitating' environment. The conceptualization of ego-splitting is then our diagnosis of what goes wrong when the environment is not 'facilitating'. Freud first attempted this on the basis of 'instinct theory'. Fairbairn pioneered its revision in terms of 'object-relations' theory. The important thing is that psychoanalysis has now arrived at insights which could make possible something better than a dreary repetition of the ghastly dehumanizations of man that make up so much of human history; if only the elements of stability among mankind can give time for these insights to work over a series of generations, to present the children of the future with a better chance of being human than any generation has hitherto had. The whole of Winnicott's work, and of psychoanalytic work with children everywhere, is dedicated to the task of making that possibility at least available.

BIBLIOGRAPHY

Abraham, K. (1911), 'Notes on the psychoanalytical investigation and treatment of manic-depressive insanity and allied conditions', in *Selected Papers* (London, Hogarth, 1927).

Apfelbaum, B. (1965), 'Ego psychology, psychic energy, and the hazards of quantitative explanation in psychoanalytic theory', *Int. J. Psycho-Anal.*, **46**.

—— (1966), 'On ego psychology: a critique of the structural approach to psychoanalytic theory', *Int. J. Psycho-Anal.*, **47**.

Balint, M. (1952), *Primary Love and Psychoanalytic Technique* (London, Hogarth; New York, Liveright).

Bibring, E. (1953), 'The mechanism of depression', in *Affective Disorders*, ed. Greenacre (London, Hogarth; New York, Int. Univ. Press).

Bion, W. R. (1962), *Learning from Experience* (London, Heinemann).

Carstairs, G. M. (1963), *This Island Now* (London, Hogarth).

Colby, K. M. (1955), *Energy and Structure in Psychoanalysis* (New York, Ronald).

Dicks, H. V. (1939), *Clinical Studies in Psychopathology* (London, Arnold).

Edel, L. (1955), *The Psychological Novel* (London, Hart-Davis).

Erikson, E. H. (1950), *Childhood and Society* (London, Hogarth; New York, Norton, 2nd edition, 1963).

Fairbairn, W. R. D. (1931), 'Features in the analysis of a patient with a physical genital abnormality', in *Psychoanalytic Studies of the Personality* (1952a).

—— (1941), 'A revised psychopathology of the psychoses and psychoneuroses', *Int. J. Psycho-Anal.*, **22**, and (with amendments) in *Psychoanalytic Studies of the Personality* (1952a).

—— (1943), 'The repression and the return of bad objects', *Brit. J. med. Psychol.*, **19**, and (with amendments) in *Psychoanalytic Studies of the Personality* (1952a).

—— (1952a), *Psychoanalytic Studies of the Personality* (Amer. title: *An Object-Relations Theory of the Personality*) (London, Tavistock; New York, Basic Books).

—— (1952b), 'Theoretical and experimental aspects of psychoanalysis', *Brit. J. med. Psychol.*, **25**.

—— (1954), 'Observations on the nature of hysterical states', *Brit. J. med. Psychol.*, **27**.

—— (1958), 'On the nature and aims of psychoanalytical treatment',

Int. J. Psycho-Anal., **39** (wrongly quoted in the Bibliography of my previous volume as **29**).

—— (1963), 'Synopsis of an object-relations theory of the personality', *Int. J. Psycho-Anal.*, **44**.

FLUGEL, J. C. (1945), *Man, Morals and Society: A Psycho-Analytical Study* (London, Duckworth; New York, Int. Univ. Press).

FOULKES, S. (1965), 'Group psychotherapy: the group-analytic view', *Proc. 6th Int. Congress of Psychother*, ed. Pines and Spoerri (New York and Basle, Karger).

FREUD, A. (1936), *The Ego and the Mechanisms of Defence* (London, Hogarth, 1937; New York, Int. Univ. Press, 1946).

FREUD, S. (1913), 'On beginning the treatment', *Standard Edition of the Complete Psychological Works of Sigmund Freud*, **12** (London, Hogarth).

—— (1920), *Beyond the Pleasure Principle. Standard Edition*, **18**.

—— (1922), 'Two encyclopaedia articles', *Standard Edition*, **18**.

—— (1923), *The Ego and the Id. Standard Edition*, **19**.

—— (1933), *New Introductory Lectures on Psycho-Analysis. Standard Edition*, **22**.

—— (1937), 'Analysis terminable and interminable', *Standard Edition*, **23**.

—— (1940), *An Outline of Psycho-Analysis. Standard Edition*, **23**.

GELLNER, E. (1959), *Words and Things* (London, Gollancz).

GILL, M. and BRENMAN, M. (1959), *Hypnosis and Related States* (New York, Int. Univ. Press).

GITELSON, M. (1952), 'The emotional position of the analyst in the psychoanalytical situation', *Int. J. Psycho-Anal.*, **33**.

—— (1965), 'Heinz Hartmann', *Int. J. Psycho-Anal.*, **46**.

GUNTRIP, H. (1960), 'Ego-weakness and the hard core of the problem of psychotherapy', *Brit. J. med. Psychol.*, **33**.

—— (1961), *Personality Structure and Human Interaction* (London: Hogarth; New York, Int. Univ. Press).

HARTMANN, H. (1939), *Ego Psychology and the Problem of Adaptation* (New York, Int. Univ. Press; London, Imago, 1958).

—— (1960), 'Towards a concept of mental health', *Brit. J. med. Psychol.*, **33**, and in *Essays on Ego Psychology* (1964).

—— (1964), *Essays on Ego Psychology* (New York, Int. Univ. Press; London, Hogarth).

——, KRIS, E. and LOEWENSTEIN, R. M. (1946), 'Comments on the formation of psychic structure', *Psychoanal. Study Child.*, **2** (London, Hogarth; New York, Int. Univ. Press).

HEIMANN, P. (1952), 'Certain functions of introjection and projection in early infancy', in *Developments in Psycho-Analysis* by M. Klein *et al.* (London, Hogarth).

Hinsie, L. E. (1944), 'The schizophrenias', in *Psychoanalysis Today*, ed. S. Lorand (New York, Int. Univ. Press).

Holt, R. R. (1965), 'Ego autonomy re-evaluated', *Int. J. Psycho-Anal.*, **46**.

Home, H. J. (1966), 'The concept of mind', *Int. J. Psycho-Anal.*, **47**.

Horney, K. (1945), *Our Inner Conflicts: A Constructive Theory of Neurosis* (New York, Norton; London, Kegan Paul, 1946).

Hutten, E. H. (1956), 'On explanation in psychology and physics', *Brit. J. Philos. Sci.*, 7.

Jones, E. (1957), *Sigmund Freud: Life and Work*, vol. 3 (London, Hogarth; New York, Basic Books).

Klein, M. (1932), *The Psycho-Analysis of Children* (London, Hogarth).

—— (1960), 'A note on depression in the schizophrenic', *Int. J. Psycho-Anal.*, **41**.

Laing, R. D. (1960), *The Divided Self* (London, Tavistock).

—— (1965), 'Practice and theory: the present situation', *Proc. 6th Int. Congress of Psychother*, ed. Pines and Spoerri (New York and Basle, Karger).

Livingstone, R. (1928), *Greek Ideals and Modern Life* (Oxford Univ. Press).

Loewenstein, R. M. *et al.* (1966), *Psychoanalysis—A General Psychology: Essays in Honor of Heinz Hartmann* (New York, Int. Univ. Press).

Macmurray, J. (1961), *Persons in Relation* (London, Faber).

McDougall, Wm. (1905), *A Primer of Physiological Psychology* (London, Dent).

Malan, D. (1963), *A Study of Brief Psychotherapy* (London, Tavistock).

Mayer-Gross, W., Slater, E. and Roth, M. (1954), *Clinical Psychiatry*, 1st edition (London, Cassell).

Nacht, S. and Racamier, P. C. (1960). 'Depressive states', *Int. J. Psycho-Anal.*, **41**.

Pattee, F. L. (1915), *American Literature since 1870* (New York, Centry Co.).

Rangell, L. (1965), 'The scope of Heinz Hartmann', *Int. J. Psycho-Anal.*, **46**.

Rank, O. (1924), *The Trauma of Birth* (London, Paul, Trench, Trubner, 1929).

Rapaport, D. (1951), 'The Autonomy of the Ego', in *Psychoanalytic, Psychiatry and Psychology*, ed Knight and Friedman (New York, Int. Univ. Press, 1954).

Riviere, J. (1952), General Introduction to *Developments in Psycho-Analysis*, by M. Klein *et al.* (London, Hogarth).

Rosenfeld, H. (1960), 'A note on the precipitating factor in depressive illness', *Int. J. Psycho-Anal.*, **41**.

SCOTT, W. C. M. (1960), 'Depression, confusion, and multivalence', *Int. J. Psycho-Anal.*, **41**.

SEGAL, H. (1964), *Introduction to the Work of Melanie Klein* (London, Heinemann).

SPITZ, R. (1957), *No and Yes* (New York, Int. Univ. Press).

SULLIVAN, H. S. (1955), *Conceptions of Modern Psychiatry* (London, Tavistock; New York, Norton).

SWAN, M. (1952), *Henry James* (London, Arthur Barker).

SZASZ, T. (1956), 'Is the concept of entropy relevant to psychology and psychiatry?' *Psychiatry*, **19**.

TAYLOR, C. (1964), *The Explanation of Behaviour* (London, Kegan Paul).

WINNICOTT, D. W. (1955a), 'Metapsychological and clinical aspects of regression within the psychoanalytical set-up', in *Collected Papers* (1958b).

—— (1955b), 'The depressive position in normal emotional development', *ibid.*

—— (1958a), 'The capacity to be alone', in *Maturational Processes and the Facilitating Environment* (1965b).

—— (1958b), *Collected Papers* (London, Tavistock; New York, Basic Books).

—— (1962), 'The aims of psychoanalytical treatment', in *Maturational Processes and the Facilitating Environment* (1965b).

—— (1963), 'Communicating and not communicating leading to a study of certain opposites', *ibid.*

—— (1964), Correspondence: 'Love or Skill?' *New Society*, February.

—— (1965a), *The Family and Individual Development* (London, Tavistock).

—— (1965b), *The Maturational Processes and the Facilitating Environment* (London, Hogarth).

—— (1966), 'The split-off male and female elements to be found clinically in men and women' (unpublished).

—— (1967), 'The location of cultural experience', *Int. J. Psycho-Anal.*, **48**.

ZETZEL, E. *et al.* (1960). Symposium on depressive illness. *Int. J. Psycho-Anal.*, **41**.

—— (1965), 'The theory of therapy in relation to a developmental model of the psychic apparatus', *Int. J. Psycho-Anal.*, **46**.

INDEX